Researching and Writing a Dissertation:
A Guidebook for Business Students

We work with leading authors to develop the
strongest educational materials in management,
bringing cutting-edge thinking and best
learning practice to a global market.

Under a range of well-known imprints, including
Financial Times Prentice Hall, we craft high-quality print
and electronic publications which help readers to
understand and apply their content, whether
studying or at work.

To find out more about the complete range of our
publishing, please visit us on the World Wide Web at:
www.pearsoned.co.uk

Researching and Writing a Dissertation: A Guidebook for Business Students

Second edition

Colin Fisher

with

John Buglear

Diannah Lowry

Alistair Mutch

Carole Tansley

FT Prentice Hall
FINANCIAL TIMES

An imprint of **Pearson Education**

Harlow, England • London • New York • Boston • San Francisco • Toronto • Sydney • Singapore • Hong Kong
Tokyo • Seoul • Taipei • New Delhi • Cape Town • Madrid • Mexico City • Amsterdam • Munich • Paris • Milan

Pearson Education Limited
Edinburgh Gate
Harlow
Essex CM20 2JE
England

and Associated Companies throughout the world

Visit us on the World Wide Web at:
www.pearsoned.co.uk

First published 2004
Second edition 2007

ISBN: 978-0-273-71007-3

British Library Cataloguing-in-Publication Data
A catalogue record for this book is available from the British Library

10 9 8 7 6 5 4 3 2 1
11 10 09 08 07

Typeset in Sabon by 30
Printed and bound by Ashford Colour Press, Gosport

The publisher's policy is to use paper manufactured from sustainable forests.

Contents

Acknowledgements

I tried the patience of my friends at Nottingham Business School by constant requests for feedback. They replied with good humour, useful feedback and new material. I wish to thank Alistair Mutch, Diannah Lowry, John Buglear and Carole Tansley especially for writing whole sections of this book. John and Carole have written completely new sections for this second edition. All the contributions by colleagues are acknowledged in the text. Among other colleagues, and ex-colleagues who have moved to other universities, I wish to thank are Jim Stewart, Tony Woodall, Val Caven, Denise Fletcher, Sue Kirk, Suzanne Tietze and John Leopold. Many thanks also to Christos Athanasoulis for his helpful advice. Tony Watson deserves particular thanks. It was only when I was writing the first edition of the book that I realised what an influence he has been on my thinking in the 20 and more years we had worked together at Nottingham Business School. Nevertheless, neither he nor any other colleague is responsible for errors or misunderstandings that might have found their way into this guide.

Much of any practical wisdom to be found in this guide comes from the many postgraduate students I have worked with at Nottingham Business School when they were doing their dissertations. Many thanks are due to them. In particular I want to thank Alastair Allen who allowed me to use some of his research material to illustrate points about conceptual framework building.

Publisher's acknowledgements

We are grateful to the following for permission to reproduce copyright material:

Figure 0.3 Reprinted by permission of Sage Publications Ltd from Gill, J. and Johnson P. (2002) *Research Methods for Managers*, 3e © Paul Chapman Publishing, 2002, Exercise 1.3, Exhibits 2.2, 3.1 and 3.2 photographs by Raj Shirole; Table 1.2 reprinted by permission of Sage Publications Ltd from Silverman, D., *Interpreting Qualitative Data: Methods for Analysing Talk, Text and Interaction*, © Sage, 1993; Exhibit 1.9 from Managing, crafting and researching: words, skill and imagination in shaping management research, *British Journal of Management*, Vol. 5 (Special issue), pp. 77–97, Blackwell Publishing (Watson, T.J., 1994); Exhibit 2.6 image of Bentham's Panopticon from Bentham Papers 115/44, University College London; Figures 3.1, 3.2 and 3.8 reproduced with the permission of T.J. Watson; Figure 3.3 from Bad apples in bad barrels: a causal analysis of ethical decision-making behaviour, *Journal of Applied Psychology*, Vol. 75, No. 4, pp. 378–385, American Psychological Association (Trevino, L.K. and Youngblood, S.A., 1990); Figure

3.9 from *Kabbalah: Traditions of Hidden Knowledge*, Thames & Hudson Ltd (Z'ev ben Shimon Halevi, 1979); Figure 3.10 from Ethical stances: the perceptions of accountancy and RM specialists of ethical conundrums at work, *Business Ethics: A European Review*, Vol. 8, No. 4, p. 241, Blackwell Publishing Ltd (Fisher, C.M., 1999); Table 4.2 from Brouse, Suzannah H. (2002) J. Advanced Nursing, Vol. 37, No.6, 607 in: Silverman D. (1993) *Interpreting Qualitative Data: Methods for Analyzing Talk, Text and Interaction*, 2e David Silverman © Blackwell Publishing, Table 4.4 from *Research Methods for Business Students*, Financial Times Prentice Hall (Saunders, M., Lewis, P. and Thornhill, A., 2002); Figure 4.8 from *Reason by Numbers*, Pelican Books (Moore, P.G., 1980) copyright © Peter G. Moore, 1980; Figures 4.14, 4.15, 4.16 and 4.17 Screenshots from Minitab software, © Minitab Inc.; Figure 4.25 Screenshot from SPSS software; Figure 4.3 *Interaction Process Analysis* Bales, R.F. (1950) © University of Chicago Press; Exhibits 4.35, 4.36 and 4.37 Screenshots from NVIV07 software, NVIVO is designed and developed by QSR International Pty Ltd. NVIVO is a trademark or registered trademark of QSR International Patent pending; Table 4.5 from *Statistics without Tears*, Penguin Books (Rowntree, D., 1991), © Derek Rowntree, 1991. Figure 5.1 An Aztec map of Tenochtitlan, Bodleian Library, University of Oxford, MS. Arch. Seldon.A.1, fol.2r; Figure 5.2 A Spanish map of Tenochtitlan, from *www.newberry.org/media/Azrecismages.html*, The Newberry Library, Chicago; Figures 5.6 and 5.7 from *Does Business Ethics Pay?*, Institute of Business Ethics (Webley, S. and More, E. 2003), Exhibit 5.13 reproduced with the permission of J. De Mey. Figure 6.1 from *Business Ethics and Values: Individual, Corporate and International Perspectives* Fisher, C.M. and Lovell, A. (2006) © Pearson Education.

The Quality Assurance Agency for the extract 'The QAA's Descriptor for a qualification at Masters (M) level' from *The Framework for Higher Education Qualifications in England, Wales and Northern Ireland*, © The Quality Assurance Agency for Higher Education, 2001; and The Times Literary Supplement for the extract 'Why it's fun to be smart' by Eisaman Maus as published in *The Times Literary Supplement* 25 May 2001, © The Times Literary Supplement. Exercise 2.2 from *Resource Allocation in the Public Sector: Values, Priorities and Markets in the Management of Public Services*, Routledge (Fisher, C.M., 1998); Chapter 3 example of conceptualising and theorising in a study of organisational culture based on *Organisation, Culture and the Management of Change in the National Health Service*, PhD dissertation, the Nottingham Trent University (McNulty, T., 1990) reproduced with permission of T. McNulty; Chapter 3 extract from Transforming former state enterprises in the Czech Republic, *Organisation Studies*, Vol. 16, No. 2, p. 215, Walter de Gruyter (Clark, E. and Soulsby, A., 1995); Exercise 5.7 from *A Handbook of Structured Experiences for Human Relations Training*, Pfeiffer, J.W. and Jones, J.E., ©1975 John Wiley & Sons, Inc. This material is used by permission of John Wiley & Sons, Inc.

In some instances we have been unable to trace the owners of copyright material, and we would appreciate any information that would enable us to do so.

Chapter 0 ● ● ● ●
Introduction

Although this book is clearly a textbook, it is intended to be used more like a tourist guide; a book to be used by readers as a guidebook to researching and writing a dissertation. It is written in a rather more informal manner than many textbooks because it focuses on what the reader needs to know rather than on the debates in the academic literature.

This introduction is Chapter 0. Such a quirky way of beginning the numbering of chapters needs to be explained. The guide is structured around six stages in the process of researching and writing a dissertation. These stages in turn reflect the six criteria that typify the standards that dissertations are marked against. The guide contains a chapter for each of these stages-cum-criteria. I wanted each of them to have the appropriate number, Chapter 1 for stage 1 and so on. This meant that the introduction that precedes the chapters had to be Chapter 0.

Calling the introduction Chapter 0 does not mean it is empty of content. It is quite important to read this chapter if you are going to get full value from the guide, because it will achieve the following:

● identify the assessment targets you need to hit for the dissertation to be passed;
● introduce you to methodological issues that can cause students problems if they are not understood;
● explain the structure of the guide and introduce you to further resources.

Contents

● ● ● ● Who is this guide for?

The first readership for the guide is all those doing an MBA, or an MSc or MA course in a management or business topic, and who have to write a dissertation as part of their studies. That said, many of the topics and skills the guide covers are relevant to anyone who has to research and write a dissertation or a long, research-based paper as part of their programme of study. The guide will be of use to undergraduates doing final-year dissertations and also to DBA and PhD students.

● ● ● ● What does doing a dissertation involve?

Most MBA and Master's in management programmes include a major project in which the students identify an issue of managerial, organisational or business concern and research it. However, different business schools demand different things in the research component of their MBA and other Master's programmes. Most commonly students will be required to write a dissertation, which is a report on a major piece of primary research (normally between 15,000 and 20,000 words long) which gives an account of a student's investigation into a business or managerial issue, provides an analysis of the research and presents the conclusions that are drawn from it. In addition to, or instead of, the dissertation, students may be required to write one or more of the following:

- a **proposal**, which is a document that defines what the project is about, explains why it is important and describes how it is to be carried out;
- a **paper**, which is a short (normally around 4,000 to 6,000 words) document suitable for presentation to an academic conference or journal;
- a **management report**, which is a shorter document (2,000 to 4,000 words) that is suitable for presentation to managers and decision makers and that is designed to persuade them to adopt the recommendations you make.

This guide focuses on the proposal and the dissertation but it also gives some help on writing papers and reports.

Some other key terms are used frequently in the guide and it will be useful to define them before we proceed:

- A **project** means all the activities that go towards completing a dissertation.
- A **thesis** is an argument or a proposition supported by evidence and literature.

A Master's degree in a business or management subject brings together an academic concern for theory and understanding with a managerial concern for analysis, planning and action. A dissertation should be written primarily for an academic audience, and it will be marked by academics. However, it should also contain elements that address the concerns of those in the organisations whose problems were the subject of the dissertation. Getting this balance right is one of the skills needed to write a good dissertation.

The aims of the dissertation, and of the proposal and the conference paper if you are required to do them, will vary from institution to institution and you will need to become very familiar with those that belong to your course. However, the following example would not be atypical.

The objective of the dissertation is to give the student an opportunity:

1. to plan, research and write up a project that improves understanding of a significant managerial, business or organisational matter, and that, if appropriate, provides recommendations or findings upon which action can be determined;
2. to learn how to undertake a major project that requires you to:
   - be focused on a complex and important issue;
   - undertake effective and competent primary research;
   - integrate theory and practice;
   - incorporate understanding taken from a critical review of the appropriate literature;
   - base your dissertation on sound analysis and arguments; and
   - be sensitive to the requirements of the different audiences for the dissertation.

The focus of the project is often a matter for you to decide. It may be on any of the following:

- a part of an organisation, or a comparison between parts of an organisation;
- a single organisation;
- a comparison between two or more organisations;
- a study of an industrial or commercial sector;
- a study of a managerial function or profession.

The process of doing a dissertation

In practice, doing a dissertation is not a sequential process in which the completion of one stage leads neatly to the next. There are often false starts and returns to earlier stages of the project to reconsider the focus and the aims. Many of the stages of doing a project will be pursued in parallel. While you are reading for the literature review you may also be setting up contacts for interviews or drafting a questionnaire. However, there is a basic logic to the process and this can be used to explain the contents of this guide. This logic is shown, as a series of stages for convenience, in Figure 0.1. In addition to this introduction, the guide contains six chapters. Each of the chapters deals with one of the stages shown in Figure 0.1. Taken together, the chapters will lead you through the processes of researching and writing your dissertation.

Figure 0.1 has three dimensions. The time dimension runs vertically. The height of the cube represents the length of time you have to complete your project and dissertation. The other two dimensions are as follows:

thinking — finding out

confusion — confidence.

Here is a description of the progress of an average project using these dimensions.

Phase 1 – Choosing a topic and designing the project

At the start, students are confused about what they are going to study for the project and how they are going to do it. In the first phase, thinking about choice of topic and what approach to research is going to be adopted leads to finding out about possible topics and investigating the

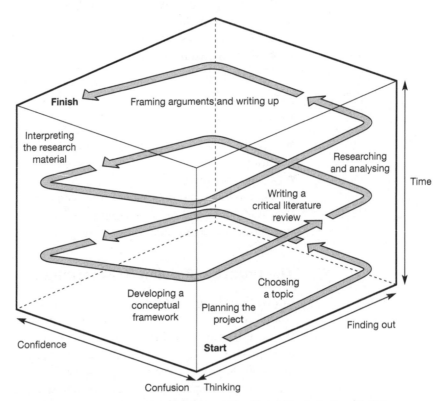

Figure 0.1 The processes of researching and writing a Master's dissertation

range of research methods available. The combination of these activities increases students' confidence, but not hugely. They are still a little fazed at the end of this first phase but they should have a clearer idea of what they want to research, why it is important and how they are going to do it.

Phase 2 – Writing a critical literature review

The next phase involves searching for books, academic papers and other materials that are relevant to the project, so quite a lot of energy at the early part of this phase goes into finding out what resources are available. Although finding materials is satisfying, there is a tendency to think that the information they contain can be transferred into one's brain by some osmotic process that does not involve actually reading the stuff. This stage, of course, involves reading the material, making notes on it and thinking about it. In particular the various theories and frameworks drawn from the literature need to be criticised and evaluated to see which are academically robust enough to be used in your project. The reading and thinking normally mean that students have increased confidence in their project by the end of this phase.

Phase 3 – Developing concepts, conceptual frameworks and theories

As a result of their increasing confidence, students feel ready to move into the next phase, which is developing a conceptual framework. This is a 'map' that draws together the concepts that the students will use to guide their research and that suggests how they are related. Conceptual frameworks are normally modifications and developments of models and theories found in the literature. When a conceptual framework is decided upon it gives a great boost to students' confidence. They feel in control of their project because they can see where it is going. However, once it is drafted, and they think about the framework some more, little doubts and worries creep in and the confidence begins to seep away. Then it is time to get into the next stage – of doing the research work.

Phase 4 – Collecting and analysing research material

Some thinking is needed at the start of the research phase of the project. Students have to decide in detail how they are going to conduct the research and organise the practical aspects of, for instance, conducting interviews or focus groups, identifying people to send questionnaires to and so on. But the bulk of this stage is about finding out. When students start to collect their research results it often boosts their confidence as they conclude that they will have enough material to write their dissertation.

Phase 5 – Interpreting research material and drawing conclusions

After a heap of research material has been collected it then remains to make sense of it – to interpret it. This can be a daunting task and initially there can be an increase in confusion as students think about what the material means. But some hard thinking and interrogation of the research material usually result in students finding out more about their topic. The interpretation stage involves choosing an interpretive grid that will, most likely, be developed from the conceptual framework that was developed during an earlier stage of the project.

Phase 6 – Forming arguments and writing up the dissertation
In the final stage the students formulate their arguments arising from all their work and shape them into a written dissertation. The process therefore moves away from 'finding out' towards 'thinking' – although it is interesting to note that students often only find out what they mean when they start writing up the project. If all goes well, by the time they have finished writing up the students will have confidence in their project and their dissertation.

The six chapters in this guide are designed to help you through each of these stages. Their contents are briefly summarised below.

Choosing a topic and designing the project   Chapter 1
- Identifying a topic
- Drafting research objectives
- Planning the research and the project
↓

Writing a critical literature review   Chapter 2
- Searching the literature
- Summarising and précising the literature
- Evaluating key concepts and theories
↓

Concepts, conceptual frameworks and theories   Chapter 3
- Identifying key concepts
- Drafting conceptual frameworks
- Theorising the material
↓

Collecting and analysing research material   Chapter 4
- Choosing and designing research methods
- Conducting the research
- Analysing, sorting and classifying the material
↓

Interpreting the research material   Chapter 5
- Honesty of argument and language
- Interpreting research material
- Drawing safe conclusions
↓

Framing arguments and writing up the dissertation   Chapter 6
- Arguing a thesis as well as writing a dissertation
- Structuring the dissertation
- Producing documents in accordance with the style guide

What does working at Master's level mean?

Studying at Master's level requires an extension of the academic skills you may have used when you were doing diploma-level studies, as well as the development of some new ones. In this section I identify these new skills and abilities and indicate which of the chapters in this guide are intended to help you develop them.

Methodology

Having a general familiarity with some of the philosophical issues and arguments about the process of research. The study of these philosophical aspects is known as methodology. It is not expected that you should become a philosopher. It is expected that you acquire sufficient knowledge of methodology to prevent yourself from making errors such as using inappropriate research methods that will be incapable of answering the research questions you have asked.

See *Jargon, 'isms' and 'ologies'* in this chapter, *Designing your project* in Chapter 1 and *Choosing an interpretive grid* in Chapter 5.

Theorising

Attempting theoretical innovation. No one expects Master's students to create new theories (although it is wonderful if they do). On the other hand, neither are they expected simply to take theories from the literature and use them uncritically. You should look for opportunities to develop, modify or adapt the theories you take from the literature. This is often necessary because you may take a theory that was developed in one field of study, or in one context, and try to use it in different circumstances. The theory may need adaptation, or at the least review, before it is relocated. Belbin's (1981) theory of team effectiveness, for example, was derived from studies of managers, yet I have seen many people attempt to use it with production staff without checking the theory's validity on the shop floor.

See Chapter 2 and *Framing conclusions and recommendations* in Chapter 5.

Dealing with complex and ambiguous matters

Developing novel analyses and arguments. At diploma level, students face the task of understanding a management technique or approach so that they can apply it. At Master's level the intention is that complex and intransigent issues and problems should be studied. This implies that existing management techniques will be inadequate for solving such problems. Therefore, you will have to develop your own ways of thinking through the problem. Techniques will be helpful but in addition you will have to use your own thinking skills to analyse the issues and present arguments as to how the problem should be studied.

See Chapter 5 and *Writing a thesis, not just a dissertation* in Chapter 6.

Learning to learn

Reflecting on your learning. Often this means being willing, as part of doing the dissertation, to challenge the unthought-of assumptions and values that constrain our thoughts and actions. To use the current managerial jargon, you should think 'out of the box'. Another way of learning how to learn is to provide a review and critique of how you tackled the Master's project. It is generally reckoned a good idea to keep quiet about your mistakes when writing up your dissertation. This is itself a mistake. At Master's level, errors are for learning from. If you made a mistake in good faith (as opposed to laziness or sloppiness) then report it in the dissertation and show how you have learnt from it. This should gain you extra marks. If, for example, after you have completed a questionnaire survey you decide it would have been better to do in-depth interviews, then explain, in the dissertation, why you have come to this view and how you would tackle such issues differently in the future.

See Chapter 5.

Undertaking a Master's dissertation requires you to develop your skills of analysis and argument; abilities that C. Wright Mills, a sociologist, called intellectual craftsmanship (see Exhibit 0.1).

Exhibit 0.1

C. Wright Mills 'On Intellectual Craftsmanship'

In 1959 C. Wright Mills added to his book *The Sociological Imagination* an appendix entitled 'On Intellectual Craftmanship' (in 1959 it was unexceptional to use sexist terms). The craft skills he identified are still those that underpin the ability to do academic work, at whatever level.

Do not separate work from life

This is especially important for people doing MBA or similar dissertations because they are likely to be researching the context they work within. His point is that ideas and insights from life can often provide the trigger or clue for theoretical understanding of the issues we are researching. He suggests, for example, that when we find ourselves feeling very emotional, perhaps angry, about something that happened at work; if we take the trouble to identify and analyse the cause of that anger then that effort can lead to thoughts that can become the basis of research. He recommends that all researchers keep research journals in which their occasional thoughts and ideas can be collected to be mulled over at a later time.

Reasoning before emprical research

Wright Mills took a stronger line on this than many Master's supervisors could agree with. He thought empirical research a tedious necessity. 'Now I do not like to do empirical work if I can possibly avoid it' (Wright Mills, 1959). You will almost

Exhibit 0.1 *continued*

certainly have to do empirical work to complete your dissertation but Wright Mills' general point, that it is wise to do some reading, thinking and theorising before doing the empirical research, is still relevant. For him, reasoning consisted of:

- identifying elements and concepts;
- deciding the logical relationships between them, 'building little models'; and then
- deciding what critical issues need to be tested by empirical research.

This process is referred to, in this book, as conceptual framework building and is explained in Chapter 3.

Getting ideas

Imagination, according to Wright Mills, was what distinguished the scientist from the technician. Imagination can be encouraged in a number of ways. Challenging common sense explanations is a good starting point. A second method is to consider very carefully the words that are used to discuss the topic of the research. The 'learning organisation' was a frequent topic of research (recently it has been superseded by knowledge management). A careful dissection of the meanings of the two words – learning and organsation – will raise questions to be researched. Is learning, for example, a tangible thing that can be stored or is it a process that cannot? The third way of releasing imagination is to throw all your ideas, which you have carefully classified and organised under neat labels, into the air, allow them to fall randomly, and then re-sort and re-classify them.

Framing a thesis

Wright Mills made an important distinction between topic and theme. A common problem among students doing a dissertation is that they settle upon the topic of their research (a hard enough task) but do not go on to identify the themes of their research. A theme is a big idea or line of argument that gives shape to a dissertation and helps to separate the important research material from the unimportant. A good conceptual framework should help you identify your themes – you may have several – and this may involve choosing an interpretive perspective or lens (this is explained in Chapter 5).

Writing in a clear and simple language

Wright Mills pointed out (which management and business students already know), that many academics in the field write in a deliberaely obscure manner that appears to be intended to make the book or article seem cleverer than it is. Students should not emulate this but should, instead, write in a straightforward manner.

Be a good craftsman

A good intellectual craftsman, according to Wright Mills, avoids rigid and set procedures. They realise that research is not a matter of simply following a recipe. In this book I do give rather a lot of recipes for doing this or that aspect of researching and writing a dissertation. This is because one has to start somewhere. But the recipes are just that – a start, a guide. Do not treat them as the final word on the matter. You have to make the methods your own and become your own methodologist and theorist.

● ● ● ● The assessment criteria

In formal terms Master's students have to show, in their proposals, papers and dissertations, that they have achieved a number of learning outcomes in order to pass the module. You should adopt a degree of instrumentality (by assuming the objective of the exercise is to pass the dissertation and gain the Master's degree) and study the learning outcomes and assessment criteria that your business school will use in marking your dissertation.

There is an independent body, the Quality Assurance Agency for Higher Education (QAA), which, among other things, sets the qualification descriptors for academic degrees in the United Kingdom. All MBAs and Master's in management programmes may base their learning outcomes for assessing dissertations on the descriptor, which is shown in Exhibit 0.2.

The learning outcomes and assessment criteria used in the business school where I work are used here to illustrate what the demands of a dissertation are. They are probably not very different from those of your institution, but if they are you should obviously work towards those that will be used to mark your dissertation.

Exhibit 0.2

The Quality Assurance Agency for Higher Education's descriptor for a qualification at Master's (M) level: Master's degree

Master's degrees are awarded to students who have demonstrated:

1. a systematic understanding of knowledge, and a critical awareness of current problems and/or new insights, much of which is at, or informed by, the forefront of their academic discipline, field of study, or area of professional practice;
2. a comprehensive understanding of techniques applicable to their own research or advanced scholarship;
3. originality in the application of knowledge, together with a practical understanding of how established techniques of research and enquiry are used to create and interpret knowledge in the discipline;
4. conceptual understanding that enables the student:
   - to evaluate critically current research and advanced scholarship in the discipline; and
   - to evaluate methodologies and develop critiques of them and, where appropriate, to propose new hypotheses.

Typically, holders of the qualification will be able to:

(a) deal with complex issues both systematically and creatively, make sound judgements in the absence of complete data, and communicate their conclusions clearly to specialist and non-specialist audiences;

Exhibit 0.2 *continued*

(b) demonstrate self-direction and originality in tackling and solving problems, and act autonomously in planning and implementing tasks at a professional or equivalent level;

(c) continue to advance their knowledge and understanding, and to develop new skills to a high level; and will have:

(d) the qualities and transferable skills necessary for employment requiring:
- the exercise of initiative and personal responsibility;
- decision making in complex and unpredictable situations; and
- the independent learning ability required for continuing professional development.

Source: The Framework for Higher Education Qualifications in England, Wales and Northern Ireland. © The Quality Assurance Agency for Higher Education (2001).

The learning outcomes and assessment criteria

The following are the learning outcomes for a dissertation module.

At the completion of this module students will be able to:

1. define the objectives of a research project and plan a valid and practicable project to meet the objectives;
2. carry out a critical literature review that provides a structure and focus for the dissertation;
3. define concepts and structure them in ways that give a useful theoretical shape to the dissertation;
4. design and apply appropriate research methods and analyse the research material systematically;
5. frame, and argue for, a clear thesis in the documents and draw safe conclusions;
6. write a clearly structured, adequately expressed and well-presented dissertation.

This guide has been structured so that each of the six chapters deals with one of these learning outcomes.

The learning outcomes set the standard for what students have to achieve. However, they do not define the criteria that markers will use to decide whether a student has reached an appropriate level of achievement against each of the learning outcomes. These criteria can be seen in Table 0.1, called the assessment matrix. A number of points need to be made about this table:

- The matrix is for assessing a complete dissertation. If you also have to submit a written research proposal or an academic paper for assessment, then probably only some of the criteria would apply.
- The matrix identifies a number of levels. Most are self-explanatory. The borderline fail level needs explanation, however. A student who is marked 46–49 per cent is classified, in some institutions, as a borderline fail. This indicates that the dissertation would only need relatively minor changes and improvements to bring it up to pass standard. In some programmes it may be possible to show this improvement at a viva voce examination.

Table 0.1 Assessment criteria for postgraduate dissertations in business, organisational and management studies

	Identify a research question and design a project to answer it	*Write a critical literature review*	*Define working concepts and conceptual frameworks to give structure to the work*	*Collect and analyse research data efficiently and effectively*	*Interpret findings sensitively as a basis for making recommendations for action that are practicable and sound*	*Write reports and dissertations that are persuasive, well structured and well written*
80–100% Excellent	An excellent proposal that would be awarded a grant if it were sent to a research funding body	The literature review is itself a significant contribution to the literature	Significant additions to the theoretical and conceptual understanding of the subject	Makes a contribution to the development of methods for collecting and analysing research material and/or methodological debate	Complex and sophisticated interpretation of the material. The conclusions are based on the findings but transcend them. Subtle understanding of action in organisations	A work of art written with style and wit. Strong arguments that refer back to each other.
70–79% Very good Distinction level	Clear and specific about research question, project design and research methods. These three elements are shown to be well coordinated and an appropriate admixture	The literature is cogently described and evaluated from novel or complex perspectives	An attempt, not necessarily wholly successful, is made to theorise beyond the current state of the literature	Modifies and develops methods for collecting and analysing research material in a way that reflects methodological understanding	Interprets the findings in a sophisticated manner. Conclusions are firmly based in findings but show a creative spark. Implementation plans show an awareness of the interaction of understanding and action	Clear and persuasive arguments expressed in good plain English in a well-structured document

Table 0.1 *continued*

60–69% Good	Well-defined research question. Sensible project design and clear plans for conducting the research	The literature is cogently evaluated using positions already available in the literature	A conceptual framework is developed, or an existing one adapted, in context of an evaluated literature	Uses methods of gathering and analysing research material well and shows an understanding of methodological issues	Uses techniques for interpretation but in a mechanical way. Conclusions based well on findings. Practical schemes for action	Either expressed well or technically correct but not both. Clear structure adequately argued
50–59% Competent Pass level	Clear research question. Explicit ideas on design and methods but there are some issues about the fit between question, design and methods	Good description of the appropriate field(s) of literature. Some general criticisms made but no close evaluation of concepts	Concepts are clearly defined and appropriate. They are set in the context of the literature	Methods for gathering and analysing research material are used competently	Treats the findings as straightforward and unproblematic. Conclusions have some connection with the findings. Action plans are general but prescriptive	Adequate expression but a noticeable number of mistakes. Argumentation is sometimes replaced by assumption or assertion
46–49% Borderline fail	Identified an interesting topic but the research question is very broad and the details of the project are hazy	Inadequate or limited description of the appropriate field(s) of literature, and/or no criticism or evaluation	The definition and use of theoretical concepts is confused. No attempt at theoretical synthesis or evaluation	Methods for gathering and analysing research material are used in a confused and unsystematic way	The occasional insight takes the place of interpretation. Conclusions have a tenuous link with findings. Action plans are simple exhortations or lacking	Sentences often do not make sense. Uses bullet points to disguise a lack of arguments
≤ 45% Fail	The focus, purpose and method of the project are unclear	The author appears to have read little and understood less	No conceptual or theoretical discussion of any value	No primary research of any value	Provides no evidence that they know what this outcome is about	Scrappy presentation, illogical structure. No arguments or silly ones

● ● ● ● # Jargon, 'isms' and 'ologies'

If you are studying for a Master's qualification you have to come to terms with the 'isms' and 'ologies' that are appropriate to your study. This means you will have to read and understand some books and articles that are relevant but difficult. To have a Master's degree in a subject means that you have a mastery of that subject. You cannot have mastery if there are some books and articles that are relevant to it that you declare out of bounds because you consider them too difficult.

Consequently you will have to learn to understand some difficult jargon. Part of the purpose of this guide is to make that task a little easier when it comes to the jargon of doing research. To use a term that was mentioned earlier, an awareness of the methodological issues surrounding research is necessary. There are a number of methodological terms you may come across, and what follows is a brief introductory comment on some of the major ones.

A dissertation is founded on research, which is an effort to find things out. Unfortunately there is a dispute between researchers about what it is possible to discover by research. The argument is not restricted to the business and management field. It is a general one about the nature of knowledge. The proper title for the study of the nature of knowledge is epistemology. The epistemological debate has a long history and it is unlikely that the matter will be resolved during your work on the dissertation. It thus remains a dangerous current that threatens to drag you off course as you try to steer your research efforts. This danger is the reason for having a sufficient knowledge of methodological and epistemological issues. An awareness of the currents and tides in this area will help you keep out of danger. The methodological argument affects all aspects of doing a dissertation and its impact can be seen in all six chapters of this guide. In this introduction an attempt is made to provide an understanding of the broad issues in the arguments about methodology so that the more careful arguments in the later chapters can be more easily understood.

A number of different methodological approaches to research are shown in Figure 0.2. This is a slightly quirky analysis based on the way I have made sense of methodology. If you wish you can skip this and move on to Figure 0.3, which classifies methodological approaches using a framework based on the literature.

In Figure 0.2 the research approaches are plotted using coordinates from two axes or dimensions. The first dimension concerns the relationship between the knowledge it is possible for us to have about the world external to us and that world itself. At one end of the spectrum it is thought that our knowledge is an exact reflection of the world. At the other end of the dimension the world is thought to be largely unknowable and that what we can know is patchy. There are two intermediate positions plotted between these two extremes.

The terms 'orthodox' and 'gnostic' will be used to describe the other dimension in Figure 0.2. These are not terms you will find elsewhere in the literature on research methods. They are taken by analogy from early divisions in Christianity. However, the different views of the world taken by the orthodox and the gnostics can still be seen in modern perspectives on research. Some idea of the positions taken by the two sides can be gained from Exhibit 0.3.

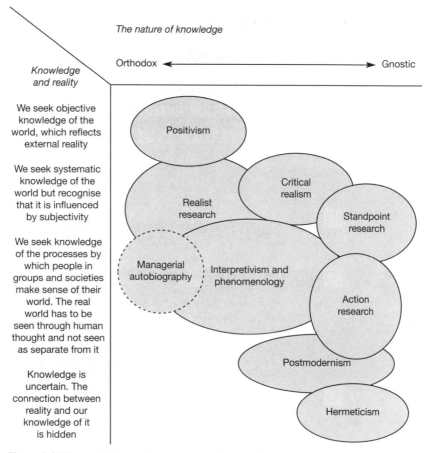

The nature of knowledge

Orthodox ←——————————→ Gnostic

Knowledge and reality

We seek objective knowledge of the world, which reflects external reality

Positivism

We seek systematic knowledge of the world but recognise that it is influenced by subjectivity

Realist research

Critical realism

Standpoint research

We seek knowledge of the processes by which people in groups and societies make sense of their world. The real world has to be seen through human thought and not seen as separate from it

Managerial autobiography

Interpretivism and phenomenology

Action research

Knowledge is uncertain. The connection between reality and our knowledge of it is hidden

Postmodernism

Hermeticism

Figure 0.2 The main forms of management research

	Non-recognition of the relevance of human subjectivity	**Recognition of the relevance of human subjectivity**
Ontological realism ↕ **Ontological nominalism**	Positivism	Methodological pluralism
		Realist research
		Critical realism
		Standpoint research
		Action research
	Not a possible combination	
		Interpretivism

Figure 0.3 Methodological choices
Source: adapted from Figure 10.2, Gill and Johnson (2002:196).

This distinction will be used to map out some of the major methodological disagreements in research. It is hoped this will give you a starting point for your methodological understanding. If you are not interested in the source of the analogy then ignore Exhibit 0.4.

Exhibit 0.3

The orthodox and the gnostic

Orthodox	Gnostic
There is an objective truth	Truth is subjective
Truth is simple and transparent	Truth is hidden
Truth is an agreed body of knowledge	Truth is gained through personal struggle
Conformance and obedience	Challenge and diversity
Language is transparent	Language is ambiguous

Exhibit 0.4

Orthodoxy and Gnosticism

The Orthodox view of Christianity is to be found in the Bible. Orthodox in this sense refers to the position of all the institutional churches such as the Catholic, the Eastern Orthodox and the Anglican churches. It used to be thought that the books included in the Bible, the canon, were the main Christian texts. It was known that there were various heretical texts in the early years of the Church but that these were marginal. But in 1945 a peasant found pots buried in the Egyptian desert that contained ancient scrolls. These turned out to be early Christian gospels that in most cases had never been heard of before, such as the Gospel of Thomas, the Gospel of Philip, the Gospel of the Egyptians. They were written in the second century AD.

These gospels suggest that there were two early versions of Christianity and that each saw the world and the truth in very different ways. The Orthodox gospels see the world as a good place that has a real existence. The task of humankind is to use it well and live according to the rules and values preached in the gospels. Salvation comes from obedience to the rules of the Church; through obedience to rules that are clear and apply to everyone. The Gnostic gospels see the world differently. Gnosis is a word of Greek origin that means knowledge. But it is different from technical knowledge. It is insight into oneself or others gained through intuitive self-examination. The Gnostics cared little about the physical world. They saw it as a snare and an illusion. The important thing was for individuals to develop their own souls through reflecting upon their own subjective processes of thought and understanding. By increasing their inner perfection they could become close to God. Gnostic knowledge was hidden and not easily found. Acquiring this knowledge called for moral worth and intellectual effort.

For Gnostics the world was dominated by chance and irrational forces. Individuals have to learn how to cope with an uncaring world. The Orthodox view was expressed through institutions, through churches, whereas the Gnostics approached religion from an individualist perspective. There were many different forms and sects of Gnosticism. Unsurprisingly, the Orthodox spent most of their time, in the early centuries of Christianity, fighting the Gnostics. The Gnostics spent most of their time squabbling among themselves. Historically the Orthodox prevailed over the Gnostics. Pagels (1982) provides a good introduction to Gnosticism.

Figure 0.3 classifies the different methodological approaches in a more conventional manner by using a framework developed by Gill and Johnson (2002: 173). It is worth remembering that while innovation may be appreciated in a dissertation, it should be innovation that develops what is in the literature and not innovation that starts afresh with a clean sheet. In Gill and Johnson's framework the two dimensions are:

- whether human subjectivity is recognized or ignored;
- whether what is being researched is thought to have an objective existence (realism) or focuses on the subjective meanings that individuals and societies use to make sense of their world (nominalism, see p. 281.)

The research approaches shown in Figures 0.2 and 0.3 are now discussed in more detail.

Positivism

Auguste Comte (1798–1857) coined the term 'positivism' in the nineteenth century. It was a statement about the power of science and of rational thought to comprehend and manipulate the world. It rejected the metaphysical and subjective ideas and was interested only in the tangible. Positivism holds that an accurate and value-free knowledge of things is possible. It holds out the possibility that human beings, their actions and institutions can be studied as objectively as the natural world. But positivism's emphasis on tangible things is important in this regard. It may be possible to study scientifically the tangible aspects of human activity – behaviours, speech – but not of course the intangible – the internal interpretation or motivation of those externals. Behaviourism was an example of this approach from psychology. Its heyday was in the 1960s and 1970s, and behaviourists held that psychology should be the study of people's observable and quantifiable behaviour and that no regard should be given to their internal processes of consciousness.

The intention of positivism is to produce general (sometimes called 'covering') laws that can be used to predict behaviour, in terms of probability at least, if not with absolute certainty. These general laws would form an open and orthodox body of knowledge, and the positivist method would be the standard approach for all scientific endeavours. It has often been assumed that traditional social science is positivist; however, some (such as Tilley, 1980: 28) argued that it is possible to have an objective, scientific social science without taking a fully fledged positivist stance, a view that is discussed in the next section.

There is no doubt that in some cases, such as mathematical models of crowd behaviour in shops and stadiums and models of market behaviour, a hard scientific approach can be invaluable. However, there are problems with these methods. They can, for example, predict only the average behaviour, not the behaviour of individuals; and in many situations understanding particularities is as important as understanding the norm. Another issue is that many choices and assumptions have been made when developing such models, and these choices open the door for the researchers' values and preferences to enter into the research process. Many researchers argue that research into the social and institutional world cannot be value-free, and that the aspiration for social researchers to become hard scientists such as chemists is not achievable (Robson, 2002: 22–23). Probably it would not be possible for MBA students working on their dissertations to adopt an extreme positivist stance, if for no other reason than that they are likely to be researching their own organisations and therefore are not the disinterested observers that scientists are supposed to be. We will not spend too much time on positivist approaches to research in this guide.

Realist research

Realist research is an approach that retains many of the ambitions of positivism but recognises, and comes to terms with, the subjective nature of research and the inevitable role of values in it. Realism still aims to be scientific but makes fewer claims to knowledge that perfectly mirrors the objects of study. Researchers with this stance recognise that things such as 'strategy' and 'job satisfaction' cannot be measured and studied in the same way as can chemical and physical processes. However, they do believe that a worthwhile attempt can be made to fix these subjects and treat them as if they are independent variables. Realist research has therefore been placed in the top right-hand quadrant of the framework in Figure 0.3.

As an example, let us imagine someone is interested in human resource development (HRD) because they think it is an underrated function of management. They suspect that uncertainty about the values of HRD may contribute to its low status. They wish to rectify the situation by researching the core values of HRD. Taking a realist approach they know that there has been much argument over the definition of HRD but this does not prevent them from believing there is a thing called HRD that can be defined and measured. They send out questionnaires to HRD practitioners and use the responses to identify several core values that define the basis of HRD practice. While they recognise that individual HRD practitioners may have different reactions to these core values they believe that HRD has an existence separate from these individual reactions and that it is possible and sensible to talk about HRD's values. Realist research puts things into categories and labels them, although it is possible to argue about whether the right categories ('should we call it HRD?') have been chosen.

Realist researchers claim to be orthodox. They want to discover the mechanisms that bring about events and they are concerned that their theories should be verifiable and have some generalisability. Miles and Huberman (1994: 5) expressed this position well:

> We think that social phenomena exist not only in the mind but also in the objective world – and that some lawful and reasonably stable relationships are to be found between them. The lawfulness comes from the regularities and sequences that link together phenomena. From these patterns we can derive constructs that underlie individual and social life ... [we] do not use 'covering laws' or the [ ] logic of classical positivism.

Realist researchers often seek to offer generalisable explanations but they are less likely (than positivists) to offer predictions.

Realists like Miles and Huberman often use qualitative methods although if they can then add some quantification to their qualitative material (for example, counting the frequencies with which findings can be classified under different headings) they have no objection to doing so. However, because the realists recognise the role of subjectivity, all theories have to come with a health warning because different researchers with different values will propose competing theories. The existence of competing, or even of complementary, explanations is one of the features of realist research. Tilley (1980: 33) argued (based on the writings of Karl Popper (see p. 44)) that such disagreements are inevitable and they may even be based on bias or prejudice. Nevertheless, it is still possible to have an objective social science. This is because the explanations that researchers propose are only ever provisional and they become the subject of scrutiny and testing by other researchers. In the long run this critical debate will drive out the inadequate explanations. The dangers of researchers' subjectivity are counterbalanced by debate and review.

Many MBA students will take a realist approach when doing their dissertations.

Critical realism

Critical realism, as its name implies, shares the ambitions of realism and so, in Figure 0.3., it is placed in the same quadrant as realism. However, in the terms used in Figure 0.2 it takes a more gnostic than orthodox tack. This is because it adds the notion of layers or stratification into our understanding of knowledge. Critical realists argue that there is a level of reality below the everyday levels of events and our experiences of them (see p. 285). It is at this level that the mechanisms that drive events in the world exist. Unfortunately our knowledge of this level is not direct; it can only be inferred. So, as with the gnostics, there is a claim that there is a level of reality that is not easily accessible because it is hidden from common view. As Miles and Huberman (1994: 5) expressed it:

We look for a [ ] process or mechanism, a structure at the core of events that can be captured to provide a causal description of the forces at work … The fact that most of these constructs are invisible to the naked eye does not make them invalid. After all, we all are surrounded by lawful physical mechanisms of which we're, at most, remotely aware.

To discover this level of reality requires honest and intelligent people to work hard at the problems and to become adept at discovering these mechanisms. The need for honesty arises because those who do critical realist research into business and management may discover bad things that ought to be made known and have action taken to correct them. There can be a moral component to the critical realist approach. Managers doing dissertations as part of their management education may not feel it is their role to provide such a moral critique of the market and institutional context within which they make their living. Nevertheless, it is a valid approach to management and business research and suggestions for (and examples of) its application are provided in this guide.

Managerial autobiography

This is not really a research approach at all, and so it is marked out with a dotted line in Figure 0.2. However, it is a common body of literature that MBA students are often drawn to. The category is constituted of all those books in which a successful entrepreneur's or chief executive officer's work experience is written down and presented as a clear orthodoxy for those who wish to achieve business success. As this knowledge has not been discovered by an objective type of research, but unashamedly bases its claim to be heard on its very subjectivity, it has been placed at that point on the vertical scale of Figure 0.2 where knowledge is seen through the prism of subjectivity.

My experience of supervising MBA students suggests that this is not a good route for them to take in their dissertation. The student who announces that they wish to use the dissertation as a vehicle for distilling their wisdom, drawn from their experience over many years of a certain industry, often struggles. Their research becomes an apologia or a justification of their actions and a chance to do down those who have opposed them.

Interpretivism and phenomenology

There are many terms for this approach to research. 'Interpretivism' is the one that will be used in this guide, although 'phenomenology' is the preferred term of many textbooks. Other terms used are 'constructionism' and 'naturalistic research'. (Concerning the spelling of interpretive, the *Oxford English Dictionary* also allows interpret*ative*.)

This approach is placed near the bottom of the vertical scale because researchers who take this position believe that reality is socially constructed. This means that our understanding of 'reality' is not a simple account of what is; rather, it is something that people in societies and groups form from the following:

- their interpretation of reality, which is influenced by their values and their way of seeing the world;
- other people's interpretation;
- the compromises and agreements that arise out of the negotiations between the first two.

Imagine you work in the procurement division of a large multinational and you are invited to an evening at a casino and dinner at a very expensive restaurant by a senior manager of an overseas company that wants you to give it a large contract. The casino is real and so are the restaurant and the food and wine, although the wine makes the other things seem a little less real. But there is another level of reality, which is – what do you think is really going on? Is the evening's entertainment just a friendly gesture, is it seen as a social obligation because it is what is expected in the senior manager's home country, is it a blatant bribe or is it a mixture of all these things and more? An interpretivist researcher would also be interested in the clues and process by which you decided what the 'reality' of this situation was. Interpretivist researchers are interested in the particularities of a situation, although they will categorise and label the processes for dealing with particulars ('how can we generalise about how people decide what to do in such situations?').

As researchers cannot claim to be studying an objective reality (which exists but is less interesting than the way people make sense of it), they study the following:

- the different accounts people give of issues and topics;
- people's accounts of the process by which they make sense of the world.

Interpretive research has been classified as gnostic in Figure 0.2 because it does not accept the existence of an orthodox or standard interpretation of any particular topic. Rather, it emphasises plurality, relativism and complexity. It is an attempt to understand the processes by which we gain knowledge and so it has affinity with the original gnostic search for one's true self. A feature of interpretive research is that you cannot understand how others may make sense of things unless you have an insightful knowledge of your own values and thinking processes. In research terms, this knowledge is known as reflexivity (see p. 299).

Interpretive research is not as common as realist research in MBA dissertations but it can be the basis of fascinating projects. It is discussed in some detail in this guide.

Action research

Action research is a further development of interpretive research that goes further towards the gnostic. I have to be careful with this claim, though, because there are different forms of action research and not all would fit my categorisation. Nevertheless, one major theme of action research is to seek to understand things by changing them, by experimenting with something new, and then by studying the consequences of the action and using them to reflect on one's values and preconceptions (that is the gnostic bit) before then taking new action. Although there are practical problems in choosing action research as the basis for a project (not least being whether the year that students typically have to complete their dissertation is sufficient to have a few cycles of action and reflection), it can lead to very worthwhile projects and is discussed in this guide.

Standpoint research

In Figure 0.2 standpoint research fits between critical realism and action research and in Figure 0.3 it is placed in the top right-hand quadrant of the framework. Standpoint research starts from the position that there is injustice in the world and that particular groups (the most commonly focused on are women, gays and ethnic minorities) are most likely to be the subjects of such injustice. The point of research is not to understand the injustice but to stop it. This approach to research takes its inspiration from Marx's (1968: 30) 11th thesis on Feuerbach: 'The philosophers have only interpreted the world, in various ways: the point, however, is to change it'. Morwenna Griffiths (1998), who is an educational researcher, puts a similar point of view more simply in the title of one of her books, *Educational Research for Social Justice: Getting off the Fence*.

Standpoint research has some of the characteristics of critical realism because researchers seek to identify the deep structural causes of social injustice. It shares with action research the intention of making the world a fairer place by changing it through the process of raising people's consciousnesses.

One feature of standpoint research is that it believes that the standard techniques and approaches to research are part of the problem. The standard methods of research, from a feminist perspective, for example, can be seen as marginalising women, by treating them as a separate category. Mirchandani (1999) studied female entrepreneurs and noted that whether their behaviour was entrepreneurial was defined by comparison with male entrepreneurs. This type of analysis might make female entrepreneurship appear to be a subsidiary, or even odd, form. Some feminist researchers have also rejected many of the traditional forms of research because they do not allow women to speak in their own authentic voice and so re-inforce the injustices that beset them.

Postmodernism

The postmodern stance sees nothing in the social and intellectual world as tangible or fixed. At this vantage point fragmentation is accepted as part of the human condition. In Lyotard's (1988: 46) famous phrase there is 'incredulity towards metanarratives'. This means that the large ideological schemes, such as capitalism and communism that used to dominate people's thinking, no longer have credibility. In the postmodern view there are no eternal truths or values. What we think of as objectively true emerges through discourses that are embedded in power and knowledge relationships where some have more influence on the outcomes of the discourses than others. But what emerges is in any case uncertain because the language we use is opaque and carries no single, clear messages (Legge, 1995: 306). For this reason postmodernism is shown in Figure 0.2 at the end of the 'knowledge and reality' spectrum that represents the belief that our knowledge of reality is uncertain.

The words we use to express our values have no fixed meaning. Statements have to be treated as texts and deconstructed. *Différance* is Derrida's device for exploring the limitless instability of language. One aspect of *différance* is that no word has a positive meaning attributed to it; it has meaning only to the extent that it is different from other words. Another aspect is deferral because the meaning of one word is always explained by reference to another and the search for meaning can involve a complex chain of cross-references as one chases a word through a vast thesaurus. Let us take an innocuous statement about public management:

> The first steps to achieving accountability for performance must be to clarify objectives and develop a recognised approach to measuring and reporting performance.

> (Dallas, 1996: 13)

This is enough to cause a deconstructionist to salivate. Postmodern researchers seek to decode dialogue to show that it can only lead to aporia. This is a term from classical rhetoric that is often used in postmodern writing. It means being in a state of bewilderment and confusion as to what it is right and good to say or do. Such a concern for getting underneath the surface meaning of words is the reason why postmodernism is shown on the gnostic end of the 'orthodox/gnostic' scale in Figure 0.2.

Most of the words in the sentence do not have an unambiguous or uncontested meaning. Accountability, for example, can only be defined by relating it to other words such as hierarchy, responsiveness, transparency and so on. Accountability may be viewed from different discourses such as political accountability, audit and accounting, consumer rights and investigative journalism. If we had the time to explore this sentence in detail and to plot its webs of signification we would find that the sentence could mean almost anything. The search for meaning may not be endless; but the end will be terminal confusion rather than clear understanding. The function of deconstruction is to reach a final impasse.

Deconstruction is not intended to overcome fragmentation but simply to map the instabilities, paradoxes and aporetic states that define it. From this position there is no hope that the fragmented values can be put back together again. As Harvey (1989) expressed it, disapprovingly, postmodernism

> swims and even wallows in the fragmentary and chaotic current of change as if that was all there was.

(Harvey, 1989: 116)

Hermeticism

Hermeticism takes its name from Hermes Trismegistus, an apocryphal pre-Christian Egyptian priest whose books were probably actually written in Alexandria in the third century AD. It is often linked with the cabbala (see p. 134) with which it shares a belief that all things in heaven and earth are linked in a harmonious whole but that the knowledge of these connections is secret and esoteric and can only be accessed by a few adepts. Everyday knowledge, by contrast, is seen as fragmented and confused. You do not often find hermeticism in writing on business and management but Gibson Burrell's (1997) book is an example. Burrell (1997: 101) alludes to his text as a cabbalistic one.

In hermetic thought, connections between things are seen as symbolic and spiritual rather than rational and analytical. The idea of overlapping concentric circles replaces the linear form that we associate with rational analysis. The orthodox model of industrial development, for example, sees economic growth as happening in a linear fashion as one stage inevitably leads to a further, and higher, stage. Hermetic thought could see these stages being leapfrogged as, in an actual instance, old cottage-industry forms of work are allied to modern information technology and communication methods to bring products and services to a post-Fordist international market (Burrell 1997: 101–100[1]). This might be small craft producers using the Internet to sell their products globally. In this process the old and the new are intermingled. The modern does not replace the old. Hermeticism focuses on symbolic relationships between things that seem or look alike (see p. 134). This probably is reflected in the liking of many modern management thinkers for metaphor. A metaphor is a judgement that one thing is equivalent to another, which is a symbolic link. It

---

[1] The page numbers are in reverse order because this part of Burrell's book is to be read from back to front.

follows that if machines are metaphors for organisations, then organisations should be treated in the same way as machines because, in some non-rational way, a machine is a microcosm of the organisational macrocosm.

However, in this guide we will ignore the two extremes of positivism and hermeticism and focus on the intermediate approaches to research.

The descriptions of the various approaches to research are something of a caricature, and specialists will take exception to many of its claims. It will be necessary in later chapters to take a more sophisticated view of these matters. But understanding has to start somewhere, and an over-generalisation is as good a point as any. This problem is a version of the hermeneutic circle. Hermeneutics is the theory of interpretation concerned with the meaning of texts. The hermeneutic circle is a claim that you cannot understand the entirety of a thing until you understand its details; but you cannot understand the details until you understand the entirety. This is certainly true of research methodology. If it is of any comfort, I have been studying this subject for some time but my understanding of it is still developing!

How to use this guide

This guide covers all the main areas relevant to doing a dissertation and associated pieces of work. It is divided into six chapters. They are intended to form a sequence but they can be used in any order. There are many themes that appear in several if not all chapters.

This guide is only a guide, however, and should not be seen as a set of dogmatic rules that you break at your peril. It is also an informal guide, and so its tone is often relaxed. Good guides often reflect their author's prejudices. Whether this guide is good is up to others to decide – but it is certainly opinionated. A certain sceptical or ironical tone also creeps into the text. This is normally at places in the guide where the subject matter is one on which there is no consensus. At these points the irony is a signal to the reader. You, the reader, will be unsure whether my text is to be taken seriously or not. You will have to think through the issue and come to your own conclusion.

The guide offers many examples of how to tackle problems when doing a dissertation. It also provides many 'five easy steps' instructions on how to do things. These illustrations and recipes are mostly designed to stimulate your own thought processes and are not to be followed slavishly. Try to avoid falling into the trap shown in the box.

The role-modelling vicious circle
Supervisor: 'You need to develop a conceptual framework.'
Student: 'How do I do that?'
Supervisor: 'Well, a conceptual framework means [etc. ...]'
Student: 'Uh?! Give me an example ...'
Supervisor: 'For example, take this concept and that concept and put them in this 2 × 2 table and ...'
Student: 'That's good. Can I use it?'

The guide is also a collection of materials that were to hand. The post-modernists would call such a collage by the French term *bricolage*. This is not a problem. Room is left for you to develop your own approach by following the leads you find in the research literature. To the extent that the guide is a collage, it will resemble your own project, in which you have to make a convincing assemblage – of the pieces of research you have done, the material from the literature, the stuff you learnt on other courses or at school years ago and the ideas and the bees in bonnets collected over the years – as you write your dissertation. It is possible to take the work seriously while also taking a wry sidelong look at its nature. Taking things seriously is often no more than taking oneself too seriously.

For these reasons you need to supplement your study of the guide with reading in the literature on research methods in business, management and organisational studies. In particular it will be necessary for you to read further on the specific research techniques you plan to use in your project.

Suggested reading

Each of the chapters in the guide includes suggestions for further reading in its particular specialist area.

There are a number of general textbooks for people researching in managerial, organisational or business topics. The main recommendation is Alan Bryman and Emma Bell, *Business Research Methods* (Oxford: Oxford University Press, 2003). It is authoritative and detailed and provides many examples from published research studies. Other useful general textbooks are:

Easterby-Smith, M., Thorpe, R. and Lowe, A. (2002) *Management Research: An Introduction*, 2nd edn, London: Sage.

Gill, J. and Johnson, P. (2002) *Research Methods for Managers*, 3rd edn., London: Paul Chapman.

Saunders, M., Lewis, P. and Thornhill, A. (2006) *Research Methods for Business Students*, 4th edn, Harlow: FT Prentice Hall.

Other recommended books

Bell, J. (1999) *Doing Your Research Project: A Guide for First-time Researchers in Education and Social Science*, 3rd edn, Buckingham: Open University Press.

Blaxter, L., Hughes, C. and Tight, M. (2002) *How to Research*, 2nd edn, Buckingham: Open University Press.

Jankowicz, A.D. (2000) *Business Research Projects*, 3rd edn, London: Paul Chapman.

Remenyi, D., Williams, B., Money, A. and Swartz, E. (1998) *Doing Research in Business and Management: An Introduction to Process and Method*, London: Sage.

References

Belbin, R.M. (1981) *Management Teams: Why They Succeed or Fail*, London: Heinemann.

Burrell, G. (1997) *Pandemonium: Towards a Retro Organisational Theory*, London: Sage.

Dallas, M. (1996) 'Accountability for Performance – Does Audit have a Role?', in *Adding Value? Audit and Accountability in the Public Services*, London: Public Finance Foundation and Chartered Institute of Public Finance and Accountancy (CIPFA).

Griffiths, M. (1998) *Educational Research for Social Justice: Getting off the Fence*, Buckingham: Open University Press.

Harvey, D. (1989) *The Condition of Postmodernity*, Oxford: Blackwell.

Legge, K. (1995) *Human Resource Management: Rhetoric and Realities*, London: Macmillan.

Lyotard, J-F. (1988) *Le Postmodernisme Expliqué aux Enfants, Correspondance 1982–85*, Paris: Editions Galilée.

Marx, K. (1968) 'Theses on Feuerbach', in K. Marx and F. Engels, *Marx and Engels Selected Works*, London: Lawrence & Wishart.

Mirchandani, K. (1999) 'Feminist insight on gendered work: new directions in research on women and entrepreneurship', *Gender, Work and Organisation*, vol. 6, no. 4: 224–235.

Miles, M.B. and Huberman, A.M. (1994) *Qualitative Data Analysis: An Expanded Sourcebook*, London: Sage.

Pagels, E. (1982) *The Gnostic Gospels*, Harmondsworth: Penguin.

Quality Assurance Agency for Higher Education (QAA) (2001) *The Framework for Higher Education Qualifications in England, Wales and Northern Ireland. Annex 1: Qualification Descriptors*. Available online at: http://www.qaa.ac.uk/crntwork/nqf/ewni/2001/annex1.htm#4 (accessed 20 July 2003).

Robson, C. (2002) *Real World Research*, 2nd edn, Oxford: Blackwell.

Tilley, N. (1980) 'Popper, positivism and ethnomethodology', *British Journal of Sociology*, vol. 31, no. 1: 28–45.

Wright Mills, C. (2000) *The Sociological Imagination*, Oxford: Oxford University Press (first published 1959).

Chapter 1

Choosing a topic and designing the project

Contents

● ● ● ● Introduction

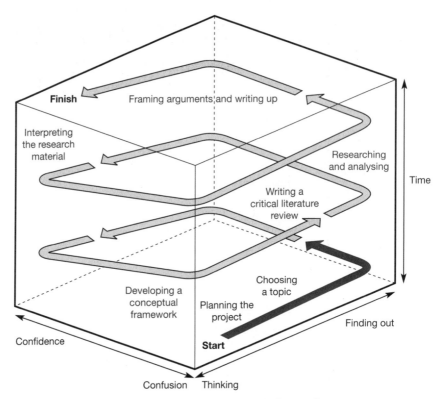

Finish   Framing arguments and writing up

Interpreting the research material

Researching and analysing

Time

Writing a critical literature review

Choosing a topic

Developing a conceptual framework

Planning the project

Finding out

Confidence

Start

Confusion   Thinking

The processes of researching and writing a Master's dissertation

If a man begins with certainties, he shall end in doubts; but if he will be content to begin with doubts, he shall end in certainties.

Francis Bacon (1561–1626), quoted in Schott (2002: 115)

This first chapter is designed to get you started on your Master's research and, if this is needed on your course, to help you write a project proposal. It is divided into three parts:

1. Choosing a topic to research and framing the research questions or objectives.
2. Designing the project. Deciding the style of research you are going to use and making the broad-brush decisions about how the project will be tackled.
3. Writing a proposal document.

Learning outcomes for the chapter

1 Students will be able to choose and define an appropriate topic for their dissertation.
2 Students will be able to frame practicable and feasible research objectives or questions.
3 Students will be able to make choices appropriate to their research objectives when designing the broad outline of their project and research methods.
4 Students will be able to recognise and respond to ethical issues that may be anticipated in their research project.
5 Students will be able to write a research proposal that defines the research topic clearly and specifies the research plan.

Choosing a topic

This is a critical stage in doing a Master's dissertation. If you fail to think about a topic in a systematic manner then you will be frustrated by your indecision and you will risk running out of time to complete the dissertation on schedule. If you make a poor choice then it may be difficult to score well against the marking criteria. The suggestions made in this section are designed to minimise the chance of either of these things happening. As this stage is so critical it is important to discuss your shopping list of possible topics with your tutor and to use your tutor as a sounding board to help you formulate your proposal.

Some of you, depending on what course you are doing, will have to make choices of two topics – a topic for your conference paper and a topic for the dissertation.

Criteria for choosing a topic

There are a number of factors you need to take into account when choosing the subject of your Master's project.

Interest and relevance

You should choose a topic that interests and even possibly excites you, otherwise you will have trouble sustaining the motivation and commitment necessary to complete the project. It should also be of interest to some external audience as well. This might be your own department or organisation, it could be a profession or it could be the wider business and management community. Problems are sometimes met when the student's boss or organisation wants them to research a topic they can raise no enthusiasm for. Should this happen, you need to discuss the situation with your tutor.

Durability

Will the project last the length of the course? Organisations are capable of making very rapid changes in direction and policy. It may be that the topic you choose could become obsolete because of a change in organisational strategy, ownership or other events. Try to choose a subject that will still be relevant in a year's time.

Breadth of research questions

Is there enough substance to your topic? A primary school head teacher, who was doing a Master's in education management, told me the following:

> I have been listening to what you said about choosing a relevant topic. The most important issue in my school, the thing that is limiting the effectiveness of the teaching we do, is the chaos and confusion that is our teaching resources storeroom. Therefore, I am going to do the sorting out of the resources room for my dissertation.

Important though it may have been, the issue was simply not broad enough to sustain the work needed for a Master's dissertation.

A more likely problem is that the chosen topic is too broad and you will find yourself flailing around and unable to get a purchase on it. It is important to consider whether the topic is too big for the time and energy available to be spent on the project.

Topic adequacy

Check the assessment criteria used on your course, against which your work will be marked, and ask yourself whether the topic you have in mind will enable you to do well against the criteria.

Access

You may have an excellent topic in mind, but unless you can get access to the people who can answer your research questions, whether by question-naire, interview or whatever, then the project will be a non-starter. Even if you think the people to whom you need access will agree in principle, the time and effort necessary to secure the access may be too much. If your research is going to take place in the organisation in which you work, the problem may not be too great. But if you need to research third-party organisations, you should assure yourself that you can get the access. Even if you want to send out questionnaires to a general sample of managers you may have trouble getting a list of names and addresses to which you can send the questionnaire. Mailing lists are valuable and you may have to pay for them.

Micro-politics

Whenever you research a business issue there is a danger that you may become a partisan in the management debates and politics that surround it. This will be a more important matter if you are studying a topic within your own organisation. You need to be sure that pursuing the project will not get you into political hot water with those in the organisation who can do you harm. Sometimes people choose to do a project that involves organisations other than the one they work for because the political situation in their own organisation (imminent takeover, boardroom battles and so on) is too dangerous.

Risk and security

Bearing in mind the previous criterion, you cannot avoid all risk. If you choose a topic that is totally safe it will probably be so bland that neither you nor anyone else will be interested in the outcomes. You need to strike a balance between risk and safety that you can live with.

Resources

Literature – make sure there is enough written about your topic, or about the general academic field in which it is located, for you to be able to do the critical literature review. This should not be a problem. A common difficulty these days is too much literature, not too little.

IT, software and skills – your topic may require access to, and skill in, various software packages. These may include NVivo, SPSS, Minitab and Snap for Windows. You may be able to access the software through the computer network of the institution you are studying at. If you do not know how to use the software, make sure you have time to learn. Brief introductions to some of these software packages are given in Chapter 4.

A six-stage process for choosing your topic

What follows is a six-stage process for you to follow when choosing your topic. Even if you have a topic in mind, it will probably be helpful to lay out your idea using these steps.

1. Identify broad topic and academic discipline(s)

The starting point is to decide your broad area of interest. It might be, to give some examples:

- implementation of mission statements and strategy in multinational companies;
- the problems caused by a lack of cooperation between GPs and other health professionals in primary care;
- performance-related pay and flexible benefits.

It is quite likely that your interest in the topic will be driven by a need to come up with some answers to problems or difficulties that you or others in the organisation are troubled by. These are strategic questions that concern what ought to be done in a particular situation. An example would be: 'What should we do to improve the company's competitive position in international markets?'

It is important not to confuse such questions with research questions. Strategic questions are not research questions. Research questions can be answered by doing research; strategic questions cannot be answered by doing research. Strategic questions can only be answered by an act of judgement and will. A manager faced with a strategic question has to use all they know to help them make a judgement about what it is best to do. No matter how much research has been done, it will not of itself identify the correct answer. Some issues require no research at all; they simply need someone to take action. These issues make poor subjects for dissertations.

It is worth considering in more detail why strategic questions are different in nature from research questions. Strategic questions concern the future – what should be done? This is why they are not research questions. You cannot research something that has not yet happened. You can only research things that are or have been. (Although you can, of course, research what people *think* might happen in the future; see p. 160.) The reason this is so can be found in the general philosophical rule that you cannot derive an *ought* from an *is*. Put in more practical terms, no matter how much analysis of the current situation you do, it cannot logically tell you what ought to be done next. Peters and Waterman (1982) reported that some companies thought analysis could determine right action and fell into the trap of 'paralysis by analysis'.

However, at this early stage of the topic-identification process, strategic questions are important because they often provide the managerial motivation for the project. At the end of the project and the dissertation the student should return to these questions and, on the basis of the new knowledge and understanding they have acquired through their research, exercise their judgement and decide what the best way forward would be in relation to the strategic questions they identified at the start.

2. Determine the scope

This is very often a practical matter of where you can get access. You need to decide whether you will be:

- studying one part of an organisation;
- making a comparison of several parts of an organisation;
- studying one organisation;
- making a comparison of two or more organisations;
- studying a sector.

Clearly the scope of the study will have an impact on the sorts of research questions you can ask and answer. You will not be able to discover whether performance-related pay generally increases organisations' financial performance if you only study one company. You could, however, explore staff's response to performance-related pay by studying a single organisation.

As a general rule it is sensible to have a comparative element in your study. It makes it easier to find things to write about. Comparing one thing with another trebles the amount of your material. Instead of just discussing one thing, you can describe two things and then discuss their similarities and differences. More importantly, comparison creates contrasts that make it easier to see things clearly.

3. Brainstorm issues, puzzles and questions

Now go into brainstorming mode and list as many different issues, problems and questions that arise from the broad topic area as you possibly can. Do not evaluate them by saying, 'No, that's not important.' Just make the list as long as possible. For reasons that will become obvious in the next section I recommend that you write the issues on Post-its™ – one issue per Post-it (see Exhibit 1.1).

At this stage you will find you should be asking research questions rather than strategic questions. Research questions are those to which it is possible, in theory at least, to go out and find answers. Research questions mostly refer to what is happening or what has happened. They are concerned with describing and explaining what is, not with proposing what should be done. So, although you cannot research what should be done to improve international competitiveness (to use the example given earlier), you could research:

- what other companies in similar positions have done to improve their international competitiveness and what the outcomes were; and
- what the company has tried in the past and how well it worked.

However, while you may not be able to research what ought to be done, you could research what people at the present moment *think* should be done. You can research respondents' views about the future.

> ### Exhibit 1.1
>
> ## Doing it with Post-its
>
>
>
> I find using Post-its very helpful for the sorting and sifting stage because they can be easily moved around as you decide how best to cluster them.
>
> Write all your issues and questions on Post-its, making sure to put only one issue or idea on each. Find a flat surface and stick your Post-its on it in random order.
>
> When that is done consider them and begin to move them around so that you can cluster together all those issues that seem similar or related. Then put the clusters in order by showing one cluster as a sub-set of another, for example. You need time and space for this task. In the photograph I was doing the task in a dingy flat in Azerbaijan on a wet weekend while working on a university project. The lack of distraction made thinking easier.

4. Map and structure the issues

Now you have a pile of issues, they need structuring and organising.

Sort and cluster all your research issues and questions in a relevance tree or hierarchical diagram. The relevance tree provides a map of all the issues and questions you could research under your broad area of interest. Note that in Figure 1.1 the question at the top of the tree is a strategic question, whereas all those beneath it are research questions.

You can then decide which of the issues you *are* going to research. The two circled areas in Figure 1.1 represent two of the many possible projects. One would concentrate on how the different regional offices of the organisation (China and the Far East, Central Europe, India and South-East Asia and so on) respond to corporate strategy and research how such differences are handled. The other project would emphasise the different regional management cultures that may exist within the multinational company and study how this can lead to different understandings about what strategy is and what its role is.

This form of analysis is particularly useful if you have to choose a topic for a conference paper as well as a topic for a dissertation. Using the tree diagram you can circle the two topics and use the tree to help you define the connections between the two projects.

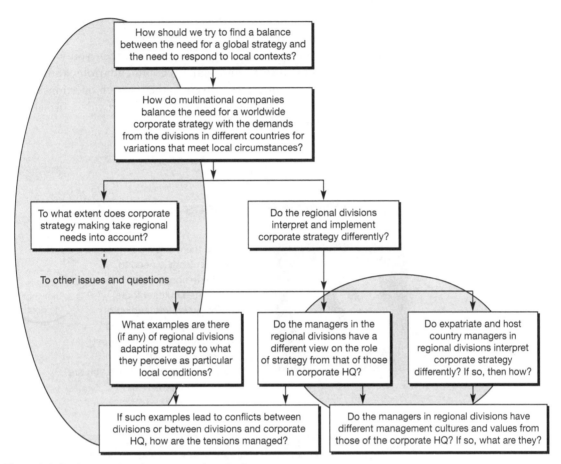

Figure 1.1 A relevance tree for a research project

5. Conduct a reconnaissance

Having arrived at a clear view about what your research topic is going to be, it is sensible to discuss it with others. Discuss it with tutors, colleagues and other managers to see whether they agree that the issue is important and coherent. You should also do an initial trawl of the literature, if you have not already done so, to see what work others have done on the issues that concern you.

6. Frame your research question(s)

The final stage is to ensure that you are clear in what you are doing by framing your research question in plain English.

The suspicion is that if you cannot ask your research question without using management jargon, then you are probably not clear what you are asking and you need to think about it some more. If your research question resembles this – *I am addressing the issues relevant to leveraging human resource competency to produce turnaround to world-class status and to diagonally integrate professional functionalities* – you probably do not know what you are talking about (see Exhibit 1.2).

Once you have found answers to such questions, then you will be in a position to draw conclusions and make recommendations about what should be done in the future. The answers to the research questions cannot dictate what action should be taken but they should provide a firmer basis for judgement and decision making.

Exhibit 1.2

Framing research questions

- Express them in plain English as a question.
- 'There is clearly a need to investigate how tourists [on escorted cultural tours] develop an understanding of transient destination images.' *This is how not to do it!*
- They must intrigue and interest you.
- They must be open.
- Avoid assumptions – unless you are researching them.

Exercise 1.1

Your research question

Identify a topic for your project and dissertation by working through the six stages recommended above. Within the general topic chosen, identify:

- a broad 'what should we do about x?' strategic type of question that responds to managerial or organisational issues and concerns; and
- one or more research questions that say what you want to find out;

and frame them in language that would be understandable to an interested lay person in a pub who has asked about your research.

If you have tried all of the above but are still having trouble choosing the topic for your dissertation, then try morphological analysis. Exhibit 1.3 is a series of lists. The first list can be updated or changed to suit your personal preferences. Just enter a series of current business and management topics that interest you. Then step back, shut your eyes and stick a pin at random in each of the lists. You can then read off a description of a project you might do. For example, you could do an ethnographic account of the implementation of BPR in a number of organisations. If you do not like that idea, put the pin in again until you arrive at an acceptable project.

Exhibit 1.3

Morphological analysis

Topic	Aim	Design	Focus
Business process re-engineering (BPR)	Classification	Action research	Professional or interest group
Globalisation	Explanation	Ethnographic accounts	Single organisation
Internal markets	Technique development	Mathematical models	Several organisations
Business excellence model	Forcasting	Comparative analysis	Industrial sector
Business ethics	Evaluation	Case study	Single project

Exercise 1.2

Construct your own morphological analysis chart. Most of the items in the second, third and fourth columns will probably be reusable. It is the first column that will have to be remade to suit your particular interests and situation. Once the chart is complete, choose items at random from each list to identify possible projects.

● ● ● ● Designing your project

A research proposal is not just a document in which you identify the purpose and focus of your research. It is also a place where you describe the broad nature and style of the project you are going to undertake. You will need to make decisions on the following matters, each of which will be discussed in some detail:

● methodological stance – understanding, action or both;
● your role as researcher;
● breadth or depth – survey or case study;
● main research methods to be used;
● ethical considerations.

Methodological stance

This is a difficult issue because there are many explanatory grids that can be superimposed on methodological matters in an attempt to understand them. The grids share many common features but they also have their own peculiarities. This confusion, which you will discover readily enough in the literature, makes the subject a difficult one – for tutors as well as for students! In this chapter a particular framework will be used to discuss the issues but we will return to the matter in later chapters where other perspectives will be used to clarify the problems of methodology.

Methods and methodology

A brief word of warning is necessary before we go any further. Many tutors, but not all, take exception to the use of the word 'methodology' when the word 'methods' would be quite sufficient. They believe, and they are probably correct, that people merely use the word because it is big and sounds impressive. Mostly, when you are discussing such things as how you used a questionnaire and why this was more suitable than interviews, you are discussing methods. So you do not need to call it methodology. Methodology has a particular meaning. An 'ology' of course is the study of a whole academic field. It is a stepping-back from a subject and a consideration of it at a broader and deeper level. Methodology is the study of methods and it raises all sorts of philosophical questions about what it is possible for researchers to know and how valid their claims to knowledge might be. What we are about to discuss is indubitably methodology. Methods are considered later in this chapter and in Chapter 4.

Understanding and action

Management and business research is different from research in many other subjects because it has both an academic and a practical purpose. Academically such research should contribute to knowledge and understanding about management. Practically it should help managers do their jobs. Management research is about both knowledge and action. The relationship between knowledge and action, however, is not straightforward. There are at least five ways in which people envisage the relationship, as shown in Table 1.1.

Ivory tower research

This probably has little place in management and business research but it is here for the sake of completeness. From this perspective it is argued that there is no connection between knowledge and action. Knowledge is of value in itself and it does not have to be justified by practical application. It is enough that research adds to the body of knowledge. It can lead to antiquarianism, which is a name for what happens when collectors of

Table 1.1 Five ways of understanding the relationship between understanding and action in management research

The philosophers have only interpreted the world, in various ways: the point, however, is to change it.

(Marx, 1970: 30)

Type of research	Understanding and action	Characteristics
Ivory tower	Knowledge is valuable in itself; it does not necessarily lead to action	Antiquarianism Intellectual elegance
Realist research	The research identifies and evaluates options for action	Structured variables Reductionism Cause and effect Statistical analysis
Interpretive ethnographic research	Understanding provides a context for thinking about action but does not specify it	Dialogic structures Participant observation Explores meaning Deals with complexity
Action research	Changing our knowledge and understanding constitutes action	Gnosis and reflection Small-scale projects Deals with personal relationships and values
Critical social research	Changing the mass's knowledge of their position to bring about social change	Radical action Raising mass consciousness

intriguing facts and trivia build up a cabinet of curiosities that amuses and appalls in turns but that is devoid of practical use. It can also lead to an emphasis on intellectual elegance as an end in itself. I have a susceptibility for this weakness and you may find one or two examples of antiquarianism in this guide.

Typical ivory tower project

Although not many students would do such a project for their MBA or Master's in management dissertation, an example might be *Marketing Strategies in the Airline Industry 1972–1995*. It would probably not do for an MBA dissertation because its focus is entirely historical. Something like *The Use of Rhetorical Figures of Speech in Board Meetings* would be borderline. It could be made appropriate to an MBA or Master's in management dissertation, but it would probably have insufficient practical relevance to be suitable.

Realist research

The case was made in the introductory chapter that realism and positivism, although they are often claimed to be the same, should be treated as separate approaches (Johnson and Duberley, 2000: 149). Many textbooks treat the two as the same thing. This is not necessarily a problem. I am not arguing that they are completely different, merely that it is helpful to draw a distinction between the two. The realist researchers into management believe, with the positivists, that the knowledge we gain through research can accurately mirror reality itself, although they think the mirror image may be distorted by the intrusion of subjectivity into the process of knowing.

It has been argued in the introduction that decisions about what ought to be done in any situation cannot be logically derived from what we know about the situation. Only human judgement and determination can make the link between knowledge and action. However, the realists tend to believe that the knowledge we acquire can give good indications of what should be done. This is because such research looks for associations between variables, and where possible tries to establish chains of cause and effect. Typically, research in this mode would involve structuring a problem by breaking it into its constituent parts. The relationship between these parts would then be studied, looking for recurrent patterns and associations. These patterns would then be used to establish principles or laws that could be used to select among a series of possible solutions to the problem. If the research indicates, for example, that outsourcing IT operations tends to be associated with reduced costs and improved quality of services, and it is probable that there are no other factors that might explain the changes, then it would be sensible to use this knowledge as a basis for future decision making.

Measurement and statistical methods are often sensible ways of establishing whether there are associations between variables. But it is not the case that all realist research must be statistical. In practice much realist research is based upon a comparison of qualitative case studies, which are analysed to see whether there are any connections between variables. This approach has one advantage over purely statistical approaches. Statistics can show that some variables are associated, and that changes in one are associated with predictable changes in the other. It can even give the probability that the association is a true one and that it is not caused by chance or by the unseen intervention of other variables. But it cannot prove cause and effect. It cannot define the mechanism by which one variable brings about a change in another. Qualitative case studies that provide a broader and deeper understanding of processes may give an opportunity to work out the ways in which one variable is causally linked to others. The disadvantage of a case-based approach is that there is often too small a sample of cases to claim that the links of cause and effect identified apply generally.

The realist approach to research is probably best understood through an illustration. Let us say that the problem to be researched concerns increasing rates of sickness and absenteeism in an organisation. The problem has to be structured by breaking it down into parts. This is often done by identifying variables. The researcher will try to identify dependent variables, which move in regular ways as other, independent variables change. The statistics on sickness and absenteeism are studied to look for patterns and associations between the many variables involved. It might be that the figures go up at times when the organisation is busy. One possible cause of increasing absenteeism might therefore be stress. There are other possible causes – the tendency to take Fridays off might suggest that people are getting more satisfaction from their social life than they are from their work. Questionnaires might then be sent to staff to measure their levels of stress and job satisfaction. These statistics can then be compared with the absenteeism figures and correlations and associations noted. These statistical models tell the researcher whether the patterns are significant or merely the result of chance. A relationship between the variables can be used to predict whether certain actions will reduce absenteeism and sickness. If there is a stronger relationship between absenteeism and stress levels than between absenteeism and job satisfaction then the obvious answer to the problem is to do things that will decrease stress at work. A number of options will be devised and evaluated to see which ones would work best. Management research, within this understanding of it, leads directly to clear recommendations for action.

This example illustrates one of the worries that researchers have about realist research. It takes complex things such as the experience of stress and reduces it, simplifies it, to an index number. In a similar manner, realist researchers will use questionnaires to 'measure' people's attitudes towards a thing. Whether such measures are valid is a matter of debate. It can be argued that they miss the point, which is to explore the complex and dynamic ways in which people form and modify their opinions within the developing social contexts they find themselves in. In plainer language, people's attitudes may be flexible and change according to whom they are talking. It is for this reason that those who take a purist positivist approach, such as the behaviourists (see p. 17), avoid dealing with internal processes, for example motivation, satisfaction and attitudes.

Realist researchers form and test hypotheses about patterns of association between selected data. Hypotheses are treated as possible explanations rather than as fixed laws, as positivists sometimes claim scientific laws to be. An example of this process can be taken from Northcote Parkinson (1961: 90), who hypothesised, perhaps with his tongue in his cheek, that just before organisations collapse they spend a fortune on upgrading the reception areas of the office block or, in extreme cases, building a palatial new corporate HQ: 'It is now known that a perfection of planned layout is achieved only by organisations on the point of collapse.'

He gives the British Empire in India as one illustration of this particular Parkinson's law. The British built an entire imperial capital city at New Delhi and completed it just as the campaign for Indian independence was fulfilling its aims. Northcote Parkinson identifies cases in which this association can be seen, and explains why he thinks there is a causal connection between the two sets of observed facts. However, a hypothesis can only ever be tentative because the realist researcher seeks evidence that would disprove the hypothesis. Once this is found, a new hypothesis has to be developed and tested to destruction in its turn. This is the hypothetico-deductive method, as described by Karl Popper (2002a, 2002b). He pointed out in a famous example (Popper, 2002a: 27) that if the hypothesis is that all swans are white, then merely counting white swans does not prove the hypothesis, because no matter how many white swans you find there is always the possibility that the very next swan you see will be black. The problem is the common one that you cannot prove a negative, and the hypothesis that all swans are white presupposes that no swans are black. Of course the danger is that if you believe the hypothesis, you might not believe that the black swan you see can really be a swan. The intention of holding tentative explanations only until they are disproved chimes well with the cautiousness of realist research (see Exhibit 1.4).

Exhibit 1.4

Nullifying a hypothesis

There may be a black swan hiding somewhere. The proper research strategy is to hunt for black swans, and until you find one your hypothesis holds.

The hypothetico-deductive approach is at the heart of realist research and deserves a little more explanation. I will simplify it into a number of steps:

1. Identify your research question. What is it that you are interested in?
2. Generate some ideas. From the literature and/or your own experience, identify the key concepts or variables that are involved in the subject of your research. Begin to speculate about how they relate to each other. Do changes in one variable cause changes in others? Are the variables related by being different points on the same dimension? This stage is closely related to developing a conceptual framework, a process that is discussed in detail in Chapter 3.

3. Develop testable hypotheses. A hypothesis is a speculation about one or more variables that can be tested to see if it holds true. If I am interested in what affects whether managers make ethical or unethical decisions in difficult circumstances, I might develop a series of hypotheses such as:

- younger managers are more ethical than older managers in their decisions;
- managers with religious convictions choose ethical options more often than those without such convictions.

However, these hypotheses will be useless unless I can find a way of testing them. It is also probably a good idea not to have too many hypotheses. Too many often lead to a confused and ill-focused dissertation.

4. You then have to choose some measures for the variables in the hypothesis. If I take the hypothesis mentioned above about the relationship between age and the ethicalness of a person's decisions, then I need to identify a measure for each variable. Age is easy enough but ethicalness of decisions is tricky. I would probably look to see whether anyone has already developed a questionnaire or inventory that assesses a person's propensity to take an ethical decision. There are several such tools mentioned in the literature, although I would have to seek their authors' permission to use them. The persistent question when choosing a measure is whether it actually measures the thing I am interested in. Often we have to choose proxy measures. These do not measure a thing directly but measure a property associated with the thing. We might choose to measure an organisation's tendency to act in a corporately responsible manner by whether it has a published policy on corporate responsibility and whether it is regarded as responsible by its peers (see p. 279). Neither of these measures is a direct measure of corporate social responsibility, because it is possible to have a policy and yet not abide by it, and the perceptions of the organisation's peers may be wrong. Nevertheless, these measures may be acceptable in the absence of anything better.

5. The next stage is to collect data to test the hypothesis. This may by done by taking data from existing databases, by conducting fieldwork, by sending out questionnaires or by preparing some case studies. In principle, data could be collected by longitudinal studies or quasi-experiments. This would normally involve collecting data before and after a significant event in an organisation. This is often difficult for students to do in the timescale of their projects.

6. The next stage is to analyse the data to see whether they support or refute the hypothesis. This may involve the use of some statistical technique. These are discussed in Chapter 4.

7. If the analysis shows that the hypothesis is not true then, although negative results are generally less enthralling than positive ones, the finding is

still worthwhile. In this case the researcher should return to the beginning and develop a new hypothesis to explain the phenomenon he or she is researching. Of course there may not be time to do this within the typical MBA or Master's project, and the task is simply identified as one to be done at some unspecified future date. If the hypothesis is supported then it would probably still be worthwhile to see how it compares with other explanations that other researchers have developed.

Sometimes a false negative result can be thrown up. This is technically known as a type 1 error. (Type 2 errors are when a false hypothesis is accepted.) In the management field this can happen because the relationships between variables are more complicated than the statistical techniques being used can cope with. The research into whether there is a relationship between job satisfaction and job performance may be a case in point. Many of the studies into the matter were done in the 1960s and 1970s and they generally showed a lack of a relationship. Iaffaldano and Muchinsky (1985), who conducted a study of studies, found an average correlation coefficient of only 0.17 (see p. 217 for help in interpreting correlation coefficients). Researchers generally concluded that levels of performance were not much affected by job satisfaction. More recent work has indicated that the lack of a linear relationship does not mean there is no relationship between the two variables. Katzell *et al.* (1992: 210–212) argued that both job performance and job satisfaction were determined by a large number of variables and that the lack of a linear relationship between them did not mean that there were not important relationships between them that were moderated by other factors. They tested this proposal using a path analysis technique and argued that intervening factors (such as goal setting and job involvement) create indirect causal links between job satisfaction and performance. Somers *et al.* (2001) used a different technique (neural nets) but also found non-linear relationships between work attitudes and job performance. They concluded that the relationship between satisfaction and performance might be higher than previously claimed but only under optimal conditions, when all the other factors impinging on performance were right.

This discussion suggests that, certainly at the Master's dissertation level, some hypotheses should not be followed up, not because they are uninteresting but because they would involve more statistical firepower than is available to the average Master's student. This may not necessarily be a bad thing because it is at least arguable that if you need excessively fancy statistics to prove your hypothesis, then it may be a little 'iffy' anyway. I was once sitting in the shade of a large striped umbrella on a Welsh lakeside. It was a hot day and there were many flies in the area. I noted casually to my companion, who was a hard-bitten scientist and positivist,

'Have you noticed how all the flies settle on the red stripes in the umbrella and not on any of the other coloured stripes? You don't need higher mathematics to prove that hypothesis.' He replied: 'If you need sophisticated statistics to prove your hypothesis, it probably isn't true anyway.'

Realist research proceeds by elimination, by rejecting hypotheses. If you were applying this approach to decision making, for example selecting a new software system to buy, you would form a list of options. You would then compare the options against your requirements (cost, quality, reliability and so on) and eliminate the options one by one. The last remaining option would be the best one. The realist approach can therefore also be used in that part of your project where you are choosing recommendations. Each possible recommendation becomes a hypothesis, which can be checked out.

Typical realist research projects

A typical project might centre on identifying factors that encouraged or constrained the introduction of teamworking and quality circle methods in a manufacturing plant. The research might be based on case studies of three or four companies that had tried to make these changes. In such a project, much of the research material may be qualitative, based on interviews and participant observation, although some statistical and documentary sources might also be used. Other realist projects might be more determinedly statistical. A questionnaire might be used, for example, to provide data on whether respondents' perceptions of the degree of fairness with which they are treated by their employer is associated with their ethnic origin, their age or their sex. The completed questionnaires would be analysed to see whether people in any of the demographic categories said they were discriminated against more often than the average for all respondents. A number of statistical techniques would be used to decide whether any variations in respondents' answers were significant or were merely random.

Interpretive research

People who take an interpretive approach to research see the link between understanding and action as an indirect one. Improving understanding and knowledge does not reveal the best actions to take. The link between understanding and action is mediated through people's thinking, values and relationships with each other. The role of capricious human understanding and will, in formulating understanding and in constraining the translation of understanding into action, means that knowledge cannot provide clear prescriptions for action. However, understanding a situation should help us to use our judgement to arrive at a better, if not necessarily the best, choice of action.

The link between understanding and action is seen as indirect because the world is complex and options for action are not always clear. The complexity emerges in two particular ways in an interpretive approach to research. The first is a concern for meanings and interpretations. While structure may be just as important to this form of research as it is to realist research approaches, it is of a different kind. The realist forms structures out of variables; the interpretivist forms structures out of interpretations. These are used to explore how people's sense of their world both influences, and is influenced by, that of others. In realist research the links between variables are cause and effect relationships. In interpretive research the links between interpretations are **dialogic**. That is to say, people develop their ideas through debate and conversation with themselves, in their heads, and with others. The researcher tries to map the range and complexity of views and positions that people take on the topic of the research. If I were researching staff appraisal I would try to explore the range of views that people took. It might be anticipated that managers and staff might have different views. It might also be the case that both groups have conflicting views. Some things about appraisal might fill them with expectation; other things about it would fill them with anxiety. People may have different views according to the context in which the question was being asked. If I asked a manager about their views on appraisal when they were doing the appraising, the answer might be different from the views they might express about appraisal when they were the one being appraised.

Interpretive research seeks people's accounts of how they make sense of the world and the structures and processes within it. Ernest Gellner was a positivist by temperament but he had a sufficient understanding of interpretive approaches to be able to parody it. The following quotation is taken from a book review he wrote.

A layman observing a member of his own society might say 'John sat down'. Trite, banal you may say. But how wrong you are. Wait till a good interpretivist gets to work. For a human being, a member of a culture *sitting down* is not just an account of a physical condition ... According to the interpretivist a man knows he is sitting down, which means that he has the concept of sitting down, which he has acquired by taking part in a community with a certain culture. [ ] To sit is to place one's bum on a chair. [ ] It is not just a physical object, it has a meaning, linked to a whole range of related meanings: chairs are not to be sat on in the presence of certain superiors without permission, or, in certain circumstances before grace being said. Some chairs are thrones, others reserved for members of religious hierarchies, others, without existing physically, define their nominal possessors as professors. You cannot think of a chair without tacitly associating yourself with the political, religious and academic ranking of your social order. Only by understanding the chair you sit on as one specimen of all these others, can you understand a culture. The same operation can be done on *bum*. You cannot sit without such a concept, but you cannot possess such a concept without immediately also knowing that this is a part of the anatomy which must in most contexts remain covered. [ ] To be a member of a culture says the interpretivist is to internalise its taboos.

Every time you sit down, you tacitly invoke the ultimate binary oppositions of your culture. You probably did not realise this; but now you know.

As a matter of fact, I don't think that this bit of interpretive anthropology is untrue, though I somehow don't expect that it will be acclaimed as an outstanding specimen of the genre.

(Gellner, 1993: 4)

Interpretive researchers often take a processual perspective. This is the second way in which interpretive research recognises complexity in the subjects of research. It is an attempt to generalise about how meaning is developed through human interactions. The approach has been used to discuss the managerial role (Watson, 1994a), the management of change (Dawson, 1994) and strategic planning (Mintzberg, 1994). I have used it in a study of business ethics (Fisher and Lovell, 2000: Ch. 5). From the processual viewpoint the world is seen as an ambiguous place that people have to struggle to make sense of (Watson, 1994a: Ch. 1). A processual study of a subject necessarily emphasises uncertainty and complexity. In his description of a processual analysis of the management of change, for example, Dawson (1994: 3) characterised the approach as follows:

- Processes are not linear and sequential; rather they are 'complex and dynamic'.
- There are competing 'histories' or interpretations of events and issues.
- Processes cannot be viewed synoptically because random events 'during the process of change may serve to impede, hasten or redirect the route to change' (Dawson, 1994: 170).
- Politics and political processes are integral to an understanding of issues.

Exercise 1.3

The park bench

You can try this for yourself. Focus on the picture of the park bench. What range of images and associations does it conjure up for you? When you have thought of some, consider them and identify the messages park benches give out about the people who sit on them. Do these messages tell us anything about the culture of the society in which the bench is sited?

Suggested answer
Let us think about the park bench. Most people think of contrary images. On the one hand, drunks and derelicts dossing on the park bench. On the other hand, young mothers with their children in buggies in the park (nannies and prams if you are old-fashioned). Here we have images of endings and beginnings. Here we have the eternal contradiction between the promise of life and its dire reality. From a park bench we can induce the wider dilemmas of being human – well, almost!

A complex understanding of a subject can only be achieved through a close involvement with the subject of research. Interpretive researchers are often participants in the processes they are studying. They sometimes approach their research topics in as open a manner as they can manage and try to let theories emerge from their research material, in what is known as the grounded approach to research, rather than begin the study with a ready prepared set of theories. Others bring a toolkit of theories that they dip into to find frameworks to help them explain what their research has discovered, as illustrated in Exercise 1.4 and discussed on p. 123.

Exercise 1.4

Group formation – using theory to explain research material

1 Imagine you are doing research into group behaviour at work.
2 Read up on the theory of group formation. Buchanan and Huczynski (2001: 297–300) is a good text.
3 Next time you are at a group event consciously make yourself alert to the behaviour that the group exhibits.
4 After the event write down your account and impressions of what happened.
5 Use the theory of group formation to explain what was happening at the group event.
6 Does the use of theory enable you to provide a more systematic account of your experience? Did it give you any new insights?

When you read up on these matters in the literature you will find this approach to research, or aspects of it, described by different names. Other names you are most likely to come across are 'phenomenology' and the 'hermeneutic tradition'.

- **Phenomenology** is a particularly difficult term because people give it many different definitions that share some common features but that also express many nuanced differences (Remenyi *et al.*, 1998: 95). The term is now used loosely but in its original formulation, by Schütz (1967), it was the study of how things appear to people – how people experience the world. In particular it was the study of how these common-sense intuitions and knowledge of society feed back into social action and so contribute to the moulding of society. The phenomenologists' approach is to urge people to forget (or bracket) their acquired ways of understanding the world and to look at phenomenon afresh, as themselves. It is therefore a critical and a subjective approach. As used by Schütz, phenomenology originally meant identifying how much of a person's understanding of an object came from the object itself and how much came from the person's subjectivity. However, the term phenomenology has acquired a wider meaning '... at least in the English speaking world. Here phenomenology is generally seen as a study of people's subjective and everyday experience' (Crotty, 2003: 83). In this sense it is very close to the definition we have given to interpretivism.
- **Hermeneutics** is a general term for the process of interpreting human actions, utterances, products and institutions. In past times it referred to the glossing of biblical texts. In modern social science use the term has been expanded to include a wide variety of texts.

Sociology has generated many specialist approaches to this type of research. Here are a few:

- *Ethnographers* try to explain cultures, including organisational cultures, by writing accounts of their subjective experiences of living and working in the culture being studied over a considerable period of time.
- *Grounded theorists* suggest that people's subjective understanding of their worlds should be theorised by studying the themes that people use in giving accounts of their lives and world. Researchers look for these themes and categories in the interviews and observations collected during the research. The researcher then develops theories based upon these themes. Academic understanding, they argue, should not be based on theories chosen in advance of the research (see Chapter 3).
- *Ethnomethodologists* are a sub-variety of phenomenologists. They study how, in everyday trivial interactions, people give rational accounts of what are essentially practical actions in their attempts to understand social interactions (Reed, 1992: 150–155).
- *Reflective practitioners* are professionals who systematically improve their understanding of their professional worlds through reflection, with the support of their professional peers, on their professional activities (Schön, 1983).

Typical interpretivist projects

Many dissertations that focus on an aspect of organisational or occupational culture adopt an interpretivist approach. If a student worked in a transnational company, for example, they might be interested in how local managers, in the different countries in which the company traded, perceived and managed commercial risk taking. In a UK context, in the public sector modernisation is a major item in the government's agenda. An interpretivist might try to explain how different stakeholder groups within a public service might interpret and value the idea of modernisation. The analysis of the research material, which could include both qualitative material from focus groups and interviews as well as statistical data from questionnaires, would focus on the differences in the views of the various groups and the processes by which these issues were debated and views changed. They might draw upon the work of Weick (1996) (see p. 282) and his concept of enactment to understand the processes of sense making that surround the issue of modernisation. Enactment is part of the process of making sense from equivocal information by selecting and editing information through discussion and interaction with others.

Action research

Action research is different from the processual, the positivist and, to a lesser extent, the realist approaches to research. It focuses on the individual researcher's understanding and values relating to the research issue. It further proposes that the only way the researcher can improve and challenge their understanding is by taking action and by learning from experience. From this perspective the belief is that action, or behaviour, can only be changed by changing a person's values and beliefs, and that values and beliefs can only be changed by testing them in action. Action and understanding become enmeshed together in a cycle of learning in which there is a constant movement between reflection and action. Action research therefore combines a focus on action and experimentation with a concern for challenging and developing personal values. In action research the cycle might begin with a researcher using their experience (values) to decide on a course of action designed to solve a problem. The action is tried out and the researcher monitors and studies the consequences of the action, particularly the consequences as seen by other people who are affected by the change. They then reflect on their findings and this may cause them to change or develop their values and beliefs. Because they now see things differently when they next use their experience to decide on a course of action, they inevitably decide to act differently.

Action research tends to focus on small-scale but important issues such as the ways in which a team implements a policy or an individual's professional or managerial practice. It becomes risky to apply this approach to large-scale change projects. A major information system could not be implemented using an action research approach because mistakes would be too costly, and action research involves learning from mistakes.

The nature of action research is a matter of debate. Those who write about it from a background in teaching and education often take a different view from those who write about it in the context of management studies. Most educationalists share many points of view with the interpretivists. Reg Revans (1983), however, who initiated action learning in a management context, often proclaimed himself a positivist. The sensible conclusion is that, in terms of action research's view of the relationship between understanding and action, action research is developing its own unique approach to research methodology that has the following characteristics:

- confronting data from different perspectives;
- closely and iteratively linking reflection and action;
- incorporating reflection and development of values;
- involving holistic and inclusive reflection;
- developing the researcher's competency;
- testing of individual findings through critical professional discussion.

> ### Exhibit 1.5
>
> # Definitions of action research
>
> *The linking of the terms action and research highlights the essential feature of the method: trying out ideas in practice as a means of improvement and as a means of increasing knowledge.*
>
> (Kemmis and McTaggart, 1982)
>
> *Action research is about improving practice rather than about producing knowledge.*
>
> (Elliott, 1991)
>
> Both of these definitions are quoted in McNiff *et al.* (1996: 9, 10), which is a useful and practical guide to doing action research for management students, despite being set in an educational context.

Typical action research projects

Occasionally an action researcher focuses on their own managerial practice. A manager or team leader, for instance, might develop their leadership practice through action research. They would change their leadership style, perhaps following the precepts of a particular theory, and use the feedback from their staff to adapt and further develop their leadership values and behaviours. More commonly, an action research project would be concerned with wider changes. For example, an organisation may have decided to provide mentors in support of a major new ICT implementation. Action research could be used to develop the method and values that would be appropriate for mentors in that particular context.

Critical social research

Researchers who profess the critical social research approach believe that the purpose of research should be to change society for the better. Central to this approach is the idea of false consciousness. This is a Marxist notion that describes the tendency of the proletariat to fail to recognise the nature of its self-interest. More generally it is any form of ideology or self-imagery that is held to be inappropriate to the real or objective situation of an actor. Crudely expressed it means that in organisations, employees are being exploited but are oblivious to their situation. The task of critical social research, therefore, is to reveal the deep and hidden structures at work behind the façade of false consciousness. Once the proletariat becomes aware that they are oppressed, that they are not so much being empowered as being exploited by such things as business process re-engineering and just-in-time production methods, for example, then they will rise in revolt. This is not a form of research that would necessarily find favour with people on management courses but, if used in moderation, in a dissertation it adds piquancy to the analysis.

Exhibit 1.6

The Humanities Curriculum project

This illustration provides a good example of the link between action and challenging personal beliefs.

The Humanities Curriculum project was an approach to teaching secondary school children. It was designed to expose students to controversial issues. The teacher was to be relieved of the task of giving facts and allowed to concentrate on chairing students' discussions on the issues. Short 'provocative' documents would be used as handouts to provide students with the basic facts and materials.

One teacher reported he was having trouble with the project. The students read the materials but no discussion started. The teacher assumed that the students were having problems understanding the materials. So, using his best judgement and having discussed it with the project researcher, he reverted to giving mini-lectures to explain the content of the documents. However, in the spirit of action learning, the researcher (R) decided to talk to the students (S).

R: 'Well, what do you think of this new approach?'
S: 'I don't like it.'
R: 'What don't you like about it?'
S: 'We don't like these documents, these materials, we don't like them.'
R: 'So what don't you like about them? Are they too difficult to read?'
S: 'Oh no! Oh no! We can read them.'
R: 'Can you all?'
S: 'Of course we can read them.'
R: 'So what's the problem then?'
S: 'The problem is we disagree with what they say.'
R: 'Oh! Good. You actually disagree with what they say?'
S: 'Yes.'
R: 'Well, then you can express your disagreement in class.'
S: 'The teacher wouldn't like it.'
R: 'Well, why wouldn't the teacher like it?'
S: 'Because the teacher agrees with what the documents say.'
R: 'How do you know that the teacher agrees with what these documents say?'
S: [Looking very surprised at the stupidity of the question] 'The teacher wouldn't give you the documents in the first place if he didn't agree with them, would he?'

(Altrichter, 1993)

The researcher had his assumptions and beliefs challenged by the feedback he received from the students. When he discussed the situation with the teacher, this new perspective would cause the teacher to try a new action in the next cycle of implementation. The teacher's and the researcher's beliefs about the pupils had changed, and so consequently would their actions. Action research is about gnosis – the Greek word for knowing oneself through self-criticism and reflection.

Critical social research can take other radical perspectives, such as feminism, rather than a Marxist one. A more careful review of this approach is provided in Chapter 5.

Critical social researchers object to positivism (but not so much to realist research, of which it is a variant), the interpretive approach and action research. From a critical perspective, interpretivism is seen as giving more importance to understanding the world than changing it. Positivism is viewed as a tool for reinforcing oppressive structures and action research is rejected because it ignores the need for big, radical changes and concentrates on small-scale and individual change.

Typical critical research projects

These are fairly rare in MBA and Master's in management programmes but they are by no means precluded. A radical critique approach might be used to study executive pay and remuneration in large public companies. The possibility could be explored that the differentials in pay between the top managers and others in such companies could arise from deep-seated and structural class conflicts. This would be in opposition to the opinion that such differences are simply the result of competition in the market for scarce entrepreneurial competency. An example of a radical critique approach can be found in Porter (2002).

Methodological pluralism

The FAQ at this stage is: 'Can you mix and match these approaches to research?' It is often easiest if you choose just one. It reduces the complexity of the chapter in your dissertation on methods and methodology. It also keeps you out of the line of sight of academic snipers, from all camps, which are in a state of constant low-level warfare with each other. While tutors and lecturers may take different methodological positions, you may be encouraged to adopt whichever approach you wish as long as you show it to be a sensible approach for answering the research question you have set yourself.

It is possible, however, with care, to combine some of the approaches. It has already been suggested that a dash of social criticism might add some spice to an otherwise standard piece of realist research. The big question is whether it is possible to combine realist research and an interpretive approach. Gill and Johnson's (1997: 135–136) line on this debate is persuasive. They argue that if you take a realist stance, then aspects of an interpretivist approach could be brought in as a useful adjunct to the research. But they also claim that the reverse is not true. If you are doing interpretivist research, then there is no way that an element of realism (or even more seriously an element of positivism) can add to it. This is because taking a positivist perspective would undermine the methodological basis of the interpretivist approach. The realist position – that what is observed is real and can be, more or less, directly studied and measured – flatly contradicts the interpretivists' belief that our knowledge of the world is socially constructed – which means that understanding derives from the social processes of debate and power that take place between people.

How is it possible for realist research to find a place for interpretivist styles of investigation? Gill and Johnson (1997) argue that positivist (and realist) research identifies associations between variables, between antecedent variables and consequences. They might find, for example, that there is a relationship between people's stress levels and their absenteeism levels. But having identified the pattern positivism can say little more. It does not explain why the pattern is there or how the antecedent factor exerts influence on people's actions. This is because the link between the two variables, in this example stress and absenteeism, is the way in which people make the link in their own minds, in their subjective processes. Realism has no way of studying people's accounts of these processes, but interpretive approaches do. Interpretivist approaches can be used to create a quasi-causal account of how the two variables interact. In brief, interpretivist research can convert the pattern of associations found by positivist work into a quasi-causal connection. Realist research shows there is a connection; interpretivism gives a possible description of how the connection may work.

There are at least two ways in which interpretivism may be called in to aid realist research:

1. As described above, a researcher may start off with a piece of realist research that identifies an association between two variables, then use an interpretive approach to understand the causal connection, the mechanism, which shows in all complexity how the different aspects interact.
2. The other possibility uses the ease with which interpretivist research generates hypotheses about the associations between variables. In this case interpretivist research is a ground-clearing operation that precedes a piece of realist research. A researcher might start with a piece of interpretive research that, say, creates all sorts of hypotheses about the causes of absenteeism and then do a piece of realist research to see whether these hypotheses hold true in general.

Exercise 1.5

Deciding on your research approach

When you are designing your project you will need to decide which of these approaches to research is going to be the dominant one in your project.

What approach would be the most appropriate one for your chosen project topic, and why?

The remaining decisions you have to make when designing your project all relate to the big decision about methodological approach that has just been considered.

The researcher's role

The roles that a researcher may take in relation to the people and the organisations they are researching will depend on whether they are a member of the organisation they are researching and on the research approach they have adopted. Figure 1.2 identifies four research roles, each of which has its own advantages and disadvantages.

	Visible	*Invisible*
Involved	Previleged observer – judge	Covert participant observer – spy
Non-involved	Academic – a harmless drudge	Fly on the wall

Figure 1.2 **Researchers' roles**

The judge
This is a researcher who is studying an organisation in which they are involved and they have told those being researched that they are being studied. This role has the advantage of being open and honest and therefore giving those being studied a chance to put their point of view to the researcher if they fear they are being misinterpreted. The disadvantage is that those being studied may become uneasy and modify what they say and how they behave. They may even become annoyed that the researcher appears to be putting themselves in the privileged position of someone who has the right to judge, to express opinions about, their doings.

The academic – a harmless drudge
The academic is a researcher who is studying an organisation in which they have no involvement except as someone who has been kindly allowed access so that they can gather information for their dissertation. The advantage is that the academic is seen as someone with no axe to grind; but there is the danger that those being studied may try to use the researcher to support them and their projects in the organisation's politics. The main disadvantage is that your project may well be low in the organisation's priorities and you may not be given the access and the time you need.

The covert participant observer

This is someone who works in an organisation so that they can study it, but the people they are studying do not know they are being researched. There has been a long line of such ethnographic studies, as nice middle-class researchers get jobs in fish-gutting factories to report on life in the lower depths. The research can be rich and fascinating. The question is whether it is ethical to study people who have not given informed consent. There is a danger that the researcher might foment situations just to increase the 'human interest' quality of their research material.

The fly on the wall

These researchers try to be invisible but are not necessarily secretive. They might, for example, have permission to observe a meeting. Although their physical presence will be unmistakable, by their demeanour and their quietness, they hope those at the meeting will forget they are there. As they cannot affect what they are observing, the ethical problem, while still important, is of a lesser degree. The fly on the wall can use secretive methods of course. A researcher studying consumers' behaviour in a supermarket might use video recordings of shoppers taken without their consent by video cameras that also have a security function.

Breadth or depth

The issue is whether the researcher is trying to obtain a broad and representative overview of a situation, in which case a survey approach would be appropriate, or an in-depth understanding of particular situations, in which event case studies would be appropriate.

Random surveys of a suitably large sample allow you to determine what is average and what the variations around the average are, to a definable level of statistical confidence. They also allow you to examine the relationships between the things you measure in the survey and to establish whether any associations or correlations are significant or just random effects. Surveys require the researcher to distinguish, in advance of the study, the phenomena that are to be studied from the contexts that influence or affect the phenomena. Surveys therefore are not efficient means of studying the complexity of things in particular.

Case studies enable you to give a holistic account of the subject of your research. In particular, they help the researcher to focus on the interrelationships between all the factors, such as people, groups, policies and technology, that make up the case studies. As Yin (1994: 13) points out, at first it may not be apparent which things are the phenomena and which are the contexts. Yin identifies the following characteristics of a case study.

- It investigates a contemporary phenomenon within its real-life context, especially when the boundaries between phenomenon and its contexts are not clearly evident.
- It has a single site, such as a team or an organisation, but many variables.
- A case study uses a variety of research methods and can happily accommodate quantitative data and qualitative material.
- Case study researchers tend to use theoretical propositions developed prior to the study to guide the data collection.

A case study is written up as an account or a narrative. In other words, you are required in a case study to tell the story of what happened from as broad a perspective as is necessary. The case study form is also very adaptable. You could write up case studies of any of the following:

- individual events in a manager's working life (when a case study would more likely be called a critical incident);
- a process, such as the development and launch of a new product;
- an organisation or part of an organisation in relation to some particular issue, such as use of the Internet;
- the making of a decision (sometimes called decision tracing).

There are many other variations and possibilities.

Case studies inevitably lack representativeness. It cannot be claimed that what happened in one case is typical of all cases. In many instances the power of the case study lies in its capacity to provide insights and resonance for the reader. However, it is not true to claim that case studies lack generalisability. Tony Watson (1994b) argues that case studies do enable generalisations to be made about organisational processes. A case study approach could be used to show, to use an invented example, that power struggles between senior managers influences the extent to which a company acts in a socially responsible manner. It could not be used to show whether this factor increases or diminishes responsible behaviour; it could work either way. Yin (1994: 10, 30–32) makes a distinction between statistical generalisations and theoretical generalisations, and points out that the first type cannot be derived from case studies but the second type can. So, if you have researched a case study in which managers who are tall behave in a particular manner, and refer to their stature as something that explains their behaviour, you cannot make a statistical generalisation that all tall managers behave in a particular manner. But you might make the theoretical generalisation that height is a factor that should be considered when generalising about managerial behaviour. If you were to undertake multiple case studies, and they also showed height to be a factor, then your theoretical proposition would become stronger. You might also be able to use the case studies in the same way as a scientist uses experiments; to check out whether tall managers do have similar behaviours as leaders or whether any similarities of behaviour could be equally well explained by other theories, for example that tall managers are more likely to be male and that the effect being observed is about sex and not about height.

You need to be as systematic and rigorous when doing case study research as you are for all other types of research. In particular, you should pay attention to the following:

- Do not rely on one particular type of evidence but use a mixture.
- Research the substance of the case study from the different perspectives of the various interested parties or stakeholders.
- Develop a formal procedure or protocol for use in gathering information so that your material is collected in a uniform manner.
- Keep systematic records of your material that could be reviewed by someone wishing to double-check your work.
- Find a way of creating an audit trail that links your findings and conclusions about the case study to your raw research material.
- Allow your thinking about the case study to be influenced and changed by the material you gather and record your changing views.
- Be aware of bias in the information you obtain from interviewees or from documents and questionnaires. Documents can be slanted and interviewees might give you selected titbits in the hope of settling old scores, for example.
- Do not allow the delights of telling a good human-interest story get in the way of telling the truth as you see it.

Choice of research methods

When designing your project you have to make some general decisions about the research methods you are going to use. These are the most commonly used methods:

- interviews
- questionnaires
- panels, including focus groups
- observation, including participant observation
- documents
- databases.

Detailed descriptions and accounts of their advantages and disadvantages are given in Chapter 4.

It is tempting, but wrong, to make an easy connection between research methodology and particular methods. It is often assumed that realist research means using quantitative research methods and materials (questionnaire surveys and databases) and interpretive research uses qualitative material and methods (interviews, documentary exegesis). These assumptions are wrong: first, because it is possible to use any of the research methods to produce either quantitative material (numbers) or qualitative material (words) and, second, because you can use qualitative material as part of a realist project and you can certainly use numbers to illuminate interpretive research. In practice you can use any of the research methods in any of the approaches.

This is not to deny that realist researchers and interpretivists may prefer to use the same research methods in different ways. Silverman (1993) has explained some of the possibilities by comparing qualitative and quantitative forms of research (see Table 1.2).

Table 1.2 Approaches and methods of research

Method	Positivist	Interpretivist
Observation	Preliminary work	A major component of the research
Documentary	Content analysis	Understanding categories
Interview	Large random samples, fixed-choice questions	Small samples, open-ended and unstructured questions
Questionnaire	Large random samples, fixed-choice questions	Used for initial mapping, open-ended questions

Source: Silverman (1993: 9).

Let us take a couple of examples. Someone doing a realist piece of work may well use interviews. But it will be the sort of interview where the interviewer has to read the questions from a pre-prepared script without deviation. The questions will be pre-coded so that the interviewee will be given a number of possible answers to choose between. An interpretive researcher using interviews, however, would begin the interview with only the broadest view about how the conversation might develop and may indeed encourage the interviewee to determine the direction in which the discussion flows. Sometimes realist and interpretively inclined researchers use the same combinations of research methods but in different sequences. An interpretive researcher writing a case study in an organisation might well use a questionnaire at the start of the project to get an overall 'feel' for the subject they are studying. But the questionnaire would remain a preliminary and a subsidiary method. A realist researcher might well start a study with open-ended interviews that will be useful to them when they design their highly structured questionnaire to be used with a large sample of respondents. When we consider documentary methods, an interpretive researcher might study the use of metaphor in an organisation's documents whereas a positivist might count the relative frequency with which the words 'customer' and 'profit' are used.

Ethical considerations

When you are doing your research you should not treat people unfairly or badly. You should not harm people, or use the information you discover in you research to harm them, or allow it to be used to do harm. This may sound alarmist and you should not assume that you will be beset by such problems when you are doing research. Nevertheless, it is sensible to anticipate whether any such difficulties might occur. Indeed, most universities now have research ethics codes and research ethics committees and it may be that you have to apply for formal ethical approval for your project before you start the research. It is best to go to the website of the institution where you are enrolled and find its code or policy on research ethics and governance and the details of the approval procedure you may need to go through. When you are planning your project it will be sensible to schedule in the time needed to obtain ethical approval. One practical problem is deciding the stage of the project at which ethical approval should be sought. It rather depends on whether the approval is in principle (to determine whether there is something about the project that is inherently unethical) or concerns the conduct of the research (is it being conducted in an ethical manner?). If it is in principle then the approval can be sought at the beginning of the project. If, as I think will be more likely, the approval concerns research practice then approval can only sensibly be sought after the literature review has been started and the research instruments (questionnaires, interview schedules, case study protocols and so on) have been drafted.

The following points rehearse some of the ethical issues and dilemmas you may come across.

Negotiating access
Negotiating terms of reference with organisations

If you are doing the project in a particular organisation it is often necessary to agree terms of reference for the project. Managements tend to have preferred solutions to the problems you are asking to research (or that they are asking you to research) and you need to ensure that the terms of reference give you scope to investigate the issues from a wide range of perspectives and come to your own independent conclusions.

Right to privacy

There is no obligation on anyone to assist you in your research. This raises the question of just how much pressure ('Oh! Come on – do it to help out an old friend!') it is proper to put on someone to cooperate. I once, many years ago, arranged a research interview with a key informant as part of a consultancy project I was doing for a large company. His first words were:

I don't think it's right that they should have brought some outsider academic like you in to do this project. I have already done much of the preliminary work for this project and I should have been allowed to take the project forward. I do not wish to cooperate but I did want you to know how I felt about the situation.

I admit that I blagged an interview from him largely by probing why he was so angry and nowadays I would probably just thank him politely for his time and leave. What would you have done in this situation?

Access to personnel or case records

It may be that you think that the data you need for you project can be found in the personal files that organisations may keep about its staff or its clients, for example hospital patients. It would only be ethical, and legal, to use such information if you have the approval of both the organisation that holds it and, more importantly, of the individuals that it relates to.

Confidentiality agreements

A principle of all academic research, including that done by students, is that the research is published, or otherwise made available to the public, so that others can learn from and criticise the work. As Master's students often research organisations, often the one they work within, this might involve organisationally or commercially confidential information being made public. In such situations organisations might insist that the university for which a student is writing the dissertation should sign a confidentiality agreement. Most universities have standard agreements that can be used. These normally state that the dissertation will not be openly available to any member of the public who asks to see it for a number of years. During that time the dissertation will only be made available with the written agreement of the organisation.

Informed consent

Informed consent is perhaps the key issue in research ethics. No one should be a participant or a source of information in a research project unless they have agreed to be so on the basis of a complete understanding of what their participation will involve and the purpose and use of the research. Sometimes informed consent is implicit, as when someone takes the trouble to complete and return a questionnaire. However, even in these cases it is sensible to make consent explicit by including on the face of the questionnaire a statement such as the following:

> By completing and returning this questionnaire you are giving your consent for the information it contains to be used in the research project. The

information will be stored anonymously and securely. When the information is used in any publication produced during the research project no individual or organisations involved in the project will be identified.

In other projects, which are ethnographical, or based on participant observation, the issue of informed consent may be tricky. If the subjects of the research know they are being studied they may change their behaviour and so defeat the purpose of the research. In these cases it may not be sensible to obtain explicit consent before the research begins. Some codes of research ethics, such as that of the British Sociological Association (2002), do in such situations approve of research done without prior informed consent. If this is so it is important that consent should be obtained after the research has been conducted but before it is analysed or written up.

The easiest way to obtain informed consent is to prepare a *participant observation sheet* that you can give to each participant as you seek their consent and a *consent form* that the participants can sign and that you can keep as a record. Exhibit 1.7 gives an example of a participant information sheet and a consent form.

Exhibit 1.7

Example of a participant information sheet and a consent form

PARTICIPANT INFORMATION SHEET

PERFORMANCE MEASUREMENT AND MANAGEMENT: GOOD GOVERNANCE AND ACCOUNTING BASED REWARDS SYSTEMS

Principal researcher:

[contact details of researcher]

Invitation

You are being invited to take part in a research study. Participation in the project is entirely voluntary. Before you decide it is important for you to understand why the research is being done and what it will involve. Please take time to read the following information carefully and discuss it with others if you wish. Ask us if there is anything that is not clear or if you would like more information. Take time to decide whether or not you wish to take part.

Thank you for reading this.

What is the purpose of the study?

To find out whether the use of performance measurement and performance related pay systems in the public sector may lead to problems in managers' and professionals' use and presentation of information; and to identify the systems and contexts that minimise these problems.

Exhibit 1.7 *continued*

Why I have been chosen

You have been chosen because you are a senior and experienced manager within the public sector with experience of working with performance measurement and/or performance related pay systems. About 50 managers will be asked to complete a questionnaire and a further 30 managers will be interviewed.

Do I have to take part?

It is up to you to decide whether or not to take part. There are two ways of participating. If you do decide to:

1 be interviewed you will be given a copy of this information sheet to keep. You will also be asked to sign two copies of a consent form, one of these will be for you to keep and the other will be kept by the research team. If you decide to take part you are still free to withdraw at any time and without giving a reason.

2 complete a questionnaire you will be given a copy of this information sheet to keep. You will give your consent to participation in the research project by completing the questionnaire and returning it to the research team.

You will normally only be asked to take part in one of the two aspects of the research (interview or questionnaire). Which one you will be asked to take part in will be chosen randomly. If you decide not to take part in the aspect of the research you have been invited to, you may be asked if you would participate in the other aspect. If you volunteer to take part in more than one aspect that will be fine.

What will be my involvement if I take part?

Your involvement will differ according to whether you

- are interviewed;
- complete a questionnaire

The research interview will normally last about an hour. It will be in two parts. In the first part you will be asked about the performance measurement systems used in the part of the public sector you are working in and whether any performance related pay systems apply. In the second part you will be asked to give examples of any incidents you have observed or been involved in at work:

- where these systems have led to problems in managers' and professionals use and presentation of information; and
- where these problems have been effectively dealt with;
- and where they have not.

You will be asked if you agree to the interview being audio-recorded. If you do not agree to this the researcher will take written notes during the interview. If you do agree you may still ask for the tape recorder to be turned off at any point during the interview.

The questionnaire survey involves you filling in a questionnaire about managerial behaviours in relation to performance management systems, using your knowledge, experience and expertise. The questionnaire you complete will be analysed, along with those of other experts, to obtain an initial, average view of all the experts. You will be sent a further questionnaire that gives these results from all of the experts (who will be anonymous) and you will be invited to complete the questionnaire again, taking into account the views of your fellow experts. This process may be repeated but you will not be asked to review your thoughts in response to the views of the other experts more than twice.

Exhibit 1.7 *continued*

Will my taking part in this study be kept confidential?

Yes. At no point will your identity, or indeed the identity of the Trust or other organisation you work for, be revealed to anyone other than the academic supervisors and examiners of the project. Your name will not be recorded on any of the research notes that are made and kept as part of the research. All notes, tape-recordings and any other materials will be kept in secure storage. There will be nothing in any materials they may have access to that could identify the participants in the study or the organisation they work for.

What will happen to the results of the research study?

The research will be written up as an academic dissertation. It will be stored in the archives at [name of institution] and will be available for inspection on request [state what the arrangements are at the institution at which you are studying].

Who is organising and funding the research?

The research is being undertaken as part of a programme of academic study at [name of institution] leading to the award of [title of degree].

Who has reviewed this study?

This study has been reviewed by the Research Ethics Committee of [name of institution].

Contact for further information

[contact details]

CONSENT FORM

THE GOOD GOVERNANCE OF
PERFORMANCE MEASUREMENT AND MANAGEMENT SYSTEMS

Principal researcher:

[contact details of researcher]

Please initial box

1 I confirm that I have read and understand the information sheet dated [date] for the above study and have had the opportunity to ask questions. ☐

2 I understand that my participation is voluntary and that I am free to withdraw at any time, without giving any reason. ☐

3 I agree to take part in the above study. ☐

--------------------------- --------------------- ----------------------
Name of participant   Date   Signature

--------------------------- --------------------- ----------------------
Name of researcher   Date   Signature

Data collection stage
Objectivity and disinterestedness

This may be impossible but you have at least to make a pretence of trying – unless of course you are acting as an action researcher or a social critic researcher.

Deception

Some very famous psychological and sociological research has involved deceiving the research subjects. They were not told the truth about the purpose of the research. Deception is of course unethical. Some research, such as Milgram's (1963), has used deception in that the people being researched were told that the subject of the research was one thing when it was in fact something quite different. Milgram's experiments discovered things, in this case about people's willingness to subject themselves to authority, that otherwise would not have been known and it can be argued that this addition to psychological knowledge justified the deception. Such a justification rests on one particular ethical perspective: that actions are justified if their beneficial results outweigh their negative consequences. Other ethical perspectives could be used to argue that such research demeans the dignity of the people being studied and reduces them simply to the status of means to someone else's ends, and that this is wrong.

Most Master's students, however, are unlikely to need to use outright deception. It is more probable they may be tempted by the lesser ethical offence of being economical with the truth. One of my students, for example, set up an experiment to study the impact of different styles of screen warning page that told employees to use the Internet only for work purposes, and not to misuse the facility. Different employees were presented with different warnings every time they logged on. What they did not know was that their subsequent use of the Internet was being monitored (to see whether they were visiting eBay, for example) so that the effectiveness of the different warnings could be measured. This economy with the truth raised questions of invasion of privacy, informed consent and deception. It is also an aspect of a wider ethical debate about the extent to which organisations are entitled to monitor possible misuse (employees using the Web for private purposes when they are at work) or illegal use (downloading paedophile pornographic images on to computers at work). There are not necessarily straightforward answers to the ethical issues raised by research activities but they should be thoroughly considered in the dissertation.

Confidentiality and anonymity

Anonymity means changing the names and locations (but not, I think, the sex) of informants. Confidentiality means not revealing your sources. You need to make it clear that confidentiality does not mean that the material will not be used. You need to make it clear to participants in your research what you mean by anonymity and confidentiality.

Normally these issues do not cause problems; but what if, in the course of your research, you unearth unprofessional practice in a social services department, say, or illegality in an international business operation? Would it be right for you to break your promise of anonymity and confidentiality and report the matter?

Permission to use video or voice reorders

If you are doing interviews, especially exploratory or semi-structured ones, you will normally want to record the interview so that you have a complete record of both what is said and the tone and manner in which it is said. You must ask the interviewee for permission to record. You should also say that you will turn off the recorder at any point during the interview if the interviewee asks you to do so.

Storage of data

All researchers must comply with the requirements of the Data Protection Act (1998) that can be found at: http://www.opsi.gov.uk/acts/acts 1998/19980029.htm. It sets down some principles concerning the collection and use of personal information, which includes information about people's opinions as well as more factual material such as age and sex. The principles are:

- Personal data shall be processed fairly and lawfully.
- Personal data shall be obtained only for one or more specified and lawful purposes, and shall not be further processed in any manner incompatible with that purpose or those purposes.
- Personal data shall be adequate, relevant and not excessive in relation to the purpose or purposes for which they are processed.
- Personal data shall be accurate and, where necessary, kept up to date.
- Personal data processed for any purpose or purposes shall not be kept for longer than is necessary for that purpose or those purposes.
- Personal data shall be processed in accordance with the rights of data subjects under this Act. This entitles a person to see any information that is held about them.

- Appropriate technical and organisational measures shall be taken against unauthorised or unlawful processing of personal data and against accidental loss or destruction of, or damage to, personal data.
- Personal data shall not be transferred to a country or territory outside the European Economic Area unless that country or territory ensures an adequate level of protection for the rights and freedoms of data subjects in relation to the processing of personal data.

The Act limits the amount of time that organisations can retain personal information and it gives people the right to access any information that is kept on them. The Act makes some exemptions in the case of research; data may be stored indefinitely and if the data are anonymous the research respondents do not have a right of access to it.

It is good research practice in any case to be meticulous in recording and storing research data. You should not only keep the raw data appropriately; you should also keep any analysis documents so that it would be possible to create an 'audit' trail between the data and the findings and conclusions.

Practitioner/researcher

What precautions or mechanisms may be necessary to prevent you exploiting the privilege that this role gives you? You might want to consider some of the options discussed in Chapter 5 (pp. 299–301).

The reporting stage
Misuse of research

One possible ethical difficulty is that the research could be used to do harm to those who cooperated with it. A frequent issue is when the managers, who gave access permission for students to conduct research in their organisations, try to influence the content or tone of the dissertation. A more invidious form of this problem is when researchers write up the research in a way that will please the sponsors because they expect it will be required of them. A less common possibility is that the sponsors may try to use the research to support positions that the researcher thinks may be harmful to others.

Homan (1991) is a useful guide to the ethics of research.

Exhibit 1.8

Ethical approval procedures for researchers conducting studies within the National Health Service (NHS)

Some organisations, notably the NHS, require researchers, and students doing a dissertation as part of an academic programme, who wish to do a project that involves their staff or patients as research participants to obtain ethical research approval in addition to any ethical approval that might be obtained from the partici-pating university. This is a time-consuming process. It involves the following stages:

1 Completion of an online application form. The form, and online guidance, can be found at the website of the Central Office for Research Ethics Committees (COREC) at http://www.corec.org.uk/applicants/index.htm. This form requires full details of all the research methods that will be used.
2 Attend at the appropriate Local Research Ethics Committee (LREC) to dis-cuss and defend the application. They may require changes to the proposal before they give a favourable ethical opinion.
3 Having obtained LREC approval, the researcher must then apply for Research & Development approval from all NHS Trusts within which research is to be conducted. This involves completing a form. There is a national form (available at https://www.rdform.org.uk/) but some Trusts also have a local form.
4 When R&D approval has been obtained, the researcher needs to obtain an honorary contract with the Trust where the research will be conducted unless they are already an employee of the Trust.
5 It is normally required that before potential research participants (i.e. the people whom the researcher wishes to interview or send questionnaires to) can be approached and asked for their consent, permission must be obtained from their line managers to ask them to take part in the research.

Writing the research proposal

When you have been through the six-step process and thought about the design of your project, it might be helpful to summarise your research project. The Watson Box can be used for this purpose. It provides a useful framework for structuring your written research proposal.

The assessment criteria, which can be seen in the introductory chapter, identify a number of features that markers will be looking for in a pro-posal document:

- The 'what' and the 'why' of the proposal are clear and specific.
- The three elements of:
  - the research questions;
  - the research design; and

– the research methods
  are well integrated.
● The proposals for the research methods are sensible and practicable.

The Watson Box helps you ensure that you have met these criteria.

Exhibit 1.9

The Watson Box

What?	Why?
What puzzles and intrigues me? What do I want to know more about or better understand? What are my key research questions?	Why will this be of enough interest to put it on the library shelves or present to my organisation? Is it a guide to practitioners or policy makers? Is it a contribution to knowledge?

How – conceptually?	**How – practically?**
What models, concepts and theories can I draw upon? How can I develop my own research questions and create a conceptual framework to guide my investigation?	What research methods and techniques shall I use to apply my conceptual framework (to both gather and analyse evidence)? How shall I gain and maintain access to information sources?

Source: Watson (1994b)

Exercise 1.6

Completing the Watson Box

Use the blank Watson Box provided to write a summary of your research proposal.

What?	Why?

How – conceptually?	**How – practically?**

You have, of course, freedom to structure your research proposal (if you have to write one) as you please, but should you need guidance, the following structure covers most of the issues.

- Introduction
- The objectives and purpose of the project (what?):
  - A brief overall description of the project's context.
  - The strategic question that guides the project.
  - The objectives of the project.
- The justification for the project (why?).
- The research questions (what? – again, but in more detail):
  - Identify and discuss the research questions that you will answer in the project.
  - If you are taking a realist research approach you might frame your research question as a hypothesis. A hypothesis is a speculation about an association between two or more variables. It is important that the hypothesis can be tested by research to see whether it can be disproved.
- An overview of the appropriate literature:
  - Mapping the main writers in the field and their arguments.
  - Definition of key concepts and outlining of conceptual framework if necessary and possible. (This is the *how – conceptually?* quadrant of the Watson Box.)
- Research design:
  - What methodological approach are you going to adopt?
  - Research methods, samples, methods for analysing research material.
- Practical and ethical issues:
  - Does the research raise any ethical concerns that need to be resolved?
  - Are there any potential problems of research access?
  - Are there any resource issues such as access to specialist databases or particular research software?
  - Are there issues of commercial confidentially or intellectual property rights?
- A plan or timetable:
  - Consider drafting a Gantt chart (as shown in Exhibit 1.10) that plots against a timeline when the major elements of the project will be done.

Exhibit 1.10

A Gantt chart for a research project

Task	Sept.	Oct.	Nov.	Dec.	Etc.
Define topic area, strategic questions and research questions					
Literature search	←————————→				
Read literature		←————————→			
Draft and pilot interview schedule			←——→		
Obtain ethical approval from the university				←——→	
Conduct interviews etc.					←————→

If your research is going to adopt a grounded approach, then it will not be possible for you to predict what the key concepts and the conceptual framework might be.

Summary

- Use the six-stage process to think through your selection of a dissertation topic.
- Try to express your central research question as a simple and plain sentence without using academic or business jargon.
- Choose a research approach that is appropriate for your research question.
- You can mix and match your research approaches, but it is risky and you need to be sure that you understand the methodological implications of what you are doing.
- Think about how, practically, you will carry out the project so that you can write the dissertation.
- Use the Watson Box to summarise your proposal.
- Use the suggested list of headings to help you structure the research proposal.

Suggested reading

The standard textbooks recommended in the introductory chapter are the best places to start an exploration of research methodology. If you are considering using case studies as a main vehicle for your research then a look at Yin (1994) is recommended.

References

Altrichter, H. (1993) 'The concept of quality in action research: giving the practitioners a voice in educational research', in M. Schratz (ed.) *Qualitative Voices in Educational Research*, London: Falmer Press.

British Sociological Association (2002) *Statement of Ethical Practice for the British Sociological Association*, available at http://www.britsoc.co.uk/equality/63#Relationships%20with%20research%20participants (site visited 24 May 2006).

Buchanan, D. and Huczynski, A. (2001) *Organisational Behaviour: An Introductory Text*, 4th edn, Harlow: Prentice Hall.

Crotty, M. (2003) *The Foundations of Social Research. Meaning and Perspective in the Research Process*, London: Sage.

Dawson, P. (1994) *Organisational Change: A Processual Approach*, London: Paul Chapman.

Elliott, J. (1991) *Action Research for Educational Change*, Buckingham: Open University Press.

Fisher, C. and Lovell, A. (2000) *Accountants' Responses to Ethical Issues at Work*, London: Chartered Institute of Management Accountants (CIMA).

Gellner, E. (1995) 'Anything goes', *Times Literary Supplement*, 16 July: 3–4.

Gill, J. and Johnson, P. (1997) *Research Methods for Managers*, 2nd edn, London: Paul Chapman.

Homan, J. (1991) *The Ethics of Social Research*, Harlow: Longman.

Iaffaldano, M. and Muchinsky, P. (1985) 'Job satisfaction and job performance: a meta-analysis', *Psychological Bulletin*, vol. 97: 251–273.

Johnson, P. and Duberley, J. (2000) *Understanding Management Research: An Introduction to Epistemology*, London: Sage.

Katzell, R.A., Thompson, D.E. and Guzzo, R.A. (1992) 'How job satisfaction and job performance are and are not linked', in C.J. Cranny, P.C. Smith and E.F. Stone (eds) *Job Satisfaction: How People Feel about Their Jobs and how it Affects Their Performance*, Oxford: Lexington Books.

Kemmis, S. and McTaggart, R. (1982) *The Action Research Planner*, Geelong, Australia: Deakin University Press.

Locke, L.F., Spirduso, W.W. and Wilverman, S.J. (1993) *Proposals that Work: A Guide for Planning Dissertations and Research Proposals*, London: Sage.

McNiff, J., Lomax, P. and Whitehead, J. (1996) *You and Your Action Research Project*, London: Routledge and Hyde Publications.

Marx, K. (1970) 'Theses on Feuerbach', in K. Marx and F. Engels, *Selected Works in One Volume*, London: Lawrence & Wishart.

Milgram, S. (1963) 'A behavioural study of obedience', *Journal of Abnormal and Social Psychology*, vol. 67: 371–378.

Mintzberg, H. (1994) *The Rise and Fall of Strategic Planning*, Hemel Hempstead: Prentice Hall.

Northcote Parkinson, C. (1961) *Parkinson's Law or the Pursuit of Progress*, London: John Murray.

Peters, T.J. and Waterman Jr, R. (1982) *In Search of Excellence*, New York: Harper & Row.

Popper, K. (2002a) *Conjectures and Refutations: The Growth of Scientific Knowledge*, London: Routledge.

Popper. K. (2002b) *The Logic of Scientific Discovery*, London: Routledge.

Porter, S. (2002) 'Critical realist ethnography', in T. May (ed.) *Qualitative Research in Action*, London: Sage.

Reed, M. (1992) *The Sociology of Organisations: Themes, Perspectives and Prospects*, London: Harvester Wheatsheaf.

Remenyi, D., Williams, B., Money, A. and Swartz, E. (1998) *Doing Research in Business and Management: An Introduction to Process and Method*, London: Sage.

Revans, R. (1983) *The ABC of Action Learning*, Bromley: Chartwell-Bratt.

Schön, D. (1983) *The Reflective Practitioner: How Professionals Think in Action*, New York: Basic Books.

Schott, B. (2002) *Schott's Original Miscellany*, London: Bloomsbury.

Schütz, A. (1967) *The Phenomenology of the Social World*, trans. G. Walsh and F. Lehnert, Evanston, Ill.: North Western University Press.

Silverman, D. (1993) *Interpreting Qualitative Data*, London: Sage.

Somers, M.J., Dormann, C., Janssen, P.P.M., Dollard, M.F., Landeweerd, J.A. and Nijhuis, F.J.N. (2001) 'Thinking differently: assessing nonlinearities in the relationship between work attitudes and job performance using a Bayesian neural net', *Journal of Occupational and Organisational Psychology*, vol. 74, no. 1: 47–62.

Watson, T.J. (1994a) *In Search of Management: Culture, Chaos and Control in Management*, London: Routledge.

Watson, T.J. (1994b) 'Managing, crafting and researching: words, skill and imagination in shaping management research', *British Journal of Management*, vol. 5 (special issue): 77–87.

Weick, K.E. (1996) *Sensemaking in Organisations*, Newbury Park, Calif.: Sage.

Yin, R.K. (1994) *Case Study Research and Design and Methods*, 2nd edn, London: Sage.

Chapter 2

Writing a critical literature review

Contents

- Introduction
- The sources
  Searching for literature
- Mapping and describing the literature
  Describing the literature
- Assessing the quality of an article or book
- Forensic critique
  Soundness of arguments
  Evaluating arguments
- Radical critique
  The critical approach – *Alistair Mutch*
  Developing a radical critique
- Summary
- Suggested reading
- References

 Introduction

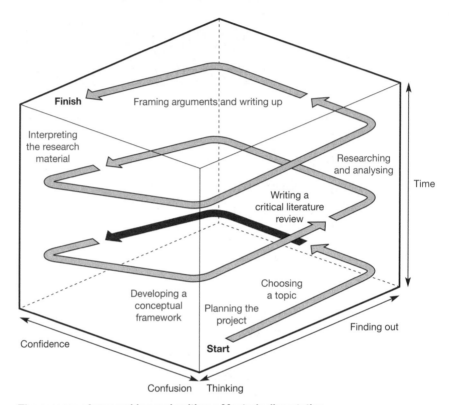

The process of researching and writing a Master's dissertation

Your manuscript is both good and original, but the part that is good is not original and the part that is original is not good.

Attributed to Dr Samuel Johnson[1]

A dissertation should include a chapter in which the literature relevant to the topic is reviewed (see Chapter 6 for a suggested list of chapters for a dissertation). It should be a critical literature review. It is the purpose of this chapter to explain what a critical review is. The criticism of the literature does not have to be as hurtful as that given by Dr Johnson in the quotation above. The purpose of criticism is not to wound but to ensure that the concepts, theories and arguments that you take from the literature to help you with the dissertation are robust. The purpose of the literature review, to take a broader perspective, is to remove the need to rediscover knowledge that has already been reported. The literature review helps you

---

[1] The quote, although often attributed to him, cannot be found in any of Johnson's published works. See http://www.samueljohnson.com/apocryph.html.

to build upon the work that has already been done in the field you are researching. To ensure that things have not been missed in the search it is important to show that you have searched the literature thoroughly and have identified most of the material that could be useful in the project. However, having found material in the literature does not mean that it is fit for use. It is necessary to subject the key materials you are going to use to a critical examination to make sure they are strong enough to sustain the use you are going to put them to in the dissertation. If you base the dissertation on invalid and poorly thought-through concepts and theories, then the whole dissertation will be weak. This does not mean that you must take on the most renowned authors and declare their arguments unsound. That might be a little arrogant. However, it may be necessary to identify the weaknesses and limitations of a writer's theories and arguments or identify their inappropriateness to the particular circumstances of your project.

It would be a good idea to look carefully at the marking scheme for dissertations that is provided in the introductory chapter and to review the benchmarks for the 'literature review' criterion. Treat this carefully, however, because the specific criteria used to mark your dissertation may be different. If you are content to be marked in the 50–59 per cent range, then it is only necessary to identify the appropriate literatures and to describe them competently. To achieve a mark in the 60–69 per cent range, a critical review of the literature is necessary. It is sufficient for this level of mark to base your criticism on those made by other writers. Even at this level, however, it would be sensible to try to form your own criticism of the work being considered. In many cases it may be that other authors have not yet written critiques of a work, in which case you will have to rely on your own resources. If the target is to be marked at a distinction level, then it is essential that you make your own evaluation of the core literature that you are using.

This chapter is divided into five parts:

1. Finding material and literature relevant to your project.
2. Guidelines for summarising and describing the literature.
3. Assessing the quality of an article or book.
4. Carrying out a forensic critique of the theories and arguments in the chosen literature. A forensic critique is an evaluation of the strength of the arguments proposed in a journal article or book.
5. Critical theory (or radical critique as it is alternatively known). This makes fundamental criticisms of management and business and is another form of evaluation of theories and arguments. It often takes a moral stance and identifies the ways in which business and management can reinforce tendencies in society to exploit and discriminate against sections of the population. The use of radical critiques in management Master's dissertations is not obligatory.

Learning outcomes for the chapter

1 Readers will be able to search library and other information resources to find appropriate literatures for their dissertation.

2 Readers will be able to map out the literatures and identify the key concepts, theories and arguments that are necessary for their project.

3 Readers will be able to make an overall assessment of the critical quality of a book or article.

4 Readers will be able to carry out a forensic critique of the core theories, concepts and arguments that they have drawn from the literature.

5 Readers will have an awareness of radical critical perspectives and be able to make radical critiques of key themes and topics presented in the literature.

● ● ● ● The sources

The first task in doing a literature review is to find some literature. You need a mixture of materials, but the precise combinations will vary from topic to topic. Try to find some material from most of the categories listed below. Students often ask: 'How many books and articles should I cite in my dissertation?' It is impossible to give a number in answer, although it can be tempting to quote a very large number to scare them and to encourage them not to ask silly questions in future. It all depends on what literature is available and how you use the ideas, material and theory it contains. It is possible to suggest that a list of references with less than 20 items is probably too short.

- *Books*
  There are three sorts of management books as far as researchers are concerned:
  - textbooks
  - academic monographs and
  - 'airport bookstall' books.
  Textbooks are useful to help you orient yourself in a field of literature and as a source of references that can be followed up. They may be recognised from their characteristic use of learning devices such as learning objectives, summaries, exercises and text boxes containing illustrative material. They should not be relied upon too heavily. Academic monographs are often difficult to read, but they do alert the reader to developments arising from recent research. These books should be used selectively. 'Airport bookstall' books are mostly written

in an accessible style and have attractive jackets. When they are not based on the biographies or experiences of successful managers, they are often distillations of more academic work. They are mostly presented in a 'can do' format, offering practical guidance for business success. Normally they have attention-grabbing titles that appear to offer solutions to all business problems. They can be assimilated within the duration of a transatlantic flight. They can be useful materials, but they should not be used uncritically because they often oversimplify and contain uncorroborated assumptions.

- *Journals*
  Journals fall into two main categories and you should use both. Academic journals contain articles that have been peer reviewed. This means that two or more expert referees approved the papers before they were accepted for publication. The general information or style pages, often on the inside of the front or back cover of a journal, should say whether it is peer reviewed. Non-peer-reviewed journals are often professional or trade journals. The articles in these journals are commonly simpler and shorter than those in the peer-reviewed journals. They can be useful for identifying trends, fashions and current concerns within business, but many are derivative and of questionable quality. Non-peer-reviewed journals should not be used exclusively. Managers doing MBAs and other Master's courses in management often look at the more academic papers in horror and declare, 'We are managers, we cannot be expected to cope with this hugely complex academic writing style.' Well, I have some sympathy because many papers do appear to be written in a style designed to fool, impress or confuse. Nevertheless, there will be much pertinent and good material in such papers and you will need to make the effort to understand them. There are some journals, such as the *Harvard Business Review*, that are academically prestigious but are designedly accessible to managers as well as to academics.

  Journals will most likely be your main source for a research dissertation, probably being more important than books. This is because the most up-to-date research and debates will be found in journals.

- *The World Wide Web*
  The World Wide Web is a very useful source of material. The better search engines can be valuable in tracking down material. The Web has to be used with care, however, because it includes both high-quality material and utter tosh. Distinguishing between the two is not always easy. In preparing for writing this guide, I found a web page on semantic differential questionnaires (see p. 197). The first few pages read very sensibly and then the web page slowly became an obsessive polemic in which semantic differentials were presented as diabolic devices that bureaucrats were using to remove the liberties of the individual.

Exhibit 2.1

The dangers of cutting and pasting from the World Wide Web

Francis Robinson (2006) reviewed a new edition of a book that describes an Indian traveller's journey through England and Ireland in the early nineteenth century. To help the reader the publisher provided an appendix describing all the key places mentioned in the book. Unfortunately the task of compiling the appendix appears to have been given to some research assistants who did all their research using search engines and the Web. This led to some unfortunate mistakes.

- St Paul's Cathedral, London, is mistaken for the Catholic Cathedral of St Pauls in Minneapolis in the USA.
- Windsor Great Park, which is to the west of London in the UK, is said to be on the south bank of the Detroit River. Windsor, Ontario, is indeed 'noted for its several large parks and gardens found on its waterfront' (Wikipedia, 2006).
- Phoenix park, which the traveller visited in Dublin, is said to be in Phoenix, the capital of Arizona.

Use of Web search engines can have the effect of undermining common sense and can give a false sense of confidence in one's knowledge.

In the public sector, where much of the material is in the form of official publications and reports, the Web can be the most convenient means of access to material. The *DirectGov* government website at http://www.direct.gov.uk/Homepage/fs/en is a good starting point.

- *Dissertations*

Business schools keep copies of past Master's dissertations produced by their students. Some are commercially confidential and cannot be consulted without the author's permission. Many students find it comforting to see others' efforts, and it may be worth asking to see some. Try to make sure that you are given ones that passed comfortably, otherwise you may gain a dangerously low impression of the standard you need to reach.

Searching for literature

Looking for literature these days is mostly an electronic activity of searching through a virtual library. Using a library's online catalogue of books and other materials makes searching for books a lot easier. It is possible to access the online catalogues of academic libraries across the country. NISS (National Information Services and Systems) provides a website of links to online library catalogues at http://www.niss.ac.uk/lis/opacs.html. The advantages of searching for journal articles and papers by using electronic library resources is that it takes much less time, you are more likely to find what you need and, if you are lucky, the papers may be available online and you can download them or print them off.

Exhibit 2.2

An electronic library

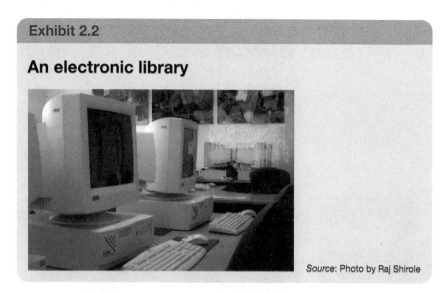

Source: Photo by Raj Shirole

You should spend some time becoming familiar with all the services that your university or institutional library can provide by exploring both the physical library and the virtual library. You may need various user names and passwords to access the latter, and the library staff will be able to help you with these. Do not become so carried away with online searching that you forget about bibliographic serendipity, by which I mean wandering around the library shelves and current journal stands, flicking through books and reading the contents lists on the back pages of journals. It is surprising how often you chance upon useful material that you would otherwise have missed. Many academic libraries have joined a cooperative scheme so that students who live or work at a distance from their university can use libraries closer to them. A website listing the universities in the scheme can be found at http://uklibrariesplus.ac.uk/.

Electronic resources

There is a range of electronic resources that might be of help. These can be searched one at a time but, increasingly, electronic libraries provide meta-search facilities that allow many databases to be searched at the same time. If you want to do a search using advanced search facilities it is often best to search databases individually and not to use meta-search engines.

Electronic journals

Most libraries will subscribe to journals that are published and/or are available online. Check out which relevant publications are provided by your library.

Exhibit 2.3

A more traditional library

Full-text databases

These are databases that allow you to make searches for materials using key words. They provide all the bibliographic details such as authors, titles, journal titles, date of publication, volume, issue and page numbers. They will also include abstracts of papers' and articles' contents. In addition, in many but not all cases they give you access to an html or pdf copy of the article itself that you can read on screen, download, print off or email to yourself. The full-text databases that you are mostly likely to use are listed below:

Business Source Premier – a good all-round database.
Emerald – includes all the journals published by MCB Press.
European Business ASAP – covers finance, acquisitions and mergers, new technologies and products, HRM, marketing and management generally.
Ingenta – a general database of papers from a number of publishers.

Universities have to buy licences to give students access to databases. Which databases universities choose to buy licences for will, of course, vary from institution to institution. You need to explore your institution's list of electronic resources to see what is available to you.

Bibliographic databases

These databases can be searched in the same way as full-text databases and provide you with all the bibliographic information and with abstracts, but they do not provide full copies of the papers and articles. If you want them you will have to find the hard copy of the journal in the library, and if the library does not have a copy you will have to order the item on inter-library loan. Some databases you might want to use are listed below:

> *Zetoc* – provides bibliographic information on journals held by the British Library.
> *PsycINFO* – covers the field of psychology, but there are many articles that are relevant to management topics.
> *Econlit* – covers the field of economics, and again there are many relevant references especially for people working on finance topics.

If you are interested in management in health care and medicine, then *Medline* may be worth consulting. If you are working in the public sector, especially in the social services, then *ASSIA* would be worth a look.

Newspapers in electronic formats

Newspapers are a valuable source of up-to-date information on many management topics. A number of newspapers are available as searchable databases in libraries. Newspapers, including the *Financial Times*, are also available as online editions on the World Wide Web.

Financial and marketing databases

Strictly speaking these are primary resources rather than secondary materials and so would find their place in the 'results and analysis' part of the dissertation rather than in the literature review. Nevertheless, here is a convenient place to mention them. *FAME* is the main financial database. It provides updated financial information on 130,000 companies in the United Kingdom and Ireland. *Mintel* is one of the main marketing databases. These or other databases will be available at your university library.

Building up your list of references

It might be worthwhile to check up on the Harvard system of referencing (see p. 343) before you start collecting material. Then you can be sure to record all the necessary bibliographic details as you identify the books and papers. This will save you much time. As I have discovered to my cost, it can take hours, after you have finished writing the dissertation, to track down the missing details (year of publication, page numbers for quotations) of material you have cited but that you forgot to record properly. This is time you can ill afford when you are struggling to get the dissertation finished by the deadline. It is much easier to be conscientious about the detail from the start. It is also worth considering whether you are going to use some specialist citation software (see p. 255) to help you with building up your bibliography.

Mapping and describing the literature

In most cases the literature search identifies a lot of material – probably more than can be sensibly dealt with in a Master's dissertation. So the next step in conducting a literature review is to map out and identify the key works and material in the literature. This exercise has two purposes. It is necessary for you to show the person who marks your dissertation that you are aware of the breadth of literature relating to your topic. But it is also necessary, for your sanity, as well as to meet the marker's expectations, to show that you can prioritise the literature and identify the key works, theories or concepts that will be of value in the conduct of your project.

Describing the literature

Describing and mapping the literature relevant to your research project is a step-by-step process that moves from the general to the specific. It is an editing process.

1. Prepare a 'map' showing the location of all the appropriate literatures

The first step involves identifying the different fields of literature that may be appropriate to the study without, at this stage, looking at any of it in detail. By literature I mean a collection of books and papers that deal with the same issues and that respond to each other in the developing debates about a topic. It follows from this definition that there will be many literatures rather than one solitary and unified literature. But it is up to you to draw the boundaries between them. This can be done by skimming through textbooks and following up the references they give, and by dipping into the journal literature via the abstracts in the bibliographic databases.

Figure 2.1 shows a 'map' of the literatures that I thought were relevant when I was planning some research into the fates and attitudes of the survivors of downsizing. The main theme of the dissertation is shown in the middle of the map in bold font. There are a number of key researchers who have written research papers specifically on the subject. There is also a large literature, mostly in journals, that focuses on downsizing as a strategy and on its financial consequences for companies. This literature suggests that the demoralisation of survivors may be a contributory factor to the poor performance of organisations post-downsizing. This link makes the downsizing literature relevant to the project. The literature on redundancy concentrates on the managerial processes involved in choosing people for redundancy. The organisational justice literature assesses such processes and evaluates them for fairness. As it is likely that people's judgements about the fairness of redundancy processes will be a factor in their reactions to it, this literature is also relevant. The literature on emotion in organisation is not directly relevant to downsizing; but because downsizing is an emotional issue there may be some insights from the literature that will be helpful in the study. Finally, in psychology there is a well-established literature on people's reactions to trauma. It suggests a sequence of reactions beginning with disbelief, moving through shock and anger and culminating with readjustment. As being a survivor of downsizing may be as much a trauma as being a victim of it, this literature might provide some helpful frameworks.

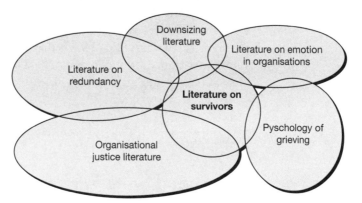

Figure 2.1 Mapping the literature

In the literature review it is important to identify the major literatures relevant to a project, without going into detail, and to explain why they might be significant. The important skill at this stage is to be able to condense or précis large volumes of literature so that the essential views or arguments they contain can be presented in a small number of words.

2. Present an argument about which literatures you are going to concentrate on

Normally the map of the literatures will contain more fields than can be managed in the literature review. It is important to reduce it to two or three. In the first step of the literature review, credit may be scored for showing an awareness of the broad scope of the literature. In this phase credit may gained by choosing the key literatures that will be helpful to the particular study being conducted. In the example of the 'survivors of downsizing study', I chose the literature on survival and the psychology of grieving and emotion in organisation as the key ones for the study I wished to do. The choice of literature will reflect the angle or perspective you wish to take on a topic.

3. Provide an overview of the chosen literature

At this stage it is necessary to give a more detailed description of the literature chosen. When you come to write up this chapter, the overview will provide the bulk of the material. It is important to think carefully about how you will structure it. The way not to structure an account of the literature is to work through a list of works one at a time. Exhibit 2.4, as a caricature, shows how not to do it.

Reading an annotated list such as that shown in Exhibit 2.4 is very boring, especially as the first sentence of each paragraph has exactly the same structure. The citations are technically correct but padded out. Do we really need to have the title of the work or the magazine spelt out in the text? The writer telling us whether they enjoyed a work does not constitute a critique, although it may be a criticism. But most importantly, there is no account given of the ideas, theories and material that are presented in the works cited.

Exhibit 2.4

How not to write a literature review

Wood (1965) wrote an article in the *Journal of Panopticon Studies* that argued that the metaphor of the panopticon was very important. The article is hard to read and uses big words.

Smith (1966) wrote a book called *Jeremy Bentham's Lessons for Modern Managers*. This is a very enjoyable read and contains many practical lessons for managers. He claims that the panopticon would be a good basis for modern office layout planning.

Jones (1967) in an article for the *Bored Accountant* magazine mentions the panopticon.

Etc. ad nauseam (i.e. until you feel sick).

Your account of the literature should be structured thematically. You should draw out of the works you are using the main themes, questions or issues that are discussed. These should become the sub-headings within the chapter. Under each sub-heading it is necessary to give an account of the relevant theories and the evidence provided in support of them. The discussion should be comparative, weighing one writer's views and evidence against those presented by others. Similarities and differences should be identified and their significance, if any, explained. One way of thematically structuring an account of the literature is shown below:

1. Identify the main 'camps', 'waves', 'schools', ideological stances or positions.

   There are always arguments and debates within a field of literature. It is necessary to describe the nature of these arguments. Identify the dominant or loudest voices in the debates.

2. Compare and contrast them.

   Decide the depth of the disagreement between the parties and their arguments. Sometimes the differences are great and significant. On other occasions the differences are trivial to all except those involved in the argument.

3. Evaluate their strengths and weaknesses.

   If the differences are significant, decide which side of the argument you believe to be stronger.

Literature reviews can often become detached from the project they are in support of. The discussion of theories and authors may develop its own momentum, and no links are made to the research questions that the dissertation is seeking to answer. The way to overcome this is to state the relevance of each piece of theory to the topic of the dissertation by using sentences similar to the following:

- Mintzberg's theory of structure in fives provides a means of analysing the organisational changes that are the subject of this dissertation.
- … this quotation mirrors the situation that has motivated the research project.
- Hamel and Prahalad's work identifies a number of factors that should be considered when researching …
- An insight into employees' responses to downsizing in my case study organisations can be gained from Broeckner's work on …
- Socio-technical theory integrates the two key aspects of this study into …

It is important to follow up these statements with an account of their significance for your project. There is nothing more frustrating to the reader than to be informed that something is 'critical' and then left without an explanation why.

If you cannot think of a way in which a piece of theory or literature aids your thinking and research into your topic, then it is likely you need not include it. A dissertation is not a place to display your encyclopaedic knowledge of a topic, unless it is relevant to your theme.

4. Provide an argument to explain and justify the shortlist of theories, concepts, frameworks or techniques that you have chosen for use in your project

By this stage a small part of the literature will have been identified that will be useful to the project. It may be down to a handful of concepts, theories and arguments. These will provide basic working materials for the project. At this stage the literature review merges into the process of developing a conceptual framework that will be considered in the next chapter.

5. Provide a critical account of the chosen concepts, theories or arguments

This is a detailed review of particular theories designed to test their fitness of purpose for use in the project.

One student was researching the introduction of teamworking at his place of work. This sentence could be found in his draft literature review chapter:

> Dunphy and Bryant (1996), for example, identify three forms of team, each of which is most suited to the pursuit of a particular aspect of performance. While simple, multi-skilled teams are thus most likely to impact most heavily on an organisation's costs, self-managed teams will have their main effects on value, and self-led teams on innovation.

At face value it appears that this piece of theory might be very helpful in understanding the introduction of teamworking into a particular organisation. It would allow questions to be asked such as whether the organisation had chosen the most appropriate form of teamworking for introduction. However, this sentence was all that was said; and it was inadequate.

A more critical and extensive account needed to be given (assuming that the theory was going to be helpful) by answering some of the following questions:

- How were the three types of teams defined? In particular, what is the difference between self-led and self-managed teams? At first glance these last two seem similar.
- How does this threefold analysis of team types differ from other writers' classifications?
- Is the claim that each type of team delivers a different strategic outcome (cost reduction, value and innovation) based on sound research?

- How well supported is it by other researchers and writers?
- Are these claims logically and consistently argued for in the work?
- How useful might this theory be to the student's own project?

The best literature reviews are those where themes and ideas are taken from the literature, evaluated, and then woven into a coherent argument about the subject matter of the dissertation.

There are three main aspects of criticising the literature:

1. assessing the quality of a article or book
2. forensic analysis
3. radical critique.

Methods and techniques that may help you with these three tasks are explained in the rest of this chapter. It is perhaps worth pointing out that the first two aspects are obligatory for all dissertations; the third, radical critique, is not necessarily expected by your markers but may still be a sensible and useful addition to your critique of the literature.

Note taking

Describing the content of the books and articles you find in your literature search means you will have to take notes. Unfortunately, simply using a highlighter pen on the book or article you are reading will not be sufficient. (It can actually be a problem in note taking if, as I have often seen, nearly all the sentences in a work are highlighted.) Highlighting is a very helpful stage in making notes but the passages highlighted need to be thought about and transferred into one's own notes using one's own words for learning to take place.

Note taking is a process of editing or 'gutting' a work to identify the key material and involves looking for the following things in the work:

- How does the work being annotated fit into the wider academic debate on the subject?
- What are the main findings, conclusions or arguments presented in the work?
- For each of the above:
  - What arguments are presented to support the finding or conclusion?
  - What evidence is presented?
  - What authorities (i.e. well-established authors) are quoted as supporting the finding or conclusion?
- Are there any particular data, arguments and/or quotations that might be useful and should be noted?
- Are there any books, articles, electronic resources cited in the list of references that might be worth chasing up?

These headings could be used to write your notes.

● ● ● ● Assessing the quality of an article or book

This first aspect of critiquing a book or article involves making an overall judgement of its worth so as to be able to decide whether it deserves a more detailed forensic critique. You need to decide whether the piece is of good quality and ought to be included in your literature review. This can be done by skim reading the piece and considering the following issues and questions.

The provenance

Some journals, and some publishers of academic books, have more prestige than others. We have already seen that some journals are peer reviewed and others are not. In general, articles in peer-reviewed journals should be more reliable than those in non-peer-reviewed publications. This is not an infallible rule, however. It would be foolish to ignore a paper just because it was published by an unregarded journal. The status of the journal is just one piece of information you have to consider. If you wish you can further establish the credentials of a journal by looking at one of the league tables of academic journals that are available. These league tables claim to rank academic journals according to their quality. The list published by Bristol Business School can be found on the World Wide Web at http://www.uwe.ac.uk/bbs/research/jlists.shtml#top.

References

The next step is to turn to the back of the book or article and look at the list of references. This will give a rough and ready guide to how well the author(s) have used the literature.

- Are there many references? But bear in mind that too many can be as much of a weakness as too few.
- Check the ratio of books to journal articles. Generally the higher the proportion of articles, the more up to date and embedded in the literature the piece will be.
- Are the journal references to well-established and regarded journals?

Precision of the writing

When you skim read the book or article consider the care that the authors take in expressing their arguments. Are there many sweeping statements or many unsubstantiated assumptions? Statements such as 'corporate real estate management is the critical factor in organisational success', especially if it comes near the beginning of a piece, is probably both sweeping and unsubstantiated; and does not suggest that great care is being taken in developing arguments. Also consider whether the key concepts used in the work have been carefully defined. For example, if someone is writing about virtual teams in organisations and claims that they can be of any size, indeed they can have an almost infinite number of members, and can be formed of anonymous participants, then the definition is so all-encompassing that the term 'virtual teams' loses most of its value. It becomes impossible to make any useful generalisations about such an amorphous concept. The more precise and careful writers are with their language, the better the quality of their work.

Description or analysis

A good piece of academic writing will have a mixture of description and analysis. Descriptive writing tells us what is but does not attempt to classify and organise the material; nor does it seek to draw any theoretical inferences from the material. A book or article that is purely descriptive is likely to be of lesser quality than one which adds analysis to description. If a researcher has conducted many interviews we do not simply want to be told what the interviewees said, although of course that is of interest, we also want to be told what is significant and what is trivial in what they said. We also need to know what insights and generalisations might be drawn from their testimonies. This often requires that the findings are discussed in the light of the theories available in the literature.

One should not be too prim about this matter. Sometimes we use an article or a book not because of its analysis or theorising but because it provides raw material, research findings, that we can use to strengthen the analysis of our own research material. Quite often we will cite a book or article because of a single fact or insight it contains and we will ignore the bulk of its contents.

Research evidence

Check whether the book or article contains research evidence that is used to support its arguments and contentions. It is perfectly proper, of course, to write a purely theoretical piece that is based on the literature. Indeed, C Wright Mills (1959: 205) in the appendix on 'intellectual craftsmanship' wrote:

> Now I do not like to do empirical work if I can possibly avoid it ... there is no more virtue in empirical enquiry as such than reading as such.

Nevertheless, research has to be conducted to resolve the matters of fact that the preliminary reading and reasoning have identified. In general terms a piece of work that includes some appropriate and well-conducted research will be more useful than a purely theoretical piece. Theoretical pieces often have one advantage to the business student, however, which is that they can provide a helpful résumé and evaluation of the literature on a particular topic.

A consideration of the preceding points should help you make a judgement about the value of a particular piece of academic writing.

Forensic critique

The term 'forensic critique' has been invented for this chapter. One of the definitions of forensic is 'pertaining to public debate'. This is relevant to the evaluation of literature because evaluation is a contribution to a public debate on arguments and theories that writers have placed in the public domain. But forensic also has an emerging definition, based on the work of forensic science, which means a minute, detailed and logical examination of evidence. This definition is also relevant to doing a literature review. Once you have identified the key concepts, theories and arguments that you will use in your research, it is important to put them under scrutiny before relying on them. So, in this section, forensic critique means the process of testing academic ideas to assess their usefulness.

There are two ways of tackling a forensic critique. The first is to identify the key arguments in a piece of work and to evaluate the soundness of the logic they utilise. The second is to scour the piece for examples of weak argumentation. Both approaches will be considered in turn.

Soundness of arguments

Books and articles contain many things: accounts, descriptions, summaries, instructions, polemics and so on. The most important item, however, is the arguments they contain. When a book or article is evaluated the main arguments it presents have to be dissected out from the bulk of the text and a judgement made about their soundness and robustness.

All arguments have three components. These can help you recognise when, in a text, an argument and not an assertion or an assumption is being presented:

- **Premises** – these are assumptions or claims that something is true or is a 'fact'. Most arguments are based on several premises, but they can be founded on one only.
- **Inference words** – these are the indicators that the writer is about to draw a logical inference or conclusion from the premises presented. Examples are 'thus', 'therefore', 'because', 'implies', 'hence', 'it follows that', 'so', 'then' and 'consequently'.
- **Conclusions** – a conclusion is an arguable statement. It is either a statement about the relationship between the premises or it is an inference about the likely consequences given the circumstances and the premises.

It should be possible, using this threefold classification and by looking for the inference words, to identify and summarise the main arguments presented in a book or an article. It may even be possible to lay out the arguments as a series of flow charts.

Judging the strength of an argument is a two-pronged activity:

- Assessing the truthfulness of the premises. In books and articles, the truthfulness, or validity, of a premise may be supported by research evidence. If this is so, then it is necessary to judge whether the research methods have been sensibly chosen and competently applied.
- Assessing the logical strength of the conclusions drawn from them. When considering the logical strength of an argument, it is likely that conclusions that are drawn deductively will be stronger than those drawn inductively. These terms need definition.

Deduction is when a conclusion is drawn that necessarily follows in logic from the premises that are stated. So a deduction does not depend on observation or experience; it is simply a matter of logic. So, assuming the premises are true, the following is an example of a logically strong piece of deduction.

Premise 1 – the selection panel thought Jane was a better candidate for the job than John.

Premise 2 – the selection panel thought John a better candidate for the job than Mark.

Conclusion, by deduction – Jane must be a better candidate for the job than Mark.

If you are evaluating a piece of theoretical writing then many of the conclusions drawn will be based on such logic. The question to be asked is whether the logic is true.

'Deduction' is a troublesome word. It has at least two meanings. In the analysis of arguments it has the meaning given here; that is, arriving at a conclusion based on logic and not on experimentation or experience. It follows (an inference phrase) that there can be no doubt about a deduced conclusion. A deduction is certain as long as the premises are true and the world is rational.[2] However, deduction is also defined as making a specific inference from a general law. This definition does not hold in this instance. In arguments, deduction can proceed from the general to the particular, from particular to particular (as in the example above) or from general to general (Hart, 1998: 82).

Induction is when a conclusion is drawn from past experience or experimentation. The assumption is made that because things have always been so, then that is how they will be in the future. The strength of inductive arguments is often weaker than that of deductions. However, the more supporting evidence there is, the stronger the probability that the inference

---

[2] The world is not always logical. In experiments on people's choices it is not uncommon for people to think, using the example given, that Jane is better than John and that John is better than Mark but also to think that Mark is better than Jane (Wright, 1984: 16; Lages et al., 1999).

is true. Deductions are certainties but inductive conclusions are probabilities. The trick is to make sure that the balance of probabilities is favourable. Consider the following example:

> Premise 1 – Companies that have the ISO 9000 certification have in the past made better supply chain partners than those that have not.

> Premise 2 – Companies that have been selected using the 'selecting a supply chain partner software' prove to be better collaborative partners nine times out of ten.

> Premise 3 – in the past, small companies have made better supply chain partners than large ones.

> Premise 4 – Skegmouth Logistics Co. has ISO 9000, has been accepted by the software and is a small company.

> Conclusion, inferred by induction – Skegmouth Logistics Co. would likely make a good supply chain partner.

When inductive arguments have been identified in a piece of writing, it is important to assess whether the conclusion is based more on wishful thinking than on a carefully judged balance of probabilities.

Exercise 2.1

Reviewing arguments

Visit the library or a bibliographic database and choose an article that interests you from a peer-reviewed journal. Read the article and draft a critical review of it. Use the following questions (based on Hughes, 1992) as guidelines:

- Identify the main arguments in the paper.
  - What is the main point of the arguments?
  - Identify the 'inference indicators', the words such as 'therefore' that indicate that a conclusion is being drawn from the evidence presented.
  - Assess the context for the argument.
- Identify the premises from which the conclusions are drawn.
  - Locate the premises in the text.
- Check the acceptability of these premises.
  - Are they well supported by evidence?
  - Are they well supported by citations from the literature?
  - Are you convinced they are true?
- Check the logical strength of the conclusions drawn from the premises.
  - Are the conclusions logically based on the premises?
  - How strong are the conclusions?
- Look for counter-arguments.
  - Could the premises support a counter-conclusion?

Evaluating arguments

Another way of judging the strength of arguments is to see whether the authors have made any of a number of well-known logical errors. What follows is a list of the most common flaws in argument, based largely on Thouless (1968) and Warburton (1996).

1. The use of emotionally toned words

'The standards of modern examinations have woefully declined. They fail *hopelessly* to prepare students for work in modern organisations. They *cripple a child's chances of later career success.*' Such arguments use a form of emotional blackmail. Who, after all, would wish to *cripple a child's chances in life*? The argument also rehashes a much used cliché in management: that if things are not modern, they are bad. It is particularly tempting to use such arguments in the early years of a new millennium – 'preparing ourselves for the challenges of the new millennium' and so on.

2. Making a statement in which all is implied but some is true

In a debate in some parts of Scotland during the early years of the past century, about whether to continue the prohibition of alcohol on Sundays, a poster proclaimed that people should vote against prohibition because any loss of liberty meant slavery (Thouless, 1968: 24). This statement is only true if all liberty is lost. The loss of only some liberty (to drink a pint of beer on a Sunday) is not the same as slavery.

3. Proof by selected instances

Where you think someone has chosen only those cases, from all those available to them, that make their point.

4. Challenging an opponent's point by extension or contradiction

In an argument over the relative merits of markets and bureaucracies in delivering public services, a person who believes that there are some services that are best delivered by private sector organisations is drawn into extending their argument into, first, that most services are best delivered so and, second, that all services are best delivered so. Extended positions are always vulnerable and can be easily demolished with a few well-chosen facts.

5. Proof by inconsequent argument

You make a statement in support of a proposition that is not logically related to it but at first glance looks as if it might be.

> This can often be ensured by making the supporting statement a reference to a learned theory of which one's opponent will be afraid to confess his [sic] ignorance, or at any rate, making the supporting statement in a

manner so obscure that one's opponent fears that it would show shameful ignorance if he confessed that he did not see the connection.

(Thouless, 1968: 43)

Fairbairn and Winch (1996: 185) refer to this ploy as crafty conflation. The following statement provides an example: 'Organisations that fail to modernise will not survive in the twenty-first century. The acceptance of flexible career patterns and of the loss of careers for life is consequentially essential for organisational survival.' This argument conflates the idea of modernisation and the acceptance of career flexibility. It is not necessarily the case that the latter is necessary to achieve the former. It may or may not be; but the point is worthy of discussion.

6. The argument that we should not make efforts against X, which is admittedly evil, because there is a worse evil, Y, against which our efforts should be directed

In the debate about the extradition of General Pinochet from the United Kingdom in 1998, one of the arguments against extradition was that Pinochet was a lesser tyrant than the Chinese leadership and that he should not be tried for crimes against humanity if the Chinese leadership was not. A failure to deal with one wrong is no reason for not acting against another.

7. The recommendation of a position because it is a mean between two extremes

There may be occasions when the mean is golden, but it rather depends on the choice of the two extremes.

8. The use of logically unsound argument

There are many forms of illogicality. Here is just one. The fact of an association between two things does not prove a causal or logical relationship. It may be that there is a statistical relationship between the number of 'quality stations' in a workplace (with their progress charts, quality awards and photos of successful quality circles) and high output. But the association does not prove that one causes the other or, if it does, which way round the causal chain works. Do the workstations cause the staff to be more highly motivated or does the fact that people are successful lead them to treasure their quality stations?

9. Begging the question

One can prove that all swans are white by refusing to accept that black swans are truly swans.

10. Failing to distinguish factual statements from opinion

The notion of facts is a little difficult to accept if you are of a postmodern persuasion. Nevertheless, it should still be possible to separate those things that are generally accepted as if they were true, and for which some research evidence can be presented, and personal opinion. In management research this error occurs when people do not distinguish between what they have discovered about a problem and their beliefs about how it can be solved, as in 'my research shows that the implementation of staff empowerment will enable the organisation to become a world-class business'.

11. Tautology

A tautology is saying the same thing twice. Stylistically it involves redundant words ('LloydsTSB Bank'). By extension a tautological argument is one in which a thing is said twice but in such a way as to make it appear that a logical deduction is being made, as in 'The increased pace of change means that things are moving faster.'

12. Inferring what should be from what the arguer thinks ought to be and assuming that something is right because it is commonly done or is useful

The fact that lots of organisations are doing 360-degree appraisals does not necessarily mean they are a good thing. Equally, the author's belief that a proposition will be of practical benefit does not mean that it is right or should be commended.

13. Changing the meaning of a term during the argument

Thouless (1968: 77) gives the following example. Crowds exhibit cruelty, unintelligence and irresponsibility. Democratic government is rule by the crowd. Therefore, democratic government is cruel, unintelligent and irresponsible. This argument involves a subtle change in the definition of the word 'crowd'.

14. The use of the fact of a continuity between two things to throw doubt on the real difference between them

Using the practical difficulty of determining where, precisely, in terms of number of staff or amount of turnover, to draw the distinction between large and small organisations to suggest that the distinction is not a useful one.

15. Disguising a lack of clear thought by the extensive use of jargon

Too much use of business and professional jargon, or of obscure and lengthy words, raises suspicions that the author is seeking to disguise their confusion and lack of clear thought.

16. The appeal to mere authority

This false type of argument is that a well-established writer in the field has said *x* and so it must be true. This should not be seen as a licence not to cite authors in your dissertation. The error is when an author is cited as a lazy substitute for making a case or presenting an argument.

17. Argument by imperfect analogy

'The keen edge of intellect will be blunted by too frequent use.' This might be a tempting maxim for a hard-pressed MBA student. However, most intellects are honed, not blunted, by use. Too frequent a resort to argument by analogy can lead to a hermetic paranoia in which everything is seen as part of a vast and secret conspiracy. Read Umberto Eco's (1989) novel *Foucault's Pendulum* for an insight into the places such thinking can lead. (The reference is to Leon Foucault (1819–1868) and not to the Michel Foucault who is discussed on p. 112; although Eco no doubt intended any confusion that might have arisen.)

18. *Ad hominem* arguments

Attacking the arguer and not the arguments. This is normally resorted to when a critic can find no weak points in an argument and so argues that the writer is a bad person and that for this reason their arguments should be discounted. In 2001 and 2002, for example, there was a correspondence in a literary journal about Foucault. The debate was started by Tallis (2001) and continued by Hargreaves (2002) and Sennett (2001), among others. Foucault was accused of deliberately infecting his partners with AIDS. It was also alleged that he did not believe in objective truth. This led to an implication that the latter justified the former. In such debates, arguments about a person's theories and arguments become confused with arguments about the morality of the person.

19. The use of persuaders

Fairbairn and Winch (1996: 182) describe these as 'words and phrases that are put into an assertion illicitly to persuade the reader to accept what is said by other than rational means'. For example, 'Surely all accountants must realise that their job is one of the most important in the country' or 'It is the exception that proves the rule.'

There are some criticisms commonly made of books and articles that are not fair. One is 'death by a thousand snips'. This is done by accumulating a large number of petty errors, an author's name misspelt here, a date wrong by one year there and so on. The overall effect is to cast doubt on the author's arguments without actually challenging them. It is a form of *ad hominem* criticism because it is challenging the author's abilities rather than their arguments. Another unfair criticism is to claim that the themes the author has chosen to focus on are the wrong ones. This is tantamount to saying the author should have written a different book or article from the one they chose to write.

Exercise 2.2

Evaluating arguments

Study the argument made in the extract from my book on public sector management (Fisher, 1998) shown below, entitled 'On heaps'.

Identify the key points in the argument.

Write a précis of the piece in less than 200 words. The piece is 1,438 words long.

Using the list of flaws in arguments given above, identify as many examples of suspect or improper forms of argument as you can.

Do bear in mind that we all use weak arguments, sometimes out of laziness, sometimes because we have not spotted the flaw and are convinced by the arguments, and sometimes deliberately as a way of ensuring we win the current round, at least, of an argument. This situation ensures that flawed argument spotting is an easy target and it can lead to

a cast of mind in the reader such that he looked only for faults, ambiguities and omissions, in order to show the writer to be muddled and incompetent. We recommend that you avoid this approach in your own writing. Scholarship is not, or at least should not be, a form of blood sport. The first business of the reader is to try and understand what is going on in a passage, *then* to subject it to measured evaluation.

(Fairbairn and Winch, 1996: 208)

So, approach this exercise as a means of testing your own abilities rather than as a criticism of the passage's author.

ON HEAPS

Academic books can be written in two ways, they are either holes or heaps. When a hole is dug all the earth has to be removed and, in the case of specialised holes such as archaeologists' trenches, the spoil is carefully sieved and the revealed strata minutely surveyed. Similarly when a book of the hole type is written the author sifts and sorts all the material drawn from his or her academic excavations. The literature dug up is finely delineated and the past history of the field of study is revealed. This type of book has a great density of reference and citation to other authorities on the subject as the writers trace through the arguments and counter-arguments that define the academic development of their topic.

Heaps however are made by walking all over the field, picking up objects that look interesting or exotic and throwing them on to a pile. The author of a book of the heap type therefore is constantly on the look out for elegant arguments and exotic and eclectic examples and illustrations. Nennius, the author of a ninth-century *History of the Britons*, which is one of the few sources for the history of the Dark Ages, scoured monastery libraries for old manuscripts. He wrote unapologetically as the first sentence of his collection, 'Coacervarvi omne quod inveni' (Myres 1986: 16) which loosely translates as 'I have made a heap of everything I have found.' I have studied my chosen subject in a similar manner. Much rummaging through the newspapers, academic and professional journals, and through my own experiences, was necessary in the search for interesting nuggets. Nennius at least had the excuse that, if he had not made his heap, our knowledge of British history in the Dark Ages would have been slighter than it is. Heap making is less excusable in the late twentieth century when we are in danger of suffocating under the mountains of information and data available to us. I justify the use of a heap-making method by claiming that heaps are intrinsically more fascinating than holes because they have a denser concentration of meaning and a wider range of content.

The writer of a heap book is a collector, an antiquarian. A collection is defined by the similarities between its elements. Often the content of the collection is based on little more than the idiosyncratic interests of the collector. If you visit Sir John Soane's Museum in London you will see crammed into a town house a heap of Canaletto and Hogarth pictures, cameos, medals, Etruscan vases, gargoyles, architectural capitals, a skeleton and an ancient Egyptian sarcophagus. The linking theme of the collection is simply that all the objects interested John Soane. Heap books, which also show a diversity of content, can be identified by their eclectic indexes. The subject index to Watson's (1994) book on management contains the following items under 'H': Hawthorne experiments; heaven; hedgehogs; Hill, Benny; human nature; humour and hymn sheets. The book you are now reading includes references, inter alia, to potholing, the Hegelian dialectic, the regulation of public utilities, Dante's *Inferno*, school dinners, critical illness insurance, the history of the British Raj in India, public sector policy making and the case of the heart patient who smoked.

Heaps can be fascinating but they are meaningless without a strong linking theme that brings together all the disparate parts. Unfortunately heap makers often get bored when they arrive at this part of collection building. John Aubrey was an antiquarian collector who, in pursuit of his obsession, made a vast heap of biographies of his contemporaries in the seventeenth century. But on his own admission the heap was disorganised and chaotic because he 'wanted the patience to go through [the] Knotty Studies' (Lawson Dick 1972: 18) necessary to put the heap into order. The classical teachers of rhetoric stressed the importance of putting materials and collections into order.

So in speaking however abundant the matter may be, it will merely form a confused heap unless arrangement is employed to reduce it to order and give it connexion and firmness of structure.

(Quintillian, 1986: 3)

If care is not taken however the order that is imposed on a heap may be based on similarity rather than on logical connection. Early renaissance thinkers, by way of illustration of the danger, believed that the bulbs of the orchis plant were a remedy for medical complaints of the testes because they looked like a pair of testicles (Eco 1992: 51). The hermetic idea of signatures and correspondences, which proposes that a similarity, of shape for example, between two things must mean that there is a deeper and functional relationship between them, is a very powerful one. It follows, from a hermetic style of argument, that if market principles are right for the economy at large (the macrocosm) then they must also be right for the public sector; and relations, say, between a doctor and patient (the microcosm) should be based on the same economic principles as the relationship between large multinational companies. But other approaches to the doctor:patient relationship emphasise differences rather than similarities. Commentators such as Smith and Morrissy (1994), who see the relationship between patients and doctors as a fiduciary one, in which economic considerations should play no part, objected when market devices such as indicative drugs budgets were introduced into general practice.

Heap makers often assume that, because all the items in their collection share at least one thing in common, there must be some greater significance to the similarities. The bigger the heap becomes the greater is the proof it provides of hermetic links. The assumption of correspondences can be detected in the large heap of organisations that have been privatised since the late 1980s (including British Steel, Amersham International, British Airways, the water companies, The Royal Ordnance factories, international airports and British Rail). They may have been similar in that they all had paying customers; but this disguises the many differences between them that needed to be taken into account when deciding whether and how they ought to have been privatised.

There are many other examples of argumentation by hermetic signature, or similarity, in the field of public sector management. The morphological resemblance between a school canteen and a greasy spoon café for example does not necessarily mean that they should be run on the same lines. It is possible to argue that the similarity between them is insignificant and misses the main issue, which is that school canteens are designed to meet school children's needs for nutritionally balanced meals whilst greasy spoon cafés are there to meet a demand for comforting stodge. I came across another example of this type of thinking when attending a seminar on quality in the provision of care for people with learning difficulties. The technique being discussed was PASS, programme analysis of service systems (Wolfensburger and Glynn 1975). The presenters were explaining a particular method, based on the use of photographs,

Exercise 2.2 *continued*

for alerting care staff to the quality implications of their habitual working methods. They showed a picture of a room and invited the audience to say what it was used for. All agreed that it was a nursery for under five's. It was of course a day room for adults with learning difficulties, but the decoration of the room reflected the staff's unconscious view that their clients behaved as, and should be treated as, kids. In particular there were several posters on the wall showing chimps being naughty, throwing toilet rolls down the toilet pan and suchlike. The staff had put the posters up to 'make the place more cheerful'. The trainers' photographs were used to jolt staff into an awareness of the inappropriateness of their assumptions and behaviours for the task of creating a good environment for the clients. In other words they were pointing out that an apparent metaphorical or morphological similarity between the behaviour of the clients on the one hand and children and chimpanzees on the other was not a sound basis for planning the clients' care.

Unless care is taken the throwing together of materials in a heap can lead to uneconomic and misleading connections and conclusions being drawn. The danger is increased because, in writing this book, I have wandered across many academic fields in which I am not an expert. This book has been put together as a heap and the reader is warned to look out for errors that may have arisen from drawing conclusions from items, which, coincidentally, happen to be found contiguously in the pile. But I hope that the reader will find in this heap enough interesting things to include in their own collection of heuristics, examples and insights concerning public services.

(Fisher, 1998: 23–25) Reproduced with the permission of Thomson Publishing Services.

Suggested answers

1 The key arguments of the piece can be summarised as follows:

Premise 1. Academic books are either of the hole or heap type.
Premise 2. Heap-type books are disorganised and confused collections of materials.
Inference. Heap-type books need to be organised into structured collections.

This leads to a further argument:

Premise 1. Heap-type books are collections of materials.
Premise 2. Collections are mostly structured and classified according to the similarities between the objects and materials in the collections.
Premise 3. Similarities can be mistakenly thought to imply logical links of cause and effect.
Inference. Heap-type books will draw false connections between things that lead to mistakes and misunderstandings.

That in turn leads to a final argument:

Premise 1. Heap-type books can be misleading and dangerous.
Premise 2. Heap-type books contain interesting and insightful materials.
Inference. Heap-type books may be worthwhile but have to be read with care and caution.

This is only one of several possible interpretations of the arguments in the piece.

2 The following is a précis of the piece. It contains 186 words.

Academic books are composed of a heap of materials gathered together either from many places or from a careful excavation of a hole into a seam of material. The author of a heap book, such as this one, collects materials that interest him or her from a wide range of sources. This method makes heap books more interesting than books based on holes.

Heaps can be fascinating but they are meaningless without a strong linking theme that brings together all their disparate parts. Heaps, or collections, are often structured according to the similarities between the objects contained in them. Similarities between things can be mistaken for causal links between things. For example, the similarity between public utilities, caused by them all having customers, does not necessarily mean that privatisation, which may work for some of them, would work for all of them.

Exercise 2.2 *continued*

Unless care is taken, the collecting and classifying of heaps of materials in a book can lead to uneconomic and misleading conclusions being drawn. The insights that may come from a heap book have to be considered carefully lest they lead to dangerous conclusions.

3 Identification of weak arguments used in the piece:

Flaw 2 – making a statement in which all is implied but some is true:
It is implied that because in some cases similarity (particularly similarity of shape) is misleading as an organising principle, then all kinds of similarity are misleading. This is not necessarily so. It is further implied that hermetic similarity is the common organising principle of all heaps. There is no evidence given that this is so and it is admitted by implication that there may be other principles on which heaps can be classified.

Flaw 3 – proof by selected instances:
A number of cases are piled up – privatisation, school dinners, services for adults with learning difficulties – to prove that connections of similarity are misleading and dangerous. There may be just as many examples that show argument by similarity to be sound and effective.

Flaw 5 – proof by inconsequent argument:
The orchis and testes example of argument by similarity is intended to raise a chuckle because it is nonsense. This can distract from the fact that this example may not be logically related to the consequent examples of privatisation and school dinners. Just because there is no similarity in the first case does not mean that there is not in the latter cases.

Flaw 8 – logically unsound argument:
It is argued that most heaps are organised according to the similarities of the material in the heap. It is further argued that this type of thinking can be dangerous and misleading. Nevertheless, it is argued in the final paragraph that heaps are acceptable because they are interesting. This seems a dangerous inference given the weight of the arguments for the view that heaps are dangerous.

Flaw 16 – the appeal to mere authority:
There is a heavyweight use of authorities here, including ancient Roman ones such as Quintillian. Tony Watson's book is also quoted as an example of a heap book, thereby suggesting that such an approach to writing a book is acceptable. Generally there is a lot of name-dropping in the piece.

Flaw 17 – argument by imperfect analogy:
The key analogy is seeing academic work as being like archaeology. It is implied that those archaeologists who minutely excavate and stratify a trench on a dig are more systematic than those who walk the fields picking up shards of pottery and other finds. The analogy is incorrect because field-walking archaeology is not treasure hunting, since it can be done in a rigorous and systematic manner. The analogy does not fit the case being made about the writing the two types of books.

Flaw 19 – the use of persuaders:
In the seventh paragraph of the piece, the phrase 'it was of course a day room for' is intended to draw the reader into an awareness of the unacceptability of the stereotyping that was being reported.
The piece also suffers from a problem, identified in Chapter 6 as a common one among historians (one of whom the author of this piece clearly once was), of meandering down obscure byways that interest the author but are uninteresting to most readers.

● ● ● ● Radical critique

There is a managerialist mainstream in business, management and organisational studies that accepts the necessity of the capitalist system and concentrates on making it work effectively. The system, the mainstream writers would argue, is to the benefit of all and it is only necessary to focus on making small improvements. There is an alternative view that challenges the system itself. This critical perspective appears in several of the chapters in this guide. It appears as standpoint research in Chapter 0, as critical theory in Chapter 1 and as critical realism in Chapter 5. Even if you do not accept the generalised critique of modern society that this approach makes, it can provide an interesting perspective on management issues that can raise difficult questions for mainstream researchers.

The critical approach

Alistair Mutch

What do we mean by the word 'critical'? In one sense we would expect all academic work to be critical; that is, we should always be questioning our assumptions and approaches. This kind of questioning has been discussed in the previous section. However, the word has tended to be appropriated by those who would use it in a broader sense. This sense is of challenging the basic assumptions on which our social world is organised. It is also, to a greater or lesser extent, used to indicate a need for radical change in these basic principles.

The approach originally associated with this sense of the word is Marxism. (Indeed, one current approach, the 'Frankfurt School', attempted to appropriate not only the word 'critical' but also the word 'theory'. If you see the two together as Critical Theory you will know what is being attempted – and you will see the difference that capitalisation can make!) In this respect, Marxism can be seen as continuing the Enlightenment project. This was the powerful intellectual tradition that emerged in the late eighteenth century. It stressed the importance of Reason and Science (they were fond of capital letters too) over religion and tradition as ways of knowing the world. To this faith in the power of ideas to reveal the truth about the world Marx added a radical political dimension. We have become much more sceptical about notions of truth, and more sophisticated currents in modern Marxism have dropped notions such as 'false consciousness' (the idea that the only reason for the lack of radical change was people holding the 'wrong' ideas – for a discussion see Callinicos (1987) and p. 109 of this book). However, Marxism has lost what was once a dominant position in the 'critical' camp, with other voices now being heard.

Exhibit 2.5

The Frankfurt School and Jürgen Habermas

The Frankfurt School was an institute for social research founded in Germany in 1923. Its members argued that the development of capitalist society in the twentieth century called for a revision of Marxist theory, a task they undertook, to some degree, by a return to the Hegelian dialectic. Hegel's (1770–1831) influence, which had become lost in the materialism of Leninist and Stalinist thought, was rediscovered in Marx's earlier writings. Leninist Marxism shared with positivism a belief that history could be explained through the automatic operation of powerful forces. The critical theorists wanted to reintroduce the role of human critical and reflexive understanding into revolutionary change. The most celebrated contemporary member of the Frankfurt School is Jürgen Habermas. He continued the School's critique of purposive or instrumental rationality, which leads to a concentration on technical means, to the neglect of ethical purposes, and proposed a theory of communicative rationality that aims to create consensus and collaborative institutions within society.

Habermas holds that disagreement can be resolved rationally through debate which is free of compulsion, in which no disputant applies pressure to another, and in which only the strength of the arguments matter. This calls for linguistic skill but it also requires a critical self-reflection in which those involved in a debate challenge their own arguments at:

- The objective level – at which a statement is tested against an observed state, checking, for example, whether the statement that 'the balance sheet does not add up' is true.
- The inter-subjective level – when a statement is made and heard it creates a social relationship between the hearer and the speaker. At the inter-subjective level it has to be questioned whether this relationship is legitimate. If the statement that the balance sheet doesn't add up implies, without evidence, that the listener is accused of cooking the books then the relationship may be unfair; especially if the speaker is the listener's boss.
- The intra-subjective level – at which a speaker has to consider whether their speech sincerely or authentically mirrors their internal thoughts and values.

It is these processes of validation that Habermas refers to as discourse. Habermas's theory of speech acts is helpful when forming radical critiques and an interesting introduction is provided by Pusey (1993).

One of the most important of these critical voices has been that of feminism. Reacting both to material social changes and to the failure of Marxism to address these changes, feminism has brought a new set of challenges, in this case to received gender roles. This has meant shifts in both the topics examined and the way in which they are examined. Again, there are many currents within feminism. Some strive for change within existing arrangements, arguing for the need to change organisations to release the talents of women (and make them better places for men). An example of a writer in this tradition who has had influence within the 'mainstream' is Rosabeth Moss Kanter. Others reject what they see as patriarchy and call for more fundamental change – Pollert (1996) has a useful overview. One impact of feminist writings has been to emphasise the importance of identity in current critical writing.

Identity is central in the intellectual tradition of postmodernism. This spurns what it calls 'grand narratives' such as Marxism (that is, in their terms, theories that purport to have 'all the answers'). Instead, it stresses the fragmentation of current life that is composed of a shifting kaleidoscope of fluid identities. An influential thinker has been the French social theorist Michel Foucault (see Exhibit 2.7 on p. 112). His emphasis on power as a property of networks and relationships has been a strong influence on thinking in many areas, not least the field of management. It has led to a focus on the micro-politics of local situations and to a divorce between critical analysis and prescriptions for change. This has led to charges (from more traditional critical theorists, such as Marxists) of academic self-indulgence and a loss of relevance. For others, however, this is a realistic adjustment to the contemporary social world and a cause for celebration. What it does seem to produce is complex and difficult language and a tendency to agonised introspection. (For an attempt to reconcile these forms of critical thinking by direct application to management, see Alvesson and Wilmott, 1996.) Other social theorists try to steer something of a middle way. Some of these, such as Giddens (lots of work, but see 1990 for a short introduction) and Castells (2000), have important things to say about the nature of the world of work, even if sometimes their detail fails to convince. Finally, the tradition known as Critical Realism (more appropriation! see p. 284) claims to be clearing the way for a more transparent use of concepts – Reed (1997) and Savage *et al.* (1992) provide some applications in the management field, although these are 'works in progress'.

What does all this mean for management researchers? It means that there is a rich body of resources upon which to draw. A little recognised aspect of management history is the way in which ideas that are now mainstream (in change management, for example) had their origins on the left (Cooke, 1999). Alternatively, the challenging of basic assumptions can help, even if it ends up by confirming your belief in the soundness of those assumptions. Some of these areas, notably feminism, have had more direct impact on the management field. It is helpful to be aware of the nuances that lie behind the use of this little word 'critical', as you will come across it all the time in the academic literature. This simply reinforces the need for you to be sceptical and challenging in your use of such literature – in a word, to be critical!

Developing a radical critique

To summarise the above discussion: a radical critique is one that challenges assumptions and conventional ways of doing things. It normally does so from a moral stance based on perceptions of injustice; so, for instance, a radical critique could be Marxist (justice to the workers) or feminist (justice to women) or green (justice to Gaia) or based on an anti-globalisation position that would incorporate all of the preceeding. This section looks at how a radical critique of a managerial theme might be constructed using a loose Marxist perspective. Remember, radical critiques are not a necessary part of a literature review.

A (rather caricatured) view of the stages of argumentation followed in the laying out of a radical critique is presented here. This is one of the occasions in this book (discussed on p. 25) where a complex mode of thought is presented as if it could be reduced to a recipe and a simple set of instructions. It cannot: but it is hoped that the following example helps you to develop an understanding of critical analysis. The case of computerisation of administrative and clerical work is used as an example to illustrate the process.

Stage 1 – identify a conventional position

Take a conventional and standard argument that is used in the literature and in public debate. Waddington (1977: 16) created the acronym COW-DUNG, which stands for 'the conventional wisdom of the dominant group' – OK, it does not quite work as an acronym but it defines the concept well. A few years ago, for example, it was widely held that the increasing use of computers in the fields of clerical and administrative work would make employees' lives more interesting by removing the drudgery from their work.

Stage 2 – problematise it

Problematising the issue means revealing that the issue is more difficult than commonly thought and probably raises questions of values or ethics. Computerisation may make work more interesting, but management does not want information technology for this reason alone. Management also wants to improve efficiency and profits and this means making staff redundant as computers do more and more of the work. This process causes that which was straightforward to appear morally ambiguous.

Stage 3 – identify contradictions and negations

Look for contradictions and negations within the process or issue being studied. A negation is a self-destructive feature of a process. Computers are meant to make life more interesting for staff by taking away the boring chores from their work. But computer software not only does sums and clerical chores – it can also make decisions by comparing particular situations against decision-making guidelines. Computers can remove decision making from people and so make their work less interesting and less responsible. Computerisation also disempowers staff by removing their discretion to amend procedures. Staff have to work in the ways required by the software. By enabling management to monitor their work rates, staff are put under an intense scrutiny that prevents them from being flexible in their work methods and rates (i.e. if staff are working on computers, then it is easy for management to see how many transactions they have processed in a shift). So, in summary, computerisation was meant to make employees' lives more interesting and ends up making them less so. This is a form of dialectical analysis that is discussed further on p. 303.

Stage 4 – spot the effects of false consciousness (this is an optional stage)

False consciousness may be out of fashion (see p. 105) but it is often a useful element in a radical critique. False consciousness arises when the opposite of what people want is happening but they do not realise it. It is a Marxist concept to describe the tendency of the proletariat to fail to recognise the nature of its interest. More generally it is any form of ideology or self-imagery that is held to be inappropriate to the real or objective situation of an actor. So, for example, imagine you have interviewed a number of clerical staff whose work has been computerised. To your surprise they tell you that they feel the process has made their work more interesting because they have learnt new skills. They have learnt how to use the new software, but they remain oblivious to the fact that the software is insidiously removing responsibility, self-control and higher-level skills from their jobs.

Stage 5 – end with an aporia

Aporia means being in a state where everything is so complex and ambiguous that you are at a loss about what to do. The critique is ended with a view that something is wrong but that it is difficult to see what can be done about it, short of changing human nature and sensibility. Things, you argue, are so complicated that anyone who believes there can be a quick fix for the issue must be deluded. Here is a typical example taken from a paper that gives a critique of the idea of business ethics:

> The problem I find it impossible to address in the rest of the paper will be what options are left for a project like 'Business Ethics' if all the above are accepted. It would simply be inappropriate for me to tie up a paper like this at the end as if I really did have a magical solution to these problems.

(Parker, 1998: 35)

However, there is often a final claim that our increasing understanding of the complexity of things will enable humanity to become better. Parker ends his paper in such a way:

> Recognising the paradoxes within 'Ethics' and 'Business Ethics' is one way to stop these words from having so much hold on us. Perhaps we can begin to develop ways of expressing our dreams and nightmares that do not fall back into the *agon* so easily.
>
> (Parker, 1998: 35)

It may not be easy to see quite what this means (the use of the word 'agon' makes it difficult – it means the endless arguments between different and incomparable ways of viewing a topic), but as an ending it sounds upbeat – in an ambiguous sort of a way.

Stage 6 – appropriate references and citations

Try to make references to Michel Foucault and/or Jürgen Habermas in the text. Surprisingly, references to Jeremy Bentham, the eighteenth-century utilitarian philosopher, and his notion of the panoptican, published in 1791 but more accessible in Božovič (1995), are also well received. The panopticon was a design for a circular prison. The cells were to be set around the circumference of the building and at the centre there was to be a watchtower. This design would allow a warder to observe all the prisoners with ease. An additional element in the design was a series of baffles and blinds. These meant that the warder could see the prisoners but the prisoners could not be sure whether they were being observed. The effect of the panopticon is that inmates would behave as if they were being observed even though they did not know whether they were. The risk that they could be under observation was sufficient, Bentham argued, to modify their behaviour.

The idea of the panopticon was adopted by Foucault as a metaphor for the way that organisations and institutions seek to control individuals. It works well as a trope for analysing information technology in offices. When an employee is working at a computer terminal that is networked to others in the organisation, it is technically possible for the management to monitor the employee's work. The employee knows that they may be being monitored, but they can never be sure whether they are. The metaphor works even better with roadside speed cameras, which reduce average speeds because drivers do not know whether the box really does contain a camera. So they proceed on the basis that it might. A panopticon therefore provides a very efficient method of social control.

The following citation of Foucault, citing Bentham, achieves a double whammy effect: 'The contemporary popularity of Foucault's version of the panopticon seems to illustrate something rather profound' (Parker 1998: 31). The panopticon is discussed in Foucault (1991).

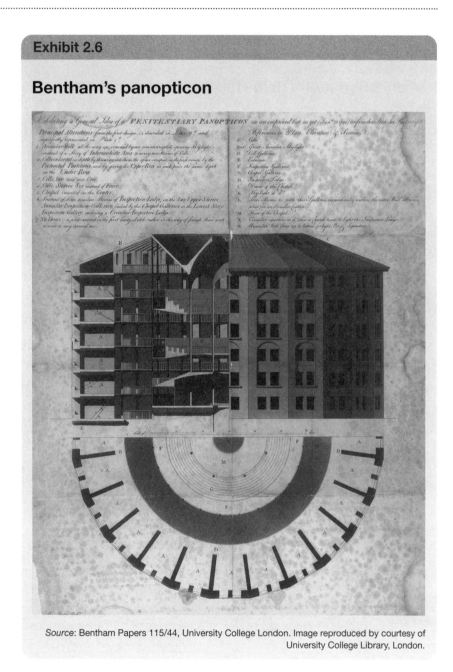

> **Exhibit 2.6**
>
> # Bentham's panopticon
>
> *Source*: Bentham Papers 115/44, University College London. Image reproduced by courtesy of University College Library, London.

The six stages of radical critique are simply a teaching aid. No one would follow such a mechanistic process in their writing. Nevertheless, these different aspects can be found in academic papers such as Parker (1998). If you have the time and inclination, you might want to locate the six stages in his article.

Exhibit 2.7

Michel Foucault (1926–1984) and genealogies

Michel Foucault (1926-1984) was a French philosopher. His work is here labelled as critical theory; but his work cannot be easily categorised. His work developed over time and in this exhibit I will deal with that aspect of his work known as his genealogical phase, which is associated with his (1991) book *Discipline and Punish*. In this book he explored how people acquire power through the development and use of discourse within human institutions such as prisons. Genealogies are accounts of the intertwining of power and knowledge, which means that what we call knowledge cannot be seen as based on absolute truths. Genealogies spread across different forms of knowledge, which are all brought to conform to, and to reinforce, certain power relations through the general acceptance of key themes. Except that this process of conformance is never quite complete and there is always room for disputes over knowledge. Foucault's essay *Nietzsche, Genealogy, History*, originally published in 1971 (an English translation is available in Rabinow (1984; 76–100)), is used here to identify the key themes of genealogy. The use of these themes in an example of management research is then discussed.

Rejection of rational and linear progression in knowledge and morals

Foucault's notion of genealogy descends from Friederich Nietzsche's (1844–1900) *On the Genealogy of Morals*. Both Foucault and Nietzsche wanted to defeat the idea that the development of morality was a linear and progressive story. They also rejected the idea of an *Ursprung* – an original basis for morals, which presupposes an original essence of a thing that pre-existed the search for it. A belief in an origin also creates a false discipline dedicated to discovering it. The idea of an origin is a chimera.

> A genealogy of values [ ] and knowledge will never confuse itself with a search for 'origins'.
>
> > (Foucault, 1984: 80)

Rather a genealogy explains how the idea of an origin is constructed and changed over time as a way of legitimising a particular set of power relationships.

Descent

A second term, taken from Nietzsche, which Foucault discusses, is *Herkunft*. This means descent and in nineteenth-century Germany it often referred to the descent of a racial group. Foucault disassociated it from race and saw it as the history of the complexity of a descent, a descent that had many origins and shows the self not to be a coherent whole but a network of fragmented pieces:

> genealogy does not pretend to go back in time to restore an unbroken continuity that operates beyond the dispersion of forgotten things; its duty is not to demonstrate that the past actively exists in the present, that it continues secretly to animate the present.
>
> > (Foucault, 1984: 81)

Genealogy represents the fragmented and contradictory meanderings of our attempts, often mistaken, to make sense of things: 'Truth or being does not lie at the root of what we know or what we are, but the exteriority of accidents.'

'Descent attaches itself to the body'

The idea of the human body being the site of knowledge is very common in Foucault's work. He sees a link between the body, power and knowledge: 'Genealogy, as an analysis of descent, is thus situated within the

Exhibit 2.7 *continued*

articulation of the body and history.' What does this mean? Could it be something as simple as what you eat, the quality of one's diet, is determined by the networks of power and knowledge? Foucault certainly mentions food and digestion as important aspects of inscription. Of course, Foucault is greatly famed for more direct inscriptions of genealogy on to bodies, such as the ways that people were incarcerated in prisons and asylums and in his discussion of the panopticon (see p. 110).

Emergence

The idea of emergence is necessary to make this articulation, of knowledge and power on the body, work. What emerges is conflict and power. So, for example, the idea of asceticism emerges during a period of decadence. It is the antithesis of luxury and it takes the form of domination, of some men over others. The rules are imposed on bodies. Ascetic rules, for example, impose a monastic severity on monks' bodies. Those who have dominance create rules that reinforce that domination: 'humanity installs each of its violences in a system of rules, and thus proceeds from domination to domination' (Foucault, 1984: 84).

Knowledge and power

A genealogy is an explanation of how knowledge is created and changes in ways that maintain the dominance of some groups over others. As conflicts challenge established order then knowledge adapts and changes to maintain the dominance. This knowledge is presented as if it has some ancient and powerful origin that legtimises it whereas knowledge actually develops haphazardly but with a purpose:

> But if interpretation is the violent or surreptitious appropriation of a system of rules, which in itself has no essential meaning, in order to impose a direction, to bend it to a new will, to force its participation in a different game, and to subject it to secondary rules, then the development of humanity is a series of interpretations. The role of genealogy is to record its history: the history of morals, ideals, and metaphysical concepts, the history of the idea of liberty, or of the ascetic life, as they stand for the emergence of different interpretations.
>
> (Foucault, 1984: 86)

The genealogist uses history in three ways:

1 The parodic and the carnivalesque. Mocking traditional historical attempts to show human development as a rational working out of a preordained original essence or truth.
2 The disassociative. 'The purpose of history, guided by genealogy, is not to discover the roots of our identity but to commit itself to its dissipation' (Foucault, 1984: 95). Genealogy reveals the invented nature of what we take to be knowledge.
3 The sacrifice of knowledge, 'recognising that all knowledge rests upon injustice (that there is no right, not even in the act of knowing, to truth or a foundation for truth) and that the instinct for knowledge is malicious (something murderous, opposed to the happiness of mankind)' (Foucault, 1984). In short, history cannot be an objective recounting of how things were.

History traditionally has sought to show how humanity has developed its own proper moral essence in a linear and straightforward trajectory from a single source or origin. Genealogy, contrarily, sees that development of humanity as being fragmented and full of twists and turns. Knowledge is not an objective thing, as traditional history suggests, but rather it is a series of systems of rules by which domination of one group over another is expressed. This domination, this knowledge, is physically written on people's bodies. As power shifts knowledge is reinterpreted but always in a way that sees power and knowledge joined in a network that challenges the happiness of mankind. The task of the genealogist is to tell the story of these shifting networks of power and knowledge.

Exhibit 2.7 *continued*

An example of a genealogy in managerial literature

Calás and Smircich (1991) wrote a genealogy of theories of organisational leadership in which they explored how these ideas were associated with ideas of seduction and control. They argued that the role of academic writers on organisations has been to create knowledge for other members of society. They analysed four classic management texts: Barnard (1938) *The Functions of the Executive*, McGreggor (1960) *The Human Side of Enterprise*, Mintzberg (1973) *The Nature of Managerial Work* and Peters and Waterman (1982) *In Search of Excellence*. Their argument proposes that each of these authors appears to take a different view of leadership so that it seems that ideas about leadership develop in a linear and progressive fashion. However, the genealogy disassociates the development of these theories from any notion of rational development, and shows that this sense of progress is illusory. Rather, the theories are a series of attempts to bolster the same power relationships that have existed during the last hundred years, and which are themselves disassociated from any development of such original ideals as justice.

All of these writers, according to Calás and Smircich, keep in place a set of practices and ways of thinking that maintain a certain set of power relationships between leaders and the led. The continuities link to the idea of sexual seduction, which of course is a power relationship in which the powerful gain control over the less powerful in ways in which the weaker appear to agree to their domination. Seduction is a power that is written on the bodies of the oppressed. It therefore disassociates the identities of the seduced who believe themselves free but are not. Calás and Smircich (1991) analyse the four texts to show how the language of academic writing on leadership has resonances in the language of seduction. They notice many *double entendres* in the books on leadership. Mintzberg identifies liaison as one of the managerial roles but liaison is also defined in the dictionary as an illicit sexual union (Calás and Smircich, 1991: 586). These perhaps are the parodic and carnivalesque aspects of the genealogy. The genealogy of leadership means that leadership can only be discussed in terms of male domination and it leaves no space for the topic to be explored from a feminist perspective. The purpose of writing the genealogy is to seek its dissolution and to challenge the injustice of leadership.

Radical critique has a jargon and a style of expression of its own. This can be difficult for the novice to penetrate, and it would take much practice to acquire it. Nevertheless, a lack of linguistic pretension should not prevent you from trying this type of analysis, especially as it often carries a ring of truth. You may test this out for yourself by doing Exercise 2.3.

If you find it too difficult to write a radical critique there is a website at http://www.csse.monash.edu.au/other/postmodern.html that produces randomly generated critical essays. Luckily it produces a new essay every time you click on the site, and the reader has no control over the topic of the essay, otherwise you might be tempted to use this facility.

Some people critique critical theory. The most recent cause célèbre was an article written by Alan Sokal (Sokal and Bricmont, 1999). In the paper he parodied the writing style of critical thinkers and deliberately introduced scientific misconceptions and mathematical blunders. This did not prevent the paper from being accepted and published in a well-respected academic journal. If you wish to know more about the debate that the publication of the article started, visit http://www.physics.nyu.edu/faculty/sokal/.

Make a radical critique

1 Choose a fashionable concept or package within your field of management, e.g.
   - relationship marketing
   - enterprise resource planning (ERP)
   - Investors in People (IiP)
   - quality assurance.
2 Construct an outline radical critique of it.

Suggested answer
I will use Investors in People as an example. I am not necessarily arguing that the following radical critique is true, but it might be.

1 The conventional view of IiP is that it is a worthwhile attempt to encourage organisations to invest more in the training and development of their staff and to set up performance management systems that focus those skills, and staff's inventiveness and commitment, towards the achievement of organisational goals. IiP is a set of standards that may be used to assess whether an organisation has achieved these objectives. So important is this purpose that the government set targets for the percentage of organisations that should be accredited against the standard.
2 But this all assumes that employees and the organisation share the same goals. If they do not, then IiP might just be a means of silencing dissenting views in the organisation and, through such devices as appraisal interviews, bring their activities under closer managerial scrutiny. Whether IiP is actually beneficial for employees becomes an issue.
3 There are a number of ways in which the implementation of IiP might contradict its formal aims:
   (a) Organisations were originally assessed for IiP against a list of items in a checklist. This led to a mindset in which gaining IiP became a bureaucratic hurdle in which getting ticks in boxes was more important than delivering better training and development and engaging employees in developing the organisation. To be fair to the IiP programme, an attempt was made to make the assessment process less bureaucratic.
   (b) Government pushed quite hard for organisations, especially public sector organisations, to adopt the standard. There was a possibility that organisations sought it because they felt obliged to fly the IiP flag and put the logo on their letterhead and not because they were committed to investing in their people.
   (c) All the effort put into gaining IiP accreditation may divert an organisation's attention from providing the training and development that investment in people demands. While HRD staff are focused on IiP preparations, they cannot be doing training.
4 However, if you talk to people in organisations they mostly say that IiP is a good thing. This may be because they do not see the threat to their best interests or, in the case of many managers, it may be that they do not think highly of IiP but feel that they must toe the party line that it is a good thing.
5 We might conclude that IiP exhibits the classic dysfunctions of bureaucracy whereby the means – the checklists and the logos – become more important than the ends – developing people and organisations. This syndrome might be thought unavoidable and therefore it is hard to know what to do to prevent the problem.
6 We could certainly use the panopticon as a metaphor for IiP and thereby find an excuse for quoting Bentham and Foucault.

Summary

Do

- identify and discuss key and landmark studies – include as much up-to-date material as possible;
- get the details right;
- try to be reflexive – examine your own bias and make it known;
- critically evaluate the material and show your analyses;
- use extracts, illustrations and examples to justify your arguments;
- be analytical, critical and evaluative in your review;
- make it interesting.

Don't

- omit classic works or discuss core ideas without reference;
- discuss outdated or rubbish stuff, or only old material;
- use concepts to impress or without definition;
- produce a list of items, even if annotated: a list is not a review;
- accept anything at face value or believe everything that is written;
- only produce a description of the content of what you have read;
- drown in information. (Based on Hart, 1998: 219.)

Suggested reading

The best book on the topics covered in this chapter is Hart (1998). Fairbairn and Winch (1996) is also useful on the subject of literature and critical evaluation. Warburton (1996) is good on logical traps.

References

Alvesson, M. and Willmott, H. (1996) *Making Sense of Management: A Critical Introduction*, London: Sage.

Barnard, C. (1938) *The Functions of the Executive*, Cambridge, Mass.: Harvard University Press.

Božovič, M. (ed.) (1995) *The Panoptican Writings: Jeremy Bentham*, London: Verso.

Calás and Smircich (1991) 'Voicing Seduction to Silence Leadership', *Organization Studies*, vol. 4, no. 4: 567–602.

Callinicos, A. (1987) *Making History*, Cambridge: Polity.

Castells, M. (2000) *The Rise of Network Society*, Oxford: Blackwell.

Cooke, B. (1999) 'Writing the left out of management theory: the historiography of the management of change', *Organization*, vol. 6, no. 1: 81–105.

Eco, U. (1989) *Foucault's Pendulum*, trans. W. Weaver, London: Secker & Warburg.

Eco, U. with Rorty, R., Culler, J., Brooke-Rose, C. and Collini, S. (eds) (1992) *Interpretation and Overinterpretation*, Cambridge: Cambridge University Press.

Fairbairn, G.J. and Winch, C. (1996) *Reading, Writing and Reasoning: A Guide for Students*, 2nd edn, Buckingham: Open University Press.

Fisher, C.M. (1998) *Resource Allocation in the Public Sector: Values, Priorities and Markets in the Management of Public Services*, London: Routledge.

Foucault, M. (1991) *Discipline and Punish: The Birth of the Prison*, trans. A. Sheridan, London: Penguin.

Giddens, A. (1990) *The Consequences of Modernity*, Cambridge: Polity.

Hargreaves, J. (2002) Letter to the editor, *Times Literary Supplement*, 1 January.

Hart, C. (1998) *Doing a Literature Review: Releasing the Social Science Research Imagination*, London: Sage.

Hughes, W. (1992) *Critical Thinking*, Peterborough, Ontario: Broadview Press.

Lages, M., Gigerenzer, G. and Hoffrage, U. (1999) *Intransitivity of Fast and Frugal Heuristics*, Working Paper in Economics. Available online at: http://netec.mcc.ac.uk/BibEc (accessed 6 July 2001).

Lawson Dick, O. (ed.) (1972) *Aubrey's Brief Lives*, Harmondsworth: Penguin.

McGreggor, D. (1960) *The Human Side of Enterprise*, New York: McGraw-Hill.

Mintzberg, H. (1973) *The Nature of Managerial Work*, Englewood Cliffs: Prentice Hall.

Myres, J.N.L. (1986) *The English Settlements*, Oxford: Oxford University Press.

Parker, M. (1998) 'Business ethics and social theory: postmodernizing the ethical', *British Journal of Management*, vol. 9, September: 27–36.

Peters, T.J. and Waterman R.H. (1982) *In Search of Excellence*, New York: Harper & Row.

Pollert, A. (1996) 'Gender and class revisited; or, the poverty of 'patriarchy''', *Sociology*, vol. 30, no. 4: 639–659.

Pusey, M. (1993) *Jürgen Habermas*, London: Routledge.

Quintillian (1986) *The Institutes of Oratory*, vol. 3, trans. H.E. Butler, Cambridge, Mass., and London: Harvard University Press and William Heinemann.

Rabinow, P. (ed.) (1984) *The Foucault Reader. An Introduction to Foucault's Thought*, London: Penguin.

Reed, M. (1997) 'In praise of duality and dualism: rethinking agency and structure in organizational analysis', *Organization Studies*, vol. 18, no. 1, 21–42.

Robinson, F. (2006) 'Not safely enough. A review of *Westward Bound. Travels of Mirza Abu Taleb*', *Times Literary Supplement*, no. 5379, 5 May 2006: 29.

Savage, M., Barlow, J., Dickens, P. and Fielding, T. (1992) *Property, Bureaucracy and Culture: Middle-class Formation in Contemporary Britain*, London: Routledge.

Sennett, R. (2001) Letter to the editor, *Times Literary Supplement*, 28 December.

Smith, L.F.P. and Morrissy, J.R. (1994) 'Ethical dilemmas for general practitioners under the UK new contract', *Journal of Medical Ethics*, vol. 20, no. 3: 175–180.

Sokal, A. and Bricmont, J. (1999) *Fashionable Nonsense: Postmodern Intellectuals' Abuse of Science*, New York: Picador.

Tallis, R. (2001) 'The truth about lying: a review of *The Liar's Tale: A History of Falsehood* by J. Campbell', *Times Literary Supplement*, 21 December.

Thouless, R.H. (1968) *Straight and Crooked Thinking*, London: The English Universities' Press Ltd.

Waddington, C.H. (1977) *Tools for Thought*, St Albans: Paladin.

Warburton, N. (1996) *Thinking from A to Z*, London: Routledge.

Watson, T.J. (1994) *In Search of Management: Culture, Chaos and Control in Managerial Work*, London: Routledge.

Wikipedia (2006) 'Windsor, Ontario', *Wikipedia*. Available on the World Wide Web at http://en.wikipedia.org/wiki/Windsor,_Ontario (accessed 15 May 2006).

Wolfensburger, W. and Glynn, L. (1975) *Program Analysis of Service Systems*, Toronto: NIMR.

Wright, G. (1984) *Behavioural Decision Theory: An Introduction*, Harmondsworth: Penguin.

Wright Mills, C. (1959) *The Sociological Imagination*, Oxford: Oxford University Press.

Chapter 3 ● ● ● ●

Concepts, conceptual frameworks and theories

Contents

● ● ● ● Introduction

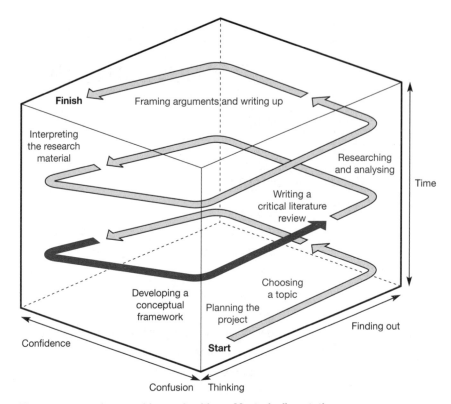

Finish

Framing arguments and writing up

Interpreting
the research
material

Researching
and analysing

Time

Writing a
critical literature
review

Developing a
conceptual
framework

Choosing
a topic

Planning the
project

Finding out

Confidence

Start

Confusion   Thinking

The processes of researching and writing a Master's dissertation

*'Here is a lovely face, a Madonna face. What eyes! … I wish I could make out the
story. There is certainly a story. What can this all be?'*
'The fewer theories you form the fewer blunders and dreams you will make.'
'But we must form theories – we cannot remain awake and not do so.'

Captain Gresley and Mr Ralph on discovering the ancient frescoes in the
Buddhist cave temples at Ajanta, India, in 1836 (Keay, 2000: 149)

The purpose of this chapter is to explain what theorising means and to
give you some help in defining concepts and formulating a conceptual
framework for your dissertation. Theorising is not an added extra in the
process of doing research. It will be argued that theorising gives shape and
structure to your research. The first stage in theorising is clarifying the
terms, or concepts, that you will use to describe the subject of research.
The second stage is providing a description of the relationships (i.e. a conceptual framework) between the concepts being used. The third stage is
using the conceptual framework to develop theories that explain the patterns and connections that you have found in your research material.

Exhibit 3.1

Ajanta cave painting

Source: Photo by Raj Shirole

The conceptual development phase of doing a dissertation is largely a thinking stage but it does prepare you for undertaking the finding out, the research phase, of the project. Initially it represents a movement from confusion to certainty. When you draft a conceptual framework that seems to work, it gives you a sense of control over the project. You know what you are trying to do. It may take several attempts to arrive at the conceptual framework, and so you may go round the cycle from confusion to confi-

Exhibit 3.2

The Ajanta caves

Source: Photo by Raj Shirole

dence and back again several times. However, the first burst of confidence wears off and uncertainty sets in until you can start the next phase and can test the framework out against the findings from your research.

Try not to dodge dealing with theoretical issues by claiming that the topic of your research is intensely practical and that it needs no top dressing of theoretical concerns. Always remember John Maynard Keynes' aphorism:

> Practical men, who believe themselves to be quite exempt from any intellectual influences, are usually the slaves of some defunct economist.

(Gross, 1987: 116)

This chapter is divided into three parts:

1. Why developing conceptual frameworks is important.
2. Techniques for developing conceptual frameworks.
3. Some examples of conceptual frameworks.

Learning outcomes for the chapter

1 Readers will understand the importance of concept definitions, conceptual frameworks and theorising in a Master's dissertation.
2 Readers will be able to define their concepts and relate them to the appropriate literature.
3 Readers will have sufficient examples of conceptual frameworks to be able to think imaginatively when developing their own frameworks.
4 Readers will be able to use their conceptual frameworks to guide the primary research phase of their projects and to structure the analysis presented in the dissertation.

● ● ● ● The roles of theory and conceptual frameworks

Defining your concepts and creating a conceptual framework are means of simplifying the research task. These two processes help you clear away all the issues and materials that are not germane to your topic and research question and they also provide a 'map' of your field of study. It helps you to find your way around your research material and it provides structure and coherence to your dissertation. Conceptual frameworks are also discussed in Chapter 5 where their role as interpretive grids is discussed. In that chapter it is stressed that conceptual frameworks are chosen by the researcher. Consequently, it must be understood that there are always alternative frameworks that could be used to guide and analyse a research project and that the chosen framework might be wrong. Students must always be alert to the possibility that they may have to modify, adapt or even replace their conceptual frameworks as their project proceeds.

One of the big practical questions is when in the research process you should define concepts and draft a conceptual framework. There are two main possibilities: at the beginning or at least early on in the process (let us call this the structured approach) or towards the end of the research process (using what is commonly called a grounded approach). In a structured approach you impose a structure on your research based on a preliminary theory, concept or hypothesis; you use the structure to guide your research and in particular your material collection process. In a grounded approach you collect all your material without prejudice, with no preliminary conceptual thoughts about what you may discover. When you have made a big pile of material you study it to see what concepts and frameworks emerge from the heap.

The term 'grounded theory' was coined by Glaser and Strauss (1967). It is a process that allows theory to emerge out of the research material rather than being forced out of it by the use of a predetermined idea or theory. Grounded theory implies that theory is implicit in the material and can be drawn out by an iterative process of coding and comparison (see pp. 257–8).

Exhibit 3.3

How important is the 'emergence of theory' in grounded theory?

In the years following the publication of their seminal work, Glaser and Strauss (1967) appear to have taken different lines on what grounded research is. Strauss, with a new collaborator – Corbin (Strauss and Corbin, 1990) – standardised and specified detailed stages, steps and procedures that should be followed by anyone claiming to do grounded research. Glaser published a critique of Strauss and Corbin in 1992. The argument between the two sides was over the degree to which the two approaches could be said to allow theory to emerge from data – which is the central justification of grounded theory.

Glaser argued that Strauss and Corbin were neglecting the central tenet and were placing too much importance on prior structures in their procedures for conducting grounded research.

- According to Glaser, the detailed rules and procedures specified by Strauss and Corbin for analysing data, apart from being cumbersome and difficult to recall, represented a prior structure that would force, or even torture, a theory from the material. Glaser, while also recommending stages in the analysis process, preferred a looser style of interpretation that allowed the material to speak for itself.
- Strauss and Corbin allow the research problem to be specified at the start of a project. The problem may be taken from the literature, from personal experience or even from the advice of tutors. Glaser countered that this would pre-empt the emergence of theory and that the research topic, as well as the corresponding theory, should be allowed to emerge from the data.

The arguments between Glaser and Strauss reinforce the importance of the decision about the point in time during a research project at which theory should play a role. It also suggests that there are intermediate positions between that which argues that research should always start from a theoretical proposition and Glaser's view that everything should be done to prevent any prior theorising from distorting the emergence of theory from the research material.

The tale told in Exhibit 3.4 should help to clarify the issues surrounding the problem of when to create a conceptual framework.

Exhibit 3.4

The historian's tale

I was not always a management studies person. History was my first field of study, and in particular Indian history. Many years ago I did my doctoral research on indigo plantations and peasant revolts in Bihar in the nineteenth and twentieth centuries. The research involved delving in the archives of the Secretariat of the Government of Bihar. As chance would have it there were two US history research students working in the archives at the same time. Perhaps because of the different research traditions in the United Kingdom and the United States, we followed different search strategies as we worked through the ancient and dusty cloth bundles of records tied with red tape. The Americans followed a grounded approach. They took notes of anything in the archive that had the least connection with the general field of their research. I, on the other hand, went for a structured approach. I had certain terms, or concepts, that were key to my research, such as plantation, indigo, revolting peasants and so on. I would skim the records and I became adept at spotting my key words if they were in the documents. When I came across a key term I would stop and take notes. At the end of a day in the archives I would have several pages of notes, having gone through many bundles of records, and the Americans would have reams of notes from only a few bundles.

I finished my PhD within four years and it was OK – it passed. The US students took on average eight years to complete their PhDs, but their theses were magnificent.

There is a moral to this tale. When doing research there is sometimes a trade-off between time and quality. I developed a conceptual framework for my research at a much earlier stage than did the Americans. As a consequence, my search of the archives was much more focused. My structured approach saved me time but diminished the quality of the final product. The Americans' grounded approach took them more time but the outcome was better. This was no doubt because they missed nothing in their search through the material. My focused search, however, probably caused me to miss material that could have generated new insights or theories. There is another price that is paid for taking a grounded approach. It is the frustration of not knowing until near the end of the project whether anything worthwhile will emerge from all your research work. The person who follows a structured approach has the security of knowing what the likely structure and shape of the dissertation will be before they start collecting their research material. The downside of the structured approach is, of course, that having developed an initial framework, people are reluctant to change it even when the research findings absolutely require it to be changed.

Exercise 3.1

To structure or to ground?

Consider whether a structured or a grounded approach would be appropriate to the position of someone doing a dissertation on a part-time Master's course.

Suggested answer

In general terms you are free to choose either a grounded or a structured approach to your research. You will certainly not be at a disadvantage if you choose a grounded approach if it is appropriate to your research question and if you have justified its use by reference to the literature on grounded theory. However, on practical grounds alone, it might be sensible to adopt a structured approach. MBA and Master's dissertations are normally done within a tight time schedule of between six months and a year, and there are many other pressures on the student's time during that period (other assignments and projects that have to be done for the course, job demands and family demands). A structured approach increases the student's sense of security that the project can be completed on time and some useful findings obtained.

Developing conceptual frameworks

This section will give you some helpful hints on defining concepts, drafting conceptual frameworks and theorising. These three activities can be seen as steps to be taken one after the other. To begin with, each of these steps will be defined and the sequence explained. Examples will be given to show how this might all work out in practice. Developing conceptual frameworks is not a matter of thinking up completely new things. Rather, it is done by building upon the knowledge you have acquired from doing a literature review. It could be argued that the purpose of the literature review is to provide the raw material from which the conceptual framework is built. You might come across a framework in the literature that you think is appropriate to your research without amendment. It is more likely that you need to modify or adapt frameworks from the literature to make them useful in relation to the contexts of your research and the research questions you are seeking to answer.

Defining concepts

Figure 3.1 provides a definition of concepts.

It is important to decide what are the main terms or concepts you will be using in your research and to define them clearly. You are not required to come up with definitions that are absolutely true and will hold for all time. You choose a definition that will help you to understand and explain the subject matter of your research. The definitions will largely come from

Concepts:

- are the building blocks of models and theories;
- are the *working definitions* that are used in particular analyses for which they have been devised or chosen;
- are chosen to be useful, not correct;
- are more than a 'dictionary definition'.

Figure 3.1 Concepts
Source: reproduced with the permission of T.J. Watson.

your literature review (see Chapter 2). Definitions taken from the dictionary will be too banal and general for research and theorising. *Collins Pocket English Dictionary* gives eight different definitions of 'culture', and so you still have the problem of choosing the appropriate meaning. Unfortunately you will find that the more you read, the more definitions you will come across. Let us pretend that one of your concepts was personality and that you had found thirteen and a half different definitions of it. If you try to use all the definitions in your dissertation, neither you nor the reader will ever be quite sure what you mean when you use the term. What you have to do is to explain to the reader the range of definitions that are available in the literature (giving the appropriate citations) and then choose one that seems to you the best suited for your research project. Explain to the reader that henceforward in the dissertation the term 'blah blah blah' will mean your preferred definition. Give your reasons for choosing this definition above the others.

Conceptual frameworks

Figure 3.2 provides a definition of frameworks.

In a conceptual framework, you put the concepts together as in a jigsaw puzzle. You work out how all the concepts fit together and relate to one another. The first stage of theorising identifies and clarifies concepts; the second stage concentrates on the connections and relationships between the concepts. A conceptual framework is formed of patterns of concepts and their interconnections. These relationships can be of many types.

Frameworks:

- are analytical schemes;
- simplify reality to make it easier to discuss, analyse or research;
- simplify reality by selecting certain phenomena/variables and suggesting certain relationships between them;
- are judged in terms or utility, not correctness.

Figure 3.2 Frameworks
Source: reproduced with the permission of T.J. Watson.

Cause and effect

One of the most common relationships described in a conceptual framework is cause and effect. Such frameworks are often shown as 'boxes and arrows' diagrams, such as the one in Figure 3.3. In these diagrams the item at the start of an arrow causes or influences the item at the arrow's head.

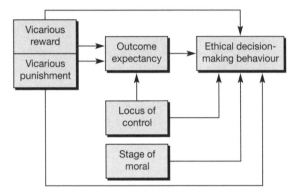

Figure 3.3 A conceptual framework for ethical decision making
Source: Trevino and Youngblood (1990). Reprinted with the permission of L.K. Trevino.

The conceptual framework shown in Figure 3.3 identifies the various factors that influence ethical decision making in management. It identifies a number of causal factors that influence whether people will act morally. If the jargon is translated, the model is suggesting that:

- seeing other people being rewarded for acting well (vicarious reward)
- and punished for acting badly (vicarious punishment);
- whether people believe they control their own destinies or are at the mercy of forces beyond their control (locus of control)
- and their level of moral development

increases the likelihood that people will make decisions that are ethical rather than pragmatic. Some of the causal factors work indirectly through intermediary factors. Vicarious reward and punishment, for example, influence people's level of outcome expectancy. This is a concept derived from motivation theory that concerns the extent to which people believe their actions will have consequences. If people believe that, at work, bad actions will not result in bad consequences, then they will not be motivated to behave well.

A conceptual framework does not have to be as complicated as the one shown in Figure 3.3. It might just be a cause and effect relationship between two factors that can be shown as a simple graph. Conceptual frameworks based on cause and effect relationships are often the basis of hypothetico-deductive research (see p. 45) because they are the source of the hypotheses that such research seeks to test. The arrows in Figure 3.3 can be converted into a series of hypotheses (for instance, that the higher a person's level of moral development, the more likely they are to take ethical decisions) that can be tested.

Stages in a process

In some conceptual frameworks the concepts are related because they are stages in a process. These relationships are also often illustrated by 'boxes and arrows' diagrams. However, in these cases the relationships are not based on cause and effect but on logic and proper order. The management control loop is an example. It starts, in its simplest form, with planning and then proceeds through the stages of doing, monitoring and revising the plan. This sequence is a logical one because to do the stages in any other order would be a nonsense.

Kolb's theory of the learning cycle (Kolb *et al.*, 1995) is an example of a staged process type of conceptual framework. He identified four styles of learning:

● active experimentation
● reflective observation
● abstract conceptualisation
● concrete experience.

These four learning styles were linked in a cyclical process (and so the theory can be shown diagrammatically as a circle, as in Figure 3.4). Effective learning requires going through a complete cycle.

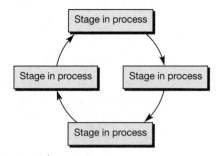

Figure 3.4 A cyclical process framework

Hierarchical relationships

In many conceptual frameworks, concepts are related because they occupy higher or lower positions on a scale or in a hierarchy. Maslow's (1954) much quoted hierarchy of needs is a good example. The sequence of human needs, going from the lowest to the highest, was as follows:

- physiological needs
- safety needs
- belongingness needs
- esteem needs
- self-actualisation.

If you like presenting your conceptual frameworks in diagrammatic form, then hierarchical relationships can easily be shown as a triangle, with the higher needs at the apex and the lower needs at the base of the triangle, as in Figure 3.5.

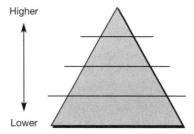

Figure 3.5 A hierarchical framework

Maps and coordinates

Places on maps are found by using coordinates. By reading off the coordinates on the vertical and horizontal scales of the map, you can locate the place you want to find and see how it lies in relation to other places. In a similar fashion you can define the relationships between concepts by plotting them against a series of coordinates. Most commonly, conceptual frameworks use only two scales, as do most maps. In a two-by-two matrix, or table, each scale or axis is divided into two, as in Figure 3.6. These are a very common form of conceptual framework.

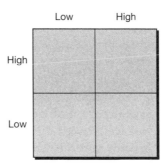

Figure 3.6 A two-by-two matrix

Of the many hundreds of these, the most famous is probably the Boston Consulting Group strategic matrix (Stern and Stalk, 1998). The matrix is used to assess the levels of investment needed by different strategic business units. It uses two axes:

- rate of market growth
- relative market share.

These axes are each divided into high and low. Business units that have both high market share and a high growth rate are the **Stars** and should be supported. Those with low growth rates but high market shares are **Cash Cows** and can be relied upon to generate income without much investment. If a business unit has a small share of a slow-growing market, it is classified as a **Dog** and it would be better if the company withdrew from this business. Business units that have a small share of a fast-growing market are difficult because they represent a gamble, and investing in them may pay off but there is no guarantee.

Of course there can be more than two coordinates. Reddin's (1970) model of managerial effectiveness uses three and so can be drawn as a cube. The figure used at the start of each chapter in this guide is also a conceptual framework that uses three coordinates:

- time
- degree of certainty or confusion
- thinking and finding out.

Even multi-dimensional matrices could be used. However, these are easier to express in databases than they are to draw on sheets of paper.

Pairs of opposites

Concepts may be related by being pairs of opposites. The idea of duality is a very powerful one in academic work. It is the notion that the world can be divided into competing forces that are in continuous tension because neither force is strong enough to abolish the other and because each force is incomplete without its opposite. This sounds very abstract but there are many practical examples of such pairs in studies of management and organisations. Leadership studies are often structured on polar opposites such as transactional and transformational leadership and relationship-oriented and task-oriented leadership behaviour. Leaders have to find a balance between these competing demands because none of the elements in the pairs can be effective on their own in all circumstances.

The force field analysis based on the work of Lewin (1951) uses the idea of competing forces as a tool for thinking about change. The status quo is seen as a point of equilibrium between forces pushing for change and forces resisting change. These forces do not necessarily come in pairs but they are often matched. So staff's fear of the new may be counterbalanced by their enthusiasm for novelty. A force field is shown graphically in Figure 3.7.

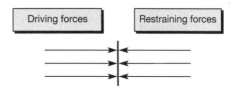

Figure 3.7 A force field diagram

Exchange and equilibrium

The idea of equilibrium, which is present in force field analysis, leads to other forms of relationships. Concepts may be related through a mechanism of exchange that leads to a balance or equilibrium between them. Tony Watson (1994: 110–111) developed the idea of 'strategic exchange' as the key conceptual framework for his research on management and strategy. He defined it as follows:

> The main strategic thrust of all organisations is one of strategic exchange to achieve long term survival (with profitability, market share and all the other typical strategic concerns as means towards this).

Every organisation has a number of stakeholders, and it exchanges resources with them in ways that enable both the organisation and its stakeholders to meet their objectives. One particular set of stakeholders are the individuals who work for an organisation, and Watson developed a conceptual framework that shows the process of strategic exchange between individuals and the organisation they work for. The exchange between individuals and organisations is conceptualised as an implicit contract. This is not formalised but it expresses the understanding that each party has of its obligations to, and expectations of, the other party.

The idea of an exchange relationship is a common one in business and management. It is associated with the ideas of equilibrium and trade-offs. This is the basis of much economic analysis. In markets exchange is the process by which a balance or equilibrium is achieved between buyers and sellers. Equilibrium is arrived at by the players deciding the point at which they are willing to trade off one thing for another. The buyer will decide that their wish to have the thing they want to buy now is more important than trying to get additional discount. Their wish to have the product and their wish for a discount balance, cancel each other out. The idea of trade-offs and balance can be found in many managerial conceptual frameworks. Kaplan and Norton's (1992) idea of the balanced scorecard in performance management is one illustration. The point of the technique is that managers do not achieve one set of targets merely at the expense of a worsened performance against other targets. Rather, the managers have to balance achievements against a number of possibly contradictory areas of performance.

Similarity

Sometimes concepts are related because they are similar. A conceptual framework can consist of groups of like themes that are clustered together. A famous example is the McKinsey '7 S' model. This is a framework for evaluating the effectiveness of an organisation. It incorporates the following seven concepts:

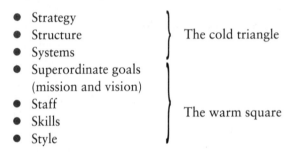

- Strategy
- Structure   } The cold triangle
- Systems
- Superordinate goals
  (mission and vision)
- Staff   } The warm square
- Skills
- Style

The first three are clustered together and are called the 'cold triangle' and the last four are grouped as the 'warm square'. The cold concepts are all analytical and impersonal, whereas the items in the warm square are all intangible and human. Cold and warm are matters of value and emotion. In other words, the similarities within the two clusters are matters of sensibility rather than of measurement. The relationships between concepts in a framework may, as in this case, be metaphorical or symbolic.

Things to watch out for

Although most of the examples of conceptual frameworks I have given can be shown as diagrams, they do not have to be. A conceptual framework can be expressed adequately in words alone. In fact one common problem is that students show their conceptual framework simply as a diagram. This is normally inadequate. A written explanation of the diagram, and in particular an explanation of the relationships between the concepts, is also required.

There are a number of common mistakes made when creating conceptual frameworks:

- Students' conceptual frameworks are often too complex and busy, and so you need to keep Occam's razor (explained on p. 309) to hand. The razor is the principle that you should keep things as simple as possible. Over-complex frameworks and diagrams are impossible to understand and lead markers to the conclusion that the student has greater facility with the graphics capabilities of word processors than they have with conceptual thinking.

- Sometimes the problem with a conceptual framework is that it does not specify what the relationships between the concepts are. If you have drawn a conceptual framework and the meaning of the arrows in it is ambiguous, or if you have a two-by-two matrix without scales on the vertical and horizontal axes, then you need to do some more work on it.
- Sometimes the proposed conceptual framework is too general and is not related to the research question that the project is seeking to answer. This can happen when a student draws a conceptual framework from the literature. It may provide a good map of the literature in the field but it may not be sufficiently specific to help answer the research question.

Theories

Figure 3.8 gives a definition of theories.

Developing theories is the third and final step in the process. This is often an aspiration and it is not always achievable in a Master's dissertation. It is perfectly possible to pass at Master's level with a dissertation that does not extend to developing theory. But, having said that, theorising does not necessarily mean inventing new theory. For most of us, theorising means adapting and developing existing theories. That does not seem such an impossible challenge. In management research, modifying or developing a theory often means adapting a theory developed in one context, say marketing, and applying it in another field.

Theories:

- are, in general terms, ideas about how phenomena relate to each other;
- are, more specifically, ideas about how particular events or actions tend to lead to others or are brought about by them;
- are generalisations;
- are the inductive heart of scientific study.

Figure 3.8 Theories
Source: reproduced with the permission of T.J. Watson.

Theories are an attempt to draw generalisable findings from specific instances. That is what the word 'inductive', in this context, means. Seen from another perspective, theories are attempts to explain research findings. Conceptual frameworks provide generalisations about processes, about the interaction of the concepts, whereas theories provide hypotheses about the outcomes of these processes. A conceptual framework might identify age and sex as factors linked with the propensity to take decisions that are ethical rather than dubious. Theory would show how these factors can explain the behaviours of different groups. It would provide an account of why senior women managers, say, respond, or are likely to respond, to situations in a different manner from, say, younger male managers. Of course, at this stage the conceptual framework and any related theories will be based on the literature review, the research having not yet been done. They remain, therefore, as a hypothesis or as a series of hypotheses.

Seeking inspiration: using your 'intellectual baggage'

In general the ideas for your conceptual thinking will come from the business and management literature. However, you can draw ideas from a much wider field. Often ideas and frameworks that you have come across in other academic subjects (and lots of people doing postgraduate studies in management have studied other subjects for their first degrees) can be adapted for use in a business or management dissertation.

An extreme example of borrowing from other fields can be taken from my research into business ethics. I had been browsing in a bookshop and came across a picture book on Cabbala and Jewish mysticism (Halevi, 1988). A central aspect of Cabbala is a diagram known as the tree of life. Within this diagram there are ten *sefirot*, a term that can be translated as spheres or stages of consciousness. These *sefirot* link God, the highest universal principle, with the material world. Look at the diagram in Figure 3.9, which represents the 'tree of life', very carefully. It is, at root, a 'boxes and arrows' diagram. There are ten circles (11 if you include *Daat*) that are connected by arrows. It is, in the terms used in this guide, a conceptual framework.

The tree of life also has similarities with force field analysis. The *sefirot* are arranged in three pillars. The left-hand pillar represents restraint, the right-hand pillar growth and expansion and the middle pillar a balance between the two others (Besserman, 1997). As in force field analysis, it supposes a dynamic between opposing forces that have to be mediated through a series of stages. Cabbala proposes, in what is known as the lightening flash, a sequence in which the forces of expansion and restraint are triggered and the tensions are resolved.

At the time I was doing research into the responses of financial and human resource management specialists to the ethical dilemmas they experienced at work. As it happens I had identified ten different forms of response and I was trying to see how they all interrelated and connected with each other. As the number of research categories matched the number of *sefirot*, I started to wonder whether the one could be mapped on to the other. It should have been possible because, according to the Cabbalists, the tree of life represents the underlying nature of everything. Some of the ethical responses in my analysis were clearly defensive, others were assertive expressions of people's values, and yet others were balancing, compromising positions. After much thinking the conceptual framework shown in Figure 3.10 emerged. You do not need to read the details of the diagram. The purpose of showing it is to give evidence of the transferability of theoretical frameworks.

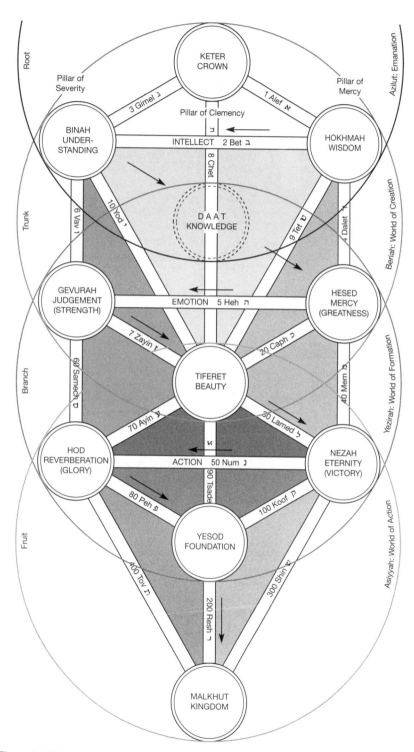

Figure 3.9 The tree of life

From *Kabbalah: Tradition of Hidden Knowledge* by Z'ev ben Shimon Halevi, published by Thames & Hudson Ltd, 1979, London. Reproduced with permission.

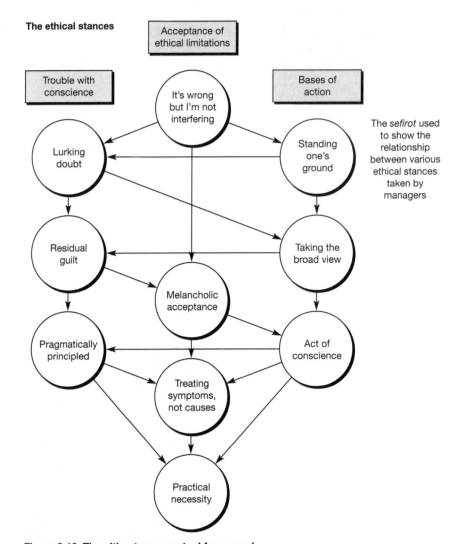

The ethical stances

Figure 3.10 The ultimate conceptual framework

Source: reproduced from Fisher (1999) with the permission of Blackwell Publishing Ltd.

This was all done with my tongue firmly in my cheek. I am normally sceptical about New Age and mystical ideas. I am not a Cabbalist. However, the conceptual framework of the *sefirot* was intriguing and its dynamics can be applied to many situations. Despite the oddity of the conceptual framework, it was published (Fisher, 1999).

An encouragement and a warning

Take heart – you do not need to do anything this complicated. But do keep your mind open to all possibilities. Conceptualisation and theorising are the hardest but also the most satisfying parts of doing a dissertation. The rewards are not purely intellectual. A convincing and elegant conceptual framework is the basis of many profitable pieces of intellectual property and of consultancy solutions to management problems. But developing a conceptual framework is a trial and error process. You will need to create a large pile of rejected scribblings before everything falls miraculously into place. But if you break through the thinking pain barrier, it does fall into place. If all this fails, use a conceptual framework straight from the literature, giving full citations of course.

Exhibit 3.5 provides an actual example, based on a student's piece of work, of the process of creating a conceptual framework. It illustrates how it might take several attempts before a usable conceptual framework is developed.

Exhibit 3.5

The process of developing a conceptual framework

Developing a conceptual framework involves playing around with concepts in a creative way; exploring how they might relate to each other, trying out different permutations, rejecting many and finally arriving at a framework that looks as if it will do its job. I can use an example provided by Alastair Allen (thanks to Alastair for giving permission to use his material) to illustrate this process.

The subject of his research project was the extent to which entrepreneurs and owners of small businesses (who might or might not be the same category of people) were inclined:

- to learn about environmental sustainability in business;
- take part in training and development and other initiatives concerning sustainability; and
- try to improve the environmental impact of their own businesses.

After having completed his literature review he started thinking about possible conceptual frameworks he might use. In his dissertation he described the tortuous path he had followed. At first he had thought about that cliché of conceptual frameworks – a two-by-two-matrix (Figure 3.11).

		Environmental awareness	
		Low	High
Environmental action	High	*Ill-informed activist*	*Deep green thinker*
	Low	*Blissful ignorance*	*Head in the sand*

Figure 3.11 A two-by-two matrix
Source: Alastair Allen. Reproduced with the permission of the author.

Exhibit 3.5 *continued*

While this appeared an attractive framework in terms of giving memorable labels to the ways that small business owners responded to sustainability issues, it did not give any analytical grip on why they chose to behave in these different manners, which was the question he was really interested in.

His second framework looked at how small business owners might be taken through a process designed to encourage them to act in a more sustainable fashion (Figure 3.12).

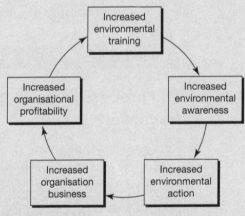

Figure 3.12 A process framework
Source: Alastair Allen. Reproduced with the permission of the author.

This was a feasible conceptual framework but it only really explained how training on sustainability should work and should influence small business owners. It did not address the complexities of their likely responses to training. They might see such training as the work of meddling do-gooders and turn against the whole idea of being more sustainable in business. The framework also incorporated a major theoretical assumption – the idea that running a business in a sustainable way will increase business profits – which had not been tested. This assumption could not be included as a basis of the conceptual framework because part of the purpose of the research was to test out whether it was a true or false assumption.

Eventually he took inspiration from the well-known force field analysis diagram (see p. 131) and which had already been used in the literature by a well-respected researcher to explore small business owners' attitudes on environmental issues. The final conceptual framework that Alastair adopted as the basis of his research was the force field analysis shown in Figure 3.13. It worked well for his project because it focused on a key issue: the pressures encouraging and discouraging small business owners from implementing sustainability training in their organisations. The complete framework was more detailed than the version shown below. The restraining and driving forces had been identified from an extensive reading of the literature.

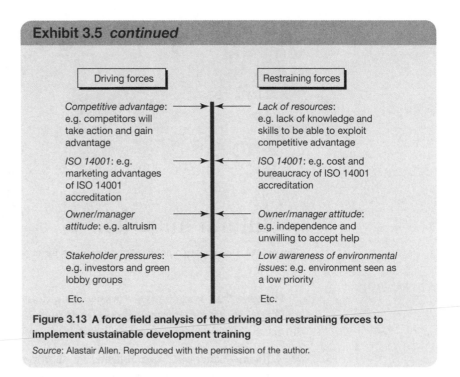

Exhibit 3.5 *continued*

| Driving forces | | Restraining forces |

Competitive advantage:
e.g. competitors will
take action and gain
advantage

Lack of resources:
e.g. lack of knowledge and
skills to be able to exploit
competitive advantage

ISO 14001: e.g.
marketing advantages
of ISO 14001
accreditation

ISO 14001: e.g. cost and
bureaucracy of ISO 14001
accreditation

*Owner/manager
attitude:* e.g. altruism

Owner/manager attitude:
e.g. independence and
unwilling to accept help

Stakeholder pressures:
e.g. investors and green
lobby groups

*Low awareness of environmental
issues:* e.g. environment seen as
a low priority

Etc.   Etc.

Figure 3.13 A force field analysis of the driving and restraining forces to implement sustainable development training

Source: Alastair Allen. Reproduced with the permission of the author.

Examples of the use of conceptual frameworks

Two examples will be given of how conceptual frameworks might be developed.

An example of conceptualising and theorising in a study of organisational cultures

This example is based on the doctoral research of Terry McNulty (1990), who received his PhD from Nottingham Trent University. As it is taken from doctoral-level work it is at a higher level of theoretical sophistication than may be necessary for Master's-level work. However, it does explain the three stages of concept definition, conceptual framework building and theorising very well. The research was into the types of organisational culture found in a number of different hospitals. The concepts needed therefore all related to the idea of organisational culture.

McNulty began by isolating a number of key concepts, some of which are shown in Figure 3.14.

Figure 3.14 Developing a conceptual framework for organisational culture

His next task was to give working definitions to all these terms, using the literature on organisational culture as his source. We will not rehearse all these definitions here but simply pick out a few:

● **Official** – sanctioned or published by the top management of an organisation. McClean and Marshall (1991) termed this the 'high profile culture'.
● **Unofficial** – values, beliefs and behaviours chosen by the staff. It is the same as McClean and Marshall's (1991) concept of 'low profile culture'.
● **Structure** – the technologies, procedures, policies and charts that define the 'architecture' of an organisation.
● **Values** – beliefs about what is good and bad and what are proper and improper ways of doing things.
● **Sub-cultures** – organisations do not necessarily have a single, unified culture. Within the organisational culture there are likely to be many sub-cultures that will differ to a greater or lesser extent from the wider corporate culture.
● **Cultural imperialism** – when one sub-culture group in an organisation gains power or hegemony over other groups.

The next stage was to put the concepts in a framework. Note that not all the concepts available to the researcher were used for this purpose (see Figure 3.15).

The two-by-two matrix is such a commonly used form of conceptual framework that it has become hackneyed. Nevertheless, it often works well. This framework has at least two functions. It can be used to define various component parts of organisational culture. It can also be used as an aid to the data-gathering part of the research. The four boxes can be used to store the information gathered during research forays into the organisation as follows:

	Structure	**Values**
Official	Mission statements, policies, objectives, organisation charts, manuals, job descriptions	Senior managers' ideas, views and visions
Unofficial	The way in which people in the organisation actually do things	The ideas, attitudes, values and opinions of everyone else in the organisation

Figure 3.15 A conceptual framework for organisational culture

- Into the official values box go all the things top managers said in interviews about their values and their vision for the organisation.
- Into the official structure box goes all the documentary evidence, such as mission statements, charts, procedures and computer software that describe how things should be done.
- Into the unofficial structure box goes all the information, from informal observations of the workplace and interviews with staff, which explain how staff actually do their job. This will include information about all the dodges and short cuts that staff use to make their jobs bearable.
- Into the unofficial values box goes the information about the staff's values and beliefs that were probably obtained by interviews and focus groups.

In the chapter of the dissertation in which these results were written up, the four boxes were used as sub-headings for describing the research findings.

The next stage involved developing theories from the conceptual framework, as in Figure 3.16.

The theory that Terry McNulty developed related the conceptual framework to the idea of organisational effectiveness. He proposed that the effectiveness, or organisational health, of an organisation would be influenced by the degree of fit between the four quadrants described in the conceptual framework. Strictly speaking, the theory was a hypothesis because the research findings would be used to test it.

Theory
If all the four quadrants complement each other, then you have an effective organisation. If the quadrants are in conflict, then the organisation will, in various ways, be ineffective.

Figure 3.16 Theorising from the framework

Exercise 3.2

Further theory making

Terry McNulty had used two other concepts in his research: strong glue culture and weak glue culture. Again, the metaphor of culture as a glue had been taken from the literature. In a strong glue culture the culture strongly binds all members of the organisation. In a weak glue culture there are greater tendencies to separation and the organisational culture is not strong enough to hold people together. He used these additional concepts to produce a further two-by-two matrix, as shown in Figure 3.17.

Official culture
(top management culture)

	Weak	Strong
Strong		
Weak		

Unofficial culture
(the culture of the
organisational sub-cultures)

Figure 3.17 Further theorising

From your own experience and common sense try to identify what the practical outcomes for organisations would be for each of the four blank boxes in Figure 3.17.

Exercise 3.2 *continued*

So, for example, what would happen in an organisation when a strong official (top management) culture meets a strong unofficial culture? What would be the consequence for a coming together of a strong unofficial culture and a weak management culture?

Suggested answer

McNulty's analysis of the outcomes in the four different circumstances is shown in Figure 3.18. You probably will not have come across the terms used in the figure because several are drawn from the historical analysis of colonialism and one comes from sociology. The analysis provides a more practical example than the Cabbala of how ideas from different disciplines can inform organisational and managerial analysis. So it is unlikely you will have used the same images or headings, but check how close your answer, expressed in your own terms, fits with the following descriptions:

● **Balkanisation or informal empire**

When the top management (official) culture is weak and there are several powerful sub-culture groups, such as doctors and nurses in a hospital, then you would expect constant feuding between the sub-culture groups as they vie for power. The political situation in the Balkans in both the nineteenth and the twentieth centuries provides a metaphor for this process. If one of the groups gains the ascendancy, then the situation will be like that of an informal empire, in which actual power lies with a sub-group, while the official power, the management, maintains control in name only. The term 'informal empire' is a historical one. In the nineteenth century, for example, Britain had an informal empire in South America. Britain was not formally the sovereign body but it controlled the economies and the other important levers of power.

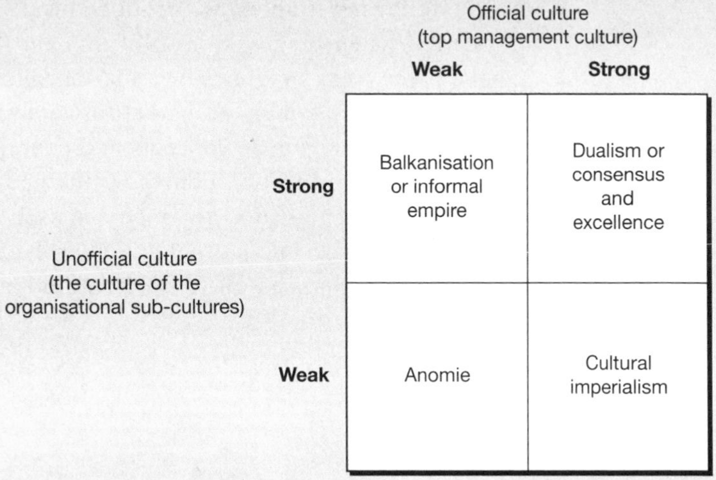

		Official culture (top management culture)	
		Weak	**Strong**
Unofficial culture (the culture of the organisational sub-cultures)	**Strong**	Balkanisation or informal empire	Dualism or consensus and excellence
	Weak	Anomie	Cultural imperialism

Figure 3.18 **Further theorising**

Exercise 3.2 continued

- **Dualism and consensus**
  When both the official and unofficial cultures are strong, there are two possibilities. The first is where the two share similar values – the organisation is unified and can aspire to excellence. If the cultures are different, then the two cultures may agree to co-exist and not to interfere with each other. For example, the doctors get on with doing the medicine and the management deals with the other staff and the premises. Dualism is a concept also taken from history. It refers to many colonial countries, in the nineteenth century, in which a modern economy existed alongside, but not interacting with, a peasant subsistence economy.
- **Anomie**
  Anomie is a term from sociology. It means a state where people have lost all sense of purpose and identity. This is likely to be the case when both official and unofficial cultures are weak.
- **Cultural imperialism**
  If the official culture, the top management, is strong but the sub-cultures are weak, then the management will have no difficulty is asserting its control over the organisation. Using another historical metaphor, this is similar to the processes of imperialism.

This second two-by-two matrix suggested another set of theoretical scenarios, which Terry McNulty then investigated by researching what was happening in a number of hospitals and units.

Another example

The following is an extract from an article by Clark and Soulsby (1995), written when they were at Nottingham Business School. The paper is about the ways organisations and managers in the Czech Republic have adapted to the coming of market forces. Study the examples of good practice in the handling of concepts and conceptual frameworks identified in the extract and think about how they might be applied to your work. The extract is presented as a model to aspire to. It was published in a well-considered academic journal and is probably at a higher level than needs to be achieved to pass the dissertation module of a Master's programme.

The study of organisational transformation

The gloss

The key concept of 'organisational form' is defined and related to other similar terms used in the literature. The authors choose a preferred definition from a range of possibilities.

Three other concepts are defined that go to make up the 'organisational form' – sub-system, structure and culture.

The concept of 'internal coherence' is introduced that links the three components. The relationship between the concepts is one of 'fit' and 'balance'.

A boxes and arrows diagram is used to explain and summarise the conceptual framework.

In this diagram the concepts are all linked together in a conceptual framework. Coherence is similar to the idea of balance. It is proposed that systems, structures and cultures tend towards a state of equilibrium.

The text

Greenwood and Hinings (1988: 296) argue that the notion of a relatively stable organisational state is a prerequisite for the study of organisational change, since it provides the starting point and an end point of a process of transition which constitutes the focus of such a study. This state of 'relative stablity' has been usefully conceptualised as a 'configuration' (Miller and Friesen, 1984) or a [design] archetype (e.g. Greenwood and Hinings, 1988). We will use the generic concept of an 'organisational form' in order to achieve some consistency in our terminology. Following Laughlin (1991) we conceive of the organisational form as being constituted by three interrelated components. These components vary in their level of abstraction and in their degree of importance for identifying the underlying nature of an organisation and the behaviour of its members (see Figure 3.19). We shall call these components the organisation's 'sub-systems', its 'structure' and its 'culture'.

[A paragraph has been omitted from here that defines the three components in more detail.]

Further, it has been argued that organisations tend towards 'internal coherence' within their organisational form. Under circumstances of successful adaptation to a relatively predictable environment, the organisation's constituent sub-systems, structure and culture will tend to be mutually consistent and supportive, leading to internal resistances to change (Miller and Friesen, 1984; Greenwood and Hinings, 1988: 297–299; Laughlin, 1991: 213). In principle, the components of an organisational form are systematically bound, by virtue of their consistent expression of its underlying values (Greenwood and Hinings, 1987: 2).

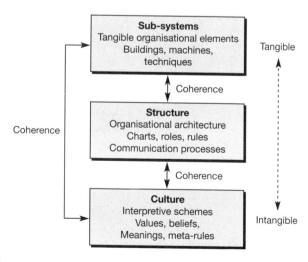

Figure 3.19

The gloss	The text

The concept of 'transformation' is introduced and related to the components in the diagram. Once again the terms are clarified in relation to similar concepts found in the literature.

The concept of 'transformation' is reserved for complete and significant changes in all three components of the organisational form. This is what Miller and Friesen (1984) call a 'quantum change'; a fundamental shift in the dominant logic or organising principles which underpin the organisational form, effecting a move to another form. Others have used the terms 'reorientation', 'revolutionary', 'radical' or 'second order' change to refer to 'change ... in the organisational "core" ... [which] is irreversible' (Levy, 1986: 10). Changes within the dominant logic are partial, incremental, piecemeal or superficial, and have attracted terms like 'convergent', 'evolutionary', 'incremental' or 'first order' (cf. Levy, 1986: 8–9; Dunphy and Stace, 1988: 322; Miller and Friesen, 1984: 223–226; see also Child and Smith, 1987; Pettigrew, 1987: 664–665). Such 'reformative' changes do not affect the cultural bedrock of the organisation, and thus leave its essential nature and reality relatively untouched. Such distinctions help to map out conceptual features of organisational change, but the analysis of its ongoing reality requires an approach that recognises the complexity of the simultaneous processes of continuity and discontinuity with the past (cf. Tushman and Romanelli, 1985; Child and Smith, 1987: 569).

The conceptual framework is used to mark off the boundaries of this study. The things the study will not do are clearly stated.

Some limitations are reported in the conceptual framework. It is signposted that the framework will be developed by adding to it the concept of human agency.

The paper is starting to develop new theory by adapting existing conceptual frameworks.

The limitations of the existing theories and conceptual frameworks are spelt out.

Some underdeveloped issues in organisational transformation

By focusing on the internal coherence of system components, and the technical fit between the organisation and its environment, the study of organisational transformation has developed within a discourse that stresses the processes of system integration and crisis. Our research on the management of organisational transformation in the Czech Republic is firmly located within this nexus of concepts, propositions and issues, but we have found certain limits to its usefulness in accounting for our observations. In particular, the current framework virtually disregards institutional processes in the environment, and, by extension, underplays key problems of social integration and legitimation. The role of human agency is especially important in looking at the behaviour of managers who are actively engaged in changing organisational systems, structures and processes.

Transformation and institutional change

As a result of its location within the contingency theory tradition, mainstream research on organisational transformation has tended to focus strongly upon the task (or technical) environment as the source of internal change. For example, 'the trigger for transformation' (Child and Smith, 1987: 575) at Cadbury was primarily identified with changes in the relationship between the firm and its markets; and 'strategic reorientations' at ICI were located in 'economic and business events' and the firm's 'operating environment' (Pettigrew, 1987: 665). While such research recognises the importance of internal culture and its symbolic relationships with external events, it still tends to underplay the role of changes in the organisation's 'institutional' environment.

The gloss

It is argued that there has been too much attention on internal 'fit' and not enough on the fit between organisational form and the wider institutional environment. Institutions in this context refers to the structures and culture of Soviet society.

The new concept of 'institutionalisation' is used to begin to extend the conceptual framework. Its implications are drawn out.

Deinstitutionalisation is linked back to the idea of a fit between an organisational form and its environmental circumstances. But it is argued that this process occurs through human agency, i.e. people in the organisation beginning to challenge and question the way the organisation is.

The new concepts of institutionalisation and human agency are added into the conceptual framework. But this time a diagram is not used.

The text

Institutionalisation is said to occur when patterns and processes take on a 'rule-like status in social thought and action' (Jepperson, 1991: 145) because they have a 'natural' and unchallengeable appearance. As a consequence of institutionalisation, organisational structures and systems, and the grounds of rational behaviour, become so taken for granted or habitualised that their underlying values and ideologies are not recognised – legitimacy is implicitly accomplished without the active intervention of human choices.

In a highly institutionalised setting, where the existing order has become part of the natural attitude, the explanation of organisational transformation requires answers to questions such as:

1. How do the underlying values, rationality and ideologies of an organisational form become revealed so that they can be interrogated?
2. How can the balance of power shift so that the values, once revealed, can be effectively challenged and opposed?

This challenge to legitimacy (in part, a process of demythologising) becomes a threat to the degree of social integration, and allows the possibility of deinstitutionalisation. As Zucker (1991: 105) argues, whereas institutionalisation can occur 'accidentally', deinstitutionalisation needs conscious acts of opposition to overcome the inertia implicit in institutional systems or networks.

It is evident that institutionalisation and deinstitutionalisation can only be properly understood as social processes at both the macro level or organisation–environment interaction, and the micro level of social accomplishment. At the former level, the process of deinstitutionalisation is related to the changing nature of the organisation's relationship with its socio-institutional environment. Patterns, practice and procedures, as well as their underlying logic, become incongruent with the assumptions of legitimacy, credibility and normality in society. At the micro level, key actors begin to question the way things are done in the organisation, and the existing customs and practices are revealed as inappropriate or non-rational – both in terms of what is required in the institutional environment, and in terms of the organisation's internal, formal coherence.

Managerial action and organisational transformation

We have argued that the dominant systems approach to organisational transformation has neglected the human and social dimensions of organisational change. We have also suggested that a key to understanding transformation from an institutional perspective lies in demonstrating the breakdown of current institutional practices and social processes of institutional reproduction by examining the social accomplishment of change at the micro level. In fact, with one or two exceptions, both the contingency and the institutionalist approaches to organisational analysis have tended to underplay those processes whereby organisational life is socially constructed.

The gloss	The text
The themes and concepts of human agency and social construction are developed.	Managers act as potentially powerful agents in the process of organisational transformation through the contribution of a complex set of cognitive, affective and behavioural influences. The choices that managers make in order to change the organisation result from their perception and understanding of the problems and constraints, their level of education, knowledge and understanding of options available to them (including knowledge of recent
The two new additions to thinking on the subject – institutional fit and human agency – are highlighted in the summary.	fashions and trends in management), and their effective power, social legitimacy and competence to get things done in the organisation. It should also be recognised that managers in any organisation will differ in the values, knowledge, experience, power and competence that they bring to bear on organisational processes.
The developments of the conceptual framework are summarised. It is argued that these developments will be useful in improving understanding of organisational transformations.	In summary, this theoretical exploration highlights the complexity of factors which affect the process of organisational transformation. It has argued for consideration of institutional as well as technical factors, and for supplementing the notions of system integration and crisis with those of social integration and crisis. The macro and micro processes of institutional change are highlighted, and it is argued that senior managers perform pivotal roles in transforming the technical and institutional relationships between the organisation and its environment, while all managers are instrumental in the re-establishment of internal coherence in the organisational form. These conceptual frameworks serve to enhance the theoretical framework within which the management of organisational transformation, in a rapidly changing and highly ambiguous societal context, can be more fully analysed.

NB The citations from the abstract have been omitted. If you are interested in the subject, as opposed to the manner in which the conceptual framework has been developed, the full references can be found in the article.

Source: Clark and Soulsby (1995). Reproduced with the authors' permission.

Summary

- Consider carefully the pros and cons of adopting a structured approach rather than a grounded approach in your use of conceptual frameworks.
- Having a conceptual framework is not absolutely necessary to gain a pass mark for a Master's dissertation; but if you do have one it repays you well in marks.
- Work through a three-stage process of defining concepts, formulating conceptual frameworks and theorising.
- You do not necessarily have to invent entirely new conceptual frameworks. You may well be able to adapt frameworks from the literature to fit a new context.
- If all else fails, then use an existing framework from the literature without adaptation.
- Use your imagination to help you in formulating a conceptual framework. Draw inspiration from the breadth of your reading and your 'intellectual baggage'.
- Use your conceptual framework to help you analyse your research material and to structure the analysis you present in the dissertation.

Suggested reading

There is no one book that I can find that focuses mainly on the subject of this chapter. Miles and Huberman (1994) is a wonderful sourcebook for ideas and possibilities for using diagrams to represent conceptual frameworks. Chapter 6 in Hart (1998) is also useful for this purpose.

Hart, C. (1998) *Doing a Literature Review: Releasing the Social Science Research Imagination*, London: Sage.

Miles, M.B. and Huberman, A.M. (1994) *An Expanded Sourcebook: Qualitative Data Analysis*, 2nd edn, London: Sage.

References

Besserman, P. (1997) *The Shambhala Guide to Kabbalah and Jewish Mysticism*, Boston, Mass., and London: Shambhala.

Clark, E. and Soulsby, A. (1995) 'Transforming former state enterprises in the Czech Republic', *Organisation Studies*, vol. 16, no. 2: 215.

Fisher, C.M. (1999) 'Ethical stances: the perceptions of accountancy and HR specialists of ethical conundrums at work', *Business Ethics: A European Review*, vol. 8, no. 4: 236–248.

Glaser, B.G. (1992) *The Basics of Grounded Theory Analysis*, Mill Valley, Calif.: Sociology Press.

Glaser, B.G. and Strauss, A.L. (1967) *The Discovery of Grounded Theory: Strategies for Qualitative Research*, New York: Aldine.

Gross, J. (1987) *The Oxford Book of Aphorisms*, Oxford: Oxford University Press.

Halevi, Z.S. (1988) *Kabbalah: Tradition of Hidden Knowledge*, London: Thames & Hudson.

Kaplan, R.S. and Norton, D.P. (1992) 'The balanced scorecard: measures that drive performance', *Harvard Business Review*, January–February: 75–85.

Keay, J. (2000) *India: A History*, London: HarperCollins.

Kolb, D.A., Rubin, I.M. and Osland, J.S. (1995) *Organisational Behaviour: An Experiential Approach*, 6th edn, Hemel Hempstead: Prentice Hall.

Lewin, K. (1951) *Field Theory in Social Science*, New York: Harper & Row.

McClean, A. and Marshall, J. (1991) *Cultures at Work: How to Identify and Understand Them*, Luton: The Local Government Management Board.

McNulty, T. (1990) 'Organisation, Culture and the Management of Change in the National Health Service', PhD dissertation, Nottingham: Nottingham Trent University.

Maslow, A. (1954) *Motivation and Personality*, New York: Harper & Row.

Reddin, W.J. (1970) *Managerial Effectiveness*, London: McGraw-Hill.

Stern, C.W. and Stalk Jr, G. (eds) (1998) *Perspectives on Strategy from the Boston Consulting Group*, London: John Wiley.

Strauss, A.L. and Corbin, J. (1990) *The Basics of Qualitative Research: Grounded Theory Procedures and Techniques*, London: Sage.

Trevino, L.K. and Youngblood, S.A. (1990) 'Bad apples in bad barrels: a causal analysis of ethical decision-making behaviour', *Journal of Applied Psychology*, vol. 75, no. 4: 378–385.

Watson, T.J. (1994) *In Search of Management: Culture, Chaos and Control in Managerial Work*, London: Routledge.

Chapter 4

Collecting and analysing research material

Contents

● ● ● ● Introduction

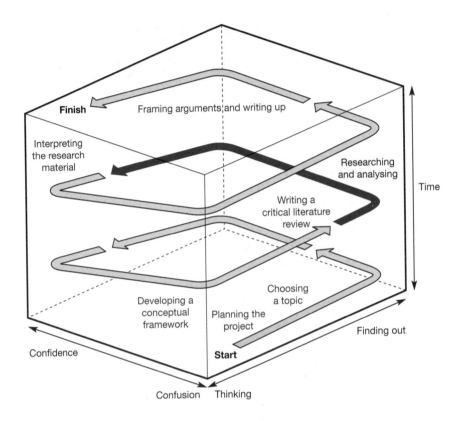

The processes of researching and writing a Master's dissertation

The great tragedy of science – the slaying of a beautiful hypothesis by an ugly fact.

Thomas H. Huxley (1870)

Research is formalised curiosity. It is poking and prying with a purpose.

Zora Neale Hurston (1942)

The previous chapters have covered:

● identifying the topic of your dissertation project;
● reviewing the literature; and
● laying down the foundations of research by defining and modelling the necessary concepts.

This chapter is about the primary research phase of the project. It deals with how to find things out by research rather than discovering things by reading the literature. It is more practically focused than some of the other chapters because it is about the technical problems of carrying out research. This phase of a project often begins with a little uncertainty as the student thinks about and plans how the research material is to be gathered. Once these decisions have been made, then the processes of finding things out leads to an increased sense of confidence in the project.

This is the longest chapter in the guide. However, it should not take you any more time than the others because, in normal circumstances, you will only need to read a portion of it. The chapter identifies two broad approaches to collecting research material. It is probable that you will use only one of these styles of research, so you need to read only those sections that deal with your chosen approach. It might just be that you are going to use both approaches, using one in a major role and one in a minor role. In that case, I am afraid, you have twice as much reading to do.

Discoverers

This chapter is about discovery, which theme leads naturally to the metaphor of geographical discovery. The analogy will help to explain two broad approaches to finding out new things. If we think of the great ages of exploration, then the images of two kinds of discoverer come to mind: explorers and surveyors.

Explorers travel into unknown (at least to them if not to the indigenous inhabitants) territory. Their mission is to make the unknown known and to make the strange familiar to those who read their books of adventure and derring-do. In the sense that they are travelling into the unknown, explorers can have no preconception about what they will find. Exploration requires an open approach. Explorers cannot, or should not, anticipate what they will find. Of course they will have preconceptions – or conceptual frameworks – that will lead them to explore one place rather than another; but they should not second guess what they might find on the basis of these preconceptions. Explorers present their discoveries in narratives, they write books and give lectures, or in modern times present television documentaries.

The surveyor often arrives at a later stage of discovery. By this time, the broad configuration of the new land and its peoples will be known. The role of the surveyor is to pin that knowledge down in a precise and reproducible form. Surveyors measure things. They produce maps, coordinates and benchmarks. Often, by the time the surveyors begin their work, it is known where the mountains are, where the rivers flow and what the customs of the inhabitants are. The surveyor finds out how high the mountains are and where precisely they are located, plots the courses of the rivers and conducts censuses of the population. It is difficult to carry out a survey if the broad contours of the subject of the survey are not already known. Without this foreknowledge it would be hard to know what questions to ask in the census or where to begin the triangulation for mapping. Surveyors can anticipate the broad shape of their findings. They present their findings in maps and tables of statistics.

The issue of concern in this chapter is not so much the methodological differences between the two approaches to research as the fact that they use different types of research techniques. Explorers do not know what they will find until they look. Surveyors on the other hand know enough about the territory to be surveyed to be able to classify and structure the things they will be measuring. Explorers are interested in the particular and are less keen to allocate everything to categories. The stock in trade of surveyors, however, is classifying things and putting them in their correct place in a scheme of classification. Explorers take an open approach to research and surveyors take a closed approach; terms that will be explained in the next section.

Exploration and ethnography

In the Victorian heyday of exploration, researchers into unknown and exotic societies were known as ethnographers. The term is still used today of people who study not obscure tribes but organisations. In management and business studies it is not generally places and territories being studied but people and their social organisations. The exotic is no longer at a distance from us but all around us in the diverse range of organisations in which we work.

Ethnography focuses on the manner in which people interact and collaborate in observable and regular ways (Gill and Johnson, 1997: 97). Another way of expressing this is to say that ethnography is the study of cultures. But the approach is also defined by the manner of the study. Ethnography sometimes requires an extended period of immersion in the culture being studied during which the researcher remains as open as they can to the experiences that surround them. Academic researchers into management and organisations become ethnographers by leaving their academic institutions and working for a time in the businesses and organisations they are studying. They become participant observers (see p. 172). This role is an easier one for part-time students on Master's courses to adopt because they, mostly, have full-time jobs and are already immersed in the organisational cultures they may choose to study. It is possible, as Master's students, to do an ethnographic study in an organisation even though you are an outsider to the organisation being studied. Ethnographers can only give accounts of their own interactions with the culture they study. They cannot claim that their accounts are replicable or generalisable. Their research is written up as case studies.

Students who are taking an exploratory approach ought to adopt open, or at most semi-structured, research tools. That is to say, they should conduct their research in ways that do not presume to know what they will discover. At its simplest it means asking open and not closed questions.

The problems latent within traditional ethnography highlight some of the problems that may be associated with open and semi-structured methods. In the nineteenth and early twentieth centuries ethnography was about westerners studying (as was then claimed) exotic and primitive cultures within colonial empires. The colonial origins of ethnography identify two of its dangers. The first is that it can be seen as patronising by those being studied. The Victorian ethnographers assumed that the societies they were studying were savage and at a lower level of development than their own. As one of the subjects of Tony Watson's modern ethnographic study of a telecommunications company said:

> Seriously though. You've told us that you are writing a book about managers, about us lot. So who is it for? I mean, you know, will thick people like us understand it?

(Watson, 1994: 1)

The second danger is that in response to the felt condescension of the ethnographer, the subjects may seek to mislead the researchers by spinning webs of false tales that they know the researcher wants to hear. Margaret Mead was a famous ethnographer who gave a lyrical account of adolescent sexuality in Samoa. Subsequently many Samoans argued that:

> the girls who they claimed plied Mead with their colourful tales were only amusing themselves, and had no inkling that their tales would ever find their way into a book.

(Freeman, 1983: 290)

These dangers do not imply that ethnographic methods should not be used. But they do indicate the importance of conducting the research and analysing the material with care. Good explorers are also open minded when they try to make sense of the new region and its inhabitants by creating frames of reference to fit them into. The less good explorers attempt to fit their new discoveries into old frames of reference. It was for this reason that the West Indies were so named on their discovery by Europeans. The explorers had found new lands with new cultures but they insisted on applying an old way of thinking, which led them to believe that they had found a new route to India and the east.

Surveyors and measurement

The surveyor who is studying organisations, businesses or economies is not so different from the surveyor who mapped new regions. They both have a faith in accurate measurement and they both use surveys as a means of measurement. It is true that in management and business the survey will often be a mailed-out questionnaire rather than a physical survey. Nevertheless, both types of survey attempt to produce a numerical or mathematical representation of the 'field' that can be used as a basis for planning and decision making. Surveyors of business and management will seek to remain detached from what they are measuring. It is not necessary to become involved with the people in an organisation in order to measure its sales turnover, its profitability, its customer churn rates and its staff turnover. It is important, however, to define very precisely the things that are to measured or counted. It is pointless, for example, to measure profitability of companies without being very precise about the accountancy rules and conventions that are to be used to calculate profit. Otherwise, when the information is to be used, it will be found that like was not compared with like. Survey research is presented as an accurate and generalised representation of the field of study.

Students taking a survey approach to their research ought to adopt a structured approach. That is to say, they should be able to define the characteristics and properties of the subjects of their study before they conduct the research so that they can accurately measure and categorise them. They should ask, mostly, closed questions.

In surveying research, what is to be researched has to be pre-planned in some detail and the measuring instruments to be used have to be well calibrated. These requirements are also the basis of the dangers inherent in this form of research. We can return to the great Victorian age of discovery to explain some of these. The British Raj in India in the nineteenth century was obsessed with surveys; every aspect of its dominion was captured in surveys and censuses. Unfortunately much of the data collected were of suspect accuracy, their collection was influenced by the political agendas of those organising the gathering and in many cases the things they measured were not useful. As one commentator pointed out, all the surveys and censuses in the early nineteenth century gave no premonition of the state of Indian popular feeling before the great Indian mutiny or rebellion in 1857 (Bayly, 1996: 221). A more insidious problem was that the mindset of the colonial administrators led them to give heightened importance to things, by measuring them, that had not previously been important. It was a Victorian assumption that some races and classes of people were inferior to others. Consequently there appeared a type of researcher, known as anthropometricians, who surveyed the peoples in India by measuring their skulls. The nasal index was a particularly important measure. These surveys allocated people to categories on a status scale according to, among other things, anthropometrical indices. Indian society had always been structured around kinship and clan. However, the formalisation of the status differences between them gave caste greater significance. Once a league table of caste status had been published in censuses, groups would organise themselves and lobby to have their position on the league table improved (Padmanabha 1978: 4). Caste became a more dominant feature in Indian social and political life than it had been before it was formalised by censuses.

Such problems resulting from statistical measurement were not reserved for the nineteenth century. The current debate about the impact of performance measurement in the National Health Service raises the same issues, about the accuracy, the objectivity and the distorting impacts of the measurements, as NHS Trusts seek to secure themselves a good position in the performance league tables (BBC, 2003). The good surveyor, then, always questions the usefulness and the accuracy of their measurements.

Structure of the chapter

You may choose to be an explorer or a surveyor, or perhaps both. The choice should depend upon which form of research will best answer your research questions.

The chapter is divided into four parts:

1. Choosing between open and exploratory research methods on the one hand and pre-structured survey research on the other. Everyone should read this part, which describes the two broad choices of approach and gives guidelines and examples to help you make your choice.
2. Collecting and analysing research material using open and exploratory research methods. This part of the guide explains the use of open and semi-structured methods. You need read it only if this is the approach you have chosen to take.
3. Collecting and analysing research material using the pre-structured, pre-coded survey approach. You need read this part of the chapter only if this is the kind of research method you have chosen to use.
4. Introduction to software for research. This part of the chapter provides brief introductions to the major software products designed for each approach. None of this part may be relevant to you. It might not be necessary for you to use software – and many students do not. If you do decide to use a package, you will need only one of the three described.

This chapter deals with both the collection of research material and its analysis. In the guide a distinction is made between analysis and interpretation. Analysis refers to putting the material in order by summarising, précising it and putting it into categories. Interpretation is the process of drawing implications and significance from the material and using them as the basis for recommendations or action. Interpretation is the subject of Chapter 5.

Learning outcomes for the chapter

1 Readers will be able to choose the degree of openness or pre-coding appropriate to their research task.
2 Readers will be able to design and use open and semi-structured research techniques in a competent manner; and/or
3 Readers will be able to design and use pre-coded and structured research techniques in a competent manner.
4 Readers will be able to analyse quantitative and survey-based material; and/or
5 Readers will be able to analyse qualitative and case-based material.
6 Readers will be able to make well-judged decisions about the appropriateness or otherwise of using software packages for analysing quantitative and qualitative material and be able to identify appropriate software packages.

The range of research methods

There is a great variety of means at your disposal to carry out the primary research phase of your Master's dissertation. A useful distinction that can be made to help people get a grasp of the range of possibilities is to contrast open, or unstructured, forms of research with pre-coded or structured ones. All this distinction means is that in the former case the answers people are likely to give to the researcher's questions are not anticipated. The researcher is open to whatever people say. In the latter case the researcher has a good idea of the likely range of answers and is more interested in the relative frequencies with which the various options are expressed. In this type of research the researcher can provide respondents with a previously prepared list of options to choose from or respond to. Each of the major research methods, questionnaires, interviews, observation and so on can be used in an open (exploratory) or pre-coded (surveying) manner. Table 4.1 shows how this can be done.

The approaches shown in Table 4.1 need explanation, some more than others.

Interviews

The ways in which interviews can be conducted in an open or in a structured manner can be easily explained:

Table 4.1 Unstructured and structured approaches to the main research methods

	Exploratory research Unstructured	< ----------------------------- >	Survey research Structured
Interviews	In-depth and open	Critical incidents	Interviewer keeps to a script and there are answer options
Panels	Focus groups		Delphi technique
Questionnaire	Lots of white space on the page		Tick boxes
Observation	Keeping a research diary	Checklists and categories	Completing an observation schedule Activity sampling
Documentary	Rhetorical analysis		Statistical analysis of themes

- The idea of an open interview is straightforward. The interviewer engages in informal conversation with the respondent about a particular area of interest. The interviewer may steer the conversation a little, by picking up on the cues and themes raised by the respondent, but generally the respondent leads the direction of the interview.
- Pre-coded interviews, in contrast, are controlled by the researcher. In these interviews the interviewer generally reads from a prepared script and is expected not to deviate from it. The questions asked are organised into a logical sequence, and for most questions the respondent is given a series of options and asked to choose a given number of them.
- Semi-structured interviews are in between these two extremes. Generally the interviewer has a schedule to remind them of the main issues and topics that need to be covered by the respondent. However, the respondent has much latitude to respond to the questions in the ways that seem sensible to them. The critical incident approach will be discussed later in this chapter but it is mentioned here because it is a form of semi-structured interview. The respondent is asked to think of occasions in their working life when they had to deal with a particular kind of issue, for example managing problem staff. The interviewee chooses an incident and then is encouraged by the interviewer to explain the incident in full detail.

Panels

Panels are a very common research method. As with interviews, they can be used in an open or in a pre-coded manner. When in open mode they take the form of focus groups. A group of people are brought together to have a free flowing, but focused, discussion on a particular topic. Gordon and Langmaid (1988) provide an accessible guide to focus groups. Figure 4.1 lists some of the issues that have to be considered when planning a focus group.

Decide what themes and issues are to be discussed

Develop protocols for use of information:
– you need to tell participants how the information they give will be used and the extent to which their anonymity will be preserved.

Decide the ideal group size:
– normally somewhere between 4 and 12 people in each group;
– add 20% for no-shows.

Choose the categories of people to take part in focus groups:
– make sure that there are no great differences in status or any other feature that might cause some participants to feel nervous or insecure and so not contribute to the discussion.

Determine how long the focus group should meet for. Normally they take between half an hour and an hour and a half. Any longer than a two-hour maximum would overstretch people's powers of concentration.

Facilitation:
– do you need someone to chair the focus group and keep the group on task? The answer is probably yes. The person chosen will need the skills and confidence to be able to manage the task.

Focus groups are normally tape-recorded, with the permission of the panel members of course. Make sure you have a good-quality microphone that can pick up the voices of people sitting around a table.

Figure 4.1 **Setting up a focus group**

The Delphi technique

The Delphi technique provides a contrast to focus groups because it uses panels in a structured manner. It was developed as a tool for futurology. It can be used to develop a consensus about the likelihood of future scenarios. It can also be used to develop a consensus on any issue that involves judgement and competing priorities.

In its classical form, a panel of experts in the subject being researched is formed. It is not necessary, indeed it is not a good idea, that this panel ever meets. A set of options or scenarios is developed (this is the pre-coding bit) and written into a questionnaire that is sent to all panel members. The panel members complete the questionnaire by entering their preferences or their judgements about the probability of each scenario. They might think a scenario has a 10 per cent chance of coming true for instance, or think that, on a percentage scale, it scores 70 per cent as an outcome to be desired. When the questionnaires are returned, the figures given by the experts are summarised as averages. The results are then fed back to the experts, in a second-round questionnaire, and they are invited to reconsider their judgements and make a new return. The idea is that by going through a series of such iterations the experts may arrive at a consensus about the issue in question.

Questionnaires

The difference between pre-coded and open questionnaires is simple. The pre-coded ones have lots of tick boxes for respondents to fill in, whereas open questionnaires have a few open questions and lots of white space for people to make their responses in their own words.

Documentary research

Research using documentary material can also take an open and a pre-coded form. In an open approach to texts and documents the researcher may be trying to understand, for example, how rhetorical techniques are used to try to persuade the reader to a point of view. Look at Exercise 6.4 in Chapter 6 for an example of this type of analysis. Other open analysts may be looking for common narrative structures that are shared by many similar documents. Silverman (1993: Ch. 4) provides an interesting account of this style of analysis. In a pre-coded study of documents the researchers may well use electronic document files or electronic textual databases to count the frequency and context of the appearance of certain key words or phrases. Sometimes, for example, the popularity of management fads can be compared by counting the number of articles and papers (using bibliographic databases to do the counting) about them that are published. For example, as the number of papers on the learning organisation has diminished, so the number on knowledge management has increased, perhaps providing evidence that the latter is eclipsing the former.

Observational research

The degrees of openness or pre-coding that can be used in observational studies will be considered in more detail. This is partly because observation provides good examples to illustrate the differences between open and pre-coded research, but also because it may encourage people to use observation, which is a relatively underused method in Master's projects, more often. A number of illustrations will be given to explain the differences between open and pre-coded research.

Unstructured observation – a very open approach with a low degree of structure

At the open end of the scale, the researcher sits, watches and listens. If the researcher were interested in customer service in a doctor's surgery, they might obtain agreement to observe and then spend a morning's session sitting quietly in the corner of the waiting room observing. The researcher should try to keep alert to the events that happen. At the end of the session they should write down in a research diary all that they saw and heard and their reactions to it. They might need to discard the early observation because it would take a while for those being observed to lose their self-consciousness about being watched. Of course some researchers might use video or audio recordings of phone calls (if the research were being done in a call centre, say) to observe their subjects clandestinely. In the 1960s, when researchers were less ethically aware, a lot of educational research into children's learning and behaviour was done by filming children in classrooms through one-way mirrors. Great care needs to be taken with the interpretation of material gathered thorough open approaches. These issues are discussed in Chapter 5.

Checklists – a low degree of structure

A move away from open observation to a semi-structured form of observation can be achieved by using checklists such as the one shown in Figure 4.2. This example is taken from a much larger document designed to help someone trying to research the culture of an organisation by observation. The checklist follows the stages in a visit to an organisation. It begins with finding the building and the look of the building and proceeds in later

---

Some things to look for

Approaching the building

1. As you approach it, what does it look like, what does it make you think of?
2. What are the surroundings like?
3. Have attempts been made to improve the building's appearance?
4. What are the access and the signposting like?
5. How easy is it to get lost?

Etc.

The visual messages inside the building

1. What impression does the reception area give?
2. What sorts of furniture and soft furnishings are used?
3. How clean is it?
4. What sorts of things are stuck on the walls?
5. How recent and relevant are the posters and notices?
6. How are rooms labelled and signposted?
7. Are there any signs that users of the building have personalised it?
8. Do different ranks or types of users have different spaces – how do they differ?

Etc.

Watching and listening to people

1. How do people acknowledge or ignore each other as they pass?
2. How do staff speak to the public, clients, each other?

Etc.

Figure 4.2 An observational checklist

pages to include how staff talk to each other, whether they have their coffee breaks together and so on. The checklist is not prescriptive. The researcher is not required to answer every question in it. It is merely an aide-memoire to jog the researcher into noting the things they might be looking for.

Categories – a medium level of structure

A slightly more structured approach to observation would be to use categories. Some of the most famous categories for observational studies are used for studying the interactions between people in meetings. Bales' (1950) scheme of categories (Figure 4.3) is one of the earliest.

To use the categories, the researcher needs to sit somewhere where they can observe the participants in the meeting. As people make contributions to the meeting, the researcher classifies the interventions under one of the 12 categories of behaviour and uses the 'five-barred gate' system to allocate the intervention to the correct participant (who have all been given identification numbers). The researcher can subsequently analyse the range of behaviours used by different participants. Different categorical schemes exist for different research topics. It is also possible to develop your own scheme of categories.

Type of contribution	Person									
	1	2	3	4	5	6	7	8	9	10
1. Shows solidarity										
2. Shows tension release										
3. Agrees										
4. Gives suggestions										
5. Gives opinion										
6. Gives orientation										
7. Asks for orientation										
8. Asks for opinion										
9. Asks for suggestion										
10. Disagrees										
11. Shows tension										
12. Shows antagonism										

Figure 4.3 A scheme of observational categories
Source: Bales (1950)

If a more structured type of observation is necessary, a pre-coded observation schedule can be used. Rutter (1979) used the schedule shown in Figure 4.4 in a study of the impact of academic ethos on schools' achievements. This is only part of the observational schedule but it gives a flavour of the overall style. By observing the minutiae of school life the researchers were able to form a measure of the rigour of academic expectations in a school's ethos (or culture as we would more likely term it today).

Activity sampling – very highly structured

Perhaps the most highly pre-coded form of observation is activity sampling. This technique can stand as an example of the opposite of open observation. To use activity sampling, researchers have to identify a limited number of conditions that they wish to research and then define them very precisely. Let us imagine that it was important to make a study of the use of peripatetic teaching styles by university lecturers. In plainer language, this is about whether lecturers teach standing up or sitting down. To research how often lecturers are on their feet when lecturing and how often they are sitting down, it would first be necessary to define the two conditions. Would a lecturer leaning against a table, for example, constitute sitting or standing? When the definitions have been sorted out the researcher would then have to take instantaneous observations of the lecturer at random points in time. Typically a researcher would have a little

This is a list of some of the things the observers had to record when they observed a lesson in a classroom:

1. The number of pupils in the class and the number who arrived after the start of the lesson.

2. The number of pencils borrowed from the researchers during the administration of the questionnaire.

3. The number of children not in correct school uniform (as defined by the school).

4. The number of children in outdoor coats or anoraks.

5. The number of broken chairs in the classroom.

6. The number of broken or cracked windows.

7. The decorative condition of the room: one point was given for each of five items and a total score assigned to each room.

8. The amount of children's work on the walls, coded from 1 to 4.

    0 = none; 1 = one-quarter of available wall space; 2 = one-half of available wall space;

    3 = three-quarters of available wall space; 4 = all available wall space.

9. The amount of graffiti, coded using the scale shown in item 8.

Figure 4.4 A structured observation schedule for the classroom
Source: Rutter (1979)

electronic gadget that beeped randomly but at a pre-set mean interval. Each time an observation was made the researcher would record whether the lecturer was standing or sitting. At the end of the research period the observations would be tallied and converted into percentages. If there were 500 observations and the lecturers were found on their feet in 300 of them, then the general conclusion that lecturers spend 60 per cent of the time standing can be drawn. Activity sampling enables researchers to measure the use of time to defined levels of statistical accuracy (of which more later – see p. 204). There are many issues in management (for example, the use of expensive plant and premises) where it is helpful to know how time is spent.

Discourse analysis is becoming used more frequently in management research and it is based on the observation and recording of conversations within organisations. Most commonly researchers work from a transcript of the recordings and try to understand the processes of communication that occur within organisations. The techniques of discourse analysis are varied and range from classifying utterances into categories and counting their frequencies to much more open and exploratory forms of analysis. It is discussed in detail on page 185.

Deciding whether to use open or pre-structured methods

The choice of research methods, whether to use interviews, questionnaires, documentary sources, and so on, was discussed in Chapter 1, and the choice between open and pre-structured was anticipated. In this chapter the issue has been given a more detailed treatment because the techniques for designing and conducting the two sorts of research approach are different. There are a number of factors that should be taken into account when deciding which approach to take:

- If you do not know what kinds of answers you will get from respondents or sources, then you should take an open approach.
- If you are looking for new ideas, then adopt an open approach.
- If you want to quantify the research material, then it is best to use a pre-coded approach.
- If you want to compare the views and experiences of a great many people, then it is easiest if pre-coded approaches are used.

Planning and setting milestones

Collecting research material is time consuming, not just because it takes a lot of your time to do the work but also because there will be lost time, such as when you are waiting for people to return questionnaires, which can delay the project. Problems in carrying out the material collection phase of a project can be the critical factor that leads to a failure to meet the deadline for submitting the dissertation. It is a good idea therefore to plan this stage of the project and to set milestones that tell you when various parts of the research phase have to be completed.

Jankowicz (1995: 76) provided estimates of standard times for some of the activities you may have to do during the project. In the case of pre-coded, survey-based work, some of the critical items are as follows:

● informal pre-testing of a questionnaire by five respondents on one site – one day;
● reaching a postal questionnaire audience by mail – one week;
● time for respondents to complete a questionnaire – two weeks;
● time for questionnaire to be received back – one week;
● time to post, complete, return 'chase-up' letters and questionnaires – three weeks;
● transcribing questionnaire results into a database (20,000 characters) – five hours;
● learning how to use SPSS – three days.

Do not assume that open and unstructured research is quicker:

● preparing a ten-item interview schedule – one day;
● pre-testing the schedule on two guinea pigs – one day;
● setting up ten interviews and sorting out cancellations – one day;
● number of interviews a day – four (five possible but tiring);
● reviewing a recording of an interview and making notes – two to three hours;
● transcribing an hour of audio-recorded interview – seven hours.

In view of these time estimates the need to plan your research work is great.

● ● ● ● Exploratory research methods

Collecting the material

Exploratory research may involve the use of a battery of research methods – interviews, observation, documents and so on. However, interviewing is the most commonly used method in Master's-level research into business and organisations and it will be used to provide examples of good practice in open and semi-structured research. After interviewing has been discussed there will be a review of a range of more specialised semi-structured techniques that can be used in exploratory research.

Interviewing

To do research interviewing successfully requires as much planning and organising as any other form of interview. The main steps in planning interviews are:

- Roughly sort and list areas of questioning.
- Edit and prioritise questions.
- Consider the methods that will be used to analyse the questions.
- Decide on which questions are going to be open and which closed.
- Put questions into sequence.
- Check the questions for relevance to your research topic – do not ask questions that are impertinent.

The first stages involve identifying the areas you could ask questions about and organising them into priority order. It is never possible to cover as much ground in an interview as you had hoped. It is helpful to know beforehand which issues are less important and can be abandoned if time runs out. Once it is known what you want to find out, it is as well to check whether there might not be a better way of seeking the answers. If you want to find out about specific cases that might be embarrassing to the respondents, past strategic decisions that went wrong, for example, you might be well advised to find the material in contemporary documentary sources and so avoid the spin that interviewees will give to their accounts of past actions.

Even if the interview is going to be very open, it is worth considering using some pre-coded elements. In-depth and open interviews can be intensive. The occasional use of pre-coded questions, with perhaps the options printed on a card that can be shown to the interviewee, can provide a welcome change of pace and style.

Some questions have to be diplomatically phrased. In these circumstances it is sensible to draft the questions before the interview. Reading them from a cue card, at least until you have done enough interviews to memorise them, avoids any stumbles or lengthy circumlocutions. Finally, bringing the planning stages to an end, it is worthwhile considering how you want to analyse the material to make sure that you are asking the right questions to produce material that can be used in the way intended.

The next stage is organising the interview:

- Script the initial questions and any that are difficult to phrase.
- Check that the language you use is simple and unambiguous.
- Prepare an interview schedule.
- Decide upon the recording method.
- Pilot an interview with someone friendly and make any necessary changes.
- Select interviewees.

- Negotiate access.
- Arrange time and place.

It is useful to write an interview schedule that contains all the main points you want to raise. If the details about the interviewee, time and place of interview are also included, and if you leave space between the main headings where you can jot down notes during the interview, then the schedule can double as a written record of the interview.

In addition to any written note, the audio-recording of the interview should also be considered. I do not think I have ever had a respondent who refused to have the interview recorded. Some agreed only on the understanding that if they asked for the recorder to be turned off at any time I would do so. The trouble with audio-recording is not so much the interviewee as the equipment – inadequate microphones, expiring batteries, jacks inadequately inserted in sockets and so on. Digital voice recorders are a great improvement on tape recorders not least because it is not necessary to change the tape cassette half way through an interview. Digital recorders also have the benefit that the voice file can be downloaded directly from the recorder to a PC. Even if you are using a digital recorder you still need to make sure that you are using an appropriate microphone that is capable of picking up the speech of both the interviewee and the interviewer. Whatever type of recording equipment you use always check the equipment before the interview. If the respondent refuses to be recorded, or if the equipment fails, write up your notes as quickly as possible after the interview. Memory fades very quickly.

It is sensible to pilot the interview schedule on some friendly respondents before conducting interviews in earnest.

Whom you interview is normally decided by purposeful sampling. This involves identifying the people who have the answers to the questions you want to ask. Often snowball sampling is used to identify people to interview. This begins by using your personal contacts to identify respondents. The people interviewed are then asked to nominate people they know who would also be good respondents. The process then snowballs, collecting more and more interviewees until you have done all the interviews you need. Even using this method, finding interviewees and negotiating their agreement to be interviewed can be a lengthy job. You also have to negotiate the terms of engagement, the subjects of the interview, how the information is to be used, what guarantees about confidentiality are to be offered and whether there will be any benefit for the interviewee. This latter may be no more than a promise to give interviewees a summary of the research when it is written up.

The place at which the interview takes place needs organising. Often, however, you will have no choice in this matter. The respondent will want to be interviewed in their office, although this is seldom ideal. It does, however, have the advantage that people will be more comfortable in their own space and you may pick up interesting clues by observing their workplace. When people work in open-plan offices it is often possible to book an interview or meeting room. These are ideal because removing people to a neutral space can encourage them to open up and to challenge their own assumptions. In the end, choosing the place in which to conduct an interview is a matter of judgement constrained by practicalities. Ask people to turn off their mobiles during the interview.

Telephone interviews

Sometimes it is appropriate to interview people over the phone. The advantages are that you can often obtain access to people by phone who would never find the time to give you an interview. It is also an efficient method to find out how a number of people respond to a specific issue. If you wanted to find out what companies thought about Investors in People, then a telephone survey of local companies would quickly give you an overview of the situation. However, phone interviews have to be kept short, and it is not sensible to use them to ask questions about complex matters or questions that require detailed or long answers.

After organising the interviews the next stage is to conduct them. The interview should include the following phases:

- Explain the project.
- Offer confidentiality, anonymity and feedback.
- Explain the timing of the interview.
- Do the interview.
- Close with thanks – ensure there is an opportunity for follow-up.

Even if the interview is open or semi-structured it is still the responsibility of the researcher to manage the flow of the interview and bring it to a satisfactory close when the agreed time is completed. The means by which a researcher can control an interview through the types of questions they ask are listed below.

Steering a semi-structured interview

- Non-committal utterances and head nods.
- Repeating interviewee's last statement with a questioning inflection.
- Probing the last utterance.
- Probing the idea just before the last utterance.
- Probing an idea expressed earlier in the interview.
- Introduction of a new question on the same theme.
- Introducing a new theme.
- Summarising conclusively.

The researcher needs to employ the normal range of question types to understand fully what the respondent is telling them. Normally a section of an interview should be begun by the researcher asking an open question. An open question invites the respondent to talk expansively rather than to deliver a monosyllabic response. Sometimes a closed questions can be used as long as it is followed by an open supplementary. 'Should the company have agreed to the merger?' ... 'Why do you say that?' As the interviewee responds to the question the researcher should ask probing questions to explore areas the interviewee is skirting around and closed questions to check upon matters of detail. It is important to be aware of the respondent's body language. If the respondent begins to show emotion when giving their answers then researchers should use reflective questions. A reflective question reflects the speaker's emotions back to them and gives them a chance to talk further about them: 'So you felt very angry and frustrated at that point in the negotiations?' These questions are often restatements of what the interviewee said but are delivered by the researcher with an inflection at the end of the sentence that makes it into a question. When the topic has been dealt with, at least to the researcher's satisfaction, it can be closed, with the researcher summarising the main points of the interviewee's response and a question about whether the summary is accurate. Be careful in the use of non-committal nods and utterance (often no more than an 'Uh-huh'). They might seem non-committal to the researcher but they may convey to the interviewee that the researcher agrees with the interviewee's point of view.

Research interviewers should show enough vivacity and interest to keep the interviewee talking but should not give away too much of their own feelings and beliefs about the subjects under discussion. This is in part to avoid leading the interviewee to give the answer the interviewer hopes for. There is a danger if the interviewer reveals their position that the interviewee will adjust their answers to fit with it. It follows that when interviewing you should not express your opinion or challenge your respondent's opinion, except in so far as probing helps you to understand it. Neither should you give advice or express agreement with the respondent. This can be difficult as oftentimes the person is only too keen to enlist you as an ally in some internal battle they are fighting in their organisation.

The following bullet points identify some common problems with interviews:

- *Don't over-schedule.* If you try to do more than five interviews a day you will be so exhausted at the end of the day you will not hear what the final respondents tell you.
- *Make the interview with the top boss the dessert rather than the starter.* Do not start by interviewing the big boss. They will be impatient, and until you have talked to others in the organisation you will not know enough to be able to evaluate and respond to what the boss tells you.

- *Find a pleasant place for the interview.* The room in which you do the interview should be quiet and uninterrupted and have comfortable chairs if possible. Do not have a desk between you and the interviewee. It is often good to sit at 90 degrees to each other with perhaps a table or coffee table, sitting in the angle, that you can both put an elbow on.
- *Do your homework.* Find out all you can about an organisation before you interview people in it – search the World Wide Web to find out what is happening to the organisation.
- *'Please give me an example'.* Interviewees mostly want to give you opinions. It is essential that you ask for examples that back up interviewees' views with details of actions and behaviours. Otherwise you may misunderstand what they are saying.
- *Don't be afraid to ask the stupid question.* In my last research project, I found myself interviewing accountants. Not being an accountant I often did not understand what they told me. The natural inclination was to pass over the misunderstanding to avoid looking like a simpleton. But when doing research interviews you have to be prepared to look ignorant or foolish. If you do not understand, ask for more explanation, and keep on asking until you do understand.
- *The devil is in the details.* You do not understand anything until you understand the detail. This is especially true if you are asking about procedures, systems and channels of communication.
- *Interview a range of stakeholders.* Make sure you interview people from all the interested parties and not just senior management.
- *Three typical statements.* It is a good idea to have an interesting question to end on that gives the respondent a chance to summarise all that they have said. It could be something like, 'Will you give me three statements that characterise [the subject of the interview]?'

The end of an interview is often the most interesting part. If an audio recording has been made of the interview, the point at which the researcher declares the interview closed and turns off the recorder is the moment when the interviewee relaxes and opens up to the researcher. These last-minute insights should be remembered and written down as soon as you are alone.

Interpretive approaches

There are many devices (sometimes called projective techniques) that can be used to tease out evidence about how people interpret and react to their organisational and work worlds. Here are the main ones that will be discussed here:

- diaries/shadowing – a life in the day of …
- life histories

- storytelling
- metaphors
- critical incidents
- personal constructs
- deframing – videos, photos, thought experiments.

Most of these techniques can be used in the context of interviews, focus groups or observation. However, they are not all suitable for all projects. You could, for example, make a collection of the metaphors that people use in describing a particular aspect of their work or organisation by doing the following:

- observing and listening to them at meetings;
- interviewing participants;
- asking members of a focus group to think of a metaphor;
- analysing the documents produced at work.

These techniques and their applications are not fixed or rigid. They can be adapted to suit circumstances. You must use judgement to decide which, if any, might be helpful to your project.

The possibilities for the use of interpretative techniques are vast. The techniques listed above will now be discussed in more detail.

Diaries/shadowing

The use of diaries to gather qualitative research material has a long pedigree. In the 1960s and 1970s many studies of the managerial role were based on diaries in which researchers asked managers to record their daily activities. Sometimes these diaries were highly quantitative and recorded how time was used. In other cases they were narrative accounts of a day's work. It may be objected that the authors can deliberately distort the content of diaries. An alternative is to shadow managers. This is time consuming and merely moves the problem from worrying about the respondents' subjectivity to doubts about the researcher's biases. David Lodge's (1989) novel *Nice Work* gives an amusing perspective on shadowing.

Diaries are a favoured technique of participant observers. Donald Roy was an early user of the technique. He worked on a factory floor to provide research material for his studies in industrial sociology. He kept a diary of his experiences. The following is a brief extract:

> On April 7th I was able to enjoy four hours of 'free time'. I turned out 43 pieces in the four hours from 3 to 7, averaging nearly 11 an hour (or $2.085). At 7 o'clock there were only 23 pieces left in the lot, and I knew there would be no point in building up a kitty for Monday if Joe punched off the job before I got to work. I could not go ahead with the next order … because the new ruling made presentation of a work order to the stock-chaser necessary before material could be brought up. So I was stymied and could do

nothing for the rest of the day. I had 43 pieces plus 11 from yesterday's kitty to turn in for a total of 54.

(Roy, 1952: 432)

Writing one's own research diary, as Roy did, can be valuable. There can be practical problems in asking others to write diaries for you. They might not be inclined to give the time and care it would demand.

Exercise 4.1

Keeping a diary

Let us assume you are researching the management of meetings. Keep a diary for a number of days in which you record your impressions of all the meetings you have attended. You might like to note your thoughts on the following matters:

- the outcomes of the meeting;
- examples of good meeting management;
- examples of poor meeting management;
- particular behaviours by participants and whether you thought them helpful;
- clichés and jargon that the groups seem to be developing.

Life histories

This is a useful technique for eliciting qualitative information from managers and professionals. The respondents are asked to tell the story of how they got to where they are in their careers and organisations. Good examples of this technique can be found in Watson and Harris (1999).

Exercise 4.2

Timelines

Let us assume you are researching career patterns and the development of managers. Identify someone to interview and ask them to draw a timeline on Figure 4.5 that plots the highs and lows of their career. Once they have drawn it, ask them to describe and explain the high and low spots. If you cannot find anyone to interview, you could draw your own timeline.

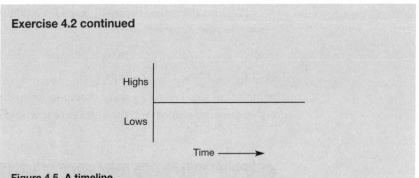

Figure 4.5 A timeline
The technique could also be used to research people's perceptions of the changes in their organisation's culture over time.

Storytelling

One consultancy project I was involved in concerned the introduction of performance-related remuneration in a medium-sized firm of solicitors. We devised a scheme for distributing a proportion of the partnership's profits to the partners according to their contribution and performance. One of the reasons the senior partners wanted performance management was because they thought many of the partners were more concerned with doing interesting work than with doing profitable work. This tension was identified by an analysis of the many stories that we heard the partners tell about each other. One particular partner figured strongly in most of the stories; but, strangely, he had different roles in them. In some stories he was cast as the villain, sometimes he took the role of the hero and sometimes he was seen as a fool.

The partner had developed a new line of business for the firm that centred around uninsured losses on vehicles. The work required little legal expertise. As it could be processed administratively, the cases could be dealt with in a high volume/low margin manner. This business generated the bulk of the partnership's profits. In a partnership, partners traditionally receive a portion of the profits in relation to their percentage ownership, not according to their efforts. So for some people the partner of whom all the stories were told was a hero because he generated profits that they all benefited from. But sometimes the other partners saw him as a villain because his indispensability to the firm meant he could blackmail the partnership into doing what he wanted. He would just threaten to leave the partnership and take the lucrative business with him. Other partners saw him as a fool because he had neglected his professional legal expertise and made himself into a mere administrator. An analysis of these stories confirmed the tensions that existed within the firm between those who took an entrepreneurial and commercial perspective and those who had a traditional, quasi-academic outlook on their profession. Stories and anecdotes can provide excellent windows into organisational cultures (Gabriel, 2000). Czarniawska (2004) is a very good introduction to the use of narratives in research.

Exercise 4.3

Heroes, villains and fools

This exercise is based on one developed by McClean and Marshall (1991). It is intended to help identify some of the key features of an organisation's culture.

Ask the respondent to recall a story, shaggy dog story, joke or anecdote that they have heard or told about the organisation. It must be one that concerns the organisation and refers to its personnel and habits. Ask them to tell you the story. Then ask them to tell you the following:

- what they think the moral of the story is;
- which of the characters in the story are seen as heroes, and why;
- which of the characters in the story are seen as villains, and why;
- which of the characters in the story are seen as fools, and why;
- what they think the stories reveal about the values and culture of the organisation.

Metaphors

One way in which you can discover the metaphors people use when thinking about something is to ask them to draw a picture or a symbol that represents, for them, the subject of the research. Some students doing a management project on managing the transition of school pupils from junior school to secondary school used this technique very successfully. First, they asked pupils who were about to move to secondary school to draw a picture of their new school. At this stage the pupils had visited the new school so they knew it to be a bright, modern building. Nevertheless, what they drew were dark halls – brooding, grey and spooky. They were again asked to draw a picture of their new school in their first week there. The pictures were still predominantly grey and grim. Only after three months, when they drew their final pictures, were the representations more realistic, light and cheerful. The team found that the drawings, through revealing the children's metaphors for their new school, threw much light on the problems of transition to secondary schools.

The same technique can be used with people in organisations. Respondents may be a little embarrassed at being asked to draw a picture and they may need a little encouragement. Alternatively you could use the 'If the organisation were an animal what sort of animal would it be?' approach. Students have used this successfully but I must admit I find this method a little toe curling.

Gareth Morgan's (1989) book *Imagin-I-Zation* is a good source for material on the use of metaphors.

Exercise 4.4

Images and metaphors

This exercise can also be used to gain insight into people's thoughts about their organisation's culture. This one, too, is based on an original exercise in McClean and Marshall (1991):

- Draw a picture that represents the culture of your department.
  - Avoid drawing an organisation chart; choose an image instead. It might be a jelly, a dustbin, a lumbering articulated truck or whatever. Trust your intuition.
- Identify the adjectives that the chosen metaphor or image suggests – slow, responsive, efficient, cold and so on.
- Then repeat the exercise for another department with which the first department interacts.
- Compare and contrast the metaphors that describe the two departments.
- How well do the two departments work together?
- Can the smoothness or the choppiness of the relationship between the two departments be explained by the comparison of the metaphors used to describe them?

Critical incidents

The critical incident technique (Flanagan, 1954) has a long pedigree in social science research. In a critical incident study the respondent is asked to think of occasions on which they dealt with the subject of the research and things went well, and other occasions when things went not so well. In one typical study, the researchers used the technique to discover the impact that Medline, a medical bibliographic database, had on doctors' treatments of their patients. They asked the following questions:

> I'm interested in recent Medline searches that were especially helpful in your work or that were unsatisfactory. I'm especially interested in searches that have had an impact on patient care.

> I'm going to ask you a series of questions about such searches, one search at a time. I want to know what circumstance led you to do the search, what the context was, what specific question or issue you had in mind, what information you wanted and why. I'll need you to be as specific as you can. If I don't understand the situation or certain terminology, I'll ask you to explain it further.

> (Wilson *et al.*, 1989)

More commonly, in management research, the critical incident technique is used to identify the critical job requirements that are the difference between doing the job correctly and doing it incorrectly. This use of the critical incidents can lead, among other things, to the development of competency frameworks (Boyatzis, 1982). As will be seen later in the chapter, critical incident information can also be analysed quantitatively.

Initially the technique was used as a means of identifying behaviour alone; but in modern uses an attempt is often made to recover the construction of meaning involved in the respondents' efforts to make sense of the issue. Ellinger and Watkins (1998: 228) describe this as a constructivist approach to critical incidents that aims to understand respondents' interpretation of their lived experience.

I have used critical incidents to research the following:

- Supervisory behaviour – 'Can you think of an incident involving managing staff that you thought you handled well/not so well?'
- Ethical dilemmas at work – 'Can you think of an incident at work that caused you a pang of conscience?'
- Evaluating management development programmes – 'Can you think of an incident at work that you thought you handled well/not so well because of things you learnt from the management development programme?'

There are of course many other possibilities.

Exercise 4.5

Critical incidents

If you were investigating an organisation's culture, here are some questions you might ask to elicit critical incidents. Try them on someone:

- Can you think of a situation at work when you knew what you would be expected to do but were unsure that this was right?
- Can you think of a situation at work when the novelty of a situation meant that there were no conventions or typical behaviours to guide your actions?
- Can you think of a situation at work when your values appeared to conflict with those of other groups in the organisation?

For each situation they can remember, ask the respondent to describe the following:

- the situation
- their thoughts and feelings about the situation
- what they did and why
- what others did
- the consequences and outcomes of the situation.

What clues do the incidents give about the culture of the organisation?

Personal constructs/repertory grids

Personal construct theory was developed by Kelly (1963). It is a theory of personality that concerns the mental models, representations or hypotheses that people use to make sense of the world. He termed these notions 'constructs'. Repertory grid was an interviewing technique he developed to identify an individual's personal constructs. The theory assumes that each individual has different constructs. The basic technique is to ask someone to compare three things – people, products, whatever – and to think of a feature or dimension on which they show differences and similarities. If you have nine elements (nine customers, for example), then you will go through the construct elicitation process for each possible combination of three from the nine. By going through a large number of comparisons, a map of a person's personal constructs can be developed.

If you were interested in MBA students' responses to different modules they are studying, you might present them, in turn, with a number of cards with the names of the modules written on them. You might randomly give a respondent cards with the following written on them:

| BUSINESS ETHICS | CORPORATE STRATEGY | MANAGEMENT ACCOUNTS |

The respondent is then asked, 'In what ways are two of these similar and different from the third?'

The respondent might reply that two involve number crunching and the third does not. The answer identifies a construct in which 'involves numbers' and 'does not involve numbers' form the opposite ends of the dimension. In this way the respondent's constructs are teased out. Sometimes you might want the respondent to focus on a particular issue. You could ask the respondents, for example, to identify what two modules have in common that makes them different from a third 'in terms of the quality of teaching'.

In the example given in Figure 4.6 the process is used to rehearse some constructs about different managerial functions. However, in this example the process has been simplified by using a comparison of two objects only to elicit the constructs. In Figure 4.6 the first column, which in practice would be longer, lists the objects (in this case, the management functions that are being studied). The arrows point to boxes in the second column. Each row is used to record the differences between two groups as indicated by the arrows. The first row compares marketing and finance people; the second compares finance and production personnel, and so on.

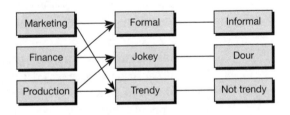

Figure 4.6 The basic mechanism of repertory grid

The second and third columns are used to record the extremes on a dimension that the respondent believes distinguishes people in different management functions. When I (acting as respondent) compared marketing people with production people I thought that fashionableness was something that distinguished them.

Stewart and Stewart (1981) is an old book but it contains a very practical guide to the use of repertory grid. A more recent guide is provided by Jankowicz (2003). In practice this basic mechanism becomes a complex and statistical process. It is best to use software to do the analysis. An introduction to repertory grid techniques and associated software can be seen at http://www.enquirewithin.co.nz.

In recent years the technique has been used, among other things, to evaluate training programmes and to identify managerial competencies.

Deframing

Deframing is a technique that, like repertory grid, assumes that people construct their view of the world through mental models. It is a way of distancing a person from their everyday experience. It requires them to look at something afresh; as if they were an alien visiting from a different planet. Video and photos can sometimes perform this role. As already mentioned in Exercise 2.2, I once went to a seminar on quality improvement in residential services for people with learning disabilities. The seminar leaders had been to many residential centres and taken photos of the buildings. They projected a slide of a room on to the screen during the seminar and asked the audience what they thought the room was used for. The room was large and light and cheerfully, if garishly, decorated. There were cuddly toys dotted about and the walls were covered with big posters showing chimps getting up to naughty tricks such as stuffing toilet rolls down the WC pan. The audience all said they thought it was a nursery. The truth was that it was a day room in a home for adults with learning difficulties. No doubt the staff had decorated the room with the best intentions to make it attractive to the users. But the photo was used to deframe the staff and to get them to see the room as clients and outsiders would see it. The photos were to help staff see how the room could reinforce damaging stereotypes that the adult users were just like children and were more trouble than a cartload of monkeys.

A common way of deframing is to look at something with fresh eyes. This is most easily done by making comparisons. Exercise 4.7 uses a comparison between perceptions in the past with current perceptions. But there are many other ways of making comparisons. Visiting similar organisations is an easy method. It forces people to challenge their own organisations because it reminds them that things can always be done differently.

Exercise 4.6

Construct elicitation

- Choose three elements.
- Elicit your constructs using the following grid.

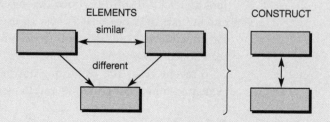

You can photocopy the grid to identify constructs from different combinations of elements.

Exercise 4.7

The newcomer exercise

This is another exercise that is based on one in McClean and Marshall (1991). It works because over a period of time we become used to the culture of an organisation and what originally struck us as strange becomes commonplace. It is only when we force our memory back to our first impressions that we realise what we have come to accept. As, by definition, culture is the values and habits we accept without thought, then this technique is excellent for making cultural values visible.

Think back to your first few days in your current organisation.

- What struck you as odd about its:
  - work practices
  - physical location and premises
  - patterns of relationships between people
  - values and priorities?
- How did it differ from your previous organisation?

Analysing the material

Imagine the situation. You have done your open-ended, in-depth interviews, you have carried out unstructured observations or whatever. As a result, you have a large pile of raw material in front of you. How do you start to make sense of it? There are two contradictory things people often discover about analysing unencoded research material. The first thing is *the law of the missing middle*. This states that students who move straight from collecting their research material to writing up the dissertation, thereby missing out the intermediate stage of sorting and sifting the material, tend to end up in a mess and a muddle. But, *the dilemma of drafting* says that researchers never really understand their material until they write it up. It is the process of writing that forces people to make sense of the material, and the significance of the material only emerges when sentences are put together.

If both of these premises are true (and they are only the result of anecdotal observation of students), then making sense of research material involves a repeated cycle of sorting and sifting, followed by writing, followed by more sorting and sifting, and so on. There are a number of devices that people use to assist them in this process (Riley, 1996).

- *Memos to self.* You write memos to yourself when you have a flash of insight (otherwise known as an epiphany or a 'Eureka! moment'). These can occur at any time, when reading, driving, interviewing, checking your research notes. It does not matter if the thoughts are fragmentary or incomplete. Jot them down informally and revisit them when you are writing up the dissertation.
- *Keeping a researcher's diary.* A researcher's diary is a very similar process to writing memos to yourself. It has the advantage that a diary is chronological and so you can use it to give an account of how your thinking has developed during the project. A diary is essential to anyone doing action research.
- *Imaginary letters to a friend.* Fix upon a friend who has no knowledge of your field of research and write them a letter in which you explain your project. Take it seriously even though you have no intention of posting it. The letter format makes you boil down your thinking about the project to a few interesting and short sentences. Because you are writing to a friend and not to an academic colleague, you will be forced to write in an informal, non-academic style. This should help to clarify your thoughts.

Coding

Before you start writing you need to draw out the usable material from all the stuff you have collected. The process for doing this has the formal name of coding. It involves identifying themes, dividing the research material into chunks or units (and excluding the great bulk of the interview material that you decide is of no value) and allocating the units to the themes. Essentially this is an indexing process. It can be done manually or it can be done using software (see the last part of this chapter – 'Software for analysing research material').

There is an important practical difficulty if your research material includes audio-recorded interviews. It is whether to transcribe the material or not. The problem is that transcribing a taped interview is very time consuming (see p. 166). The process can be especially slow if you are unused to transcribing and if you do not have the proper equipment. It is obviously best to conduct your analysis using transcripts of the interviews, but many students doing MBA and Master's dissertations will simply not have the time to prepare them. In this case it is perfectly possible to write a set of notes on each interview based on listening to the taped interviews several times.

If you have used interviews, and if you have transcripts of the interviews, you can go through the sheets using a highlighter pen, or by marking the margins in scribbles, to identify the themes that you think will be useful. If you have a tape and/or written notes, but no transcript, the simplest procedure is to listen to the tapes or scan the notes to identify the major themes or issues. In either case, create a sheet of paper for each theme and then listen to the tape again, or read the notes more carefully, and transcribe useful material from the interviews on to the appropriate sheet. Figure 4.7 shows one sheet from the analysis I carried out when I researched the role of district managers in a large service organisation.

The codes or themes can be identified by either skimming your research material, as already illustrated, or by reading the literature. You can also code for different things. For example, you could use substantive codes. Figure 4.7 uses substantive codes that concern the subject matter of the research. Alternatively 'code domains' (e.g. actions, meanings, relationships, settings, etc.) could be used. These relate to the levels at which the material can be analysed rather than the subject of the research. However the codes are defined, it is important that they remain open to modification and change. As the research progresses, understanding improves and it is necessary to modify and develop the framework.

Two other pieces of advice about coding structures:

● Organise the codes into a hierarchical order. This can be done using an 'organisation chart' form. This enables the researcher to show how some codes are subsets of others and allows content analysis to be done at different levels of aggregation.
● Use cross-references between codes. These are useful to make connections between disparate elements in the code structure that might otherwise be ignored. One simple way of doing this is to allocate units of material to a number of appropriate codes.

This might seem like a lot of work but it makes writing up the dissertation much easier. It is important at a stage in the project when deadlines loom. As you write each section of your findings, turn to the appropriate coding sheet and there you have all the information you need – the most common views taken of a matter, the extreme views, the juicy quotes – all ready for you to write up. If you have to continuously refer back to your original

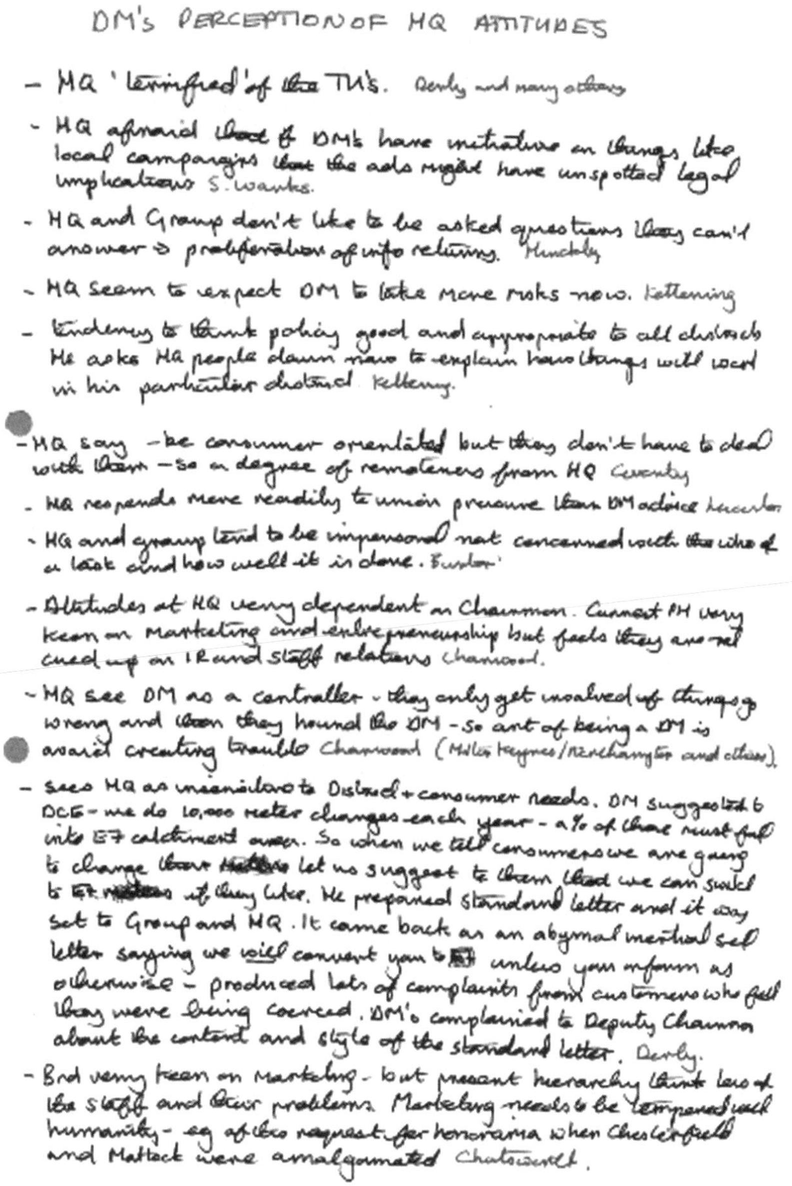

DM's PERCEPTION OF HQ ATTITUDES

- HQ 'terrified' of the TU's. Derby and many others
- HQ afraid that if DMs have initiatives on things like local campaigns that the ads might have unspotted legal implications S. Wanks.
- HQ and Group don't like to be asked questions they can't answer → proliferation of info returns. Hinckley
- HQ seem to expect DM to take more risks now. Kettering
- tendency to think policy good and appropriate to all districts. He asks HQ people down now to explain how things will work in his particular district. Kettering.
- HQ say – be consumer orientated but they don't have to deal with them – so a degree of remoteness from HQ Coventry
- HQ responds more readily to union pressure than DM advice Leicester
- HQ and group tend to be impersonal not concerned with the whole of a task and how well it is done. Buxton
- Attitudes at HQ very dependent on Chairman. Current CH very keen on marketing and entrepreneurship but feels they are not clued up on IR and staff relations Charnwood.
- HQ see DM as a controller – they only get involved if things go wrong and then they hound the DM – so art of being a DM is avoid creating trouble Charnwood (Milton Keynes/Northampton and others)
- sees HQ as insensitive to District + consumer needs. DM suggested to DCE – we do 10,000 meter changes each year – a % of these must fall into E7 catchment area. So when we tell consumers we are going to change their meters let us suggest to them that we can switch to E7 if they like. He prepared standard letter and it was sent to Group and HQ. It came back as an abysmal hard sell letter saying we will convert you to E7 unless you inform us otherwise – produced lots of complaints from customers who felt they were being coerced. DM's complained to Deputy Chairman about the content and style of the standard letter. Derby.
- Brd very keen on marketing – but present hierarchy think less of the staff and their problems. Marketing needs to be tempered with humanity – eg of the request for honoraria when Chesterfield and Matlock were amalgamated Chatsworth.

Figure 4.7 A coding sheet

research notes when writing up, the process is cumbersome and you are more likely to forget important points.

Content analysis

Content analysis is an additional step you can take when you have finished coding the material. It adds a quantitative element to the analysis of qualitative material. In a content analysis the frequency with which issues or themes appear in the material is measured.

David Silverman (1993: 165) provides an interesting example of a content analysis that is summarised in Table 4.2. He was studying the differences between private health care and NHS health care. In particular he wanted to find out how the relationship between doctor and patient differed in the two systems. He focused on ceremonial order. Two aspects of this order were whether a doctor opened a consultation with general conversation, to build rapport with the patient, and whether future appointments were made to suit the patient's diary. The research was done by observation. The consultations were recorded and then analysed. The frequencies with which the doctors chatted with the patients and took their prior appointments into account were coded, with the results that can be seen below. The use of percentages rather than words such as 'mostly' and 'infrequently' to describe the material gives the findings more punch.

Table 4.2 **Content analysis: ceremonial orders in health care**

	% occurrence of feature in private clinics (n = 42)	% occurrence of feature in NHS clinics (n = 104)
Appointments set at patients' convenience	36	10
Social elicitation	60	30

Source: Silverman (1993: 165).

Content analysis can be very useful when you have a large number of critical incidents to analyse. In a recent study I, with colleagues from Nottingham Business School, carried out a critical incident study of the ethical difficulties financial and HRM managers reported they experienced at work. A total of 240 incidents was collected. A classification of ethical problems was developed from the material in the incidents and then the incidents were classified accordingly. The results are shown in Table 4.3. In the case of this research, a content analysis is a very efficient method of highlighting the differences between the ethical problems reported by financial and human resource management specialists.

Table 4.3 **Categories of ethical issue reported by accountants and HRM specialists**

Problem type	Financial and accounting specialists (%)	Human resource management specialists (%)
Distributive justice	12.2	12.2
Economy with the truth	28.5	9.4
Confidential and privileged information	8.4	6.5
Conflicts of interest	6.9	3.7
Bullying and pressure	13.0	9.4
Bending the rules and ethical risk taking	16.8	27.1
Matters of principle	6.1	17.8
Giving and withdrawing trust	8.4	14.0
Total number of critical incidents	131	109

The difficulty with this form of content analysis is that the allocation of incidents to the categories is subjective. It is done according to the researcher's judgement. Other researchers might put some of the incidents in different categories. This is known as the problem of inter-rater reliability. One way of diminishing this problem is to ask several people to allocate independently the incidents to categories. The allocations can be compared and any incidents that the raters cannot agree upon can be excluded from the analysis.

Discourse analysis

Discourse analysis is a range of techniques and methods for analysing particular types of qualitative material, particularly documents and transcripts of speech. Tietze *et al.* (2003) is a good introduction to the approach. At some risk of caricature, discourse analysis can be said to be concerned with:

frames – the context of shared culture and beliefs within which communication takes place. Much of the focus of inter-cultural communications, for example, focuses on what happens when people from different cultural frames communicate.

genres – the form of communication practice. There are many types including speeches, jokes and emails. They all have their different rules and conventions. Some genres of course, such as email, are relatively new and rules and conventions are not yet clearly established. Such genres are often an interesting area to research.

discourses – the subject matter, topics or texts of communication. It may well be that in an organisation, for example, there are several contradictory discourses in play. It may be possible to research what happens when these discourses rub up against each other.

Exhibit 4.1

Email – a new genre

A discourse analyst might be interested to research how the development of a new genre might change the manner, tone and content of communications at work. It is estimated that 36 per cent of employees have an email address provided by their employers. As access to email and the Internet grows, so the ethical issues become more important. People are not sure what is acceptable and unacceptable use of their access to email and the Internet at work, as can be seen from the following news items. In 1998 an IT manager was sacked from her job because she had booked her holiday on the Internet, using the company's computers, during work time. In 2003 four lawyers lost their jobs at a top London law firm after circulating an email about oral sex among their colleagues; at some point it was emailed to a further 20 million people worldwide. A year later 10 clerical workers at the Royal Sun Alliance in Liverpool were dismissed after emailing a risqué cartoon involving Bart Simpson and a donkey. People have no control over

> ### Exhibit 4.1 *continued*
>
> what they are sent by email, and they may inadvertently, or so they will claim, download a pornographic image, for example. Even if they delete it immediately a record will remain, in this networked age, that they received the image. It might be difficult for them subsequently to disprove that they were simply an innocent dupe.

> ### Exhibit 4.2
>
> ## Discourses within the NHS
>
> Pollitt and Bouckaert (2000) have argued that changes in the NHS can be analysed as a conflict between a discourse of modernisation and a discourse of public service. The government's reiteration of themes such as modernisation creates a discourse that managers have to accept. As Pollitt and Bouckaert (2000: 18) pointed out, once the rhetoric of managerial improvement, known in the UK as modernisation, 'has gained hold, it can become, like other reform movements, a 'community of discourse' with its own logic, vocabulary and internal momentum'. Modernisation involves telling employees that they are valued at the same time as pointing out that their security of job tenure may be lessened, by changes in terms of employment or by their employment being transferred to a private company, for example, rather than, in the case of the NHS, downsizing. The suspicion, on the part of public sector unions, that such changes might be planned for the NHS were heightened by the government's intention, emphasised after their success in the 2001 general election, to extend the private sector's role in the NHS. Pollitt and Bouckaert (2000: 163) argued that such reforms could
>
> > destroy institutional memory, reduce the chances for survival of any 'public service ethic' and lead to a 'hollowed out' and ultimately less competent form of government. Here the basic contradiction is left naked for all to see, and the consequences in terms of morale and trust must be expected swiftly to follow.

Writing case studies and accounts

If content analysis or discourse analysis are not appropriate for your research material, it might be suitable to be written up as a case study. In a case study you give a narrative account of the subject of your study. You can draw your material from your coding sheets or your index of codes, but the skill is in blending it into a coherent story that draws together all the complex interactions and processual coincidences that constitute organisational life.

There is no commonly accepted way of analysing a case study. It is something that case study writers have to work out for themselves. This uncertainty is a feature of most qualitative research when compared with quantitative methods. In the latter case great effort has to go into planning the data collection stage (sorting out a sample, designing and testing a questionnaire and so on) but the analysis stage is just a matter of following a statistical recipe; in the former case preparation for data collection is not so complex but how to analyse the material after it has been collected is a far more complex matter. Various writers, such as Miles and Huberman (1994), have attempted to define a set of tools for analysing case study material. It is well worth trawling through their book to see if there are, among the illustrated, techniques that you can use for working up your case study.

- matrices and tables;
- flowcharts, logical dependency diagrams, cause and effect relationship diagrams;
- rating and ranking techniques;
- chronological presentation charts.

Yin (1994: 103–105) has defined two general strategies that can be adopted for analysing case studies, which he terms:

- following up theoretical propositions;
- developing a case description.

I will discuss the theoretical approach first. If, as recommended in Chapter 3, you developed a conceptual framework before you began the data collection stage of your project then the conceptual framework becomes both the guide for collecting your research material and the scaffolding that you use to write up your case study. In practical terms what you need to write up the case study is a set of headings and sub-headings and the conceptual framework can provide this. In the case study the concepts in the conceptual framework and the relationships between them become the headings in the account of the case study. Yin expressed a similar idea in a slightly different way. He argued that a conceptual framework should (in the theorising stage of conceptual framework building, see p. 133) lead to the identification of a set of theoretical propositions that speculate about possible cause and effect relationships. The account of the case study would then be written in a way that allows these propositions to be tested. A general term for this process is pattern matching and it means proposing a set of propositions that could be true; and then comparing them with the patterns of relationships that are found in the case study. A rather more sophisticated form of pattern matching involves testing out rival propositions or theories. There is a general discussion of the logic underlying these forms of analysis in Chapter 6 (pp. 321–323). If the case study has been researched without benefit of a prior conceptual framework then it is necessary to try to develop the propositions from within the case study material.

A descriptive approach to case study analysis is rather simpler but offers less by way of theorising. Description, even when compared with theorising, must not be undervalued. In some cases a descriptive case study can add greatly to the stock of understanding of an issue. When writing a descriptive case study the writer has to develop a series of themes and then use them as headings and sub-headings. I might, for example, write a case study of how a national pub chain responds to corporate social responsibility issues. The themes I would use to write the account might be as follows.

1. The company's corporate social responsibility policy and website.
   (a) Senior management's accounts of how and why it was developed.
   (b) Pub managers' perceptions of the policy and website.

2. Drinks pricing and promotions practices and the problem of binge drinking.
   (a) The national context.
   (b) The debates within the company about the issue.
   (c) How pub managers respond to the pressures of corporate social responsibility and the possibly competing demands of the performance measurement and management system.
   (d) The impact of the new licensing system under which, if a member of staff serves alcohol to a customer who is under age or drunk, both the licensee and the member of staff might be fined.

3. Staff management and employment practices.
   (a) Descriptions of good and bad employment practices.
   (b) Emotional labour issues.
   (c) Benchmarking against industry standards.

4. Strategy development.
   (a) How do senior managers and pub managers see the implications of the issues listed above for the developing strategy of the company?
   (b) What are the implications and issues for the industry as a whole?

The value of a descriptive case study lies in its identification of issues. In particular they can identify tensions and contradictions; in the case illustrated above there might well be tensions caused by the intentions of the company's corporate social responsibility policies being undermined by operational practices. There may also be contradictions between the views and values of senior managers and pub managers. Descriptive case studies can also be the basis of developing, rather than testing, theory.

● ● ● ● Survey research: pre-coded and structured research methods

Collecting the material

In this section the development and use of a questionnaire-based survey that is largely pre-coded, completed by a sample taken from a particular population, and to be analysed quantitatively, will be used to illustrate the use of pre-coded and structured techniques. The issues will be dealt with by going through the stages from deciding on the sample size to analysing the results of the questionnaire.

Sample size

The first question that worries people designing a questionnaire is 'How many should I send out?' Students' concerns about whether they can achieve a big enough sample are often a key factor when deciding whether to do a survey. As it is a critical matter, this question will be dealt with first. The answer depends on a number known as the limit or margin of error. The purpose of taking a sample is to obtain a result that is representative of the whole population being sampled without going to the trouble of asking everyone. The problem is that no sample can be guaranteed to be representative. If you could take a large number of different samples from the same population, some would overestimate and some underestimate the true figure. The margin or limit of error is a measure of this uncertainty in the representativeness of the sample.

You may not have been aware of the term 'margin of error'. But you are almost certainly aware of its importance. The US presidential election of 2000 provides a good example. In the opinion polls before the elections the results were often Gore 48 per cent and Bush 50 per cent. The margin of error on these opinion polls was +/–2 per cent. That is to say the percentage of the population likely to vote for Gore could have been anywhere between 46 per cent and 50 per cent, most likely 48 per cent. The proportion who would vote for Bush could be anywhere between 48 per cent and 52 per cent, most likely 50 per cent. The margin of error was the same or greater than the difference between the candidates. The poll results therefore could not be used to predict who might win. In the event, this proved to be a very accurate forecast.

The size of sample you need depends in part on the size of the margin of error you are prepared to accept and the size of the population from which you are going to take the sample. If there were 1,000 employees working in an organisation that you wanted to sample, and if you were prepared to accept a margin of error of +/–5 per cent, then Table 4.4 can be used to discover the number of completed questionnaires necessary.

The figures in Table 4.4 are the number of completed questionnaires you need to have returned. The number of questionnaires you send out will have to be larger. In the case of a general questionnaire, a return rate of 30 per cent would be very good. If the questionnaire was being distributed to employees in an organisation, it might be easier to chase up the questionnaires and then a return rate of 70 per cent or more might be achievable.

Sampling frame

To send questionnaires to people you need a list of the names and addresses of all the people in the appropriate population. Such a list is called the sampling frame. Finding a sampling frame may be a major obstacle. People are not inclined to give researchers access to mailing lists for free because the information they contain is valuable, and doing so may contravene data protection legislation. If you are doing the survey within an organisation, then the payroll is the most reliable sampling frame. Once the sampling frame is available, the normal process is to take names from the list randomly until you have as many as you need in the sample. This is known as probability sampling. It is the best form of sampling because all elements in the population have an equal chance of being

Table 4.4 Estimating margin of error on sample survey results

	Margin of error			
Population	5%	3%	2%	1%
50	44	48	49	50
100	79	91	96	99
150	108	132	141	148
200	132	168	185	196
250	151	203	226	244
300	168	234	267	291
400	196	291	343	384
500	217	340	414	475
750	254	440	571	696
1,000	278	516	706	906
2,000	322	696	1,091	1,655
5,000	357	879	1,622	3,288
10,000	370	964	1,936	4,899
100,000	383	1,056	2,345	8,762
1,000,000	384	1,066	2,395	9,513
10,000,000	384	1,067	2,400	9,595

Note: At 95 per cent level of certainty – this means that in 95 out of 100 times the true result will be within the range of the margin of error. There is, however, a 5 per cent chance that the true value will be outside of the range. It is possible to set different confidence levels. If a 99 per cent confidence level were needed, then many more completed questionnaires would be necessary.

Source: Saunders *et al.* (2002: 156).

included in the sample. It minimises the possibility of an unrepresentative sample. It can be a time-consuming process and so a systematic sample is sometimes used. This means taking elements at fixed intervals from the sampling frame, taking every tenth person on the payroll, for example. In the case of activity sampling (see p. 164), systematic sampling could be achieved by taking observations every half an hour, say. Of course, if the subject being studied had a natural cycle that lasted half an hour (taking a cigarette break, for example), then the sample of observations would be highly distorted. Quota sampling is a technique that aims to ensure that the sample is representative of the major groups in the population. If the proportion of women and men employees is 30:70, then a quota sample would try to reproduce this ratio in the sample. In practice it is difficult to achieve. You may send questionnaires to female and male in the desired proportions, but there is no guarantee that the completion rates will be the same for the two groups and therefore the final sample of questionnaires will not be in the correct ratio.

Many people doing Master's dissertations resort to purposive sampling because their problem is simply getting enough questionnaires filled in. This is a grand way of saying that the researcher puts into their sample whoever they can obtain access to or whoever they think may be appropriate respondents for the questions they want to ask. Students often have to resort to this technique for practical reasons. The downside is that the lack of randomness in the sample means that any calculation of the margin of error that might be done is unreliable.

One interesting development in the use of research questionnaires is the use of email and the World Wide Web to deliver questionnaires and to receive the responses. This is most easily done if you want to survey employees in a single organisation who all have access to email and the organisation's intranet. One colleague conducted a survey of employees' opinions about a new office building they had moved into. He was able to obtain the email addresses of all the employees based in the building and he sent them an email explaining what the research was about. The email contained a hyperlink to a World Wide Web page that held the questionnaire. Respondents clicked on to the link and completed the questionnaire on the screen. They were then asked to click on a button that emailed their responses to an electronic database (also on a web page) where all the returns were collected. This approach is more difficult to use for a public population because not all respondents may have access to email or the Internet and there can be problems in sending the results back to the researcher because of the different capabilities of hardware and software. Another problem of using email to return completed questionnaires is that the email will come with the sender's email address and so it is more difficult to promise confidentiality convincingly.

Exhibit 4.3

Software for creating Web-based questionnaires

There are many software packages available for helping you create online questionnaires. Here is one that was originally written by Andy Sutton and Kristan Hopkins Burke of Nottingham Trent University. It is called Autoform and details can be found on the World Wide Web at http://www.ntu.ac.uk/soc/projects/14846gp.html. Charges may be made for using it if you are not a student at Nottingham Trent University. The developers are producing a new version of the package that will have a different name but you will be able to access the new software, when it becomes available, through the same URL.

Autoform is designed for people with no prior knowledge of online questionnaires. The package is Web based so you do not need to download any software; you can create your questionnaire online. One great advantage is that Autoform produces data that is ready for use on SPSS. It means you do not have to define and set up the variable value labels yourself (a process that is explained on pp. 239–40 if you have to do it yourself).

Designing a questionnaire

There are a number of general issues to bear in mind when designing a questionnaire. They are all concerned with maximising the response rate:

- Keep the questionnaire as short as possible. Two or four sides of A4 paper would be good for research for a Master's dissertation.
- Design it to look attractive by using the capacities of your word processor.
- Give it a logical and sequential structure so that the respondent can easily see what the questionnaire is about and can follow its themes as they develop.
- Divide the questionnaire into parts that correspond to the various issues you are asking questions about. If you are going to ask for demographic information about the respondents (such as age, sex, job title or whatever), ask for it at the end of the questionnaire. People are more likely to answer personal questions if they have already invested time and effort in completing the rest of the questionnaire.
- Ask the easy questions first and the hard ones last.
- Keep any personal questions (as long as they are justified) until last.

Many students ask for too much demographic information in their questionnaires. They ask questions about age, sex, ethnicity, socio-economic classification and so on as a habitual response rather than from a genuine need for the information. There are two reasons for asking for demographic information. The first is to provide a way of checking the representativeness of the people who respond to the questionnaire. If, for example, an organisation that has been surveyed has 20 per cent of its staff working in technical jobs but only 5 per cent of those who completed the questionnaire hold technical positions, then it may be necessary to take this into account when interpreting the results. The second reason is to allow you to do cross-tabulations. This is dealt with later in the chapter, but in brief cross-tabulation allows you to enquire of the questionnaire replies whether people with differing demographic characteristics responded in a similar manner to the main questions asked.

Question formats

The next step in designing a questionnaire is to choose the question formats that are appropriate to the information being sought. A number of formats will be rehearsed here.

Dichotomous questions

These are questions that offer the respondent only two alternatives to choose between. These can only be used when the issue is clear-cut. To ask 'Is globalisation a force for good or bad in the world ... Yes/No?' is to reduce a complex issue to an absurd demand for a simple answer. The question is a large and difficult one and respondents may object to having to give a simplified response to it. The examples given below are appropriately set as dichotomous questions:

Are you   Male ☐   Female ☐

The law requires all employees to have a
contract of employment   True ☐   False ☐

Multiple choice questions

These questions normally provide respondents with a choice of three to five options and ask them to choose one. There is normally a final 'Other (please specify)' option. The skill in drafting these questions lies in giving unambiguous options that are mutually exclusive:

What sort of domestic animal would you choose as a pet?

Dog ☐   Cat ☐   Bird ☐   Fish ☐   None ☐

Other (please specify) ....

Checklists

These are the same as multiple choice questions but the respondents are allowed to tick as many items as they wish:

What aspects of the staff cafeteria do you think are unsatisfactory?

Menu choice ☐   Prices ☐   Quality of food ☐   Style and design ☐

Rating scales

These questions ask respondents to rate or evaluate a service, policy or option according to a carefully graduated scale. The respondents indicate the nature of their opinion by marking the appropriate place on the scale:

What is your opinion of the service provided by the call centre?

Excellent				Poor
1	2	3	4	5

The scale can be entirely in words. If you use verbal scales it is necessary to be careful in writing them. A sample of patients in a hospital was asked (Thompson, 1986: 95) to complete a rating scale question on the degree of boredom they experienced during their hospitalisation. Here are the results:

I was thoroughly bored throughout my stay	13%
I normally found something to occupy my time	66%
There was never a dull moment in such a busy ward	21%

The first and last statements in the scale were very extreme, of utter boredom or total exhilaration. It was not surprising that most respondents chose the mid point on the scale. The researchers redrafted the scale and gave it to the same respondents, with the following results:

I was quite bored during my stay in hospital	18%
Although I didn't have much to do in the ward I wasn't particularly bored	36%
I normally found something interesting to occupy my time	31%
There was never a dull moment	14%

This revised scale shows a much wider spread of results and differentiates between the degrees of boredom experienced by those in the middle of the distribution of opinion. These examples show how sensitive the results from a rating scale question are to the phrasing used in the scale.

It is possible, by using a technique called Behavioural Anchored Rating Scales, to attribute a numerical value to positions on verbal scales (Mohrman *et al.*, 1989). Such scales are often used in appraisal systems.

A further possibility is to use graphic symbols. You could use a smiley face ☺ to represent the positive end of a scale and a series of increasingly scowling faces for the other end of the scale.

Ranking questions

These questions ask respondents to put a number of statements or options into rank order:

Exercise 4.8

Verbal and numerical scales for rating

Jim Stewart

Step 1

Give a numerical value between 0 and 9 (where 9 = the greatest frequency) to indicate the frequencies suggested by each of the following words and phrases.

Often	...	Quite often	...
Always	...	Frequently	...
Sometimes	...	Rarely	...
Never	...	Almost always	...
Usually	...	A lot	...
Most of the time	...	Seldom	...
Occasionally	...		

Step 2

Ask a few friends or colleagues to do the same. Compare and discuss the ratings.

Suggested answer

The exercise normally indicates that the meanings of words about frequencies are not fixed and that it can be dangerous to use these words in rating scales in questionnaires. It is likely that you and your colleagues agreed that 'always' is 9 or thereabouts and that never was a '0'. However, the chances are that you and your colleagues disagreed about the values to be placed on the other words and phrases.

Indicate your order of preference for the kind of nursing you would like to do after graduation. Show your first choice as 1 and your least favoured choice as 4.

Acute care.....   Occupational.....   Community.....   School.....

Ranking questions are important because they are more useful for exploring difficult questions of priorities than are rating questions. If you wanted to find out which of five departments should bear the brunt of a major budget cut, then a rating question would probably reveal that respondents thought that none of the departments could manage with a swingeing cut. However, if respondents were asked to put the departments into rank order, according to their ability to bear a cut, most respondents would be able to discriminate between the departments.

Likert scales

These are a form of rating scale that is commonly used to ask people about their opinions and attitudes. The basic structure is to provide a series of statements, some negative and some positive in tone, and to ask the respondent to choose a position on a five-point scale between strongly agree and strongly disagree. It is this scale that Rensis Likert invented.

Statements	Strongly agree	Agree	Uncertain	Disagree	Strongly disagree
1. Training in office management improves one's promotion prospects					
2. Off-the-job training is usually too theoretical and impractical					
3. Off-the-job training is usually more like a holiday than work					

The straightforward way to use these questions is to analyse them one at a time. However, as long as the statements all relate to the same subject it is possible to use them to measure the overall opinion of an individual, or of a sample of respondents, to a particular issue. In the example shown above, the issue in question is attitude towards training. This is done by deciding whether statements are positive or negative towards training. Let us agree that statement 1 is positive and statement 2 is negative. It is then necessary to decide whether 1 or 5 on a five-point scale is going to represent a positive attitude. Assume the number 1 is chosen to indicate a positive attitude. As statement 1 is positive, a respondent who ticked 'strongly agree' will score a 1 and a respondent who ticked 'strongly disagree' will score a 5. Statement 2 is negative and so the scoring is reversed. Once all the statements have been scored, then a respondent's overall score on the statement can be calculated as a mean. If a respondent scored 20 on five statements, then their average, or mean, score would be 4. The researcher can then claim that, on a scale from 1 to 5, where 1 equals a positive attitude and 5 a negative attitude, this person has a score of 4 and therefore has a broadly negative opinion of the issue. If the scores of all the respondents are averaged, then the result is an overall and representative measure of attitude among the population surveyed.

The use of Likert statements to measure attitudes is only valid as long as the statements relate to the subject of the research. There are a number of reasons why this might not be the case. One possibility is that the researcher thinks that a statement relates to an issue but that many of the respondents see it as unrelated. Another possibility is that some respondents may see a statement as positive while others see it as negative. Statement 3 in the example shown is a case in point. Some people might think seeing training as a holiday a bad thing. Others might think it perfectly acceptable that training should be seen as a perk or a reward. If either of these situations is true, then the statement should be removed from the questionnaire because it is not a reliable indicator of the opinion being studied. There is a technique for checking the reliability of statements, known as Cronbach's Alpha, and it is available in SPSS (Bryman and Cramer, 1997: 63–65). An introduction to SPSS is given in the final part of this chapter.

Needless to say, interpretivist researchers find the whole idea of measuring attitudes laughable. They would argue that attitudes are too complex to be reducible to a single number on a scale. Billig (1996: 207–208) points out that most people are in a constant state of debate with themselves about their views on any issue and therefore their attitudes are subject to constant change and revaluation.

Semantic differential

In a semantic differential question respondents are asked to rate a single object or idea on a series of bi-polar scales. Each scale is formed from adjectives (words, which are a semantic matter) that are opposites (i.e. differential):

To me, electronic mail means:

Boring	---:---:---:---:---:---:---:	Interesting
Relevant	---:---:---:---:---:---:---:	Irrelevant
Exciting	---:---:---:---: ---:---:---:	Unexciting
Nothing	---:---:---:---:---:---:---:	A lot
Appealing	---:---:---:---:---:---:---:	Unappealing
Fascinating	---:---:---:---:---:---:---:	Mundane
Worthless	---:---:---:---:---:---:---:	Valuable
Involving	---:---:---:---:---:---:---:	Non-involving
Not needed	---:---:---:---:---:---:---:	Needed

As with the Likert scales the respondents' ticks can be given a numerical value and means can be calculated, always making sure that the scoring of the questions is adjusted to account for the mixing of positive and negative adjectives at both ends of the scale.

Open questions

It is nearly always a good idea to have a number of open questions in a questionnaire otherwise dominated by tick boxes. It is an irritation to people when they are required to respond to predetermined categories.

The provision of space for them to give an answer from their own perspective and in their own words diminishes the frustration:

	SA	A	U	D	SD	Comments
Tick box questionnaires are annoying	☐	☐	☐	☐	☐	☐

Open questions are vital when the researcher is interested in new ideas or novel points of view or cannot anticipate the likely answers.

There are a number of types of question that you should avoid. These restrictions mostly apply to asking questions in interviews as well as to designing questionnaires.

Leading questions
A leading question is one that, by its content, structure or wording, leads the respondent in the direction of a certain answer. Sometimes, as in 'Wouldn't you say...' the ploy is obvious. In other questions the leading is more insidious.

	SA	A	U	D	SD
Teachers should be praised for their managerial skills, particularly in view of the large class sizes	☐	☐	☐	☐	☐

Hypothetical questions
Hypothetical questions ask people what they would do in a particular circumstance. What people say they might do and what they actually would do are often quite different. Hypothetical circumstances are without constraint and so people answer them in terms of what it might be nice to do or in terms of what they think others believe they ought to do. It is at least possible that the overestimate of 12 million visitors to the Millennium Dome was a result of market researchers asking hypothetical questions.

Presuming questions
A presuming question is one that assumes something about a respondent. Frequently questionnaire designers make assumptions that the respondent will both understand and know the answer to their questions.

Drafting and piloting the questionnaire
If anyone manages to write a perfect questionnaire on first draft, it must be the result of sheer good luck. Most people draft questionnaires that are full of mistakes, illogicalities and howlers. The following is a good example of the mistakes people can easily make in their first drafts. It is about the staffing resources in a college of further education:

Are the staff that teach you (please tick one box only)

Male ☐   Female ☐

Half male/half female   ☐

More male than female   ☐

More female than male   ☐

It is just possible to see what the drafter meant.

The only way to prevent such problems is to pilot and test your questionnaire.

Distributing the questionnaire

Here are a few tips for distributing your questionnaire:

- Send out the questionnaire with a covering letter that includes a 'thank you' and gives instructions for returning the questionnaire.
- Repeat the 'thank you' and the return instructions at the end of the questionnaire.
- If the questionnaire is sent out by post include an SAE.
- Most of the paper on people's desk is white. Print your questionnaire on coloured paper. It will stand out and increase the chances of it being completed. Apparently, pastel colours are the best ones to use.
- Seek sympathy, but do not grovel. If you have sent the questionnaire to employees, many of them will have done courses that required them to send out questionnaires. Appeal to their sympathy for your plight to encourage them to fill in the questionnaire.
- Offer to send people who request it, perhaps by completing a tick box and contact details question on the questionnaire, a summary of the findings from the questionnaire.

Checking the margin of error

When the questionnaire has been piloted it can be useful to check the margin of error on the results. Each question will have its own margin of error and there will not be time to check every one. Choose an important question that gives a nominal answer, i.e. the answer can be expressed as a percentage. The following formula can be used to calculate the margin of error at a 95 per cent confidence level:

$$L = 2 \sqrt{\frac{p(100 - p)}{n}}$$

where L = the margin of error, p is the percentage answer to the question in the questionnaire (e.g. 30 per cent of respondents ticked 'strongly agree') and n = the number of questionnaires (the sample size).

Exercise 4.9

The attitudes towards staff appraisal questionnaire

Review the following fictitious questionnaire and identify as many mistakes and bad things about it as you can. Treat it as a first draft.

Survey into staff attitudes on the performance appraisal scheme

The organisation's Investors in People (IiP) accreditation is coming up for renewal. As part of the preparation for the visit of the inspection team this questionnaire is being sent to all staff to complete. You can return the completed questionnaire in the envelope provided to your line manager. The questionnaire is anonymous. When the results have been analysed it will provide the information necessary to show that the organisation's appraisal scheme is effective and supports our investment in you, our employees.

The questionnaire is also available on the organisation's intranet at www.skegmouthindustries.com/investorsinpeople/appraisal/survey/Ab2593602/responses/289993355/html. If you fill it in on the screen you can email it to the HRM department.

It takes just a few minutes to fill in the questionnaire and the managing director is looking for a very high response rate. Please tick the boxes as appropriate.

Part 1

1. What is your role in the organisation?

Top management team	1	Senior manager	6
Upper middle manager	2	Middle manager	7
Senior team leader	3	Team leader	8
Core worker	4	Casual worker	9
Blue-collar worker	5		

2. What age are you?

Under 12	13 to 15	15 to 21	22 to 30	30 and over
10	11	12	13	14

3. Are you   male ☐ 1   female ☐ 2

4. How would you describe your ethnic and cultural origins?

UK	☐	Indian	☐
European	☐	Pakistani	☐
African	☐	Other Asian	☐
Caribbean	☐		

Other (please specify) ....

5. Have you applied for a job outside the organisation within the last year?   Yes ☐ 10   No ☐ 11

Exercise 4.9 *continued*

Part 2

6. How many days absence have you had in the past two years? [ ]

7. Do outside interests take up much of your time?   Yes [ ]   No [ ]

8. Have you had an appraisal this year?   Yes [ ]   No [ ]

9. My appraisal was   Exceedingly helpful and beneficial [ ]

   Quite helpful [ ]

   A complete waste of time [ ]

10. Did you find

The preparatory documentation	very satisfactory	satisfactory	acceptable
The appraisal interview	very satisfactory	satisfactory	acceptable
Your performance ratings	very satisfactory	satisfactory	acceptable

How often do you?	frequently	sometimes	occasionally
11. Review your performance against targets and objectives	[ ]	[ ]	[ ]

	regularly	frequently	sometimes
12. Review your personal development with your manager	[ ]	[ ]	[ ]

	often	occasionally	rarely
13. Discuss your career ambitions with your manager	[ ]	[ ]	[ ]

Part 3 Please read the statements below; decide whether you strongly agree, agree, disagree or strongly disagree, and then circle the number below your choice.

	Strongly disagree	Disagree	Agree	Strongly agree
14. An effective appraisal scheme improves the organisation's performance.	1	2	3	4
15. The performance pay element of the appraisal scheme is fair and motivates me to perform better.	1	2	3	4
16. Without an appraisal interview my staff development needs would not be met.	1	2	3	4
17. If a peer mentoring scheme were introduced it would help me become better at my job and I would take part with enthusiasm.	1	2	3	4

Exercise 4.9 *continued*

Part 4

18. The appraisal system benefits me and the organisation because...
    (please complete the sentence in not more than 50 words)

19. What changes would you like to see made to the appraisal system?

Suggested answer

- The introduction to the questionnaire presupposes that the results will support the organisation's reaccreditation. This makes the questionnaire a series of leading questions because the respondents will know which answers they are expected to give.
- The instructions on what to do with a completed questionnaire are confusing. The lengthy URL for the web version of the questionnaire is far too complex for anyone to wish to type into his or her web browser. It would be all right if the notification of the questionnaire had been sent by email and people had only to click on to the hyperlink.
- Never suggest how long it takes to fill in a questionnaire. Some people will do it quicker and think they must have missed something. Some will take longer and think themselves 'thick'.
- The general instruction to 'tick the appropriate boxes' does not apply to all questions. Some require answers to be circled.

Q1. This is a multiple choice question but the options presented are ambiguous. Terms such as 'upper middle' have no commonly agreed definition. Other options (casual worker, blue-collar worker) could be seen as disrespectful. There is also a technical problem. The logic of the possible answers is hierarchical and it zigzags from left to right and back again; the numbers, however, proceed first down the left-hand column and then down the right-hand column. The numbers are unnecessary in any case. They are probably data input field numbers to help the staff who type the completed questionnaires into computer databases. However, they are of no relevance or interest to the people filling in the questionnaire.

Q2. The options provided leave out 12-year-old people and leaves 15-year-olds a choice of two categories to check. People over 30 years old may regard the options as a little insulting. 12-year-olds don't work.

Q3. This is probably acceptable.

Q4. The options in this multiple choice question are not mutually exclusive. A person might quite honestly tick several boxes; UK (because they are a UK citizen), European (because we are part of the European Union), Caribbean (because they were born there) and Indian (because they are Hindu and live by Indian social customs). The options do not cover enough of the range of possible responses. Several groups may feel less than pleased at being thrown together in the category of 'other Asian'.

Q5. This is the sort of question people may be uncomfortable answering unless they feel very confident of anonymity. The phrase 'within the past year' is ambiguous. Does it mean the calendar year, within the last 12 months or within the past financial reporting year?

Q6. It is most unlikely that the respondent will know the answer to this question unless it is very simple one, such as having had no days off. Questions ought not to be asked if it is suspected that the respondents will not know the answer.

Q7. This is an impertinent question. Both in the sense that it is not relevant to the subject of the questionnaire and because it is also a question to which the employer has no right to know the answer. There was probably some hare-brained notion behind the question, such as that people with strong outside interests will be less committed to work and will have a lower opinion of appraisals.

Exercise 4.9 *continued*

Q8. There is a phenomenon in the literature on appraisal known as the 'disappearing appraisal'. If you ask appraisers whether they have conducted an appraisal, they will answer yes far more often than the staff they are supposed to have appraised. The issue is whether different groups might have different under-standings of what appraisal is.

Q9. This question can only be answered if the respondent has reported that they have had an appraisal inter-view. The three options presented do not give a graduated set of responses to the question. The middle option is likely to be the mean position whereas the other two options are very extreme and are likely to occupy positions at the far end of the normal distribution 'bell' curve. In other words, the options are not very sensitive to the likely range of responses to the question.

Q10. This rating scale is so crass as to be unbelievable. I have seen it used in a feedback questionnaire on cus-tomer service in a hotel.

Q11. The rating scales in this block of questions are very loosely drafted so that the same words appear in dif-ferent places on a three-point scale.

- **Part 3**. This section uses Likert scales. However, the mid point in the scale has been left out. This raises a con-tentious point of debate in questionnaire design: whether it is acceptable to have an even number of points on a scale or whether it is always proper to have an odd number of points. The argument for even-numbered scales is that it forces respondents to take a view one way or another and this gives managers useful information. The argument in favour of odd-numbered scales is that most people take a neutral or a 'not sure' position on most issues and therefore the mid point of 'uncertain' on the Likert scale is necessary to record their position. As I heard someone say on the radio when talking about how he had felt when responding to a pollster's questions, 'What I actually thought is that there were points in favour of the thing and points against it and that both sets of arguments were open to questioning.'

  Apart from this general point it should be noted that the scale is presented 'strongly agree' first in the instruc-tions and 'strongly disagree' first in the places for the respondents' answers. This leads to a further problem. The Likert scale is presented in an order that is the reverse of that normally used. The normal order is given in the rubric to this block of questions but is reversed for the questions themselves. There is a danger that people might respond according to the anticipated, normal order and not to the actual order of the scale.

Q14. This question is tautological – an *effective* appraisal scheme can only improve an organisation's perform-ance: if it did not it would not be effective.

Q15. This is a double question. A performance pay element could be fair but not motivate, or motivate because it is not fair, or be both fair and motivating.

Q16. This question contains a double negative. This always increases the ambiguity of a statement or question. People often assume that if people say yes to a double negative question, then the opposite must also be true; i.e. if they agree with the statement in Q14 then they must believe that with an appraisal interview their development needs would be met. This is not necessarily so.

Q17. This is a hypothetical question. Seldom give credibility to the answers to such questions.

Q18. This statement belongs only in a quiz on the back of a cereal packet.

Q19. This is OK but there is not enough space given to answer it.

- **General**. The sequencing of the questions is wrong. The first questions should be about the subject of the ques-tionnaire – not, as in this case, about the respondent. Demographic questions about the respondent should be at the end of the questionnaire. There are in any case too many demographic questions. They outweigh the questions about appraisal. There is no particular reason that the questionnaire should be divided into four parts.

  The questionnaire is also unattractive and poorly designed. It would be nice if there were a 'thank you' at the end.

If you do not like formulae you can use the nomogram shown in Figure 4.8. Take a ruler and place it on the correct point on the 'number in sample' scale (using the 95 per cent confidence side of the scale); pivot the ruler until you have it on the appropriate point of the 'percentage occurrence' scale and read off the margin of error on the middle scale.

This formula, and the nomogram, can only be used on their own where the population that was sampled was very large or, what may be the same thing, the sample was less than 10 per cent of the population. They can, for example, be used for identifying the margin of error on activity sampling results (see p. 164). In this case n = the total number of observations made. As the number of points in time at which observation might be

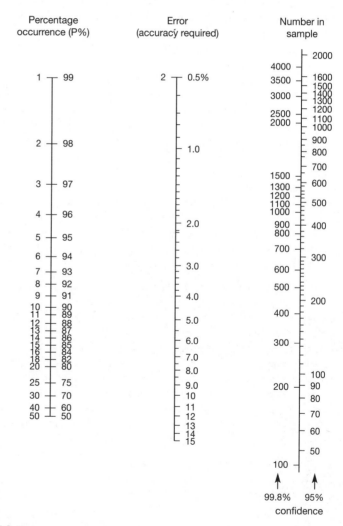

Figure 4.8 The nomogram

Source: Moore (1980: 250) and also Whitmore (1975: 126).

made is very large (you might observe every second), so we can assume that with activity sampling the sample of observations will always be a small proportion of the total time. However, with the kind of surveys and questionnaires MBA and Master's students typically do, it is quite likely that the sample will be a large percentage of the population, especially if the survey population is within a department or an organisation. There may be 400 employees in a department, for example, and it would be quite easy to survey more than 10 per cent of them. This is good news for MBA researchers. Where the sample is a relatively large proportion of the population the limits of error will be smaller than those suggested by the formula and the nomogram. Looked at obversely this means you can get the same margin of error with a smaller sample size. To work out the margins of error in this situation you add a correction element to the formula:

$$L = 2 \sqrt{\frac{p(100 - p)}{n}} \times \frac{N - n}{N - 1} \qquad \text{This last term is the adjustment element}$$

In the adjustment element, N = the size of the total population and n = the sample size.

If the margin of error is unacceptably high you will need to have more questionnaires completed to reduce it to a proper level. The following formula can be used to calculate the total number of questionnaires needed. You can of course also use the nomogram to avoid doing the mathematics.

Exercise 4.10

Margin of error

In a survey in a department of 500 employees, 200 completed questionnaires were returned. Of these, 48 per cent of the respondents strongly agreed with the statement 'Tea trolleys improve morale at work'. Use the formula to calculate the margin of error.

Answer
The margin of error on the result would be +/–5.5 per cent so the true figure will lie somewhere between 42.5 per cent and 53.5 per cent, most likely around the 48 per cent mark. If you cross-check this result with Table 4.4 you will see that it recommends that 217 questionnaires would be needed to get a margin of error of +/– 5 per cent.

The choice of an acceptable margin is up to the researcher, but +/– 2 per cent or +/–5 per cent would be conventional options:

$$n = \frac{4p\,(100 - p)}{L^2}$$

If the sample size calculated from the formula or read from the nomogram is a large percentage of the population, then the following formula can be used to calculate an adjustment factor:

$$\text{Adjustment factor} = \frac{N}{N + n - 1}$$

where N = total population size, and n = sample size calculated from the formula or read from the nomogram.

It may well be that the numbers needed to reach a low margin of error cause panic for part-time researchers for whom it may be difficult, because of shortage of time if nothing else, to obtain and process such volumes of questionnaires. One piece of good news is that if the results are highly skewed, for example if 80 per cent of respondents 'strongly agreed', then acceptable margins can be achieved with relatively smaller sample sizes. You

Exercise 4.11

Sample size

Assuming a margin of error of +/–5 per cent is acceptable, what is the total number of completed questionnaires that would be necessary to achieve it if there were 200 employees in the population and in a small pilot study 48 per cent had agreed with a statement and 52 per cent disagreed?

Answer

The total number of observations necessary to achieve a margin of error of +/–5 per cent would be 133. Let us see how this is arrived at. If you use the nomogram a proportion of 48 per cent (or as close as you can get it on the scale) and a margin of error of +/–5 per cent, this gives a sample size of 400 or thereabouts (the figure is 399 if you calculate it using the formula). As this sample size is a high proportion of the whole population – in fact, of course, it is much bigger than the size of the entire population, which is only 200! – you can apply the adjustment formula. If you put the figures into the formula you get:

$$\frac{200}{200 + 399 - 1} = 0.334$$

When you multiply the suggested sample size of 399 by the adjustment factor (0.334) it gives you a sample size of 133. If you check this with the figure suggested in Table 4.4 you will find it very close (132).

can discover this for yourself by using the nomogram. The minimum sample sizes given in Table 4.4 are 'worst case' figures because they are calculated on the assumption that the sample is equally split, 50:50, on issues.

Do not let trouble with margins of error put you off using questionnaires. The dissertation markers are conscious of the problems of obtaining large numbers of completed questionnaires, especially when the project is only part of the demands made by a part-time course on students who also have jobs to manage and friends and families to talk to. If the margins are low, dissertations are not marked down if you have made reasonable efforts to get questionnaires filled in and if you recognise the limitations that a small sample places on the results.

This section has concentrated on questionnaires as an example of pre-structured research methods. There are, of course, as suggested in the first part of this chapter, many other means of collecting quantitative material. You may have used activity sampling or obtained material from organisational or publicly available databases. The next section provides some of the basic statistical tools you might need to analyse the material.

Analysing the material: basic statistical analysis of data – *Diannah Lowry*

Introduction

'Oh no, not statistics!' we can hear you say. Do not be put off by the thought of statistical analysis. You may not be aware of it, but you are probably using statistical thinking in your everyday life. Any time you use phrases such as: 'On average I drive 65 miles a week' or 'We can expect snow at this time of year' or 'The earlier I start work on my dissertation, the better I am likely to do' you are making a (rough) type of statistical statement.

Statistics has its genesis in the somewhat contentious philosophical view that our observations of the world can never be totally accurate. Statistics thus arises out of 'caution in the face of uncertainty' (Rowntree, 1991:18), and enables us to estimate the extent of our errors when making observations and generalisations.

Moreover, statistics is not an invention of the so-called 'modern' era. Statistical thinking in one form or another has been around throughout the ages. The Old Testament tells us that the pharaohs of Ancient Egypt had a keen interest in collecting data about how many people they had available to build pyramids and fight wars, and how much wealth they could extract in taxation. Domesday Book assembled for William the Conqueror is another example of a compendium of statistics about the population and available resources. Statistics also has some origins in gambling. In the seventeenth century the French mathematician Blaise

Pascal tried to assist a gambling friend to 'figure out the odds' on the dice table. Such musings resulted in 'the theory of probability', a theory that has since revealed its explanatory and predictive powers in diverse areas such as business, astronomy, genetics and even warfare.

The examples of statistical thinking described above reveal two different types of statistical thought. The statement 'On average I drive 65 miles a week' is essentially descriptive. The statements 'We can expect snow at this time of year' and 'The earlier I start my dissertation, the better I will do' go beyond description and infer what is likely to happen in the future. There is thus a distinction between *descriptive statistics* and *inferential statistics*. The former is concerned with generalising from a sample, whereas the latter is concerned with generalising from a sample to make estimates and inferences about a wider population. How safe is it to make generalisations from a part to a whole? This is what statistics is all about: quantifying the probability of error. It is this issue that is covered below. Bear in mind that this is a section on *basic* statistical analysis, and is therefore confined in its scope to the forms of analysis you may wish to undertake. We do not expect you to become statistical masters as a result of conducting a single piece of research. If you require more detail in any of the areas discussed, feel free to consult a more in-depth guide to statistical procedures.

Now, take a breath and *relax* – it's really not that hard!

Types of variable

Samples are made up of individuals. The individuals (or 'members') in the sample may be humans, squirrels, pay rates, alcoholic beverages or whatever. All members of the sample will share some common attribute or characteristic we are interested in. In the case of employees, we may be interested in salary level, level of job satisfaction, hours worked, number of hours spent training, etc. Furthermore, each member will differ from one or more of the others on these characteristics. In looking at members of a sample we ask how they *vary* among themselves on one or more of such characteristics. Because of the variation among members, such characteristics are called variable characteristics or, more simply, **variables**.

Suppose you are thinking of purchasing a second-hand car. Can you list some of the variables that you would consider in choosing a vehicle? No doubt you would consider some or all of the following as variables of interest:

- price
- make (e.g. Peugeot, Fiat, Rover, Toyota)
- type (e.g. estate, four-wheel drive, soft top)
- colour

- age
- condition (excellent, acceptable, poor)
- mileage
- transmission type (automatic or manual)
- size of engine.

How do you evaluate each individual car, in the sample available to us, in terms of these variables? This depends on the *type* of variable.

With variables such as price, age, mileage and size of engine we are looking at quantity variables. Such variables can be either *discrete* or *continuous*.

A *discrete* variable is one in which the possible values are clearly separated from one another. Take family size for example: a family can have one child, or two or three, etc., but it cannot have 2.5 or 3.75.

Continuous variables, however, do have possible values between them. Take the variable of height as an example. A child may be three feet high this year and three feet six inches next year. In the meantime, however, they will have not just been three feet one inch and three feet two inches, but an infinite number of heights in between: 3.0001 feet … 3.00015 feet … and so on.

Discrete variables imply counting, whereas *continuous* variables require a measurement system. Now, let us go back to the variables involved in the purchase of a second-hand car. Among our car variables 'price' is discrete, since the asking price of the vehicle could be £4000.00 or for some incredibly unlikely reason it may be £4000.01; but there is no possible price between these two, or between any other two that are more than 1 pence apart. Also, given the car registration system in the United Kingdom, 'age' could also be considered a discrete variable (all 'G'-registered cars are 1990 models, etc.). Size of engine is also a discrete variable – 1.4 litre engines are distinct from 1.6 litre engines, and so on. Mileage, on the other hand, is *continuous*: the mileage may be 30,000 or 120,000 miles or an infinite number of possible miles in between.

With a variable such as 'make of car' we set up categories, e.g. Toyota, Rover, Peugeot and so on. Then we categorise each car simply by noting its name. This type of variable is called a category variable. A *category* variable such as 'make of car' is sometimes called a *nominal* variable (from the Latin *nominalis* = of a name). Other variables listed above include 'type of car', 'colour' and 'transmission type' and these are also category variables (they are also *nominal* variables).

You may have considered 'condition of car' to be a category variable, and indeed it is, since there are three categories of condition mentioned: excellent, acceptable and poor. This is, however, a different type of category variable. Since the categories can be ordered according to condition, this type of category variable is called an *ordinal* variable.

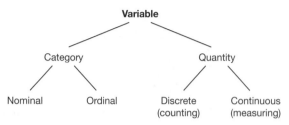

Figure 4.9 Types of data

Figure 4.9 summarises the types of variables discussed here.

As you shall soon see, different variable types require different statistical analysis, the main difference being between category and quantity variables. Before we move on, however, it is important to note that data about quantity variables *can* be converted into category data. For example, cars under 1.4 litres can be converted into 'small engine capacity', those between 1.6 litres and 1.8 litres as 'medium engine capacity', while anything over 2 litres could be categorised as 'large engine capacity'. The drawback to this sort of method is that loss of information occurs. If the numbers in each category are recorded, we lose data about exact (actual) information. This sort of sacrifice is sometimes worthwhile in order to make data easier to handle. However, the sacrifice should not be made without weighing up the pros and cons.

There is another important aspect in analysing variables. You will need to differentiate between the *independent* variable(s) and the *dependent* variable(s). The dependent variable is the variable of interest to you in your research question. Suppose, for example, that you were researching pay differentials between full-time employees and part-time employees. In this study the variable of interest is amount of salary, and this is then the *dependent* variable. It is dependent on employment status; hence employment status is termed the *independent* variable in this particular piece of research. Your software package will ask you to identify your independent and dependent variables in the course of the statistical tests you choose to use.

Summarising data and making them useful

Available software packages these days make it easy to summarise large amounts of data in diagrammatic form. For example, the most common methods of summarising categorical data include tables, histograms and pie charts. Excel and SPPS can easily facilitate these summary statistics. However, you will need to become acquainted with the software of your choice in order to produce the diagrams. Do not be concerned – these sophisticated packages include 'tutorial sessions' that clearly demonstrate how to generate the desired summary.

Summarising categorical data

Tables display data either in their 'raw' form or in percentages. From a table, it is often possible to determine the 'mode' of the sample. The mode of a distribution is the category that occurs with the greatest frequency. It is the most 'fashionable' or popular value. For example, size 7 is the mode, or modal value, in women's shoes – it is the size that most shoe shops sell in the greatest quantity.

Histograms and pie charts provide a diagrammatic view of differences in proportions. An example of a histogram is provided in Figure 4.10.

Histograms are particularly useful if you wish to compare one category with another (by comparing the heights of the columns). However, if you wish to compare each category (piece) with the total, a pie chart is more illustrative. An example of a pie chart is provided in Figure 4.11. There is a tendency to overuse pie charts in dissertations. If half the respondents to a questionnaire are male and the other half female, a pie chart illustrating the fact adds little.

Summarising quantitative data

The techniques for summarising quantitative data include the methods of determining measures of central tendency, as well as measures of dispersion. Statistical packages will calculate these measures for you. Measures of central tendency include the median and mean, while measures of dispersion include the range and standard deviation. Lets look at these a little more closely, without going into too much mathematical detail.

The median value (from the Latin for 'middle') is a kind of representative value that indicates the centre of a distribution. The median is the value that splits the distribution of data into half. There should be as many observed values greater than the median as there are less. Thus, if the following were the number of miles driven by seven postgraduate students per week:

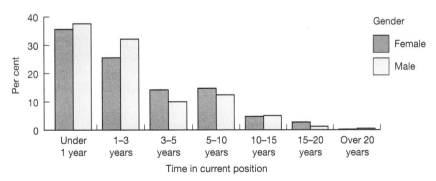

Figure 4.10 **Time in current position by gender**

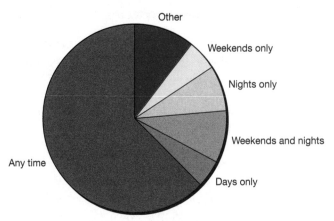

Figure 4.11 Availability for work of casual employees

| 0 | 16 | 18 | 20 | 33 | 48 | 68 |

the median here would be 20 (miles per week). That is the value with equal numbers of observations greater and lesser. When the number of observed values is even, the median is quoted as the value halfway between the two middle values. Thus, if our sample looked like this:

| 0 | 16 | 18 | 20 | 33 | 48 |

the median here would be halfway between 18 and 20 $(18 + 20)/2 = 19$; and 19 is thus the value that has equal numbers either side of it (even though no student actually drove just 19 miles).[1]

A more commonly quoted representative value is the arithmetic mean. As you are probably aware, the mean is simply the average of the sample. It is calculated by adding together all the observed values and dividing by the number of observations. As a measure of central tendency, the mean has an advantage since it is usually stable from one sample to another. However, if there are extreme outliers (see footnote), these extreme values will distort the mean. In such cases the median is preferred as a measure of central tendency.

The *range* is an elemental form of a measure of dispersion. It is a simple calculation where the lowest value is subtracted from the highest value. While it is a simple measure to calculate, we cannot put too much faith in it. It depends on just two values – the two most extreme cases. These may be outliers, and not typical of the sample. Thus, the range may provide a distorted view of the sample.

---

[1] The median is a good way of summarising data when there are a few extreme (high or low) values observed (these are termed 'outliers'). Their effect would be to distort the mean.

A more comprehensive measure of dispersion is the *standard deviation* of the sample. Identifying the standard deviation is a way of indicating a sort of 'average' amount by which values deviate from the mean. The greater the dispersion, the bigger the deviations and the bigger the standard deviation of the mean. Consider the following sets of values:

(a)   6   24   37   49   64   (mean = 36)

(b)   111   114   117   118   120   (mean = 116)

The values in (a) are more dispersed (i.e. they deviate more from the mean) than those in (b), so it is likely that the standard deviation is larger. Let us see why, by calculating how each value in (b) differs from the mean of 116:

Value:	111	114	117	118	120
Deviation from 116:	–5	–2	+1	+2	+4

We cannot take an average of these deviations, since there are negative values. In order to overcome this, we square each deviation, and thus get rid of the minus signs:

Deviations:	–5	–2	+1	+2	+4
Squared deviation:	25	4	1	4	16

The mean of these squared deviations is called the **variance**:

Variance = (25 + 4 + 1 + 4 + 16)/5 =50/5 = 10

The variance is a measure with some good uses. However, if the original values were, say, 'heartbeats per minute', then the variance would be so many 'square heartbeats per minute'! So, in order to get the measure of dispersion back into the same units as the observed values (and the measures of central tendency), we take the square root of the variance – and this is termed the **standard deviation**:

Standard deviation of distribution (b) = $\sqrt{10}$ = 3.16

The same process of calculation for (a) above reveals a standard deviation of 20. We can thus comment that the distribution of (a) is much more dispersed.

The remaining discussion on significance and specific statistical techniques is, at best, basic and brief. The intention here is not to overwhelm you with statistical theory or formulae. The remaining sub-sections merely serve to introduce you to some of the issues and methods you may like to consider in analysing your data. As stated above, you will need to supplement the materials provided here with reference to slightly more detailed texts on statistical methods, or alternatively consult the handbook that accompanies your statistics software package of choice.

Comparing samples and tests of significance

It may be the case that you wish to compare two or more samples in your research. Suppose, for example, you were interested in comparing the annual salaries of permanent and part-time workers. You may do this by comparing the mean salaries of each group. However, how do we know whether the mean salaries are *significantly* different from each other? In statistical thinking, 'significant' does not just mean 'interesting' or 'important'. A significant difference is one that signifies a real difference in populations. We will get back to this point in a minute. For now, we must consider another concept.

Researchers are expected to be cautious, and they have thus developed a cautious convention. The convention is that we test for a significant difference by asking: 'Could it be that the difference is *not* significant?' So we start out by assuming there is *no* real difference between the salary levels of permanent and part-time employees. This assumption or hypothesis is called the **null hypothesis**. This hypothesis is under attack in all research. If the difference between means turns out to be too big to be explained away as chance variation, then we must reject the null hypothesis, and we must replace it with an alternative hypothesis. The alternative hypothesis is that there is a difference between the salary levels of permanent and part-time employees.

Now, we may further hypothesise that permanent employees receive higher annual salaries than part-timers. If we are testing this, we have a *directional* research question. We are suggesting a direction of findings. This type of testing involves a one-tailed test, and you must select this option on your software package in your process of analysis. I will not go into the mathematics of one-tailed tests – it is beyond the scope of this discussion. Just remember to choose the option in your analysis. If, however, you are not suggesting any direction in your research question (i.e. suggesting the results could go either way), you will need to use the two-tailed test option in your computer analysis.

Let us get back to that somewhat significant matter of 'significance testing'. It was stated earlier that a significant difference shows a real difference in populations. But how big does a difference have to be in order to be considered significant?

The two common cut-off points in statistical analysis are the 5 per cent level and the 1 per cent level (written as 0.05 level and 0.01 level). This type of information will be displayed in the results of your computer analysis on your statistical software. A difference is less significant at the 0.05 level than at the 0.01 level. Any result of a test of significance greater than 0.05 would result in acceptance of the null hypothesis (i.e. there is no difference between the samples). A difference at 0.05 is called 'significant', while a difference at 0.001 is called 'highly significant' (both lead to acceptance of the alternative hypothesis, i.e. there is a difference between the samples).

Statistical tests for quantitative data

Comparing two means – the t-test

If you have two groups and you would like to test the difference in their mean scores, an appropriate test is the t-test. This test of means will be included as a simple option (just click the option) in your statistical software package and as such the rather complicated formula underlying the test statistic will not be included in this discussion. (Refer to a statistics text if you require the mathematical logic and formula underlying the test.) Suppose, for example, that a researcher wants to test the different levels of job satisfaction (converted into quantitative data) between permanent and casual employees. The t-test would be an appropriate test in this case. Your computer will provide you with a t-statistic and a significance level. Remember, if the significance level is 0.05 or less you can reject the null hypothesis, and conclude that one group does differ from the other in terms of job satisfaction.

Comparing several means – ANOVA (F-statistic)

Let us say the same researcher wanted to compare three groups in terms of their job satisfaction – permanent employees, fixed-term contract employees and casual employees. In this case, with more than two groups, the t-test cannot be used. Instead we use what is called an analysis of variance test (or ANOVA). As the name suggests, the test involves comparing variances to make inferences about the means. The logic of this test goes something like this: the variance of the means of the three groups will be large if the groups differ from each other in terms of satisfaction level. If the variance *within* groups is compared with the variance *between* groups, it can be determined whether the means are significantly different. You *are* lucky that your computer will do all this for you! The ANOVA test results in what is called the F-statistic (named after the British statistician R.A. Fisher). The larger the ratio of variance, the greater the value of the F-statistic. A high F-statistic usually indicates that the results are significant. Once again, however, your computer will provide you with significance levels. Remember, if the significance level is 0.05 or less you can reject the null hypothesis, and conclude that the groups differ in terms of job satisfaction.

Analysing relationships – correlations

Correlation analysis is a measure of association (relationship) between two or more variables, and is calculated from standardised measures of

Figure 4.12 Positive correlation

covariance (but do not worry too much about this latter piece of information). There are three kinds of correlation: positive, negative and zero. With **positive correlation** changes in one variable are accompanied by changes in the other variable and in the *same direction*. In other words, larger values in one variable tend to go with larger values in the other. This is illustrated in the scatter diagram shown in Figure 4.12.

However, in equally strong relationships, the two variables change in the *opposite* directions. Larger values on one will tend to go with smaller values on the other. This is called a **negative correlation**. For example, there may be a negative correlation between age and willingness to learn about statistics within a group of students, i.e. younger students may be more willing to learn about statistics, and older students may be less willing to do so.

If there were no clear tendency for the values on one variable to move in a particular direction (up or down) with changes on another variable, then it could be said that we are approaching a **zero correlation**. For example, the relationship between age and height of female postgraduate students may well approach zero correlation. A zero correlation is illustrated in the scatter diagram of Figure 4.13.

As alluded to above, correlations vary not only according to direction (+ or −) but also in strength. Your computer will calculate a numerical measure to indicate strength of the relationship, and this is called the **correlation coefficient**. It is represented by the letter r. The correlation coefficient (r) cannot lie outside the range between −1 and +1. Those two values of r represent, respectively, perfect negative and perfect positive correlation. When $r = 0$ there is no correlation at all. The closer the correlation gets to +1 or −1 the stronger the correlation; the closer it gets to 0 the weaker it is. Table 4.5 is a rough guide to interpreting correlation coefficients.

Your computer package will be able to display a correlation matrix for you if you are investigating the correlation between a number of variables. An example of a correlation matrix is provided in Table 4.6.

Figure 4.13 **Zero correlation**

Table 4.5 **Interpreting correlation coefficients**

Correlation coefficient	Strength
0.0 to 0.2	Very weak, negligible
0.2 to 0.4	Weak, low
0.4 to 0.7	Moderate
0.7 to 0.9	Strong, high, marked
0.9 to 1.0	Very strong, very high

Source: Rowntree (1991:170).

To illustrate correlation from Table 4.6, management skills is related to promotion satisfaction, organisational commitment is related to management skills, and organisational commitment is related to job satisfaction.

A serious word of caution needs to be included here: correlation does *not* imply causation. If variables X and Y are correlated, this may be because X causes Y, or because Y causes X, or because some other variable is affecting both X and Y, or for a mixture of these reasons, or the whole relationship may be a coincidence.

This perhaps requires further explanation. Consider the following: no matter how highly correlated the rooster's crow is to the rising sun, the rooster does not cause the sun to rise. Another example is that it has been found that there is a high correlation between lecturers' salaries and alcohol consumption over a number of years. This does not indicate that lecturers drink, nor does it indicate that the sale of alcohol increases lecturers salaries. A more likely explanation is that both salaries and alcohol *co-vary* because they are *both* influenced by growth in national income and/or population. So, variables can be statistically related, but not causally related (when this is the case, they are usually termed *spuriously related*).

Table 4.6 Correlation matrix of size, location and work context factors with satisfaction, organisational commitment, intent to stay and performance commitment

	1	2	3	4	5	6	7	8	9	10	11	12	13
1. Size	1.0												
2. Location	.07	1.0											
3. Work scheduling	.14	.01	1.0										
4. Wage satisfaction	.15	.02	.47*	1.0									
5. Social integration	.02	.04	.26	.28	1.0								
6. Promotion satisfaction	.05	.13	.48*	.32*	.33*	1.0							
7. Management skills	.03	.09	.62*	.41*	.34*	.61*	1.0						
8. Involvement	.11	.10	.02	.01	.12	.08	.03	1.0					
9. Intent to stay	.06	.02	.34*	.20	.11	.20	.25	.13	1.0				
10. Organisational commitment	.01	.06	.46*	.34*	.31*	.49*	.64	.07	.39*	1.0			
11. Satisfaction	.03	.01	.44*	.34*	.33*	.34*	.44	.04	.39*	.61*	1.0		
12. Work commitment	.00	.01	.19	.09	.08	.18	.31	.08	.18	.45*	.26	1.0	
13. Performance commitment	.00	.03	.17	.09	.13	.20	.23	.05	.27	.35*	.35*	.18	1.0

Statistical tests for categorical data

Comparing proportions – the chi-squared test (χ^2)

This is one of the most widely used categorical variable tests in the social sciences. The symbol is the Greek letter *chi*, pronounced 'kye' as in 'sky'. This test informs us as to whether the collected data are close to the value considered to be typical and generally expected, and whether two variables are related to each other. Suppose we wish to see if there were any signs of correspondence between an applicant's gender and whether or not they have had prior work experience. Essentially the data obtained in a study (observed frequencies) are compared with expected data (expected frequencies), and the actual differences determine the level of significance. An example of these is provided in Table 4.7.

The steps involved in the chi-squared test go something like this (again, do not worry – your computer does it for you). First, a contingency table is constructed. Then observed frequencies are identified and expected frequencies are ascertained. Expected frequencies are subtracted from the observed frequencies – these differences are then squared and divided by the number of expected frequencies. Your computer will provide you with a chi-squared statistic and will indicate its level of significance.

Table 4.7 A contingency table

Obtained frequencies: work experience

	Yes	No	Total
Male	70	30	100
Female	50	50	100
Total	120	80	

Expected frequencies: work experience

	Yes	No	Total
Male	60	40	100
Female	60	40	100
Total	120	80	

Cross-tabulation is often used to analyse questionnaire results and chi-squared can be used in association with it. Cross-tabulation is the comparing of respondents' answers to one question in a questionnaire in relation to their answers to other questions. Most commonly respondents' replies to questions on the substantive theme of the research are compared with the respondents' demographic characteristics such as their age, sex, length of service and so on. Cross-tabulation can best be explained by example. Let us imagine a staff satisfaction survey in a large organisation. One question might ask whether people thought they experienced discrimination at work because of their ethnic origin, sex or disability. The question might use a rating scale.

| I am treated fairly on grounds of sex, race or disability | | | I have been treated unfairly on grounds of sex, race or disability | |

1	2	3	4	5
69.2%	14.7%	10.9%	3.2%	1.9%

The results (shown above) would probably be regarded by management as positive. It might, however, be thought interesting to cross-tabulate the results with answers to the question about the sex and ethnic origin of the respondents. Table 4.8 gives the results when analysed according to whether respondents saw themselves as a member of an ethnic minority group.

An inspection of Table 4.8 suggested that people who considered themselves to be in an ethnic minority ticked the 'treated fairly' end of the scale less often than those who did not consider themselves to be in an ethnic minority. When the other parts of the scale are considered, which all imply a degree of unfairness, the 'ethnic minority group' always scored higher than the non-ethnic minority group. While the survey may show that discrimination is not a major problem, the cross-tabulation suggests that the ethnic minority group sees it as rather more of an issue than the non-ethnic minority groups do. But are these differences statistically significant? The chi-squared test can be used to provide an answer.

The use of chi-squared begins with a *null hypothesis*, which is that there is no association, or difference, between the responses to the two questions in the cross-tabulation. A null hypothesis means that the responses to one question are not associated with differences in responses to the other question. SPSS reports the value of a chi-squared test for the above data as 13.557 with a significance level of 0.009 (on a probability scale of 0–1). The significance level is the probability that the null hypothesis is true. In this case the probability is 0.009, or 0.9 per cent. The significance level of 0.009 is smaller than 0.05 and smaller than 0.01. The differences are therefore significant at the 0.01 level. In other words, we can say that at the 99 per cent confidence level the null hypothesis is probably not true. There is a less than 1 per cent chance that it might be true. As researchers we would be willing to say that the null hypothesis is not true at the 0.05 per cent confidence level, which would mean there was a 5 per cent chance of the null hypothesis being true. It can be concluded with a known degree of statistical confidence that there is an association between being, or not being, a member of an ethnic minority and the degree of discrimination respondents believed they suffered. If you want   to know more about chi-squared, and SPSS, see Bryman and Cramer (1997: 168–172).

Table 4.8 **Cross-tabulation**

				Q. 78 Do you consider yourself in an ethnic minority?		Total
				Yes	No	
Q. 56	Fairly	1	count	41	868	909
			% within Q. 78	53.2%	70.5%	
	Fair	2	count	14	178	192
	treatment		% within Q. 78	18.2%	14.5%	
		3	count	14	127	141
			% within Q. 78	18.2%	10.3%	
		4	count	6	36	42
			% within Q. 78	7.8%	2.9%	
	Not fairly	5	count	2	22	24
			% within Q. 78	2.6%	1.8%	
	Total		count	77	1,231	1,308
			% within Q. 78	100%	100%	

Exercise 4.12

Cross-tabulation

The table below shows the results of a cross-tabulation between answers to the question 'Are you female or male?' and answers to the rating scale question on discrimination on grounds of sex, race or disability. Inspect the figures and decide whether men and women have responded differently to questions about discrimination. You do not need to do a chi-squared test but you might want to calculate a few percentages.

				Q.74 Are you male or female?		Total
				Female	Male	
Q.56	Fairly	1	count	713	189	902
	Fair treatment	2	count	150	44	194
		3	count	110	31	141
		4	count	33	10	43
	Not fairly	5	count	19	6	25
	Total		count	1,025	280	1,305

Answer

Inspection suggests that the null hypothesis is true. When the percentages of men and women responding to each of the categories in the rating scale are calculated it is clear that there is little difference between the two sexes. Neither group feels more discriminated against than the other. The chances are that the null hypothesis is true. This is supported by the chi-squared test. When the chi-squared test is used the probability of the null hypothesis being true (the significance level) is 0.973, or 97 per cent. It is much higher than the 0.05 level and so the differences are not significant at that level.

There is a rough and ready, but quicker, way of looking for statistically significant differences between percentages. In Appendix II of Oppenheim (1992) is a set of three nomograms that can be used for making a quick check on whether there are any significant differences between percentages. This would be perfectly adequate for many applications in Master's dissertations.

Final word

This section on basic statistical analysis has attempted to cover a lot of material in a fairly short space. Hopefully it will provide a neat introduction to some tests available to you on current statistical software packages. Just another gentle word of caution. Over the years it has been pointed out that 'there are lies, damned lies, and statistics'. Daryll Huff's (1991) book title *How to Lie with Statistics* conveys this message rather well. So let us finish off this section with a succinct quote from Rowntree (1991: 190):

As a consumer of statistics, act with caution; as a producer, act with integrity.

● ● ● ● Software for analysing research material

Jankowicz (1995: 76) argued that the break point at which it becomes sensible to use software to analyse your results is 100 questionnaires. I might prefer to use software if there are more than 30 questionnaires. Certainly, if you anticipate doing cross-tabulations, then the use of software is almost a necessity. Doing cross-tabulations manually is very time consuming as the questionnaires have to be frequently sorted into different sub-categories and the percentages recalculated. There are a number of pieces of software that you might use to analyse the results from your questionnaires or any other quantitative material. If you were interested only in simple and descriptive statistical analysis of your material, then Excel would be perfectly adequate. If you wanted to carry out cross-tabulations, then Excel is not so useful. It can handle cross-tabulation by using pivot tables, but it would probably be easier to use one of the other packages. Minitab and SPSS, two packages for analysing quantitative data, are introduced. Software is also available to help with the analysis of qualitative material. Most people using qualitative material for MBA and Master's dissertations do not use such specialist software. However, a brief guide to software tools for exploring qualitative materials is included in this part of the guide.

Using Minitab and SPSS to analyse survey results – *John Buglear*

In this section you will find guidance on the use of two statistical packages: Minitab and SPSS. They are similar in many respects, not least the wide variety of facilities they offer; from modest bar charts to sophisticated multivariate analysis. Of the two, Minitab is generally easier for those unfamiliar with statistical work, but SPSS is probably more widely available.

The instructions below are designed to demonstrate some of the procedures and facilities of the packages to the new user. **Bold** type is used for text or figures that you should see on your screen and *italic* type for characters that you should enter. The data that form the basis of the tasks are listed in Table 4.9.

Table 4.9 **Example data**

A researcher has surveyed a random sample of members of a professional institute. Each respondent completed a questionnaire used to find out about their gender, age, current salary (in £000), and whether they had been promoted within the last 5 years. They were also asked for their reaction to a proposed new name for the institute by giving a rating of either 1 for 'strongly approve', 2 for 'approve', 3 for 'disapprove', and 4 for 'strongly disapprove'. Thirty completed questionnaires were received. The results are as follows:

Gender	Age	Salary (£000)	Promotion	Rating
M	43	46	Y	1
M	29	35	Y	4
M	55	57	N	3
M	31	38	Y	3
M	37	52	Y	3
M	58	40	N	3
M	49	60	N	2
M	30	32	N	1
M	26	34	Y	3
M	35	40	Y	3
M	42	45	N	2
M	51	56	Y	4
M	29	30	N	3
M	47	42	N	1
M	62	45	N	1
F	37	41	N	1
F	25	30	N	4
F	42	47	Y	4
F	28	34	Y	2
F	33	36	N	3
F	39	45	Y	1
F	26	32	N	4
F	45	40	N	1
F	27	35	Y	4
F	38	47	N	1
F	49	43	N	4
F	36	50	Y	2
F	31	37	N	3
F	44	42	N	1
F	39	38	N	1

Minitab

Minitab is a general-purpose statistical package originally developed for academic use by staff at Penn State University in 1972. Since then it has become widely used in business; at the time of writing, some commercial applications, including those at Ford, 3M and Toshiba, are described at the Minitab company website, http://www.minitab.com. Look for such examples by clicking the **Resources** tab then **Case Studies and Customer Success Stories**.

The package is relatively straightforward to use, thanks to its educational origins. The most recent version is Release 14, which is in Windows format. Data can be entered directly into Minitab worksheets, or read from (and written to) Excel, Quattro Pro, 1-2-3, and dBase files. Output can be printed directly, copied and pasted into Word or PowerPoint, or assembled in a file using the ReportPad facility in the package. The ReportPad file can subsequently be accessed and edited in Word.

Data entry, editing, and storage

When you enter Minitab there is a short loading sequence following which you should see a screen that has two sections; it should look like Figure 4.14. The upper half is the **Session** window. It should display the date and a welcome message. The **Session** window is where the output you generate will be shown, with the exception of graphical output, which is displayed in separate windows superimposed on the default screen.

In the lower part of the screen there is the **Worksheet,** where you can enter and store data. The **Worksheet** looks like a spreadsheet since it consists of numbered rows and columns, but there are important differences. In a spreadsheet you can enter titles, names and formulae freely because you define the data you wish to analyse by their column and row location. In Minitab you will be defining the location of data you want to analyse using only its column location. This makes using the analytical procedures easier, but it does mean that you have to ensure that only the data you want to analyse are entered into the column. You can give each column a name but you must enter the name in the unnumbered cell at the very top of the column where you want to store your data, immediately beneath the column number (**C1** or **C2** etc.).

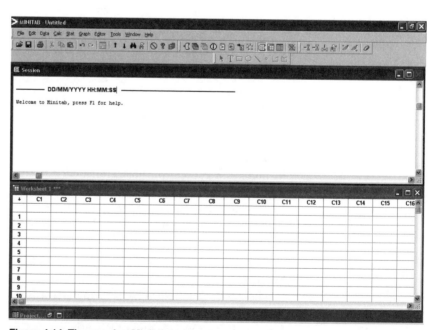

Figure 4.14 The opening Minitab screen

Keeping names and punctuation marks out of data columns is especially important when you are dealing with numerical data that you want to analyse arithmetically, such as by calculating the mean. If you put an alphabetic character or a punctuation mark, other than full-stops which are accepted as decimal points, in one of the numbered rows of the column, the column designation **T** (for text) will appear next to the column number at the head of the column. If you ask the package to calculate the mean of such a column you will find that it will not allow you to do so. Be particularly careful not to insert commas in data consisting of large values; you may think of the number as 23,456 but you must enter it as 23456.

At the very top of the screen you will see a menu bar of function headings (**File, Edit, Data,** and so on) that release draw-down menus when clicked. These menus list the tools the package provides.

When you have identified these features of the screen enter the data in Table 4.9 into the first five columns (**C1** to **C5**) of the worksheet. Put the names of the five variables in the unnumbered cells at the top of the columns. Two of the variables are non-numeric (Gender and Promotion); as you enter the first values of these variables you should see the column designations of **C1** and **C4** change to **C1-T** and **C4-T**.

When you have entered the data the top of your worksheet should look like Figure 4.15.

If you make a mistake in entering the data you can amend the contents of a cell by clicking on the cell and typing in what you want to store in the cell. If you miss out a value click on the worksheet cell that you want to be BELOW your insertion, click **Editor** on the menu bar and select **Insert Cells**. A new cell will now appear into which you can type the missing value. If you want to delete a cell, click on the cell concerned then click **Edit** and **Delete Cells**.

The letters F and M in the first column stand for Female and Male. It is faster to enter the data in abbreviated form but we can alter them to 'Female' and 'Male' so that interpreting the analysis is easier:

↓	C1-T	C2	C3	C4-T	C5
	Gender	Age	Salary	Promotion	Rating
1	M	43	46	Y	1
2	M	29	35	Y	4
3	M	55	57	N	3
4	M	31	38	Y	3

Figure 4.15 **The upper section of the worksheet**

- Click **Data** on the menu bar and from the draw-down menu select **Code**.
- Pick **Text to Text** from the sub-menu.
- In the dialogue box specify *C1* as the column to **Code data from columns** then click in the space below **Into columns** and type *C1*.
- Enter the **Original values** (F and M) and **New** values (Female and Male), putting *F* and *Female* respectively in the left- and right-hand side spaces of the first row and *M* and *Male* in the second row, as shown in Figure 4.16.

Repeat the procedure for the Promotion data, replacing *Y* with *Yes* and *N* with *No*.

Now the data has been amended it is timely to save it.

- Click **File** on the menu bar and choose **Save Current Worksheet**.
- In the **Save Worksheet As** window that appears click ▼ to the right of the **Save in** box and pick the appropriate drive and folder.
- Type an appropriate file name in the box to the right of **File name** and click the **Save** button.

Leave the package then re-enter and retrieve your worksheet:

- Click **File** on the menu bar and choose **Exit**.
- Re-enter the package, select **File** from the menu bar and click **Open Worksheet**.
- In the window that appears click the ▼ button to the right of the **Look in** box and select the appropriate drive, folder and file.

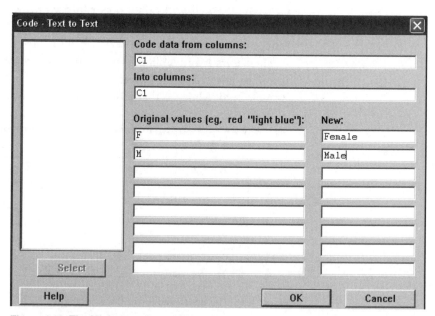

Figure 4.16 The Minitab coding window

- Click **Open** and subsequently click **OK** on the message informing you that the data will be added to the worksheet.

Your data should appear in the on-screen worksheet.

In statistical work it is sometimes useful or necessary to pick a random sample from a data set. Try selecting a random sample of 12 from the sample of 30:

- Click the **Calc** draw-down menu and choose **Random Data**.
- From the sub-menu select **Sample From Columns**.
- In the dialogue box specify that you want to **Sample** *12* **rows from columns** *C1–C5* and **Store samples in** *C11–C15* and click **OK**.

Check that your sample of 12 is stored in columns 11 to 15.

Tabulation, diagrams and summary measures

Produce a simple tabulation of the gender data:

- Select the **Stat** draw-down menu and choose **Tables**.
- Click **Tally Individual Variables** in the sub-menu.
- In the dialogue box that appears type *C1* in the space below **Variables** and click **OK**.

The upper part of the screen, the **Session** window, should now contain a table like Table 4.10.

Enter this table into the ReportPad:

- Right click on the table.
- Choose **Append Section to Report** from the menu that appears.

Check that the Report does contain the table by pressing the Ctrl, Alt and R keys and inspecting the **Project Manager** screen that appears. You can also access the Report by clicking on the Show ReportPad icon, which looks like a notepad, at the top of the screen, or by clicking the **Project Manager** tab to the bottom left of the screen.

While you are looking at the Report contents, click the **File** draw-down menu; it should include options to **Print Report** and **Save Report As**. To return to the default screen, minimise the **Project Manager** screen. Note that you cannot delete the **Project Manager** screen; it remains live throughout your session, storing information about the work you carry out.

Table 4.10 Tabulation of gender

```
Tally for Discrete Variables: Gender
```

Gender	Count
Female	15
Male	15
N =	30

For a two-way tabulation of the gender and promotion data:

- Select the **Stat** draw-down menu and choose **Tables**.
- Click **Cross Tabulation and Chi-Square** in the sub-menu.
- In the dialogue box that appears, type *C1* in the space to the right of **For rows:** and *C4* to the right of **For columns:** then click **OK**.

The **Session** window should now contain a table like Table 4.11. The message **Cell Contents: Count** at the bottom specifies that each figure in the table is the number of respondents whose details accord with the row and column designations of the cell.

Table 4.11 **Two-way tabulation of gender and promotion**

Tabulated statistics: Gender, Promotion

Rows: Gender Columns: Promotion

	No	Yes	All
Female	10	5	15
Male	8	7	15
Female	18	12	30

Cell Contents:		Count	

Construct a simple bar chart for the gender data:

- Select the **Graph** draw-down menu and choose **Bar Chart**.
- In the first window check that **Counts of unique values** appears under **Bars represent** and that the **Simple** chart type is highlighted then click **OK**.
- In the next window type *C1* in the space below **Categorical variables,** then click **OK**.

After a short delay your bar chart should appear. It should look like Figure 4.17.

If you want to alter the title, axis labels or scaling you can do so interactively:

- Double left click on the default title, **Chart of Gender** and the **Edit Title** window should appear.
- In the space below **Text:** to the bottom of the window type *Gender of respondents* then click **OK**.
- Similarly double left click on the default vertical axis label, **Count,** and type *Number of respondents* in the space below **Text** in the **Edit Axis Label**.

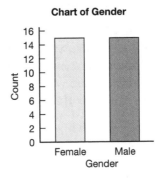

Figure 4.17 **Simple bar chart of the gender data**

- To alter the vertical scale double left-click directly on the vertical axis, when the label **Y Scale** will appear, and in the **Edit Scale** window untick the lower, **Maximum**, box below the **Auto** setting under **Scale Range**.
- Type *20* in the space to the right of **Maximum** then click **OK**.

The chart should now look like Figure 4.18.

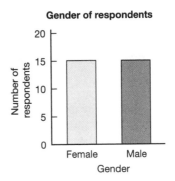

Figure 4.18 **Amended simple bar chart of the gender data**

Try storing your graph in the ReportPad:

- Right click on the graph.
- Click **Append Graph to Report** on the menu that appears.
- Access the ReportPad by clicking **Project Manager** tab and look for your graph.

Close the **Project Manager** screen and delete the graph by clicking the **X** in the top right-hand corner of the graph window. You will be asked if you wish to save it; click **No**. Try repeating the procedure to obtain a bar chart for the promotion data in C4.

Construct a stack bar chart for the gender and promotion data:

- Click the **Graph** draw-down menu and select **Bar Chart.**
- In the first window check that **Counts of unique values** appears under **Bars represent:** and highlight the **Stack** chart type, then click **OK.**
- In the next window type *C1 C4* below **Categorical variables (2-4, outermost first)** then click **OK.**

The graph that you see should look like Figure 4.19. You can use stack bar charts to demonstrate possible associations between qualitative, or category, variables. Here the diagram illustrates that a greater proportion of the men have responded 'Yes' when asked about promotion.

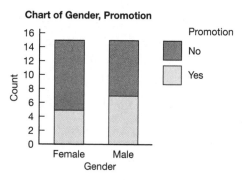

Figure 4.19 **Stack bar chart of the gender and promotion data**

Repeat the procedure but now try typing *C4 C1* below **Categorical variables (2-4, outermost first)**. You should find that the bars now represent gender and the components of them, promotion. Another variation is to have a vertical scale that measures percentage of respondents; repeat the sequence but now click the **Bar Chart Options** button in the second window. Tick **Show Y as Percent** and select **Within categories at level 1 (outermost)** then **OK.**

An alternative form is the cluster bar chart. In this the secondary categories are represented as bars that are clustered together by their primary categories. Go through the procedure for a stack bar chart but now highlight the **Cluster** chart type in the **Bar Chart** window.

Produce a histogram for the age data:

- Select the **Graph** menu then **Histogram.**
- In the first window check that the **Simple** diagram type is highlighted then click **OK.**
- In the next window type *C2* in the space below **Graph variables** then click **OK.**

In the histogram that appears the blocks are situated above the mid points of the classes. Double left click on one of the blocks then in the **Edit Bars** window that appears click the **Binning** tab. Change the **Interval Type** from **Midpoint** to **Cutpoint** then click **OK**. Your diagram should look like Figure 4.20.

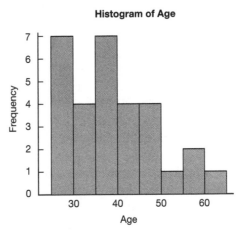

Histogram of Age

Figure 4.20 **Histogram of the age data**

You can use the **Interval Definition** section of the **Edit Bars** window to alter the number and width of the classes. The title, axis labels and vertical scale can be adjusted interactively using the same procedures used above to produce Figure 4.18.

A useful alternative to the histogram, especially if you need to compare two or more distributions, is the boxplot. This device is based on order statistics: the median, the quartiles, and the minimum and maximum values. Produce a boxplot for the salary data:

- Select the **Graph** menu then **Boxplot**.
- In the first window check the **Simple** plot type is highlighted, and click **OK**.
- In the next window type C3 in the box below **Graph variables** then click **OK**.

The diagram that appears should look like Figure 4.21.

Boxplot of Salary

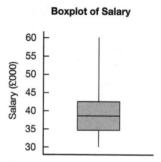

Figure 4.21 **Boxplot of the salary data**

In Figure 4.21 the salary distribution is depicted against a vertical scale by means of what is known as a box and whiskers plot. The box at the heart of the diagram has a line across the middle. This line represents the median of the distribution, about 40, i.e. £40,000 in this case. The upper and lower edges of the box mark the positions of the upper and lower quartiles respectively. The vertical line above the box extends to the maximum value, 60, and the line below the box extends to the minimum value, 30.

Repeat the procedure but this time click the **With Groups** plot type and in the next window type *C3* in the space below **Graph variables** and *C1* in the space under **Categorical variables for grouping (1-4, outermost first)** then click **OK**. After a short time you should see a diagram like Figure 4.22 with two boxplots plotted on the same pair of axes, one representing the salaries of female respondents, the other the salaries of male respondents. The greater height of the boxplot on the right reflects the wider spread of salaries among the men. In fact the major distinction between the two plots is the extent of their upper sections, representing the data between the median and maximum values. This shows a greater spread of salaries among the higher paid half of the men compared with the higher paid half of the women.

Boxplot of Salary vs Gender

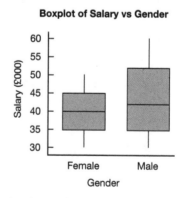

Figure 4.22 **Boxplot of salary by gender**

You might like to change the vertical scale by left-clicking on the vertical axis and in the **Edit Scale** window untick both **Auto** settings under **Scale Range** and insert appropriate values, such as *0* and *70* in the **Minimum** and **Maximum** boxes respectively. Which scale you use is in part an aesthetic question, but too large a scale range may make the object too small to interpret and too short a scale range might cut off part of your diagram. For more information about boxplots see Buglear (2005: 199–202).

Create a scatter diagram to portray the age and salary data:

● Select the **Graph** menu, then **Scatterplot.**
● Check that the **Simple** plot type is highlighted in the first window and click **OK.**
● In the second window type *C3* in the uppermost space below **Y variables** and *C2* in the uppermost space below **X variables** then click **OK.**

The diagram that appears should look like Figure 4.23. Each point in it represents a pair of values: the age and salary of a respondent. The scatter of points implies that, in general, older respondents have higher salaries.

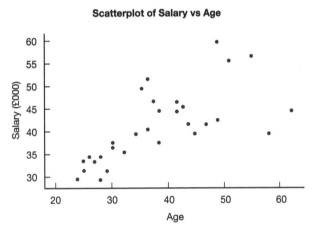

Figure 4.23 **Scatter diagram of the salary and age data**

Obtain summary or 'descriptive' statistics for the salary data:

● Select **Stat** then **Basic Statistics.**
● Pick **Display Descriptive Statistics** from the sub-menu.
● In the dialogue box type *C3* in the **Variables** space then click **OK.**

The output that appears in the **Session** window should look like Table 4.12.

Table 4.12 **Summary measures for the salary data**

Descriptive statistics: salary

Variable	N	N*	Mean	SE Mean	StDev	Minimum	Q1	Median	Q3	Maximum
Salary	30	0	41.63	1.45	7.92	30.00	35.00	40.50	46.25	60.00

In Table 4.12, **N** is the number of observations, **N*** is the number of missing values, **Mean** is the arithmetic mean, **TrMean** (not shown in table) is the trimmed mean (the mean of all values except the highest 5 per cent and lowest 5 per cent, which is intended to correct the distortion that any extreme values exert on a mean), **SE Mean** is the standard error of the mean and **StDev** is the standard deviation. **Q1** and **Q3** are the upper and lower quartiles. For more on the interpretation of these measures see Buglear (2005: 177–187, 194–199, 202–209).

Repeat the procedure but now type *C1* in the space below **By variables** (**optional**) in the **Display Descriptive Statistics** dialogue box and click **OK**. The analysis that appears in the **Session** window should show summary measures for the salaries of female respondents on one line and male respondents on another. The higher mean and standard deviation for the male respondents indicate that on average the men have higher and more widely spread salaries.

Produce a 95 per cent confidence interval for the population mean salary of all institute members:

- Select the **Stat** menu then choose **Basic Statistics**.
- Pick **1-Sample t** from the sub-menu.
- Click in the space below **Samples in columns** and type *C3* in it then click **OK**.

You should see output like Table 4.13 in the **Session** window.

Table 4.13 **Confidence interval for population mean salary**

One-sample t: salary

Variable	N	Mean	StDev	SE Mean	95% CI
Salary	30	41.6333	7.9198	1.4459	(38.6760, 44.5906)

In Table 4.13 the figures in brackets under **95% CI** suggest that we can be 95 per cent certain that the mean salary of all institute members is somewhere between £38,676 and £44,591. See Buglear (2005: 493–503) for an explanation of confidence intervals.

Bivariate analysis

Produce a contingency table for the gender and promotion data. This name is given to this type of table because it allows you to assess the extent to which the variables are associated, or contingent upon each other.

- Select the **Stat** menu and choose **Tables**.
- Select **Cross Tabulation and Chi-Square** from the sub-menu.
- In the dialogue box type *C1* in the space to the right of **For rows** and *C4* to the right of **For columns**.
- Click the **Chi-Square** button to the lower right of the window.
- In the dialogue box that appears tick **Chi-Square analysis, Expected cell counts**, and **Each cell's contribution to the Chi-Square statistic** then click **OK** and **OK** in the first dialogue box.

You should see output like Table 4.14 in the **Session** window.

Table 4.14 Contingency table of gender and promotion

```
Tabulated statistics: gender, promotion

Rows: Gender                    Columns: Promotion

                No          Yes          All
                10           5           15
Female           9           6           15
             0.1111      0.1667           *

Male             8           7           15
                 9           6           15
             0.1111      0.1667           *

All             18          12           30
                18          12           30
                 *           *            *

        Cell Contents:   Count
                         Expected count
                         Contribution to Chi-square

Pearson Chi-Square = 0.556, DF = 1, P-Value = 0.456
Likelihood Ratio Chi-Square = 0.558, DF = 1, P-Value = 0.455
```

In Table 4.14 there are three numbers in each cell. The top one, the **Count**, is the actual number of respondents giving those gender and promotion details, for instance ten respondents were female and had no promotion. The middle number, the **Expected count**, is the number of respondents that would be expected to have those gender and promotion details if gender and promotion were independent; nine in the case of female and no promotion. The bottom number, the **Contribution to Chi-square**, is based on the difference between the actual and expected values for the cell; specifically the difference squared divided by the expected value, 0.1111 for female and no promotion.

The **Pearson Chi-Square** in the penultimate row of output is an aggregate measure based on the differences between the **Count** and the **Expected count** values for all the cells in the table. The larger the differences between the expected values and the counts, the bigger the value of Chi-square will be, and the larger the differences, the more evidence there is for association between the variables. The **P-value** to the right of the Chi-square figure is the probability of getting these sample results if there is no association between the variables in the population. You can interpret it simply as the probability of no association between the two variables. In this case the **P-Value** is **0.455**, so there is a 45.5 per cent chance of no association, suggesting that gender and promotion are independent. In practice only when this figure is less than 10 per cent (0.10), and by implication the chance of association is more than 90 per cent, would it be legitimate to conclude that there is association. The final row of output contains an alternative form of the chi-square calculation. Buglear (2005: 569–575) contains a fuller discussion of this type of analysis.

Suppose the gender of the last three of the fifteen males in the data set had been wrongly recorded and they were in fact females. Alter the thirteenth to fifteenth rows of data accordingly and repeat the procedure above to produce a new contingency analysis. The **P-Value**, now **0.094**, suggests that there is less than a one in ten chance that these data came from a population where gender and promotion are independent, and hence the two variables seem to be associated. The **Count** and **Expected count** of female and no promotion are now **13** and **10.80** respectively, indicating that the form of the association is that women are less likely to be promoted than men.

Towards the bottom of the output you should see the message **1 cells with expected counts less than 5**. This is a warning to alert you to the thin spread of observations in part of the table and to suggest that the results should be treated with caution. This can be a problem with variables that have several response categories.

Produce a contingency analysis for the promotion and rating data. Proceed as before but in the **Cross Tabulation and Chi-Square** dialogue box type *C4* in the space to the right of **For rows** and *C5* to the right of **For columns**. The resulting table should have a warning of **6 cells with expected counts less than 5**. The best way of avoiding this would be to obtain more data, but an alternative resolution is the merging of categories. Apply this to the rating data:

● Click **Data** on the menu bar and on the draw-down menu select **Code**.
● Pick **Numeric to Text** from the sub-menu.
● In the dialogue box specify *C5* as the column to **Code data from columns** then click in the space below **Into columns** and type *C6*.
● In the first row under **Original values** type *1:2* and under **New** type *Positive*, then in the second row type *3:4* and *Negative* respectively.

- Click **OK** and check that column six of your worksheet contains the new categories.
- Repeat the sequence for producing contingency analysis but this time type C6 to the right of **For columns**.

The output you see should have no warning message.

To measure the association between the age and salary data produce a Pearson correlation coefficient:

- Click **Stat** on the menu bar then **Basic Statistics** from the menu and **Correlation** from the sub-menu.
- Type C2 C3 in the space below **Variables** then click **OK**.

The coefficient, **0.684**, should appear in the **Session** window. This value, which needs to be considered with Figure 4.23, suggests the association between the two variables is positive but modest (Buglear, 2005: 224–234). You should always assess a correlation coefficient alongside a scatter diagram of the data; the same value could reflect a broad but even scatter or a tight scatter with prominent outlying values.

Obtain a regression model for the relationship between age and salary:

- Select the **Stat** menu then **Regression**.
- Choose **Regression** from the sub-menu.
- In the dialogue box that appears type C3 in the space to the right of **Response** and C2 in the space to the right of **Predictors** then click **OK**.

The **Session** window should contain output like Table 4.15.

Table 4.15 Regression model of the salary and age data

Regression analysis: salary versus age

The regression equation is
Salary = 20.7 + 0.539 Age

Predictor	Coef	SE Coef	T	P
Constant	20.729	4.350	4.77	0.000
Age	0.5392	0.1087	4.96	0.000

S = 5.88088   R-Sq = 46.8%   R-Sq(adj) = 44.9%

Analysis of Variance

Source	DF	SS	MS	F	P
Regression	1	850.59	850.59	24.59	0.000
Residual Error	28	968.37	34.58		
Total	29	1818.97			

Unusual Observations

Obs	Age	Salary	Fit	SE Fit	Residual	St Resid
6	58.0	40.00	52.00	2.35	−12.00	−2.23R
7	49.0	60.00	47.15	1.55	12.85	2.26R
15	62.0	45.00	54.16	2.74	−9.16	−1.76 X

R denotes an observation with a large standardised residual.
X denotes an observation whose X value gives it large influence.

In Table 4.15 the **regression equation** is the equation of the straight line that best fits the data. The **R-Sq** figure suggests that the proportion of the variation in salary that can be explained by age, **46.8%**. The **Unusual Observations** at the end of the output do not fit the regression model particularly well, the first two are outliers, and the third is detached from the general location of the data. Refer to Buglear (2005: 237–244) for more extensive coverage of regression models.

You might like to try to identify these unusual observations on a plot of the regression model.

● Select the **Stat** menu then **Regression**.
● Choose **Fitted Line Plot**.
● In the dialogue box type C3 in the space to the right of **Response (Y)** and C2 in the space to the right of **Predictor (X)**.
● Click **OK**.

The graph that appears will be like Figure 4.24.

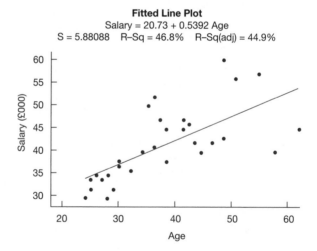

Figure 4.24 Fitted line plot of the salary and age data

Leave the package by clicking on the **File** and choosing **Exit**. Before the package allows you to finish your session you will be presented with a message asking if you want to **Save the project**. In Minitab the word project means all the output you have produced and all the data in the worksheet(s). Since your current session is an exercise rather than an analysis of your research there is no need to save the project.

You can find more information about Minitab on the company website at http://www.minitab.com. The company usually offers a free 30-day trial of the package, which you can take up through the website. For more on using Minitab, try Joiner, *et al.* or McKenzie and Goldman (2004).

SPSS

SPSS, the initials of its original name (Statistical Package for the Social Sciences), was developed by postgraduate students at Stanford University in 1968. It is widely used in both academic and commercial spheres. The businesses that use SPSS at the time of writing include BT, HSBC and Whitbread. If you want to read about such examples go to the company website at http://www.spss.com and click **Customers** at the top of the screen then look for **Customer Successes in Your Industry**.

SPSS provides a wide range of tools from basic tabulation to sophisticated multivariate analysis. The most recent version is Release 14, which is in Windows format. Data can be entered directly into the package, or read from (and written to) Excel, Lotus and dBase files. Output can be printed directly, copied and pasted into Word or PowerPoint, or stored as an output file using the **Output Viewer** facility in the package.

Data entry, editing and storage

When you enter the package you will see a dialogue box that asks **What would you like to do?** Click the button to the left of **Type in data** then click **OK**. An empty **Data View** screen appears with the cursor located in the cell in the top left-hand corner.

Type the gender of the first respondent, *M*, into this first cell then press Enter. As you do this the column width reduces and the name **VAR**, a truncation of **var00001**, appears vertically at the top of the column. This is 'Variable 1', the default name the package gives to the first column of data. Change the variable name to 'Gender' by clicking the **Variable View** tab to the bottom left of the screen and typing *Gender* in the cell below **Name**. Click in the cell below **Columns** and widen the column by increasing the number in this cell to eight. Return to the previous display by clicking the **Data View** tab to the bottom left of the screen and continue entering the gender data in the first column. Enter the age, salary, promotion and rating data in columns two to five. Click **Variable View** and type *Age, Salary, Promotion* and *Rating* in the second to fifth rows respectively below **Name**. Click on the fourth cell below **Columns** and change the number of columns for the promotion column to eight. To allow the values of the gender and promotion variables to be expanded, change the entries in the first and fourth cells below **Width** to eight. The upper part of the **Variable View** should now look like Figure 4.25.

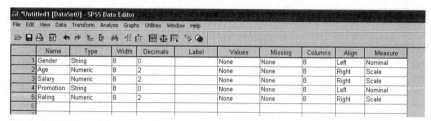

Figure 4.25 SPSS variable view screen

It is quicker to enter single characters but complete labels look better in the output. Click **Data View** and change the 'F' and 'M' entries in the first column of data to 'Female' and 'Male' as follows:

- Select the **Transform** draw-down menu and choose the **Recode** option.
- Pick **Into Same Variables** from the sub-menu.
- In the dialogue box check that **Gender** is highlighted then click ▶ . **Gender** should move to the space below **String Variables**.
- Click the **Old and New Values** button.
- In the dialogue box that appears, type *F* below **Value** in the left-hand side of the box under **Old Value** and *Female* alongside **Value** in the right-hand side of the box under **New Value** then click **Add**.
- Type *M* and *Male* as the **Old Value** and **New Value** respectively, click **Add** then **Continue**, which will return you to the previous dialogue box. Click **OK**.

The data in the column should now change. Follow the same sequence to rtecode the 'Y' and 'N' **Promotion** values in the fourth column to 'Yes' and 'No'. To keep things simple, move **Gender** out of the **String Variables** box using ◀ before moving **Promotion** into it.

Now save the amended data:

- Click the **File** the draw-down menu and choose **Save**.
- In the **Save Data As** window that appears click ▼ to the right of the **Save in:** box and select the appropriate drive and folder.
- Type a suitable file name in the box to the right of **File name** and click the **Save** button.

Leave the package then re-enter and retrieve your worksheet:

- Click the **File** draw-down menu bar and choose **Exit**.
- Re-enter the package, and in the **What would you like to do?** dialogue box check that **Open an existing data source** is selected. You should see the file name you have used in the space immediately beneath. Click on the file name then **OK**.

Your data should appear in **Data View** window.

Statistical work sometimes involves picking a random sample from a data set. Try selecting a random sample of 12 from the 30 observations in this data set:

- Click the **Data** draw-down menu and choose **Select Cases**.
- In the dialogue box choose **Random sample of cases** then click the **Sample** button.
- In the **Random Sample** dialogue box click the button on the left of **Exactly** then type *12* in the window to the right of **Exactly** and *30* in the window after **cases from the first** then click the **Continue** button then **OK**.

A column headed **filter** appears. It contains a **1** in each row (i.e. observation) that has been selected and a **0** in each row that has not. In subsequent analyses only the selected sample values will be used. To undo this, simply highlight the **filter** column and delete it.

Tabulation, diagrams and summary measures

Obtain a simple tabulation of the gender data:

- Click on **Analyze** at the top of the screen and from the draw-down menu select **Tables**.
- Select **Tables of Frequencies** from the sub-menu.
- In the **Tables of Frequencies** window that appears you will see **Gender** highlighted in the space on the left. Click the ▶ button to the left of **Frequencies for** and **Gender** should be switched to the space below **Frequencies for**. Click **OK**.

You should see a table like Table 4.16 in the **Output Viewer** screen.

Table 4.16 Tabulation of gender

	Count
Female	15
Male	15

Minimise the **Output Viewer** screen and produce a two-way tabulation of the gender and promotion data:

- Select the **Analyse** draw-down menu and choose **Descriptive Statistics**.
- Select **Crosstabs** from the sub-menu.
- In the dialogue box click **Gender** in the list of column names on the left hand side then click ▶ to the left of the **Row(s)** box. Click **Promotion** in the list of column names on the left then ▶ to the left of the **Column(s)** box then **OK**.

In the **Output Viewer** that appears you should see a **Case Processing Summary** below which is a two-way tabulation like Table 4.17.

Table 4.17 Two-way tabulation of gender and promotion

| | | Promotion | | |
		No	Yes	Total
Gender	Female	10	5	15
	Male	8	7	15
Total		18	12	30

Construct a simple bar chart for the gender data:

● Select the **Graphs** menu and choose **Bar**.
● In the dialogue box check the **Simple** chart type is highlighted, then click the **Define** button.
● In the **Define Simple Bar** dialogue box check **Gender** is highlighted, then click the ▶ button beside **Category Axis** and then **OK**.

You should see a bar chart like Figure 4.26 in the **Output Viewer**.

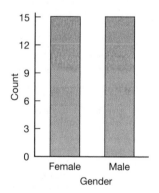

Figure 4.26 Simple bar chart of gender data

Repeat the procedure to obtain a bar chart for the promotion data, but this time:

● Choose **Interactive** from the **Graphs** menu then **Bar**.
● In the dialogue box click and drag **Promotion** into the window below and to the right of the window that has **Count** in it.
● Click the **Options** tab near the top of the dialogue box then untick the box to the left of **Auto**, leave the default setting for **Minimum** at 0 but type *30* in the window to the right of **Maximum**, then click **OK**.

A chart like Figure 4.27 should appear in the **Output Viewer**. Try repeating the sequence and changing **Maximum** to *20*.

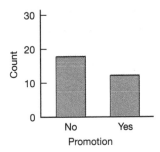

Figure 4.27 **Amended simple bar chart of the promotion data**

Construct a stacked bar chart for the gender and promotion data:

● Select **Graphs** then **Bar**.
● In the dialogue box click the **Stacked** chart type then **Define**.
● In the **Define Stacked Bar** dialogue box check **Gender** is highlighted and click ▶ beside **Category Axis**.
● Click **Promotion** and ▶ beside **Define Stacks by**, then click **OK**.

Your chart should look like Figure 4.28. Repeat the procedure providing the same instructions as before but this time click the **Clustered** chart type in the **Bar Charts** dialogue box.

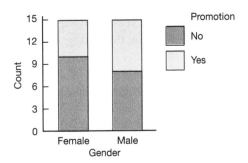

Figure 4.28 **Stacked bar chart of the gender and promotion data**

Produce a histogram for the age data:

● Select the **Graphs** draw-down menu then **Histogram**.
● Highlight **Age** then click ▶ to the left of the **Variable** window and **OK**.

The diagram that appears should look like Figure 4.29, complete with the mean, standard deviation and number of observations, **N**. If you want to edit these out double left click on the graph and the **Chart Editor** dialogue box will appear. Left click on the text you want to remove, which will become 'live' with a box around it, and press the Delete key. Click the **File** draw-down menu and select **Close**. The amended graph should now be in the **Output Viewer**.

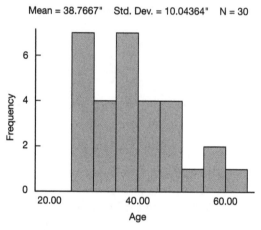

Figure 4.29 **Histogram of the age data**

Obtain a histogram of the salary data using the **Interactive** facility:

- Choose the **Graphs** menu and select **Interactive** and **Histogram**.
- In the dialogue box click and drag **Salary** into the window below and to the right of the window with **Count** in it.
- Click the **Histogram** tab near the top of the dialogue box.
- Untick the box to the left of **Set interval size automatically** and check that **Number of intervals** is selected.
- Change the number in the space to the left of **Number of intervals** to 6, and click **OK**.

A histogram like Figure 4.30 should appear in the **Output Viewer**.

The boxplot, based on order statistics, i.e. the median, quartiles, and minimum and maximum values, is a useful alternative to the histogram, especially if you need to compare two or more distributions.

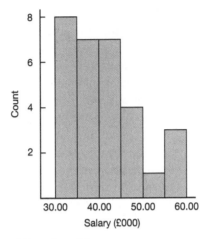

Figure 4.30 **Histogram of the salary data**

Produce a simple boxplot for the Salary data:

- Select the **Graphs** draw-down menu then **Boxplot**.
- Check that the **Simple** chart type is highlighted.
- Lower in the box, under **Data in Chart Are**, click next to **Summaries of separate variables** then click the **Define** button.
- In the dialogue box that appears click on **Salary** then ▶ beside the **Boxes Represent** window, then **OK**.

The **Output Viewer** should contain a chart like Figure 4.31.

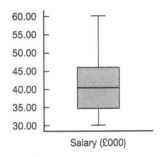

Figure 4.31 **Boxplot of the salary data**

Figure 4.31 shows the salary data against a vertical scale by means of, to use its full name, a box and whiskers plot. The central box has a band within it which represents the median of the distribution, about 40, i.e. £40,000. The upper and lower ends of the box represent the upper and lower quartiles respectively. The vertical line above the box ends at the maximum value, 60, and the line below the box ends at the minimum value, 30.

Repeat the procedure but this time under **Data in Chart Are** click next to **Summaries for groups of cases** then **Define**. In the dialogue box click **Salary** then ▶ beside the **Variable** window then click **Gender** and ▶ beside the **Category Axis** window then **OK**. In the **Output Viewer** you should see two boxplots plotted on the same axes, as shown in Figure 4.32. One represents salaries of the female respondents, the other one the salaries of male respondents. The greater height of the boxplot on the right signifies a wider spread of salaries among the males. Specifically the major contrast between the two plots is the extent of their upper sections, which represent the data between the median and maximum values. This portrays a greater spread of salaries among the higher paid half of males compared to the higher paid half of females. See Buglear (2005: 199–202) for more about boxplots.

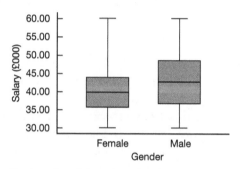

Figure 4.32 Comparative boxplot of the salary data by gender

Produce a scatter diagram to show the age and salary data:

- Select the **Graphs** draw-down menu then **Scatter/Dot**.
- In the dialogue box check that the **Simple Scatter** chart type is selected then click **Define**.
- In the **Simple Scatterplot** dialogue box that appears click on **Salary** then ▶ to the left of **Y Axis**.
- Click on **Age** then ▶ to the left of **X Axis**, then **OK**.

The scatter diagram in the **Output Viewer** should look like Figure 4.33. Each point in the diagram represents both the age and the salary of a respondent. The pattern suggests that, in general, higher salaries are paid to older respondents.

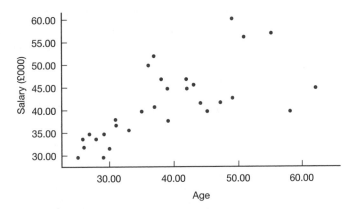

Figure 4.33 Scatter diagram of the salary and age data

Obtain summary or 'descriptive' statistics for the salary data:

- Select the **Analyze** draw-down menu then **Descriptive Statistics**.
- Pick **Descriptives** from the sub-menu.
- In the dialogue box click **Salary** then ▶ beside **Variable(s)** then **OK**.

A set of results as shown in Table 4.18 should appear in the **Output Viewer**.

Table 4.18 Summary statistics for salary data

	N	Minimum	Maximum	Mean	Std. deviation
Salary	30	30.00	60.00	41.6333	7.91978
Valid N (listwise)	30				

In Table 4.18, **N** is the number of observations, **Mean** is the arithmetic mean, and **Std. deviation** is the standard deviation. See Buglear (2005: 181–182, 202–209) for guidance on interpreting these measures.

Compare the salary data for female and male respondents using summary statistics:

- Pick the **Analyze** draw-down menu then **Compare Means**.
- Choose **Means** from the sub-menu.
- In the dialogue box click **Salary** then ▶ beside **Dependent List** and **Gender** then ▶ beside **Independent List**.
- Click **OK**.

The table that appears in the **Output Viewer** window below the heading **Report** should have the mean and standard deviation for the salaries of the female respondents along one row and those of the male respondents on another. The higher mean and standard deviation for the latter suggest that, on average, men have higher and more widely spread salaries.

Produce a confidence interval for the population mean salary of all institute members:

- Select the **Analyze** draw-down menu then choose **Compare Means**.
- Pick **One-Sample T Test** from the sub-menu.
- In the dialogue box click **Salary** then ▶ beside **Test Variable(s)** then click **OK**.

A table like Table 4.19 should appear in the **Output Viewer**. The figures on the right of the table under **95% Confidence Interval of the Difference** suggest that we can be 95 per cent certain that the mean salary of all institute members is somewhere between £38,676 and £44,591. For an explanation of confidence intervals see Buglear (2005: 493–503).

Table 4.19 **Confidence interval for population mean salary**

| | t | df | Sig. (2-tailed) | Mean difference | 95% Confidence Interval of the Difference | |
					Lower	Upper
			One-sample test Test Value = 0			
Salary	28.793	29	.000	41.63333	38.6760	44.5906

To obtain a comprehensive analysis of a quantitative variable such as salary try selecting **Descriptive Statistics** from the **Analyze** menu then **Explore** from the sub-menu. Enter **Salary** under **Dependent List** and **Gender** under **Factor List** then click **OK**. The resulting output includes a variety of summary statistics, confidence intervals, boxplots, and stem and leaf displays. For an explanation of stem and leaf displays refer to Buglear (2005: 152–157).

Bivariate analysis

Produce a contingency analysis for the gender and promotion data. This type of analysis is so called because it can be used to gauge how much the variables are associated, or contingent upon each other.

- Select the **Analyze** menu and choose **Descriptive Statistics**.
- Select **Crosstabs** from the sub-menu.
- In the dialogue box click **Gender** in the list of variable names on the left-hand side then click ▶ to the left of the **Row(s)** box. (Note that if you have produced Table 4.17 in your current session this and the next variable setting will already be there.)

- Click **Promotion** in the list on the left then ▶ to the left of the **Column(s)** box.
- Click the **Statistics** button in the **Crosstabs** dialogue box.
- In the **Crosstabs: Statistics** box tick the box to the left of **Chi-square** then **Continue**.
- Click the **Cells** button in the **Crosstabs** dialogue box.
- In the **Crosstabs: Cell Display** dialogue box tick the box to the left of **Expected** then **Continue**.
- Click **OK** in the **Crosstabs** dialogue box.

In the **Output Viewer** you will see output like Table 4.20.

Table 4.20 Contingency analysis of gender and promotion

			Promotion No	Promotion Yes	Total
Gender	Female	Count	10	5	15
		Expected Count	9.0	6.0	15.0
	Male	Count	8	7	15
		Expected Count	9.0	6.0	15.0
Total		Count	18	12	30
		Expected Count	18.0	12.0	30.0

Chi-square tests

	Value	df	Asymp. Sig. (2-sided)	Exact Sig. (2-sided)	Exact Sig. (1-sided)
Pearson Chi-square	.556[b]	1	.456		.
Continuity Correction[a]	.139	1	.709		
Likelihood Ratio	.558	1	.455		
Fisher's Exact Test				.710	.355
N of Valid Cases	30				

[a] Computed only for a 2×2 table
[b] 0 cells (.0%) have expected count less than 5. The minimum expected count is 6.00

In the upper section of Table 4.20 there are **Count** and **Expected Count** figures for each combination of gender and promotion. The former is the actual number of respondents giving those gender and promotion details, for instance ten respondents were female with no promotion. The **Expected Count** is the number of respondents that would be expected to have those gender and promotion details if gender and promotion were independent; nine in the case of female and no promotion.

The **Value** of the **Pearson Chi-square** to the top left of the lower section of Table 4.20 is an aggregate measure based on the differences between the **Count** and the **Expected Count** for each gender and promotion combination. The larger the differences between them, the bigger will be the value of chi-square, and the more evidence there is for association between the variables. The top figure in the column headed **Asymp. Sig.** is the probability of getting these sample results if there is no association between the variables in the population. You can interpret this simply as the probability of there being no association between the two variables. In this case the value is **0.456**, so on this evidence there is a 45.6 per cent chance of no association, which suggests that gender and promotion are independent. In practice only when this figure is less than 10 per cent (0.10), and by implication the chance of association is more than 90 per cent, would it be legitimate to conclude that there is association. Buglear (2005: 569–575) contains a fuller discussion of contingency analysis.

Suppose the gender of the last three of the fifteen males in the data set had been wrongly recorded and they were in fact females. Alter the thirteenth to fifteenth rows of data accordingly and repeat the procedure above to produce a new contingency analysis. The top figure in the **Asymp. Sig.** column, the probability of getting the sample results if there is no association, is now **0.094**. This implies that there is less than a 10 per cent chance that these data came from a population where gender and promotion are independent, and hence that the two variables appear to be associated. The **Count** and **Expected Count** for female and no promotion are now **13** and **10.8** respectively, indicating that the form of this association is that women are less likely to be promoted than men.

The bottom row of the output should consist of a message saying **1 cells (25.0%) have expected count less than 5. The minimum expected count is 4.80.** This is a warning to alert you to the thin spread of observations in part of the table and to suggest that the results should be treated with caution. This can be a problem with variables that have several response categories.

Produce a contingency analysis for the promotion and rating data. Proceed as before but:

- In the **Crosstabs** dialogue box click the **Reset** button.
- Click on **Promotion** in the space on the left-hand side then ▶ to the right of **Row(s)**.
- Click on **Rating** in the space on the left then ▶ to the right of **Column(s)**.

The resulting table should have a warning of **6 cells (75.0) have expected count less than 5. The minimum expected count is 1.60.** The best way of avoiding this would be to obtain more data, but if this is not feasible we can merge categories. Apply this to the rating data:

- Click **Transform** on the menu bar and on the draw-down menu select **Recode**.
- Pick **Into Different Variables** from the sub-menu.

- In the dialogue box highlight **Rating** in the list on the left, click ▶ then type *Reaction* in the space below **Name** to the top right of the box.
- Click the **Old and New Values** button.
- In the dialogue box type *1* below **Value** in the left-hand side of the box under **Old Value**.
- Tick the space to the left of **Output variables are strings** in the right-hand corner of the box.
- Type *Positive* alongside **Value** in the right-hand side of the box under **New Value** then click **Add**.
- Type *2* and *Positive* as the **Old Value** and **New Value** respectively then click **Add**.
- Similarly make *3* and *4* the existing values to be replaced by *Negative*.
- Click **Continue**, which will return you to the previous dialogue box, click **Change** then **OK**.
- The **Data View** should now contain an additional column containing the recoded values.

Produce a contingency analysis for the promotion and reaction data as before, by selecting **Descriptive Statistics** from the **Analyze** menu and picking **Crosstabs** from the sub-menu but this time remove **Rating** from the space below **Column(s)** and replace it with **Reaction**. The output should now have no expected counts less than 5.

Produce a Pearson correlation coefficient to measure the association between age and salary:

- Choose **Correlate** from the **Analyze** draw-down menu and select **Bivariate** from the sub-menu.
- In the **Bivariate Correlations** window that appears the locations of your data are listed on the left.
- Click the ▶ symbol to bring **Age** and **Salary** into the **Variables** box on the right.
- Check that the default setting under **Correlation Coefficients** is **Pearson** and click **OK**.

The coefficient, 0.684, should be in the **Correlations** table in the **Output Viewer**. This value suggests the association between the two variables is positive but modest (Buglear, 2005: 224–234). Bear in mind that a correlation coefficient should always be considered with a scatter diagram of the data as the same coefficient value could arise from different scatters of data.

Obtain the regression model for the relationship between age and salary:

- Select the **Analyze** draw-down menu then **Regression**, and then **Linear**.
- Click on **Salary** then ▶ beside **Dependent**, and **Age** then ▶ beside **Independent(s)**, then **OK**.

The analysis that appears in the **Output Viewer** should include the coeffi-cients of the regression model and the value of R^2, listed as **R Square**, as shown in Table 4.21.

Table 4.21 **Regression analysis of the age and salary data**

Model summary				
Model	R	R Square	Adjusted R Square	Std. Error of the Estimate
1	.684(a)	.468	.449	5.88088

(a) Predictors: (Constant), Age

Coefficients(a)						
		Unstandardised Coefficients		Standardised Coefficients		
Model		B	Std. Error	Beta	t	Sig.
1	(Constant)	20.729	4.350		4.766	.000
	Age	.539	.109	.684	4.959	.000

(a) Dependent Variable: Salary

In the upper section of Table 4.21 the **R Square** figure gives the propor-tion of the variation in salary that can be explained by age, **.486** or 46.8 per cent. The coefficients of the regression equation listed under **B** in the lower section of Table 4.21 tell us that the linear equation that best repre-sents the relationship between salary and age is:

Salary = 20.729 + 0.539 Age

Buglear (2005: 237–244) contains a more extensive discussion of regres-sion models.

You might like to look at the regression line superimposed on the data:

● Select **Regression** from the **Analyse** draw-down menu then choose **Curve Estimation**.
● Click on **Salary** then ▶ beside **Dependent(s)**, and **Age** then ▶ under **Variable** in the **Independent** section of the box.
● Check that the **Linear** option under **Models** is ticked then click **OK**.

The **Output Viewer** should show a scatter diagram with the best fit line superimposed like Figure 4.34. The points furthest from the line repre-sent the likely outliers, observations that appear unusual in the context of the model.

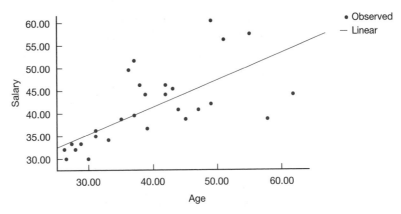

Figure 4.34 **Fitted line plot of the salary and age data**

Leave the package by clicking on the **File** and choosing **Exit**. Before the package allows you to finish your session you will be asked if you want to save your work, which is entirely up to you.

You can find more information about SPSS on the company website at http://www.spss.com. The company often offers a free trial of the package for a limited period, which you can take up through the website. For more on using SPSS output, try Bryman and Cramer (2004) and Pallant (2004).

Software for analysing qualitative material – *Carole Tansley*

Qualitative research data can be said to be made up of words rather than numbers and can be generated from a variety of different research methods, including: case studies, ethnographies, participant observation, interviews (semi-structured, open), questionnaires (structured or semi-structured), focus groups, life/career histories, discourse analysis and organisational stories. Research material can be collected in different media, including audio and video clips, and the result is usually massive amounts of data which requires careful recording and organisation. However, the benefits of this are that we end up with 'well-grounded, rich descriptions and explanations of processes in identifiable local contexts', so that researchers can identify 'a chronological flow, see precisely which events led to which consequences and derive fruitful explanation – they help researchers to get beyond initial conceptions and to generate or revise conceptual frameworks' (Miles and Huberman, 1994: 1).

Given the richness and volume of data and information involved, researchers need to think carefully about which computer software packages might be helpful in their organising, sensemaking and theorising processes. Using computers for qualitative research can not only speed up the process of retrieving, exploring and theorising material, it can also ensure that the final research report can be shown to have been produced as a result of rigorous collection and analysis processes.

There are a number of types of computer software and a number of ways in which computer software can help the researcher make sense of data. Types of software and their functions include:

- *Word processing tools.* There are many varieties and they are valuable for the production and revision of text throughout the research process. These are available on desktop PCs, notebooks and handheld computers such as PDAs (personal digital assistants).

- *Word-retrieving tools and text-based managers.* Text-retrieval and document-management systems are designed for archiving, researching and annotating large bodies of text. They enable searches through thousands of documents at extraordinary speeds. Researchers can source particular words and phrases; concepts; key words; wildcards; dates; part numbers; quantities and statistics, and searches can include substrings; proximity; Boolean and combination searches. They can also allow the examination of: selected references in contexts; conducting user-defined frequency distribution analysis; creating user-selected word lists/reference lists; and generating concordances according to a set of user-defined parameters. Programs providing some or all of these functions include: Metamorph, Sonar, WordCruncher and The Text Collector.

- *Collation, code and theory-building software.* These allow the import of text-based qualitative data, typed in any word processor, straight into the program, then support searching and annotation of segments of interest within the data, the marking of code words and the running of analyses which can be retrieved for inclusion in reports or further analysis. Examples include: NVivo 7, The Ethnograph and Atlas ti.

Tips about choosing qualitative analysis software

Choosing qualitative analysis software can take some time and effort but there are certain steps it would be sensible to undertake. First, do a search on the Internet for different types of software and take note of the functionality and features offered, including user-friendliness, flexibility, cost and what you actually get for your money. For example, does the price include a hard copy of an operations manual as well as on-screen and web-based help features, as well as having additional technical support whose cost is not too crippling? Consideration should also be given to the amount of time that needs to be invested into learning about the capability of the software because such software is powerful, supporting as it does processes of coding data in an index system, searching text or searching patterns of coding and theorising about the data.

One such system is called NVivo 7 and it comes with a detailed online help function, clear tutorials and user guides (go to http://www .qsrinternational.com/products/productoverview/NVivo_7.htm for a free 30-day online trial). In terms of style and layout, this software package has the look of Microsoft Outlook, which, if you are familiar with this popular software, will reduce the investment in learning how to navigate the different elements. Functionally, the software provides two essential purposes. First, it is a powerful and user-friendly 'electronic filing cabinet' for importing documents singly or in batches, in plain text with automatic formatting to the chosen unit of text. These documents can then be edited, extended or the notes revised. Second, it supports content analysis (counting frequencies, sequence, or locations of words and phrases) and coding on-screen by enabling the attachment of key words or tags to segments of text to permit later searching and retrieval.

In the following sections I will describe how various software (and hardware) can be used in the different stages of qualitative research.

Software tools for recording and managing bibliographies

Over the course of a research project the researcher will gather many references which need to be cited in a bibliography. These can be in the thousands and it is important to record these carefully as evidence of the statements made in the finished research report or dissertation. There are several proprietary packages on the market, the well-known ones being EndNote (see p. 346) and Research Manager. They enable:

- Organisation of references and images in a database.
- Recording of different reference types (journal articles, books, personal conversations, videos).
- Recording notes for literature review.
- Accessing and searching bibliographic databases on the Internet.
- Generation of a bibliography/references section as you write.
- Organisation of more than just text. Such software can also manage any type of generic image (e.g., BMP, TIFF, JPEG) or application file (e.g., Microsoft Excel, PhotoShop, ChemDraw) using the image and caption fields in any reference type.
- Construction of your thesis with built-in manuscript templates. With this, you can start a new Microsoft Word document based on pre-defined templates from within a package like EndNote (or you can also do this directly from Word). You can also copy and edit one of the pre-defined manuscript templates shown in your dissertation editorial style guide or, if you are writing a paper for a journal or magazine from your study, the publisher to which you intend to submit your manuscript. This opens a new document in Microsoft Word that is based on the template file, and starts a manuscript wizard to help you set up your thesis or paper.

As with all electronic databases, if they are to be effective in your research you need to use them for everything or you will find you miss that important reference and this can take some time to find when the pressure is on at the final stages of producing the research report or dissertation.

Production of field notes

When in the 'field' it is important to have appropriate equipment to hand to make sure you take advantage of that opportunity to collect information, either in formal situations such as interviews or those 'serendipitous' moments which occur where something happens or someone says something that can really make a difference to the direction of your research. Carry a handheld/PDA (personal digital assistant) to make or take notes in the field, storing them as text or recording notes, or use any voice-recording facility for meetings and impromptu discussions (always making sure you ask permission to record first). Many PDAs allow notes to be 'typed' into a word processing package using a keyboard available on or below the screen. Some also allow handwriting recognition if you need to make notes quickly. Once at home or back at work you can then synchronise the material recorded on the handheld with your notebook or desktop computer.

Analysing qualitative data

It is recommended that you analyse as you go along rather than saving all your material up for one major analysis-fest, because themes will be emerging all the time and they need to be recognised, organised and taken account of. A standardised information form is ideal for this purpose. A Contact Summary Form template is provided by Miles and Huberman (1994: 51–54), which is ideal for transferring your field notes into a more structured word-processed format by undertaking a 'first cut' data reduction exercise on what you saw, what conceptual themes seemed to be involved and any aspects or issues which might need to be followed up in the future. The file can then be saved as a rich text document in a word processing package and transferred into qualitative analysis software which allows storage coding, indexing, searching, analysis and theorising of non-numerical, unstructured research material. There are a number of these on the market but you need to make sure you go about the choice carefully.

As documents build up in the 'electronic filing cabinet', deeper analysis begins. Qualitative analysis involves four concurrent flows of activity: data reduction; data display; theory building; and conclusion drawing and verification.

Many qualitative researchers work inductively, that is by attempting to gain an understanding of the meanings the people being studied attach to events by gaining a close understanding of the research context and also with less concern with the need to generalise. There are particular challenges in theory building when working with qualitative research material.

Theory building with qualitative analysis software

Researchers working inductively often describe the theorising aspects of their research as using a 'grounded theory' approach – that is, theory that is developed inductively from an entire collection of data from the study. Grounded theorists use categories drawn from respondents themselves and try to understand the interpretations of their research subjects by making their subjects' implicit belief systems explicit.

A grounded theory approach involves the reading and re-reading of research materials in a textual database (such as a collection of field notes, although the data do not have to be literally textual – they could be photographs, video or audio files), identifying and labelling variables (called categories, concepts and properties). We can see what such a database looks like with the screenshot of an NVivo 7 extract shown in Figure 4.35.

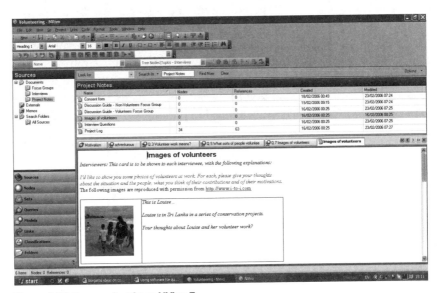

Figure 4.35 Screenshot from NVivo 7

Theory building takes place by considering changes of research emphasis as the research progresses and interrelationships develop.

This is done by the coding of segments of relevant text, then their clustering into key conceptual areas which are derived either from the data themselves or via the researcher's hypothesis and the themes considered relevant at the start of the study. The ability to perceive variables and relationships is termed 'theoretical sensitivity' and is affected by a number of things, including one's reading of the literature and one's use of techniques designed to enhance sensitivity. So a grounded theory approach consists of a set of steps aimed at producing a 'good' theory as the outcome ('good' meaning that the quality of the theory produced can be evaluated by the process by which a theory is constructed.)

Different ways of coding can be undertaken during the analysis.

Stages of coding
Open coding

When we first examine the data, we begin to assign codes to the concepts covered. This is called 'open coding'. Open coding is the part of the analysis concerned with identifying, naming, categorising and describing phenomena found in the text. Essentially, each line, sentence, paragraph etc. is read in search of the answer to the repeated question 'What is this about – what is being referenced here?'

These labels refer to things like factories, networking, friendship, micropolitics, that is, the nouns and verbs of a conceptual world. This part of the analytic process is to identify the more general categories that these things are instances of, such as organisations, social activities, social relations, social outcomes, etc.

The adjectives and adverbs are the properties of these categories. For example, about a network we might ask about its duration, its membership and its importance to each person. Whether these properties or dimensions come from the data itself, from respondents, or from the mind of the researcher depends on the goals of the research.

Borgatti (2006) points us to Strauss and Corbin (1990: 78) to consider what is implied in the following passage of text:

> Pain relief is a major problem when you have arthritis. Sometimes, the pain is worse than other times, but when it gets really bad, whew! It hurts so bad, you don't want to get out of bed. You don't feel like doing anything. Any relief you get from drugs that you take is only temporary or partial.

Borgatti explains that one thing that is being discussed here is *pain*. Implied in the text is that the speaker views pain as having certain properties, one of which is *intensity*: it varies from a little to a lot. (When is it a lot and when is it little?) When it hurts a lot, there are consequences: don't want to get out of bed, don't feel like doing things (what are other things you don't do when in pain?). In order to solve this problem, you need *pain relief*. One *agent of pain relief* is drugs (what are other members of this category?). Pain relief has a certain *duration* (could be temporary), and *effectiveness* (could be partial).

Coding can be done very formally and systematically or quite informally. In grounded theory, it is normally done quite informally. For example, if after coding much text some new categories are invented, grounded theorists do not normally go back to the earlier text to code for that category. However, maintaining an inventory of codes with their descriptions (i.e., creating a codebook) is useful, along with pointers to texts that contain them. In addition, as codes are developed, it is useful to write memos known as code notes that discuss the codes. These memos become material for later development into reports.

Qualitative data analysis software like NVivo 7 allows for allocation of concept 'nodes' called 'free nodes' which are 'standalone' nodes that have no clear logical connection with other nodes – they do not easily fit into a hierarchical structure, at least to begin with. Here, the researcher simply labels the phenomena as they are being discovered, keeping an open mind during this process to avoid the concepts inherent in the data being obscured by any predetermined theoretical basis. Figure 4.36 illustrates how NVivo 7 allows this.

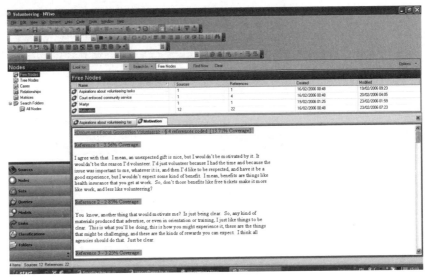

Figure 4.36 The use of free nodes for indexing

The topic of this research is 'volunteering' and we can see in the list in the upper half of the screen the themes emerging and being allocated, one of which is 'motivation' (to volunteer). In the lower half of the screen is shown which segments of text have been 'tagged', here in interview transcripts kept elsewhere but gathered as a dynamic report as the codes are allocated.

Free nodes are useful to allocate when we are not sure of the whole picture and are trying to capture emerging themes which we might explore in greater depth later through more empirical research or which we might decide to set aside, at least for the moment unless more information becomes available which shows that this is a concept or theme worthy of raising in importance.

As the researcher continues to compare the concepts being examined with those that have already been coded, he or she will begin to get a sense of hierarchies of codes. Alternatively, the researcher might already be working with a model in mind and know which concepts are relevant and how they are related to each other. In both these cases the researcher can use what are called 'tree nodes'. As can be seen from the NVivo 7 screen example in Figure 4.37, these are nodes that are catalogued in a hierarchical structure, moving from a general category at the top (the parent node) to more specific categories (child nodes) later, thus beginning to identify hierarchies of relationships between concepts. This can reduce the number of concepts to be handled and provide a stronger conceptual basis to the themes discovered.

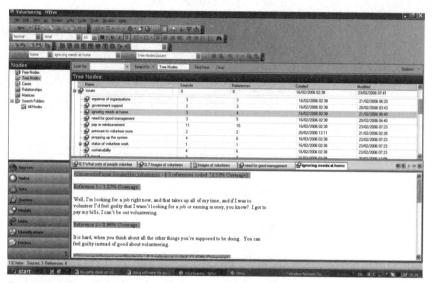

Figure 4.37 Hierarchical coding

Axial coding

As the researcher is working inductively, trying to develop ideas, concepts and theories from the data, 'axial coding' will then commence. This coding process involves examining each category in terms of the context in which it occurs, any conditions which it may have caused, any actions and interactional strategies by which it is managed or handled and the consequences which arise from the category. By examining these factors, it becomes possible to link categories and to verify the linkages by testing them against the data. It enables the researcher to 'ground' their theory on the data. The final result of axial coding is a very rich description of the phenomenon being researched.

Axial coding is the process of relating codes (categories and properties) to each other, via a combination of inductive and deductive thinking. Borgatti (2006) advises that to simplify this process, rather than look for any and all kinds of relations, grounded theorists emphasise causal relationships, and fit things into a basic frame of generic relationships. The frame consists of the following elements:

- *Phenomenon.* This is the concept that holds the bits together. In grounded theory it is sometimes the outcome of interest, or it can be the subject.
- *Causal conditions.* These are the events or variables that lead to the occurrence or development of the phenomenon. It is a set of causes and their properties.
- *Context.* Hard to distinguish from the causal conditions. It is the specific locations (values) of background variables, a set of conditions influencing the action/strategy. Researchers often make a distinction between active variables (causes) and background variables (context). It has more to do with what the researcher finds more interesting (causes) and less interesting (context) than with distinctions out in nature.
- *Intervening conditions.* Similar to context. We can identify context with *moderating* variables and intervening conditions with *mediating* variables. But it is not clear that grounded theorists cleanly distinguish between these two.
- *Action strategies.* The purposeful, goal-oriented activities that agents perform in response to the phenomenon and intervening conditions.
- *Consequences.* These are the consequences of the action strategies, intended and unintended.

In the extract on p. 258 above, it seems obvious that the phenomenon of interest is pain, the causal condition is arthritis, the action strategy is taking drugs, and the consequence is pain relief. Note that grounded theorists don't show much interest in the consequences of the phenomenon itself.

The final stage is 'selective coding', involving the integration of the categorised material into a theory which accounts for the phenomenon being researched. This integration is done by selecting one of the categories as the focus of interest and making it the 'core category' or 'storyline' around which the rest of the categories are organised. This creates a theoretical framework, which is validated against the data. So in our example, the 'storyline' could be about how pain develops or is controlled by taking particular drugs, what causes relief and what impact not relieving the pain has on the person being studied.

Data displays

Continually producing data displays is important as the research progresses. Data can be displayed in a variety of ways but doing so involves placing selected or reduced data in a condensed, organised format such as a matrix, a network or a map so that it can be examined and data can be linked by connecting segments to one another to form categories, clusters of networks of information or produce theoretical models. It is an important part of qualitative research, involving as it does the development of systematic, conceptually coherent explanations of findings and enabling the testing of any propositions or hypotheses. A theoretical framework or frameworks can then be constructed (or, if working deductively, you can focus on concepts already in the theoretical model and look for patterns and appearances). Mind-mapping software can be useful for this, as it can enable the speedy brainstorming and capture of ideas, the organisation of ideas in a view of the map and facilitate the attachment of relevant information, the creation of visually rich maps with graphics and colours and the drawing of relationships between important issues (and the software transfers to Microsoft PowerPoint slides and Word documents). Figure 4.38 shows how the maps can be built up.

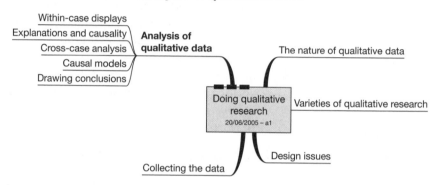

Figure 4.38 Example of a mind map

Practical tips on using software for qualitative analysis

Over the many years that I have gathered and analysed qualitative research material in the area of organisational behaviour I have found there are a number of aspects which need to be taken into consideration:

- Apart from a word processing package, it is not essential to have any of these packages. They just help with the organising process overall.
- While it is useful to have access to so many different software packages one must take care that the sourcing and learning about the use of such packages does not take valuable time one should be spending doing the actual research.
- Software and hardware can be expensive. Check out if the institution you are studying with provides free access to relevant software packages – and the tutors (virtual or real!) to show you how to use them.
- As part of the ongoing analysis, it recommended that the researcher produces memos. These written, reflective commentaries will contain detailed thoughts and observations and link them to the research as a basis for deeper understanding. These can be either to oneself for

future consideration or to send to others, such as a tutor. If these memos are stored in an analysis software package, they too can be coded, added to and changed.

- However, do not become fixated on the collection of material into databases rather than getting on with the analysis.
- In the analysis process do not allocate codes ad infinitum. I know one student who did this and ended up with over 500 codes and no idea how to pull them all together as she did not analyse as she went along.
- You need to understand the diversity of the sort of material you are working with and match the functionality of the data analysis software, for example:
  - If you are working inductively then you need software which enables fast search and retrieval, easy coding and revision and a good graphic display. If you are working deductively, say working with hypotheses, then you will need good theory-building capability.
  - If you envisage that you will be adding to/annotating some of the material (codes, memos etc.), rather than having a static collection of materials (documentation etc.), make sure the database you are using allows revising as you go along rather than having to recreate records.
  - Take account of how flexible the software is with regard to coding 'chunks' of data. Do you need to be able to code just one word, as well as sentences, paragraphs or whole pages or files? Then check out the functionality of the software in this case, as well as being able to identify the source of the document when you have undertaken a report of annotated text per code.
  - If you are collecting data from many sources or doing cross-case analyses of multiple cases, then your software needs to be good at making links between phenomena and you may need to sort these into different patterns or configurations and 'tag' and sort them using the software's functionality.
  - Decide how you would like the coded items to be displayed. By list? By matrix? By hierarchical tree diagram?
  - If you think you will continue your studies then do not see this as a one-off event, but envisage that you will be using your database and the software again, for another research project or a qualification.

Homepage URLs for the software mentioned in this section

EndNote http://www.endnote.com
Metamorph http://www.thunderstone.com/texis/site/pages/Metamorph.html
NVivo 7 http://www.qsrinternational.com/products/productoverview/NVivo_7.htm

Research Manager http://www.adeptscience.co.uk/products/refman/
reference
Sonar http://www.virginiasystems.com/
The Text Collector http://www.jaedworks.com/hypercard/scripts/text-collector.html
Wordcruncher http://www.hamilton-locke.com/Products.html

Summary

- Decide whether you will be researching as an explorer or a surveyor, or both.
- Make a careful choice about the degree of openness or pre-coding that you need to apply to the research methods you are using.
- If you are using an open or semi-structured approach you still need to plan and organise your research methods carefully.
- If you are using pre-coded techniques, choose the best question format, from those available, for each of the questions you want to ask.
- Whether you use open, semi-structured or pre-coded techniques always pilot your research tools, schedules, aides-memoires, questionnaires or whatever before using them on your main research subjects.
- If your research material is qualitative, use a coding method to summarise and précis the material. Frame the account of your material in a case study format, which helps you to identify the connections between the themes within your material.
- If your research material is quantitative, analyse it using descriptive and summary statistics. Use graphs and charts where they ease explanation but avoid overusing them.
- Use appropriate statistical tests to check the significance of your analysis.
- Consider using software packages to help you analyse your material qualitatively or quantitatively – but be careful. Deciding whether the effort needed to master the software and input the research material is justified within the short amount of time available for a part-time Master's dissertation is a fine judgement.

Suggested reading

Saunders *et al.* (2006) is the best option if you want a general guide to all the techniques covered in this chapter. For open and semi-structured research I recommend Silverman (1999). The classic work for those designing a questionnaire is Oppenheim (1992). For statistics and quantitative methods read Buglear (2000). Sapsford and Judd (1996) is a good alternative. Bryman and Cramer (2001) is based on SPSS and explains the statistical techniques well but probably goes into too much detail for most Master's students. Sapsford (1999) is helpful survey research.

Bryman, A. and Cramer, D. (2001) *Quantitative Analysis with SPSS Release 10 for Windows: A Guide for Social Scientists*, London: Routledge.

Buglear, J. (2000) *Stats To Go*, Oxford: Butterworth Heinemann.

Sapsford, R. (1999) *Survey Research*, London: Sage.

Sapsford, R. and Judd, V. (eds) (1996) *Data Collection and Analysis*, London: Sage.

Silverman, D. (1999) *Doing Qualitative Research*, London: Sage.

References

Bales, R.F. (1950) *Interaction Process Analysis*, Reading, Mass.: Addison-Wesley.

Bayly, C.A. (1996) *Empire and Information: Intelligence Gathering and Social Communication in India, 1780–1870*, Cambridge: Cambridge University Press.

BBC (2003) 'Row over NHS star ratings', BBC News (Online) 16 July. Available at: http://news.bbc .co.uk /1/hi/health/3069121.stm (accessed 16 July 2003).

Billig, M. (1996) *Arguing and Thinking: A Rhetorical Approach to Social Psychology*, 2nd edn, Cambridge: Cambridge University Press.

Borgatti, S. (2006) *Introduction to grounded theory*. Available on the World Wide Web at: http://www .analytictech.com/mb870/introtoGT.htm (accessed 10 July 2006).

Boyatzis, R. (1982) *The Competent Manager*, New York: John Wiley.

Bryman, A. and Cramer, D. (2004) *Quantitative Data Analysis with SPSS 2 and 13: A Guide for Social Scientists*, London: Routledge.

Buglear, J. (2001) *Stats Means Business*, Oxford: Butterworth Heinemann.

Buglear, J. (2005) *Quantitative Methods for Business: The A to Z of QM*, Oxford: Elsevier.

Cramer, D. (1997) *Basic Statistics for Social Research*, London: Routledge.

Czarniawska, B. (2004) *Narratives in Social Science Research*, London: Sage.

Ellinger, A.D. and Watkins, K.E. (1998) 'Updating the critical incident techniques after forty-four years', in R.J. Torraco (proceedings ed.), *Academy of Human Resource Development 1998 Conference Proceedings*, Baton Rouge, La.: Academy of Human Resource Development, Conference, Chicago, March.

Flanagan, J.C. (1954) 'The critical incident technique', *Psychological Bulletin*, vol. 1: 327–358.

Freeman, D. (1983) *Margaret Mead and Samoa: The Making and Unmaking of an Anthropological Myth*, London: Harvard University Press.

Gabriel, Y. (2000) *Storytelling in Organizations*, Oxford: Oxford University Press.

Gill, J. and Johnson, P. (1997) *Research Methods for Managers*, 2nd edn, London: Paul Chapman.

Goldman, R. and McKenzie, J. *The Student Guide to Minitab Release 14*, Reading, Mass.: Addison-Wesley.

Gordon, W. and Langmaid, R. (1988) *Qualitative Market Research: A Practitioners' and Buyers' Guide*, Aldershot: Gower.

Huff, D. (1991) *How to Lie with Statistics*, Harmondsworth: Penguin.

Hurston, Z.N. (1942) *Dust Tracks on a Road*, Philadelphia, Pa.: J.B. Lippincott.

Huxley, T.H. (1807) 'Biogenesis and abigenesis', in *Collected Works*, vol. VIII.

Jankowicz, A.D. (1995) *Business Research Projects*, 2nd edn, London: Chapman & Hall.

Jankowicz, A.D. (2003) *An Easy Guide to Repertory Grids*, London: John Wiley.

Joiner, B., Cryer, J. and Ryan, B.F. (2004) *Minitab Handbook*, New York: Brooks Cole.

Kelly, G. (1963) *A Theory of Personality: The Psychology of Personal Constructs*, New York: Norton.

Lodge, D. (1989) *Nice Work*, London: Penguin.

McClean, A. and Marshall, J. (1991) *Cultures at Work: How to Identify and Understand Them*, Luton: Local Government Management Board.

McKenzie, J. and Goldman, R. (1999) *The Student Edition of MINITAB for Windows 95 and NT*, New York: Addison-Wesley-Longman.

Miles, M.B. and Huberman, A.M. (1994) *Qualitative Data Analysis: An Expanded Sourcebook*, London: Sage.

Mohrman, A. Jr, Resnick-West, S.M. and Lawler, E.E. III (1989) *Designing Performance Appraisal Schemes: Aligning Appraisal and Organisational Realities*, San Francisco: Jossey-Bass.

Moore, P.G. (1980) *Reason by Numbers*, Harmondsworth: Penguin.

Morgan, G. (1989) *Imagin-I-Zation: New Mindsets for Seeing, Organising and Managing*, London: Sage.

Oppenheim. A.N. (1992) *Questionnaire Design, Interviews and Attitude Measurement*, rev. edn, London: Pinter.

Padmanabha, P. (1978) 'Indian census and anthropological investigations' in *Proceedings of the Xth International Congress of Anthropological and Ethnological Sciences*. Available online at: http://www.censusindia.net/library/anthro.pdf (accessed 16 July 2003).

Pallant, J. (2004) *SPSS Survival Manual*, Buckingham: Open University Press

Pollitt and Bouckaert (2000) *Public Management Reform. A Comparative Analysis*, Oxford: Oxford University Press.

Riley, J. (1996) *Getting the Most from your Data: A Handbook of Practical Ideas on How to Analyse Qualitative Data*, Bristol: Technical and Educational Services Ltd.

Rowntree, D. (1991) *Statistics Without Tears*, Harmondsworth: Penguin.

Roy, D. (1952) 'Quota restriction and goldbricking in a machine shop', *American Journal of Sociology*, vol. 57: 427–442.

Rutter, M. (1979) *Fifteen Thousand Hours: Secondary Schools and their Effect on Children*, London: Open Books.

Saunders, M., Lewis, P. and Thornhill, A. (2006) *Research Methods for Business Students*, 4th edn, London: Financial Times Prentice Hall.

Silverman, D. (1993) *Interpreting Qualitative Data: Methods for Analysing Talk, Text and Interaction*, London: Sage.

Strauss, A.L. and Corbin, J. (1990) *Basics of Qualitative Research: Grounded Theory, Procedures and Techniques*, Newbury Park, Calif.: Sage.

Stewart, V. and Stewart, A. (1981) *Business Applications of Repertory Grid*, Maidenhead: McGraw-Hill.

Thompson, A. (1986) 'What are the patients thinking?', in B. Moores (ed.) *Are They Being Served?* Oxford: Philip Allan.

Tietze, S., Musson, G. and Cohen, L. (2003) *Understanding Organisations through Language*, London: Sage.

Watson, T.J. (1994) *In Search of Management: Culture, Chaos and Control in Managerial Work*, London: Routledge.

Watson, T.J. and Harris, L. (1999) *The Emergent Manager: Becoming a Manager in the Modern Work Organisation*, London: Sage.

Whitmore, D.A. (1975) *Work Measurement*, London: Heinemann.

Wilson, S.R., Starr-Schneidkraut, N. and Cooper, M.P. (1989) *Use of the Critical Incident Technique to Evaluate the Use of Medline*, Washington, DC: The National Library of Medicine. Available online at: http://www.nlm.nih.gov/od/ope/crl.html (accessed 10 November 2000).

Chapter 5 ● ● ● ●

Interpreting the research material

Contents

● ● ● ● Introduction

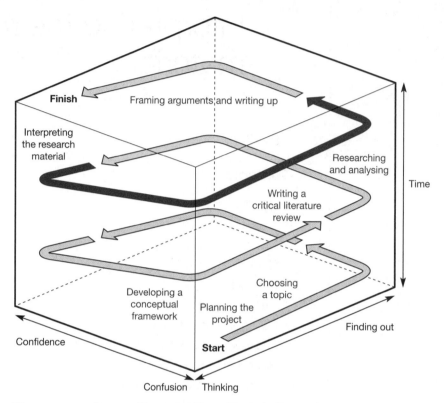

The processes of researching and writing a Master's dissertation

'What is now proved, was once only imagined.'

William Blake, *The Marriage of Heaven and Hell* (1793)

This chapter focuses on the processes and skills of interpreting your research findings and of drawing conclusions from your interpretations that are sensible and practicable. Interpretation in this chapter means deciding how robust and helpful your research findings are and the extent you might rely on them when exercising your judgement. It involves much thinking to help you 'find out' the meaning of your research findings. It can represent a loss of confidence after the buzz of certainty that comes with having completed the research phase of your project. It should be a stage in which you question everything before coming to a final statement of your interpretation and conclusions in the next 'writing up' phase of the project.

Grids and maps

To help you understand your research material you will need a map or grid (a grid is the metaphorical equivalent of the squared wire grid that archaeologists place over their excavation to help them plot the finds and accurately determine their position). The function of maps and grids is to help you distinguish what is important from what is not and help to identify the relationships between the important items.

But a grid or map is not definitive. It exists to serve a purpose; so different purposes require different maps. You can use different maps or grids; some will be plain wrong, of course, and others may throw different lights on the matter in hand. There can be no one definitive and all-purpose map. Richard Rorty made this point in relation to understanding literary texts.

> Having read Eco, or having read Derrida, will give you something interesting to say about a text which you could not otherwise have said. But it brings you no closer to what is really going on in the text than having read Marx, Freud, Matthew Arnold or F.R. Leavis. Each of these supplementary readings simply gives you one more context in which to place the text – one more grid you can place on top of it or one more paradigm to which to juxtapose it.

(Rorty, 1992: 105)

The test of the map is its usefulness. To quote Umberto Eco's (1984: 492) character William of Baskerville in his postmodern detective story *The Name of the Rose*:

> The order that our mind imagines is like a net, or a ladder, built to attain something. But afterwards you must throw the ladder away, because you discover that, even if it was useful, it was meaningless. Er muoz gelîchesame die leiter aberwerfen, sô er ir ufgestigen ... Is that how you say it?

The German saying, which is actually a quotation from the modern philosopher Wittgenstein, can be roughly translated as 'He must metaphorically get rid of the ladder the moment he has used it to get upstairs'. The point of these quotations is to suggest that it may be sensible to view the interpretation that you make of your research material as one of several that you could make; albeit you would argue that your interpretation is a useful one in the circumstances.

The same place can be mapped very differently; just as one set of data can be interpreted contrarily. Take, for example, the two maps of the Aztec city of Tenochtitlan (modern Mexico City) at the time of Cortes' conquest of Mexico. As Massey (2004) pointed out, the Spanish map shows places and spaces only; the Aztec map also incorporates time, through the narration of events and stories. The Spaniards and the Aztecs looked upon the same geographical space but interpreted it differ-

Figure 5.1 An Aztec map of Tenochtitlan

ently by emphasising different things. Consequently the maps, although of the same place, necessarily look very different (see Figures 5.1 and 5.2). Maps are useful because they help us find our way around but they are always limited because they are necessarily based on a particular perspective or projection.

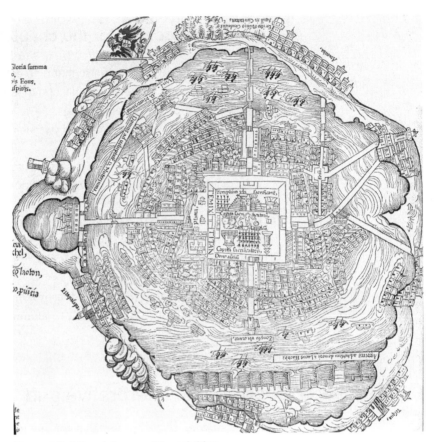

Figure 5.2 **A Spanish map of Tenochtitlan**

A key purpose of this chapter is helping you to choose an interpretive map or grid that works for your research purpose and material. The range of grids available to you is based on the range of methodological approaches outlined in Chapters 1 and 2. Indeed, you will almost certainly have chosen an interpretive grid when you developed a conceptual framework. However, when you come to interpret your research findings you need to revisit and reconsider the conceptual framework. In this chapter the intention is, by looking at how research material might be interpreted differently, to explore how you might reconsider your perspective and conceptual framework.

Learning outcomes for the chapter

1 Readers will be able to recognise that different interpretive grids can be applied to their research material and that these grids will lead to different insights and understandings.
2 They will be able to make balanced decisions about which grids to apply to their research material.
3 Readers will be able to write in a careful manner so that the claims they make are not greater than can be supported by their research and reading.
4 Readers will be able to discuss and evaluate the claims to truth and validity they make when writing a dissertation.
5 Readers will be able to draw conclusions based upon their interpretations of their research material.
6 Readers will be able to identify the problems of implementation associated with any conclusions or recommendations they might propose in the dissertation.

● ● ● ● Choosing an interpretive grid

It may be that you are of the view that for any given collection of research material there is only one correct, one right, or at the least one best, interpretation. I try to suggest in Exhibit 5.1 that there may be alternative interpretations depending upon which interpretive grid you choose to use.

Exhibit 5.1

The 'who-dunnit' and multiple interpretations

A common view of research among management students is that it involves gathering data, formulating various possible explanations of the data and then, at the end of the dissertation revealing the true explanation. This makes research seem very like detective 'who-dunnit' novels, such as Agatha Christie's Poirot stories. Poirot gathers the clues, suspects different people of the crime in question, and after using his 'little grey cells' he reveals the true culprit to the gathered company of suspects.

However, to be contrary, this may be an oversimple view of both research and detective stories. If I can persuade you that 'who-dunnits' are capable of multiple interpretation, perhaps you can accept that research material can also be 'read' from different perspectives. I shall use Agatha Christie's (1993, first published in 1927) *The Murder of Roger Ackroyd* as an example. If you do not know the story and think you might want to read it, do not continue, for the murderer's identity will be revealed.

Roger Ackroyd, an industrialist turned country gentleman is found murdered in his study. The most obvious suspect is Roger's son Ralph who is heavily in debt and who disappears immediately after the murder.

Exhibit 5.1 *continued*

But there are several other suspects, including the inevitable butler. Ackroyd had been the lover of Mrs Ferrars who had earlier, it was thought, committed suicide and who had been suspected by village gossips of having murdered her own husband. Two other key characters are Dr Roger Shepherd (who is the narrator of the book) and Caroline his sister who lives with him and keeps his house.

At the end of the book Poirot declares (in a nice postmodern twist by Agatha Christie) that the murderer is Dr Roger Shepherd. The murderer is the very person who has written the account of the case that we have been reading. Poirot argues that Mrs Ferrars had murdered her husband and was being blackmailed by Shepherd who knew of her crime. To escape the blackmail Mrs Ferrars killed herself but not before writing to Roger Ackroyd, naming Shepherd as the blackmailer. So Shepherd had to kill Ackroyd. Poirot builds his case on three clues:

- An armchair that had been moved in Ackroyd's study.
- An illogical phone call.
- Five minutes unaccounted for.

Shepherd, Poirot argues, had arranged the murder to make it seem that it occurred later than it had. He was a gadget man and knew about the latest invention, in the 1920s, the Dictaphone™, an unwieldy piece of equipment to modern eyes. After he killed Ackroyd (in the five minutes of his day unaccounted for) he set up the Dictaphone in Ackroyd's study on a timer so that much later it would play a tape of Ackroyd's voice, and those outside the study would think Ackroyd still alive. He had to move the armchair so that the Dictaphone could not be seen through the window. The last element in his plan was to pay someone passing through the village and his surgery to ring him in the evening and pretend to be calling from Ackroyd's house and asking him to attend. This gives Shepherd an excuse to visit Ackroyd and be the person to find him murdered. In the confusion Shepherd hides the Dicatphone in his capacious medical bag. He, of course, had ensured he had an alibi for the time when it was mistakenly thought Ackroyd had been murdered. All very clear; the murderer had been found.

Until 2000 when Pierre Bayard published a book entitled *Who Killed Roger Ackroyd? The Murderer who eluded Hercule Poirot and deceived Agatha Christie*. He reconsidered the evidence in the book and comes to the conclusion that Poirot was wrong. He had misread the characters, based his account of the murder on trivial clues (an armchair that had been moved a few inches) and had produced an overcomplicated account that depended on too many elements (such as a Dictaphone, which is never actually seen in the novel). Bayard pointed out that a much simpler solution would fit all the known facts. He argued that the murderer was Dr Shepherd's sister Caroline. She was a village busy-body who owed her status in the village to being the doctor's sister. She killed Ackroyd to prevent her brother being revealed as a blackmailer. Bayard argues that as a village gossip she had the knowledge to be able to plan the murder, that she had the psychological strength to murder and she had no alibi for the time of Ackroyd's murder. Bayard has done the unimaginable. He has applied a new interpretation to the clues provided by Agatha Christie and has come up with a solution that fits the facts better than the one Christie allows Poirot to make.

As if this were not enough, Bayard then proceeds to make another interpretation of the novel. This time, instead of making an alternative forensic interpretation of the evidence, he makes a psychoanalytical interpretation. When she wrote the book Christie had not invented her other famous fictional detective Miss Marple. But many of Caroline Shepherd's characteristics prefigure Miss Marple. Both were nosey older women who observed village life and applied a cool incisive logic. If Caroline is the psychoanalytical shadow of Miss Marple then the novel can be seen as a conflict between Christies' two detectives in which the female outwits the male. He takes the analysis further (one cannot help suspecting with his tongue in his cheek) to suggest that Caroline Shepherd/Miss Marple are an extension of Agatha Christie herself and so the novel can be seen as a struggle between Christie and her own most famous creation – Poirot. It seems not unusual for creators of famous fictional detectives to want to kill them off; Arthur Conan-Doyle tried, unsuccessfully, to kill off his creation Sherlock Holmes.

Following this example an important point needs to be made. That it may be possible to make different interpretations of some research material does not mean that all interpretations are equally helpful or true. Some interpretations will be just wrong or silly. As Umberto Eco (1992: 52) wrote: 'If there are no rules that help ascertain which interpretations are the "best" ones there is at least a rule for ascertaining which ones are "bad".' William of Ockham, a medieval philosopher, proposed one such rule, Occam's razor. 'Entities ought not to be multiplied except by necessity.' The simplest argument that fits the evidence will be the best one. Arguments that bring in too many unnecessary explanations will be bad. This explains why 'cock-up' theories are more likely to be right than conspiracy theories.

● ● ● ● Styles of interpretive grid and the problem of 'universals'

To understand the range of grids available to you, and to consider their implications for what you can claim on the basis of using a grid, we need to take a short detour into medieval philosophy. Although it might seem to wander off from the point, you will see later (in Exercise 5.2) that the detour has practical consequences for the interpretation of research material and for dissertation writing.

Most of management and business research deals not in tangible objects but in ideas and abstractions. If you are studying human resource management (HRM), for example, then HRM itself is an abstraction; as are many of the things you study in its name, such as motivation, empowerment and commitment. Even in the more quantitative branches of management the subjects that are studied are mostly concepts and ideas, such as strategy and consumer preferences. Ideas, concepts, abstractions are names that we give to a number of things that we believe form a set or group because they are thought to have some important feature in common. The medieval philosophers called these sets *universals*. Think of a number of chairs you have sat on. Each and every one of these is a real thing, but the concept of *chair* is an idea formed from the conjunction of all chairs.

Medieval philosophers were the first to distinguish between universals and substance. A chair has real substance. It objectively exists. If the substance of the chair you are sitting on breaks, you get a bruised backside when you fall to the floor. However, the concept or the idea of a chair, which refers to all possible chairs and not to any one particular chair, has no substance. It is a concept, an idea or, in medieval terms, a universal. Identifying the common features that link all the chairs that can exist within the universal concept of 'chair' is often difficult. The concept is something we know intuitively rather than something we can easily articulate. You might think that all chairs have four legs; but no, there can be three-legged ones. Some chairs are built as a cube and have no legs at all. The difficulty of defining the core characteristics of a universal explains why their common use in management studies makes for difficulty: people will not agree on their definition. A universal can also be understood by comparing it with its opposite, which is a proper name. A proper name is given to a thing or person, each of which is the only thing to which the name in question applies, for example the sun, France and Napoleon. Universals such as 'chair', 'cat', 'dog' and 'humankind' apply to many different things.

It is easy, when writing about management, to use terms such as 'strategy' and others shown in Figure 5.3 as if they had clear meanings and unambiguous reality. But while it is easy to claim that a substance is real, it is not so easy to make the same claim for a universal. The document I hold which says 'A Strategy' on its cover is real enough. But whether the general idea of a strategy is as real is at least open to question (Franklin, 2001).

- Research into business, organisational and managerial matters tends to be research into abstract ideas.

- The technical term is 'universal'.

- Do universals have a concrete, objective existence?

Figure 5.3 Universals

The question that faced medieval philosophers, and still faces us, was and is: are universals real? Do they have a concrete and objective existence? As universals are the subject of much of the research into management and business it is an important question to us too. The medieval philosophers had two opposing answers to the question: realism and nominalism.

The realists thought that universals were real and had an existence separate from people's thoughts about them. The nominalists thought that universals were not independent objects and were simply convenient names or labels. These ideas will be used to identify three broad forms of interpretive grid: realist, nominalist and critical realist – an approach that seeks to combine aspects of nominalism and realism; and within each of these a number of particular interpretive grids will be illustrated to show the range and diversity of grids available. These exhibits will not exhaust the range of grids available – that would be too large a task – they are indicative only. It is important to note that most people doing a Master's dissertation in the fields of business and management will opt for realist interpretive grids. However, examples of other interpretive grids are provided for those who might feel more adventurous.

Realism

The realist (or more properly the epistemological realist to use Johnson and Duberley's (2000) term) believes that universals have a reality that is independent of how people talk about them. Therefore, the concepts we use when talking about management can be real. They believe that universals (or concepts) mirror what exists in the real world. Epistemological realism is the belief that the structure of the real world is 'cognitively accessible' to those who investigate it (Johnson and Duberley, 2000: 151). Accessible does not mean that knowledge is a perfectly accurate depiction of reality (see p. 18). Realism holds that not only does the world have an objective existence, but also it is possible for people to know about it more or less objectively.

Typically an epistemological realist who was researching HRM, for example, would claim that there are things in organisations such as:

● human resource management practices;
● policies and procedures;
● patterns of behaviour; and
● the planned outcomes of HRM activity

that can be described and delineated. They would also claim that when all these features are put together they form something which all sensible people would agree is called HRM. Quite likely they would write about HRM as if it were an unambiguous thing. So they might claim that 'HRM is the key to competitive advantage' or some such.

With this belief, epistemological realists can talk about HRM in a certain way. As it has an independent existence HRM is fixed and can be measured and defined. Realists can research organisations to see which ones practice HRM and which ones do not. They can draw conclusions about whether it is a good thing or not (see Figure 5.4).

Comparative case studies are a commonly used approach in realist research. This normally involves identifying some particular (and real) features of the case studies and then using these to define the similarities and difference between the case studies. These comparisons often allow dimensions to be defined which form a conceptual framework on which the various case studies can be plotted. This, in turn, can then form the basis for drawing some conclusions or generalisations. This process, which is what Yin (1994: 30–32) termed theoretical generalisation, is illustrated by Exhibit 5.2.

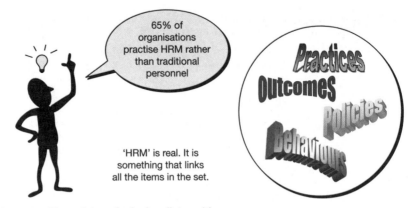

Figure 5.4 **The epistemological realist position**

Exhibit 5.2

Greenfield sites and HRM: an example of realist research

The question of whether companies that are set up on greenfield sites are more likely to break with the organisation's past and establish new approaches to HRM is explored by Leopold and Hallier (1999). They used a comparative case study method in which they researched a number of greenfield sites in Australia and New Zealand. The study built upon an earlier one that had looked at Scottish companies. For this earlier study they had developed a conceptual framework (see Figure 5.5) that identifies the possible positions that organisations developing a plant or office on a greenfield site might adopt. Organisations can either choose, on their new site, to break with the past or decide to implement their already established HR policies and practices. In terms of approach to HR they may adopt either a traditional style of personnel management that focuses on regulation and control or a more proactive policy, which seeks to create high levels of commitment among the new workforce.

The case study companies are shown plotted against the conceptual framework in Figure 5.5. It is clear that starting anew on greenfield sites does not necessarily cause organisations to break from the past and adopt new high-commitment approaches to HRM. Indeed, one of the companies simply replicated its traditional approach to HR on its new sites. One company did use the new site as an opportunity to try a new approach. However, two companies that followed a high-commitment approach were simply recreating on the new sites an HR strategy they had already tested in the rest of the organisation.

In the study the conceptual framework was useful because it could be used to show how the HR strategies initially adopted in the greenfield sites changed over time. In the cases of the two companies that sought to replicate their high-commitment approaches on the greenfield sites, management found the strategy hard to maintain. Leopold and Hallier (1999: 728) identified a 'crisis of expectations'. The proclaimed high-commitment strategy caused the new staff in the greenfield plants to have very high expectations of how they would be treated. When these expectations were not met there were pressures within the companies to move from the top left-hand quadrant of the conceptual framework to the bottom right-hand quadrant.

Exhibit 5.2 *continued*

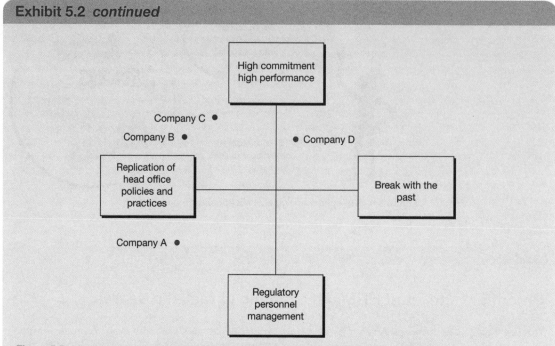

Figure 5.5 A framework for analysis of human resource management in greenfield sites

The case study approach provided a method of showing that there was no simple correlation, or cause and effect connection, between moving to a greenfield site and adopting a high-commitment approach to human resource management and industrial relations. In addition, the conceptual framework provided a way of mapping the tensions and strains within greenfield organisations and suggested how they move along the dimensions in the framework as circumstances changed.

Another common approach to realist research is to seek correlations or associations between variables. This can be attempted using more, or less, sophisticated statistical methods. The example in Exhibit 5.3 uses a very simple statistical approach.

Exhibit 5.3

Corporate social responsibility and financial performance: an example of realist research

Webley and More (2003) have sought an empirical answer to the question, does business ethics pay? They faced the technical problem that there is no single and definitive measure of ethical performance. They had to choose proxy or surrogate measures that are indicative of whether a company is behaving in an ethical and environmentally protective way. The measures chosen were:

- Whether a company has a published code of ethics that has been revised within the past five years.
- A company's rating on an index that assesses the degree to which a company manages ethical risk and whether the company is an ethical one in which to invest.
- Companies' ratings on *Management Today's* 'Britain's Most Admired Companies' survey, which is carried out by Michael Brown of Nottingham Business School.

Webley and More happily accepted that such measures did not measure the ethicalness of companies' behaviour. (Commentators have taken a satirical delight in the fact that Enron was often commended for its ethics policies.)

Webley and More showed in their analysis that companies that had a code of ethics had better ratings on both the ethical risk management and the 'Most Admired Company' league tables than those that did not. Therefore, to keep things simple all they needed to check was whether companies with a code performed better financially than those that did not.

It might have been anticipated that when Webley and More (2003) came to consider how to measure the financial performance of companies the task would be easier; but there is a wide range of possible measures. They chose four:

- Market value added (MVA) – this is the difference between what investors have put into a company over a number of years and what they would get from it if they sold their investment at current prices.
- Economic value added (EVA) – this is the amount by which investors' current income from the company is greater or less than the return they would get if they had invested the money in something else of equal risk. In other words, it is the opportunity cost of placing money in a particular company.
- Price/earnings ratio (P/E ratio) – this is the market value of shares in a company divided by the earnings investors receive from owning them.
- Return on capital employed (ROCE) – this is a measure of the returns that the capital invested in a company makes for its owners.

Two cohorts, each a little short of 50, of large companies were chosen from the FTSE 350 for the study. The results indicated, prima facie, that companies within the sample that had a code of ethics (and hence score better on the ethical risk ratings and the 'Most Admired Company' tables than those who do not) achieved a better MVA and EVA over the four-year period 1997–2000. Between 1997 and 2000 companies without a code had a greater ROCE than those that did; but by 2001 the position had reversed and those with a code performed better. The P/E ratio was more stable over the period of the study for companies with codes than it was for companies without. There is a strong indication that having a code, managing the non-financial risks of a company, and being rated by one's peers as a reputable company are associated with higher and more stable financial returns (see Figures 5.6 and 5.7).

Exhibit 5.3 *continued*

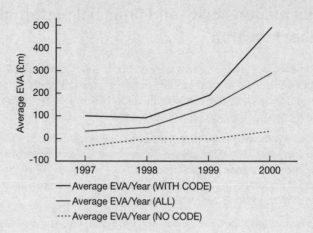

Figure 5.6 Does business ethics pay: does it add value?

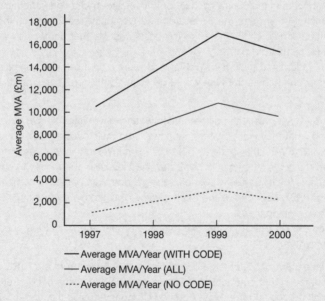

Figure 5.7 Does business ethics pay: does it enhance market value?

However, this is not necessarily proof of the business case for business ethics. A statistical association does not mean that the adoption of ethical business practices is the cause of better financial improvement. It could be the result of some different, and as yet unconsidered, factor.

Nominalism

The nominalists see universals differently from the realists. When they research an organisation they do not see undisputed facts; they see accounts and interpretations. They see themselves as researching how and why people say what they do about the subject of research, in our example case HRM. They study the accounts, arguments and statements that people make about HRM in their organisations. As people will inevitably have different opinions it follows that a concept, a universal, such as HRM, will at best be a confusion of many images. The subject can only be seen hazily as if it were being viewed through a dark glass or in a distorting mirror. Consequently, nominalists argue, what they are seeing through the glass cannot have a reality of its own; cannot in other words be a universal. They are not arguing that what is being researched is not real, just that the names we give to the things we research are not real. Modern philosophers of science often make a similar distinction. Bhaskar distinguishes intransitive objects (the things and events being studied), which are real, from transitive constructions (the shifting ways in which we understand those events and things), which are social constructions (Johnson and Duberley, 2000: 152).

Nominalists, therefore, are much more careful about the claims they make upon the basis of their research. Such researchers, investigating HRM in organisations, would not say that some organisations **do** and others **do not** have HRM. They would only go as far as to claim that most, or a certain percentage of, managers in organisations **say** that they practise HRM. This statement leaves open the question of whether what people say is mirrored by external reality. Questions about HRM, say the nominalists, cannot be answered straightforwardly because HRM is not a real thing. HRM is just a convention, a shorthand that we use in conversa-

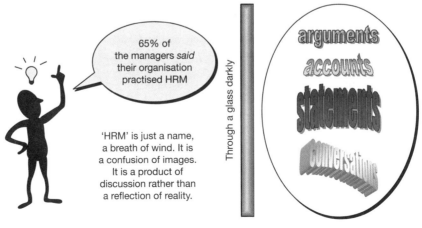

Figure 5.8 **Nominalism**

tion. One immediate consequence of writing in a nominalist mode is that sentences are longer because the ambiguities about the concepts being discussed have to be specified (as in Figure 5.8).

The next three exhibits give some examples of nominalist interpretive grids. They are not exhaustive; there are many other perspectives that might be taken. The first example, Exhibit 5.4, illustrates Karl Weick's theory of sense making.

Exhibit 5.4

Karl Weick and sense making: an example of a nominalist interpretive grid

Weick has developed a theory of sense making which provides a useful interpretive grid for nominalists interested in the way that individuals create their understandings. In his (1995) book *Sense Making in Organisations* he identified seven properties of sense making.

1 *Identity construction*. Sense making is a process by which people create a personal identity that they can present to others.
2 *Retrospective sense making*. Weick argues that people act and then make sense of their actions, not the other way around.
3 *Enactment*. People construct the reality of their organisations by how they choose to act and speak. What they say and do limits how the organisation is seen by creating the agendas for what can be said and done and what cannot ...
4 *Sense making is social*. It follows from the concept of enactment that sense making is not an isolated and individual process but a social one.
5 *Sense making is ongoing*. As situations and circumstances change then the process of sense making will adapt and change people's understandings.
6 *Sense making focuses on extracted cues*. Sense making is an editing and simplifying process. People ignore some things in the daily flow of organisational life but fix on others for use in making sense of their experiences.
7 *Sense making is based on plausibility*. People's judgements in extracting cues and enacting their sense making is based on intuitive judgements of plausibility and not on carefully calibrated rational evaluations.

Weick (1995, 2001) used his theory to explain organisational success and failure. He analysed the case study of the Mann Gulch forest fire in Montana in 1949 as an example of failure. The firefighting team mistook the extent and development of the fire; they became trapped and many died. Weick argued that circumstances made it difficult for people to make sense of what was happening and this collapse of sense making contributed to the firefighters' deaths. Their radio had been smashed and the inability to communicate with each other meant they had no access to social sense-making resources. At one point they were ordered to drop their firefighting tools; this disrupted their sense of identity; were they firefighters or victims? The fire, which they had at first seen as a small local one, which they were familiar with fighting, developed very fast into a large and fast-moving one. Their experience made this development seem implausible and the speed with which things changed made it difficult for them to extract cues. They did not know what to do to, how to enact their sense of their situation, and so they took flight but were engulfed by the fire (Weick, 2001: 465–466). In his 2001 paper Weick also gives examples where circumstances assisted sense making and allowed people to act effectively.

The next exhibit is based on actor network theory. This is not a perspective that is much seen in Master's, or indeed doctoral, dissertations, but it is an intriguing approach that students occasionally adopt.

Exhibit 5.5

Bruno Latour and actor network theory: an example of a nominalist interpretive grid

Latour, who developed actor network theory (ANT) is not keen on defining it: 'I will start by saying that there are only four things that do not work with actor-network theory: the word actor, the word network, the word theory and the hyphen' (Latour, cited in Lee and Hassard, 1999: 392).

We can say that the theory is focused on organisational processes, initially in Latour's work in the areas of science and technology, but now in a range of fields including management and organisations. We will use information technology as an example to give some small insight into ANT. ANT begins with the issue common to most forms of interpetivism. Should IT be seen as an example of technological determinism, because IT changes and controls individuals' lives in ways they cannot influence? Or should the impact of IT on people's lives be seen as mediated by, among many other things, individuals' different responses to it. ANT takes the latter view and seeks to describe the network of connections and effects between large numbers of actors. One of the novelties of ANT is that is gives to things (called actants) – objects, software and so on – the same explanatory power as it gives to people. The process of inscription is important here. When people are designing new software, for example, there will be a process of negotiation which results in a series of 'ways of seeing the world' which then are inscribed into the piece of software that then directs people who use it to think and behave in certain ways rather than other ways. Umberto Eco's (1994) famous claim that, in the field of operating systems (before the dominance of Microsoft Windows), MS-DOS encoded a Protestant way of thinking while Apple Mac encoded a Catholic world view is an example of inscription. The networks that develop may reach a state where it is difficult to reverse them; ANT, therefore, can make a contribution to the understanding of resistance to change.

Walsham and Sahay (1999) used actor network theory as an interpretive grid in their study of the role of geographical information systems (GIS) in development projects in India. The GIS projects were based on western technology and were intended to provide information on wasteland that could be used by local government administrators in developing land use. They noted that the GIS hardware, software and data were actants in the project. These actants were inscribed with western values which, to a degree, clashed with local Indian values and habits. The main values inscribed were:

- Map based. The GIS emphasised the dominance of maps as a basis for decision and action. Walsham and Sahay argued that maps were not a central aspect of Indian culture, even in finding your way to a town. The westerners wanted to use a map; the Indians preferred to ask directions from the locals.
- The GIS actants inscribed data-based, rational methods of decision making. This fitted ill with an Indian preference for intuitive decision making based on interpersonal and political relationships.
- The GIS actants were integrating mechanisms because they allowed layers of data to be projected on to the maps. The tradition in India, with deep roots in the caste system, Walsham and Sahay argued, was compartmentalism.

Walsham and Sahay then explored how the contradictions between the inscribed values of the actants and the values preferred by the Indian project partners affected the way in which the actor network developed and was maintained. The key actors included the staff of the Indian scientific institutes and the staff of the

Exhibit 5.5 *continued*

US aid agency that was promoting the projects. The developing shape of the actor network reflected the changing ambitions and expectations of those enrolled in the network. Initially the US agency staff and the Indian scientists' interests coincided. The Indian scientists wanted the American cash to buy the technology and Americans wanted local collaborators to push the projects forward. However, once the Indian scientists had the technology, their interest was to use it for pure research and not for practical problem solving, which was the intention of the American agency. Consequently the American aid agency withdrew from the project.

Actor network theory provided an interpretive grid for Walsham and Sahay's research material that enabled them to draw helpful insights into the history of the GIS projects.

Discourse analysis, which is described on pages 185–86 provides a final example of a nominalist interpretive grid.

Exhibit 5.6

Discourse analysis: an example of a nominalist interpretive grid

Tietze (2005) undertook a discourse analysis of teleworkers, that is to say, people who are required by their employers to use information and communication technologies to work from home rather than from an office. The difficulties that face teleworkers stem from the fact that 'home' and 'work' are very different frames (see p. 185 for an explanation of frames) and those involved often found working at home paradoxical. Yet they have to cope with the integration of the two. A number of discursive acts were identified that help teleworkers manage the relationship between the frames. They might, for example, use their files and paperwork to separate their work space from non-work space in their homes. They also used 'self-regulatory acts' that defined their identity as a worker. One man put a tie on when he was working at home and took it off when he had finished. Tietze noted that the discursive acts were not always successful, did not always 'take'. She noted, for example, that the space delineation acts tended to be more successful (except in households with children) whereas the 'self-regulation acts' took less often. In this paper the notion of discursive acts provides a suitable grid for explaining the quotidian details of teleworkers' lives.

Critical realism

There is a third position on the question of universals. It is the critical realist stance and it is an attempt to bring together realism and nominalism by transcending their differences. The idea that there is an objective world, and the notion that our understanding of it can only be subjective and never objective or definitive, are shown not to be mutually exclusive.

Critical realism is a stance developed by Bhaskar (Johnson and Duberley, 2000: 150–156). It proposes three levels of reality (Collier, 1994: 42–45):

- *Experiences*. This is what we see and experience of the world. This can be subjective and limited. We may 'see' things from an odd perspective or may not see things at all. This level is nominalist. Our experiences are not mirrors of reality.
- *Events*. Events are the things that happen in the world that we perceive through our experiences of them. They are the things that happen and things said and they are the second level of reality. This level represents a metaphysical realism, which is the view that the external world has a physical reality.
- *Mechanisms*. However, events do not occur out of nothing; they must have a cause. Mechanisms are the causes of events and are the third, and deepest, level of reality. The critical realists argue that there are many mechanisms existing at this level. They could be, for instance, the assumptions that constitute someone's personality, a clash of economic interests or the constraints of an organisational culture. Triggers switch on such mechanisms in complex combinations and they bring about the events that we experience. A crucial feature of mechanisms is that they cannot be directly experienced. They can only be logically inferred from events. This might be seen to make mechanisms nominalist but the critical realists argue that because they are the generative mechanisms that cause real events then they must be real too. The apparent contradiction between nominalism and realism is overcome at this deep level of reality. This third level is the 'real' reality that researchers ought to discover.

Critical realists studying HRM might observe (experience) that there are certain events that are typical of HRM. To understand these events they have to infer the mechanisms that might cause them. A good starting point might be to focus on any oddities or contradictions seen among the events as they might indicate different mechanisms coming into play (see Figure 5.9). For example, the concern for empowering employees, which HR managers often express, might sit oddly with their concentration on labour efficiency and downsizing.

If we study these contradictions they lead us to an understanding of a deeper reality that is normally hidden from view. This deeper reality is the underlying dynamics or mechanisms that are driving changes in society in general and in organisations in particular. These underlying mechanisms are often understood as the workings of the deep contradictions in capitalist society that Marxists have identified. There are some overlaps between critical realism and what is known as standpoint and emancipatory research. The latter term means that the point of research is to bring about changes in society that remove injustices. Standpoint research identifies that some groups, women and ethnic minorities for example, are more likely to suffer injustice than others and that research should be directed at identifying the underlying mechanisms that cause the discrimination and contribute to their rejection.

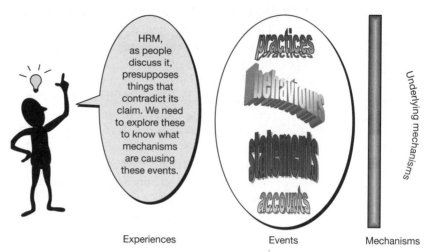

Figure 5.9 **Critical realism**

Underlying mechanisms, according to the critical realists, have a solid and real existence. Critical realism therefore combines a belief in real social forces with an understanding of the socially constructed nature of the terms (universals) that we use when discussing them.

Exhibits 5.7 and 5.8 are examples of how critical realist approaches might be used to analyse empirical material.

Exhibit 5.7

Critical realism: an example of a critical realist interpretive grid

Subramaniyam (2001) used a critical realist grid to critique the standard approach used in development projects designed to alleviate poverty, illiteracy and poor health among the Indian poor, especially those *dalit* groups who used to be known as untouchables. He called up an image of a pregnant *dalit* woman carrying water several kilometres from the well to her hut. In critical realist terms that is an event. The woman will have her own interpretation, her own experience of why she is carrying water rather than, say, using her time to make crafts to sell to a Fair Trade cooperative. She may see it as her unquestionable duty and station in life. But to understand why she is carrying the water one has to identify the underlying mechanisms that limit the events of her life, and most likely lead to her baby being malnourished and why she has a high probability of dying during childbirth. The higher castes in the woman's village depend upon an oppressed group of *dalits* to maintain their economic and status superiority. One way they achieve this is by insisting that the *dalits* live in hamlets at a distance from the main village where the caste families live and where all the resources, food supplement clinics, wells and so on are situated. This status differentiation mechanism, when associated with the physically separated condition of the *dalit* woman, causes the events in her life.

The standard development project approach, supported by the government, NGOs and aid agencies, is known as 'participatory rural appraisal' (PRA). There are variants such as participatory action research. This approach has been reduced to a series of techniques that are provided in 'toolkit' packages by agencies such as the World Bank. The toolkit includes such methods as social mapping and wealth ranking.

Exhibit 5.7 *continued*

Subramaniyam argued that these techniques only deal with the participants' experiences and events; they do not identify the underlying mechanism. They therefore miss the point and are doomed to failure. Subramaniyam then describes his own work in a particular rural area in Southern India in which he tried to avoid the limitations of the PRA approach and instead aimed at 'assisting the community to realize the "real" reasons – as opposed to the "perceived" reasons – which cause the problem and to provide them with the skills to tackle the situation' (Subramaniyam, 2001: 23).

The next example looks at a method for evaluating public services that is based on a critical realist philosophy.

Exhibit 5.8

Realist evaluation: an example of a critical realist interpretive grid

One aspect of Bhaskar's critical realism is that it argues for the existence of many mechanisms that could come into play; but which ones have an effect depends upon circumstances. Pawson and Tilley (1997) built upon this insight to develop a method of realist evaluation that is designed to evaluate public policies and programmes. It is also based upon a critique of the sort of analysis that was used in Exhibit 5.3 when conclusions are based on the analysis of the relations between just two variables (in the example of Exhibit 5.3 the relationship between corporate social responsibility and profitability). Tilley (2000) used an example, of CCTV in car parks as a means of reducing car crime, to illustrate the point. He pointed out lots of studies had been done to discover whether the rate of car crime was lower in car parks with CCTV than in car parks without. The various studies came to conflicting conclusions. Tilley argued that this is because the evaluation studies had too simple a model of public policy.

Pawson and Tilley proposed a model based on realist philosophy that had three elements that connected with each other in what they called a configuration–mechanism–outcome configuration (CMOC):

- Underlying mechanisms – there will probably be several; they are likely to be hidden and not immediately obvious to the observer.
- The various mechanisms are triggered by some contexts and circumstances but not by others.
- Outcomes. These are the desirable or undesirable consequences of the mechanisms that have been triggered by the context.

This process can be applied to the CCTV in car parks policy. One of the possible mechanisms Tilley identifies he labelled 'the nosey parker mechanism'. People see the CCTV cameras in a car park, which makes them feel secure; more people therefore use the car park, which consequently becomes busier. Because there are more people around the criminals are deterred. However, this mechanism will only be triggered in some contexts. If the car park was one that people use to park their cars while they are at work then the car park will be busy at the start and end of the working day but will be quiet for most of the day and criminals will be able to steal cars and cars' contents undisturbed. In the case of this context the outcome of CCTV will be no reduction of car crime. Other contexts may well trigger other mechanisms that would lead to a reduction in crime (Phillips, 1999).

Pawson and Tilley propose an evaluation process that involves speculation about the range of possible mechanisms and contexts, to suggest what the outcomes of the various CMOCs might be and then to set up research projects to produce data that can test out the various mechanisms. This process is similar to the abduction, deduction, induction sequence discussed in the next chapter (see p. 321).

Mixing interpretive grids

There are of course many different interpretive grids that might be used and the examples just given provide only a small glimpse into the range available. Some grids, such as those provided by the work of Foucault, have been described elsewhere in the book. Many management theorists combine several different grids when analysing their research material. Calás and Smircich (1991; see p. 114) studied some of the classical texts in management studies using a combination of Foucauldian genealogy, discourse analysis, Derrida's deconstruction and feminist standpoint research. Exercise 5.1 gives an opportunity to practise the skill of applying different interpretive grids.

Exercise 5.1

Using different interpretive grids to explain empirical material

Below is some research material gathered during an interview. Imagine you have a range of similar material. There are probably many interesting questions raised by the extract given below. Let us assume that you are interested in one only; why did Brenda choose not to blow the whistle on the discrimination practised within the company?

On the assumption that it is possible to:

- focus on different aspects of the material
- ask different questions arising from the material
- analyse the material using different theoretical grids or lenses

draft out three different interpretive grids that might be placed over the material:

- one of which is realist
- one of which is nominalist
- and one of which is critical.

The HR director

Brenda had just been appointed to her first directorship, as HR director to a retail chain. Upon taking up her appointment she realised that the company practised discriminatory policies that would be difficult to defend under equal opportunities legislation. These practices involved refusing to employ young men on the checkout tills and refusing to employ married women with young children. The employment application form required women to indicate whether they had children and, if so, their children's ages.

Brenda's attitude was that these practices had to be changed, but she would change them from within, by arguing the 'business case' rather than the 'moral case'. When asked whether she had felt the desire to reveal these practices to a wider audience, Brenda replied, 'No, I believe almost the reverse ... I will always take the business case over the moral case if I have to, because in the end it's the business that comes first, but usually the two align ... the straight moral case never wins, not against a business person who doesn't care.' Brenda had raised the issue of business ethics, and whether the company should be taking this more seriously, but was met with responses from her colleagues that ranged from 'business ethics – isn't that a contradiction in terms?' to 'Oh, come on, Brenda! Stop going all girly and nurturing on us'.

Exercise 5.1 *continued*

Very quickly after her appointment, Brenda found herself called before an Equal Opportunities Commission hearing, representing the company against a charge of discriminatory practices. She could have adopted an apologetic approach, but decided her position (as HR director) required her to defend the company. In her eyes, accepting the position of HR director entailed a sense of cabinet responsibility even though she had only just joined the company.

> So I got hauled up before the Equal Opportunities Board to justify our policies because they had had a complaint. So my view was, rather than say 'Gosh yes' and put our hands up to it and make a big fuss, my view was because you are in the organisation you are cabinet responsible, even if you have only just joined.

Brenda did a good job and the complaint against the company was not upheld. However, within the senior management team she made her views known, not so much by declaring her objection to the discrimination but by indirect, ironic, facetious or snide asides and by jokes made in meetings. The managing director (MD) always looked uncomfortable when Brenda made these remarks. He was, it appeared, a little uncomfortable with having a woman on the senior management team and often reacted by making an overenthusiastic attempt at treating her as 'one of the lads'.

Within a few weeks of the case being settled, Brenda was sacked

> because the MD thought I would blow the whistle. It was a shitty trick. He probably decided that I was just too dangerous to have on board even though the fact was that I was being supportive.

Suggested answers

A realist research grid

A realist researcher would probably conceptualise the inclination to blow the whistle, or not, as a psychological variable; let's call it propensity to whistle-blow that is influenced by a range of other variables. They would use the research interview to identify what those variables or factors might be (see Figure 5.10). They would then plan to collect data on the variables, probably using a questionnaire, so that they could then check statistically whether there are any significant relationships between the variables.

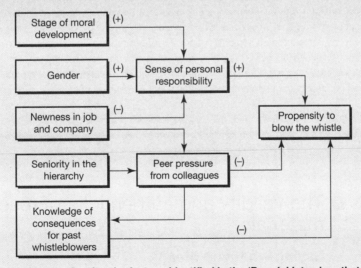

Figure 5.10 A causal diagram showing the factors, identified in the 'Brenda' interview, that may influence the propensity to blow the whistle

Exercise 5.1 *continued*

A nominalist, discourse analysis grid

A discourse analysis approach to the research question would seek to use the interview to show that Brenda, through her discourse acts, was trying to cope with, come to terms with, a dominant discourse that discouraged whistleblowing. The dominant discourse in the company might be labelled a 'business case discourse' that emphasised financial results rather than ethical or correct behaviour. This would not be unusual in the retail industry, which is traditionally driven by sales and performance targets.

It might also be considered that the discrimination against men did not fit with a discourse of discrimination that focused on injustices towards women and this may have limited the inclination to whistle-blow. Another element may have been the adversarial, quasi-judicial genre of discourse in tribunals. This would have placed Brenda in the role of an advocate with a responsibility to defend her company rather than in the role of a righter of injustice.

A discourse analysis of the interview might also note that Brenda developed some discursive acts, ironic and facetious side comments that enabled her to keep her private values and beliefs isolated from those she adopts as a manager. A discourse approach emphasises how Brenda responds to the different ways of talking and thinking about the conduct of business.

A feminist, critical, standpoint grid

> Some feminist standpoint researchers take the view that traditional research propagates masculinist notions of reason and science which men have appropriated to themselves and which exclude, marginalize and belittle women and other subordinates.
>
> Ramazanoglu (1992: 208)

The feminist belief, in contrast, is that emotion and reason, subjectivity and objectivity are inseparable. Rational analysis cannot be divorced from questions of ethics and values. In Brenda's story this might be interpreted as seeing the deliberate separation of reason and ethics enforced by the company's culture as a masculinist position; and that a feminist stance would not seek to separate the two. This separation of the objective and the subjective can be understood, to take a critical realist approach, as a mechanism which was triggered by the circumstance of a complaint to a tribunal being made by an employee. The mechanism is a deep-seated one which has developed to maintain men's positions of power over women. If this is so then Brenda is being discriminated against either by being forced to accept an uncongenial position or by being placed in a position where she feels she has to behave in a masculinist way to be accepted as a senior manager. The discrimination is exacerbated by the way in which Brenda is dismissed, for fear of her perceived feminine subjectivity, despite having behaved very loyally towards the company. Such analysis leads very easily to an emancipatory concern for using the research as a means of challenging the discrimination, both in the recruitment of staff and in the treatment of senior women managers.

None of these interpretations is fully developed; they are speculations that would need to be tested against a wider range of evidence. However, they perform the function of showing how different interpretive grids emphasise different aspects of the material and lead to different insights.

● ● ● ● The validity and authenticity of research material

Saying what you mean

When interpreting research material a major concern is the validity, or truth, of our interpretations. I will discuss later which criteria of truth can be applied. When we research and write dissertations we are mostly dealing with universals; and the discussion of realism, nominalism and critical realism raises questions of what it is possible to say validly of universals. To summarise what was discussed earlier, there a number of positions we can take on the issue of universals, including:

- They are real and more or less reflect reality and are therefore easy to define and measure.
- They are just phrases – puffs of wind, arbitrary labels – and because of this ambiguity they are difficult to define and measure. However, the ways in which people deal with this ambiguity can be researched.
- They are real but exist below the level of our direct experience and although they can be defined and specified it is a difficult intellectual process to excavate through the levels of experiences and events to identify them.

How should we write about such things? Should we write about them as if they were clear and straightforward or as if they were uncertain and ambiguous? I think, and you may disagree, that it is best to assume the precautionary principle. Which of the two situations would be worse?

- to write about universals, such as strategy or HRM, as if they were real when in truth they are not;

or

- to write about them with caution, as if they were uncertain, when in truth they are real and unambiguous.

If you take the first course you risk looking foolish; if you take the second course then the worst you will look is overcautious. On balance it might be thought best to treat universals in your dissertation as if they were dangerous and ought to be carefully caged within caveats and warnings. After all, even most modern realists do not claim that knowledge can be a perfect reflection of the real world and so even they would be a little careful with their universal concepts. As Johnson and Duberley (2000: 151) argue, 'truth must be more than outputs from a language game yet it cannot be absolute'.

One particular pitfall that Master's students can fall into is to treat the universals they are researching as if they are real when their evidence is actually nominalist in nature. Put more simply, students have often collected evidence of people's views and opinions about a thing but they write up their research as if they had objective data on the thing itself – a problem that is illustrated in the next exercise.

Exercise 5.2

Researching supply chains

Let us consider a conversation I had with a researcher a few days before writing this. He was planning some research into the efficiency and effectiveness of supply chains:

> We are looking for a correlation between lean manufacturing *attributes* (low stock levels, advanced software systems etc.) and *competitive bases* (flexibility, speed, responsiveness). At first we intended to measure these things directly. Some of them, however, are hard to measure. So we have sent out questionnaires asking managers to assess the importance of the relationship between attributes and competitive bases. Having established the relationship between attributes and competitive bases we will be able to produce a decision model to help companies find good partners for their supply chain.

The speaker is claiming his research will provide the basis of a new decision support system to help managers choose the best partners for their supply chain. Is there anything that causes you to question the honesty of this claim?

Suggested answers

The main criticism is that the researcher is claiming more for his research than can be justified. At first glance it looks like a good piece of hard scientific research. If it is possible to calculate the statistical relationship between attributes and competitive bases, companies will be able to work out which potential partner will be most competitive. Companies could measure the organisational 'attributes' of potential partners and use these to forecast which partners would be most competitive. But this is not what the researcher is planning to do. He admits that both attributes and competitive bases are tricky things because they are hard to measure. As he said, 'The trouble is each of these things, such as flexibility, can be measured in so many different ways.' Instead he is proposing to measure what managers ('who should know after all') *think* the relationship between attributes and bases is. Suddenly we are no longer dealing with hard facts, with things; we are dealing with perceptions. Perceptions are trickier than things. It is at least arguable that the feature that characterises experts in any field is that they disagree with one another. This would not matter if the researcher admitted he was only dealing with opinions, but at the end of the conversation the researcher talks as if he will have established the relationship between attributes and bases, when he will have done no such thing.

If we look a little more closely we can see that the speaker is claiming that 'attributes' and 'competitive bases' are things. They are seen as being as real and as solid as the table I am working at. They are seen as real because, in this researcher's world, there is a general acceptance of their definition and importance. But neither of these things *is* real. They are just names that the author has chosen to group together a number of other terms which he, and possibly others, think are important. Other people might choose different lists of things to put under each label. Different people may choose to define terms, such as flexibility, differently. The acceptance of this truth is implied in the researcher's admitted difficulty in measuring his terms. We might need to consider whether abstract terms, such as competitive bases, are ever real.

In summary, the research is proposing to study people's opinions on things that are more fuzzy concepts than factual, tangible objects. This does not mean the research will not be useful; much management research appropriately concentrates on perceptions and opinions. However, it is easy to claim that this type of research is more than it is.

Interpretation is a complex matter as the illustration in Exhibit 5.9 might suggest.

Exhibit 5.9

Source: Therapeutisch Bruegelconcert voor een Magrittiaanse toehoorder, by Jos De Mey.
Reproduced with the permission of the artist.

Exercise 5.3

Framing sentences honestly

Review each of the following sentences. They all assume a realist stance. Redraft them into a form of words that would be acceptable from a nominalist stance. Another way of putting it is to ask you to rewrite the following statements so that they are more honest.

1 The organisation's culture is acting as a brake on growth.
2 The majority of staff, according to the staff feedback survey, is satisfied with the leadership they receive at work.
3 HRM increases bottom line performance.
4 Does TQM work?
5 Around this time 'hard' and 'soft' HRM emerged.

Suggested answers
1 The sentence treats 'organisation', 'culture' and 'growth' as if they were all real things with clear definitions. It rather assumes, for instance, that the organisation has a single culture. It is much more likely that it has an overlapping admixture of sub-cultures. It is also unlikely that everyone in the organisation agrees with the sentiment expressed in sentence 1 of the exercise, so it is necessary to be specific about who holds this view. If we assume that this is the view of managers in the HRM department then we might reword the sentence as follows:

Managers in the HRM department argue that the culture of the organisation, as they see it, is preventing the type of growth they believe is necessary.

2 The main problem with the sentence is that putting a tick in a particular box on a questionnaire is assumed to represent the 'real' feelings of the staff. It may be that staff fibbed when they ticked the box. Maybe they had not settled their own views on the issue and ticked any box just to complete the questionnaire. It all also assumes that there is a consensus among the respondents about what good leadership is.

The majority of the respondents ticked a box that said they were satisfied with the leadership they received at work.

3 This is a bold claim. Let us assume that it is based on some survey research in which companies were asked questions about their HR management and about the financial performance. Let us further assume that there was a positive statistical correlation between the two variables. There are two problems. The first is that the sentence treats HRM as an unambiguous thing. The second is that it assumes a statistical association is the same as cause and effect.

Companies that reported that they practised HRM tended to be the same as the companies that reported higher returns on capital expended.

4 Well, it all depends on what you mean by 'TQM' and by 'work'. Again TQM is treated as if it were a real thing as opposed to being a label that is used with greater or lesser exactitude by a wide range of people. The question is so wide it is probably not possible to answer it in its present state.

5 The problem here is that 'soft' and 'hard' are being treated as if they have an independent existence from the academics and HR professionals who write and talk about them.

At about this time academic writers began to use the terms 'hard' and 'soft' when analysing the approach to managing people known as HRM.

It is possible to take this cautious approach to writing too far. If you were to add too many cautions and caveats to your sentences they would become cumbersome and you would not be able to express what you wish to say. The purpose of Exercise 5.3 is not to freeze you into immobility but to warn you against being too sweeping in your claims.

Saying what is valid

While of course it is important to say what you mean, it is as important to say something that is meaningful. This is the matter of validity. Valid means true. Truth may be too demanding a test for social science research but at the least we ought to ask, of our own research, whether:

● The concepts and terms we used to analyse and describe our research fairly represents our research material. If we say that our research, for example, tells us something about employees' commitment to their organisation, is our claim valid?

- The interpretations and conclusions we draw are robustly and logically derived from the research findings.
- Appropriate research techniques have been competently used so that we can be reasonably sure that the findings reliably and fairly represent the topic being studied.
- It would be safe to use conclusions from the research as a guide in our managerial, professional or organisational practice.

Each of these questions concerns a different aspect of validity. Each of these will be discussed in more detail and then consideration will be given to some practical proposals for securing validity for your piece of research.

Construct or measurement validity

Construct validity refers particularly to research that uses questionnaires or inventories to assess whether a person or an organisation exhibits a particular characteristic. The characteristic could be any number of things, for example, different learning styles, degree of hierarchy in an organisation or leadership styles. In the latter case the questionnaire will contain a number of statements that allegedly are typical of each leadership style and, according to the answers a respondent gives, they can be classified along a spectrum from low to high on this leadership construct. The problem of validity is whether these statements and constructs actually measure the thing they are said to measure. There are a number of statistical techniques that can be used to assess the extent to which they do so (see p. 179).

There is a similar issue in interpretive and qualitative research. Let us imagine that some semi-structured interviews have been conducted to explore the role of intuition in management decision making. The interviewees were asked to give examples, tell the story, of decisions they had made at work. The researcher, on reading the transcripts may come to the view that people are more likely to decide intuitively when the issue has a powerful emotional impact for them. If it does not, they are more likely to coolly analyse and weigh the data before reaching a decision. The problem is whether the researcher read the clues and cues in the transcripts 'correctly' when deciding whether the issue described had created strong emotions in the decision maker. The researcher may have considered frequent hard swearing in the interviewees' accounts of decision making as an indicator of emotional stress; perhaps for some interviewees it was; for others it may have been no more than a casual habit of speech. If the latter is true then the researcher's claim that they had researched the impact of a construct called 'emotional stress' on decision making would not be true. What they claimed was emotional stress might not be. In Tietze's study of teleworkers/homeworkers, discussed earlier in this chapter (see p. 284), she argued that certain actions (such as putting on lipstick and earrings) when in working mode rather than 'home' mode were discursive acts. By this she meant that they were deliberate actions designed to create a separation between work and non-work. They probably were; but there is the possibility that they were random acts or, more likely, that they were intentional acts but related to things other than the home/work distinction. When you discuss your research findings you need to show awareness of the possibility that your constructs do not refer to what you claim they do.

Internal validity

In realist research, the intention is to identify cause and effect relationships. Internal validity is concerned with whether the evidence presented justifies the claims of cause and effect. The Webley and More (2003) study (p. 279) was trying to show that being socially responsible causes a company to achieve a better financial performance. In some studies the robustness of such a conclusion can be assessed by using statistical significance tests. The Webley and More study does not use statistical methods to identify associations between being socially responsible and profitability. Instead it relies on the plain observation that companies with a corporate social responsibility policy show better financial results than those that do not. It might be that these results were a coincidence; and it would be possible to use statistical techniques to assess the probability that the findings could be explained by chance. Questions could still be asked about the validity of the conclusion without the use of statistics. For instance, even if it were accepted that there was a causal relationship between social responsibility and financial success, there remains the question of the direction of any cause and effect relationship. In other words, does being responsible cause improved profitability or do companies that are making good profits feel more relaxed about diverting some time and money into behaving well? Asking this question does not invalidate the study's conclusion but it does make it difficult to be definitive about it until further research has been done to explore the direction of causality.

When we are dealing with interpretive research and qualitative material the question of internal validity cannot be readily resolved by the use of statistical techniques. But the issue remains the same. Writers on interpretive research have suggested different tests, essentially subjective judgements, for assessing validity in such studies. Lincoln and Guba (1985: 301) suggested a credibility test – how believable are the interpretations that a researcher makes? According to Lincoln and Guba (1985: 301–319), believability is improved where the researcher has:

● Used a range of research techniques, conscientiously, and in ways that help them triangulate their findings. If you were evaluating the effectiveness of a manger training programme you might give students feedback sheets to complete at the end of the programme. But to rely on this information alone would be risky. If you were also to interview the students three months later and enquire whether the programme had caused them to behave differently as managers, and if those results tallied with the questionnaire results, then your conclusions would be triangulated and much more credible.

- Has asked others, independent from the research, to critique their research methods.
- Constantly questioned their interpretations against the data and been prepared to revise them.
- Kept their research material archived, even if it is only in a cardboard box, so that others might re-analyse their material.
- Checked their interpretations with the people (or at least the types of people) from whom they drew their raw material.

Some of these methods will be discussed in more detail in the next section.

Weick's study of the role of sense making in his analysis of the Mann Gulch forest fire in Montana (Exhibit 5.4) can provide an example. Weick argues that the effectiveness of people's actions in a particular situation is affected by the processes of sense making. The question is whether this interpretation is believable. In his 2001 paper Weick contrasted the Mann Gulch case study with a case study of civil society forming groups in Poland in Soviet times and so he can be claimed to have used a form of triangulation. He has used well-known case studies so that it is possible for other scholars to revisit the material. The explicitness with which he interpreted the case studies using his theory of sense making makes it possible to evaluate his arguments. On these grounds it can be argued that Weick's account is credible.

External or population validity

External validity, which interpretive and qualitative researchers may call transferability, using Lincoln and Guba's (1985) term, questions whether the generalisations or interpretations that a researcher has proved in a particular context apply equally well to other populations or other contexts. Belbin (1981), for example, conducted some famous research that identified eight different roles that were performed in effective teams. However, his research was conducted on management teams. External validity concerns whether these findings apply to other types of team (teams of non-managers, for example). It might also be asked whether the findings apply to management teams in other countries and cultures. Of course Belbin is not necessarily to be expected to have answered all such questions; but it is normally expected that researchers will point out that there may be contexts and populations in which their findings do not apply.

In the case of large sample research, external validity is focused on the representativeness of the sample studied:

- Is the sample large enough for the conclusions drawn from it to be applied to the whole population?
- Does the sample contain enough data from the different categories that make up the population being studied? If the sample is of employees of an organisation, does it contain enough respondents from the various organisational levels and functional departments?

If samples are small, or used to generate qualitative material rather than numbers, the question of whether findings are transferable can only be answered by judgement and not by calculation. Can findings based on three organisational case studies, for instance, be transferred to all organisations, some other organisations which are similar to the case study organisations or to no other organisations? Lincoln and Guba (1985: 316) move the responsibility for answering such questions from the researcher to the reader. The researcher does have a responsibility; it is to provide a thick and detailed enough description of the research material to allow the reader to make their own judgements about transferability. To take an example, in Exhibit 5.2 the conclusion of Leopold and Hallier (1999) is a theoretical one, that setting up on a greenfield site does not lead companies to adopt or retain a high-commitment approach to human resource management. It is a negative conclusion and so there is no reason why it would not be generalisable to all greenfield sites.

Ecological validity

Research is often done in ways that are not natural, for example psychological experiments, filling in questionnaires, taking part in role plays and simulations. Such methods raise the question of ecological validity. Do findings obtained from contrived circumstances have validity in the messy complexity of real life? Belbin, for example (see above), came to his conclusions by studying groups of managers who were making decisions in role plays on management courses. The question to be asked reflects the point, which the people who take part in such role plays always express, 'But of course I wouldn't behave like that in real life.' The 'of course' may only be an excuse for their behaviour.

Interpretive and qualitative researchers ought to be less worried by ecological validity because, they would argue, a defining characteristic of their research is that they try to do it in a real-life, or naturalistic, setting. Ecological validity is a hard matter for researchers using quantitative methods to follow because there are no statistical techniques for answering it. Not all quantitative research requires contrived situations though. Using activity sampling (see p. 164) to study behaviour at work provides quantitative data from a natural setting. As with credibility, all the researcher can do is to provide enough information about the context of their study so that the reader can come to a conclusion about the ecological validity of their findings.

Improving the validity of research findings

It follows from the argument presented in the previous section that researchers need to take care when making sense of their research material. Richard Winter (1989) has proposed a number of principles that can be applied when trying to find out what interpretations may be placed on research material. To some extent these principles mirror Lincoln and Guba's (see pp. 296–297) tests of credibility. Winter's principles are:

- reflexive critique
- dialectical critique
- collaborative resources
- risk to one's own values
- plural structure
- theory, practice and transformation.

The jargon is a little impenetrable but each of these perspectives can be explained in a practical way.

- **Reflexive critique.** Whenever we give an account of our research findings we should accept that the account would be coloured by our values, assumptions and prejudices. That is to say, our accounts are reflexive, our judgements about things 'out there' are always bent back to focus on our internal concerns and preoccupations. In a reflexive critique we recognise and explain these concerns. A reflexive critique may also cause us to reconsider our values. At a simple level a reflexive critique allows the reader an insight into the researcher's thinking and helps the reader take this into consideration when reading the researcher's account of the research. It allows the reader to apply the 'Mandy Rice-Davies test'. Rice-Davies was involved in the Profumo sex and spying scandal in the 1960s. When she was confronted in court with a witness's allegations against her, she replied, 'Well he would say that, wouldn't he?' This is a useful question to ask of any researcher's work, including your own. Van Maanen (1988) provides interesting insights on a reflexive approach to research, as does Alvesson and Skoldberg (2000).
- **Dialectical critique.** The key idea of dialectical critique is that whenever we study something there are always contradictions between the formal unity of the thing and its teeming, detailed practical aspect. If we study HRM we might begin with a formal definition of it. But when we look at how it is implemented in organisations we will find that it involves many different practices. This practical diversity may well contradict the apparent unity of the thing we have called HRM. Billig (1996) calls these two processes categorisation and particularisation. As soon as we think we have put everything into neat boxes some irritating particular

refuses to be pigeon-holed. If we take the idea of dialectical analysis a little further we may find that some of the things that are done under the name of HRM not only fail to fit neatly within the category but actually challenge the formal claims made for it. In my work, for example, I have argued that codes of ethics in organisations, which are intended to encourage staff to behave with integrity, often have the reverse effect. Staff think to themselves, 'The organisation obviously doesn't believe we can act with integrity or else they would not have asked us to commit to the code of ethics.' This perceived lack of faith in their integrity encourages staff to act as they think the organisation believes they will (Fisher, 2001: 147).

Dialectical analysis means looking for the contradictions in your research material:

- Contradictions between the big categories that bring everything together and the multitudinous detail that pulls everything apart.
- Contradictions between the formal stated purposes of people's actions and their practice and impact.

As Winter (1989: 53) puts it, dialectical critique means looking for 'unity concealed behind apparent differentiation and contradiction concealed within apparent unity'. Dialectical analysis is explained in more detail on p. 323.

- **Collaborative resources.** This principle fits well with the concept of stakeholders, which is commonly used in business and management studies. It means looking at an issue from the perspectives of the various stakeholders and involving them as resources in interpreting and understanding the research material. This may involve actually working with others in a collaborative group, or in some other way feeding back your material to others to gain their insights and readings of it.

- **Risk to one's own values.** A good researcher is willing to let the research process challenge their own values and ways of looking at things. In particular, the things at risk are:
  - the researcher's provisional interpretation of the research material;
  - the researcher's decisions about the question at issue and what the research is about; and
  - the research plan, which may well have to change as the researcher's thinking is challenged.

- **Plural structure.** If the research we have carried out recognises that there are different perspectives on an issue then it follows that when the research is written up this diversity should be recognised in the structure of the report or dissertation. In other words, the dissertation should recognise that different groups of stakeholders may well have different views and conclusions about the subject of the project.

- **Theory, practice, transformation.** Theoretical thought about managerial and business issues is good and necessary; but just as practice needs to be challenged by theory, theory needs to be challenged by practice.

The judgements and decisions that you make based upon your research should, if possible, be tried in practice or at least be capable of being tested in practice.

Winter wrote of these six principles in relation to action research. But they are useful guidelines for any type of researcher. They form a coherent series but it is not necessary that every researcher should apply all of them. I propose that you should consider applying one or two of these principles, as appropriate, when you interpret and make sense of your research material. The following exercise gives you opportunities to try out some of these principles.

Exercise 5.4

The doctors' surgery

A researcher was studying the organisational cultures of GPs' practices. He had chosen this topic because he had for long been involved with doctors as a result of his injuries from a car crash and the subsequent litigation and frequent medical examinations. One or two GPs had become his close friends and in conversation with them he had become interested in the management of primary health care.

He decided to start his study by carrying out informal observations of surgeries. He was given permission to do the work and sat quietly in waiting rooms for the duration of clinic sessions and kept a research diary in which he noted all the things that seemed to him to be of interest. A page from his research notes is printed below. You will need to know that a Lloyd George envelope is the small manila packet into which GPs traditionally stuff medical notes. A nebuliser is a device for treating a patient suffering from a severe asthma attack.

What opportunities do the materials present for applying Winter's six principles of interpretation?

Entries from a logbook written during observation of a general practice surgery

1   Driving to the practice it was difficult to identify the building, it was on a busy road, many tall shrubs were growing in front of it, and there was no obvious sign; it was also in the middle of a difficult one-way road system.

2   The waiting area (for a two-doctor practice) was 30ft by 10ft.

3   There was a noticeboard on one wall of the room giving practice information. It was cluttered and two items were over two years old.

4   Overheard conversation among receptionists: 'Mrs Jones has been in again; she's a nuisance. She said she was just passing and she thought she would see if her repeat prescription was ready, even though we told her to come tomorrow. Well it was ready, but I told her it wasn't and to come back. They start to take liberties if you aren't careful.'

5   There is a small, but well organised, practice library, which includes health education material as well as clinical textbooks.

6   Observed: a woman and child who had been waiting 15 minutes. The child was becoming agitated and whining, 'When are we going to see the doctor?' The mother replied, in a loudish voice, 'My love, you just have to wait till they are ready.' No response from the receptionist staff who had overheard the conversation.

7   In the record-keeping area I notice that pulling and returning medical notes from the racking seems to be a cumbersome and difficult activity without actually being able to say why. Then it hit me, the racking was designed to take A4 records but the notes are still kept in Lloyd George envelopes.

8   As I pass along the upstairs landing I hear a GP saying to a child and his mother, 'Hang on here a moment, I'm just going to go downstairs to get the key to Dr Y's room – he's not in today – and then I'll fix up the nebuliser for you in that room and I'll come back and check on you when I've seen my next patient.'

Exercise 5.4 *continued*

9   The administration and clerical staff, all women, wear a uniform – smart navy suits from Marks & Sparks.

10 Various community nursing staff are based in a pleasant airy office within the surgery. A GP poked his head round the door, noticed that only the school nurse was in, and exited muttering, 'Bloody health visitors, never one when you want one and then three come along together when you don't.'

11 Access to the building and the downstairs rooms is good for people with mobility problems. There is also a patient's toilet with a wide door and appropriate fitments for use by people in wheelchairs.

12 The surgery runs an open appointment system during morning surgeries. People come and wait in turn either for the first doctor available or, if they prefer, for their own doctor.

13 There is a large notice pinned up which says that the practice wants to provide a personal service and that, consequently, locums or stand-in GP's will never do night calls. These will always be done by one of the two partners.

14 The practice is well below the regional average for payments for night visits per GP according to the figures the practice manager showed me.

Suggested answer

The researcher has obviously had much experience of the health service. His particular experience of it, together with his attitude towards the NHS, may affect what he chose to record in his diary and what spin he placed upon it. A reflexive critique of the material would be helpful to the reader.

The practice has a policy of doing its night visits itself and providing a personalised service (item 13). But the figures from the health authority suggest that the GPs do fewer night visits than other GPs (item 14). This apparent contradiction might form the basis of a dialectical critique. There may be reasons, such as the following, to explain the discrepancy:

- The GPs may make the visits but forget to claim the payment from the health authority and so the visits do not show up in the statistics.
- Maybe the GPs have trained their patients not to call them at night.
- Perhaps the GPs do not put their policy into practice, and so on.

Exploring the contradiction should lead to a better understanding of the situation.

There may be room for another dialectical critique when the formal contexts provided for the patients (items 2, 9, 11 and 12) are contrasted with the manner in which patients are treated by reception staff (items 4 and 6). The physical conditions are mostly good (except item 1) but the way staff treat the patients looks less good.

One of the problems with the research material is that there is no guarantee that the observed behaviour was representative of the practice. It may have been that the reception staff were just having a bad day and that this was the reason for their lack of charm. Or it may have been that the researcher was not aware of the full context of items 4 and 6 and so he misread the situations. Given these doubts a collaborative approach would be sensible. This would mean seeking the interpretation that other receptionists, if not those particular receptionists, would place upon the events. Of course, an action researcher would argue that such research should have been carried out as a collaborative exercise in the first place with all the staff of the surgery.

As the research stands there is not much risk to the researcher's values.

There are a number of items in the diary that are capable of being interpreted differently. Item 8 is a case in point. You could argue that this is good news because here is a doctor going to some trouble to respond to the needs of a patient. A contrary view would be that it is a bad thing that the practice does not have the rooms or the procedures for dealing with this patient in anything other than an ad hoc fashion. Which view you take will probably depend on who you are. Research material such as this would clearly benefit from a plural structure when it is written up. The question of the appropriateness of putting the receptionists in uniform (item 9) might also best be considered from plural perspectives. If, for example, the surgery were in a middle-class suburban area, the uniforms might be seen as a mark of professionalism. If the surgery were in a deprived estate, the uniforms might be seen as a mark of the staff's superiority over the patients.

There is no intention that the research findings should be used to develop or transform practice within this particular surgery. Should they?

Dialectical critique

This way of interpreting research material is particularly interesting and will repay more detailed consideration. It is best explored by doing it and so here are two exercises.

Exercise 5.5

Management attitudes towards redundancy decisions

Below is an abstract from a transcript of a research interview. The interview was structured around the collection of critical incidents. The interviewees were asked about any incident at work they could recall that seemed to them to raise questions of right and wrong or of fairness in the treatment of people. In this extract two incidents are related.

Carry out a dialectical critique of the incidents. This will involve making a comparison of the two cases to see whether there are any contradictions or discrepancies in the way the interviewee thought and acted in the two situations. If there are contradictions, how might you begin to understand or explain them?

Can you think of the recent example?
The most recent example, yes, in terms of a retail business manager that currently works for the organisation and actually works for this division, who got a consistently high appraisal rating, high performance rating over the last few years. But what is required over the next three years, this person has the ability to be above, to move forward. Therefore, there is a big question mark over where that person goes.

Why does this cause you a slight pang or twinge?
Because we're talking about somebody who's perceived by the organisation as a high performer. Yet in terms of everything they do, everyday we can see that they have the inability to change, to be above, to move forward with the change in an emerging brand.

Right. How are things changing then?
Well, the whole style of the operation is changing. We have a new director and general manager and senior management team for a start. They have a different way of working. The emphasis is on empowering the staff.

And he's a traditional company person is he?
Yes, and the emphasis is moving away from control culture, control-type management, to a more loose management culture and more sales oriented and building on development in sales. This person is not interested in development and growing sales. It's more about the old control culture. 'Hit them with a big stick and sack them if they don't do what you tell them' mentality.

But he's still a good performer?
He has an excellent performance and if you look in terms of actual year-on-year profit performance he's the best achiever in the company.

In some ways this is someone who has been a good performer and has apparently done well in the company but isn't changing, and I suppose, am I right in thinking that you have a bit of a dilemma in terms of have you got to do something?
Absolutely. And also the difficulty is because he has a reputation throughout the company for that cultural aspect and that management style that nobody else wants to face him. So the fact is that we'll end up losing somebody from the organisation.

He is a symbol for the old way of doing things?
Yes, and that will also cause or create a huge employer relations issue.

Why is that?
Because he will take us to a tribunal.

Exercise 5.5 *continued*

Right.

Rightly so in terms of performance.

So you are going to do something about it? What have you decided to do?

Well, we've decided he's got to go.

Yes, what sort of mechanism are you going to use?

Well, it will be a severance. He'll have to go. We've looked at the other alternatives and there aren't any.

Effectively redundancy?

Effectively, a form of redundancy.

Because his role doesn't fit in. Is this one of the areas where you feel a bit of a clash between what you need to do for the organisation and your own values?

Well, you know, I think in terms of the organisation it's absolutely right but actually this guy has worked for the company for some time and in his own way has been committed. So I think there probably is a view that maybe over the years this person hasn't been managed properly in the past and maybe if he'd been managed better in the past then maybe we wouldn't be at this point now.

As an ex-trainer and developer, have you considered that?

Yes, we've worked on it, we've been working on it for the last six months. It's not even a runner. We're basically saying up yours, you know, as good as.

But tricky when somebody has actually got a good official appraisal record.

Yes, absolutely, no disciplinary record, no major performance issues. It's very much about management styles and culture and change.

How do you think you're going to feel when you deal with this one?

Well, I've dealt with so many that I always think that if I go home at night and sleep, my conscience is relatively clear. I have a job to do and I believe when it comes round and it's right for the business, then it's part of the job.

In a sense it sounds like you've been giving him chances and saying, OK this time you've got to change.

I think so, yes, and I believe that generally if I have to do, in fact I quite often won't do something if I don't agree with it being morally right, or I'll look for a compromise.

That's a very interesting example. What we're doing is mapping out the issues that people have to face. You just said that sometimes you just don't think they're right. Can you think of an example or a type of situation when you've had to do that?

Yes, somebody who works for me, one of the directors felt, wasn't committed enough to the organisation because they didn't work seven days a week. He told me that I needed to do something about that person and I refused point blank. I said that they actually worked more effectively than anybody else here, and now I don't intend – I refuse to do that. At the end of the day, just because you believe that we should work seven days a week it doesn't prove that they're not committed. So I actually did dig my heels in and said no, I'm not going to do it, I refuse; and we've worked around that. I did then talk to that person and let that person know how he felt about it and said, you know, you just need to think about raising your profile and meeting part way.

That's sort of a PR job? Is this an organisation which takes the seven-day-a-week line very strongly?

Different parts of the organisation.

All sorts of people do.

It's individuals really.

Can we explore a bit more why you thought that was an inappropriate line to take?

Well, I think because that person is an extremely effective member of the team and actually the output is far higher and greater, the overall output, than the average. And really it was more about profile.

Exercise 5.5 *continued*

Do you think the senior person was being fair?
No, unreasonable, totally unreasonable, absolutely.

Legally would it have been an easy thing to have done anyway?
Well, I don't legally know, but in terms of the organisation, because it's the nature of the business and because our business does operate seven days a week, then it becomes the accepted norm. If you've got pressure from a senior manager then it makes life difficult for you and then ultimately it forces somebody out. If you get a reputation within the organisation it affects your promotion opportunities or future opportunities.

Did the team member take the advice, did they up their profile? Did it work?
Hmm, it did actually. It's settled down again now but it was very difficult at the time. It put me in a difficult position. I'm a great believer in sticking to your guns and I'm a spade or shovel person.

Is that how you're known?
Yes, I have very strong values.

Is it a useful reputation to have?
Yes, it helps being female with that reputation.

Why?
I think I wouldn't have got away with it so easily if I'd been a man. It's a male-dominated organisation generally and being a fairly strong female has allowed me to manoeuvre a lot better than I would have done if I'd been a man.

You can stand your ground maybe a little bit more.
Yes, with the male members of the board and things, I am able to stand my ground a lot more.

Suggested answer

The interviewee had a formal idea that, in order to sleep at night, she always acted morally in matters of redundancy, severance and disciplinary action. She went to some trouble to point out that she was responding fairly to the merits of individual cases. She gave one example where she thought severance was right and another case (where a senior manager was pushing to have someone made redundant) when she thought such action would be wrong. So in formal terms both cases fit the category of acting from a position of principle.

The claim that she was applying consistent principles in the cases is possibly contradicted because the two cases she gave, in which she acted differently, were similar, if not identical, situations. Both incidents involved members of staff who would not adopt the values and beliefs that management wished them to adopt. In one case the manager did not fit with the culture of the new brand, and in the second the manager did not accept the macho, long hours culture. In the first case the interviewee chose to support the action proposed; in the second case she chose to oppose it. This raises interesting questions to be answered. Dialectical critique raises new questions and moves you into a deeper level of understanding.

The interviewee could have categorised both issues as questions of compatibility between individual employees and the corporate culture, and adopted a similar stance in both cases. Instead she took opposite views. There must have been some particulars that justified this position. There must have been some features that made her see the two situations as different. We cannot know, of course, what these particulars might be, but we can speculate, and there are a few clues in the interview. Here are some possibilities:

- The fact that the second person was a member of the interviewee's staff and the first person was not could account for the different responses.
- In the second incident the interviewee was apparently being ordered to get rid of the employee and the interviewee might see this as an unwarranted attack on her managerial autonomy and wished to prevent the director feeling he could order her about.
- She might herself accept the new brand culture but reject the long hours culture, and so she might particularise according to different aspects of culture.

Exercise 5.5 *continued*

- It could simply be a matter of personality; she may have little personal sympathy for the subject of the first incident but lots for the subject of the second incident.
- It is also tempting to think there may be an age aspect to the two incidents, the person in the first incident being older than the person in the second, but there is absolutely no evidence for this!

This analysis also points up the importance of follow-up and probing questions during the interview. Some of the issues listed might have been explored in the interview. Adopting a dialectical critique can develop a more complex and dynamic understanding of issues.

Dialectical contradictions can be seen in quantitative data as well, as illustrated in the following case.

Exercise 5.6

Staffing the nursery school

This is an opportunity to make a dialectical critique of some quantitative research material. The issue was to decide the appropriate staffing level for nursery schools. The staff numbers needed in any particular school was decided by applying a standard ratio of staff to the number of pupils. The question was, what should the ratio be? The education advisers were consulted and they argued that the staffing should be such that for a good proportion of every nursery session staff should be able to work with small groups of children. The rest of the session should be used for whole-group activities such as storytelling and outdoor play. They argued that the more time staff could work with small groups of children, the better the quality of the education. This belief was official policy.

An activity sampling study (see p. 164) was carried out in which the percentage of time staff spent with different group sizes of pupils was researched in eight nurseries. The results are shown in Table 5.1.

The table shows, for example, that in nursery 'a' staff spent 15 per cent of their time working one-to-one with children and 12 per cent working with a pair of children.

Table 5.1 **Analysis of nursery staff time (analysed according to the size of the group of pupils staff worked with)**

Nursery	a	b	c	d	e	f	g	h
Group size								
1	15	29	13	33	24	60	19	10
2	12	5	8	6	–	–	8	2
3	8	5	13	9	–	–	17	6
4	2	11	1	5	16	–	12	19
5	–	–	1	–	–	–	–	–
6	–	–	1	–	–	4	–	–
7	–	–	–	–	–	12	–	–
8	10	–	7	9	–	–	–	9
≥ 9	53	50	56	38	60	24	44	54
Ratio of pupils to staff	10:1	7:1	12:1	7.5:1	12:1	6.7:1	8.7:1	13:1

Exercise 5.6 *continued*

When the results were analysed an overall pattern emerged. The amount of time that staff spent with groups of four or less children was strongly negatively correlated with the staff ratio. The correlation coefficient (see p. 215) was −0.86912. A regression line (see p. 237) could be fitted to a graph of the data. The intercept was 78.98 and the slope was −3.43. Once this graph was plotted it could be used to determine proper staffing ratios. If the experts defined the optimum percentage of time to be spent with groups of four or less children then the graph could be used to say what staffing ratio would be necessary to achieve it.

But such patterns can be deceptive. Look at the data in the table again. Can you identify any contradictions in the ways in which nurseries worked with their pupils?

Suggested answer

One nursery (f) stands out from the others. Its staff used their time in a very different way from the others. They spent all their time either on one-to-one work with the children or on large-group activities. They did not do any small-group work with children. Normally statisticians would declare such a result an 'outlier' (an unrepresentative result) and exclude it from consideration. But a dialectical critique approach emphasises such discrepancies and uses them to gain a better understanding of the subject. It would question why there might be such differences. We can only speculate but it is likely that nursery school 'f' has a different educational philosophy from most of the others. It may be that this school puts more emphasis on individual attainment and believes that this can best be done by maximising the amount of one-to-one teaching. If this, or something like it, is true then we have to ask questions about whether the assumptions that we initially made about what makes a nursery school effective ought to be challenged. We would then find ourselves researching different views on the nature and purpose of nursery education.

In summary, a dialectical critiques begins with the formal policy that schools should maximise the time staff spend working with small groups of children – no doubt to develop social skills, or in management terms – team skills. It is difficult to see whether school 'f' fits in this category. At one level it does because it maximises the time spent with children in groups of four or less. But its choice to spend all this time in one-to-one work, rather than in groups, contradicts and undermines the purpose of the policy.

Framing conclusions and recommendations

Conclusions are not the same as your research findings or research analysis. Conclusions are your interpretations of the findings. By returning to the distinction made in Chapter 1 between research questions and strategic questions it is possible to identify three types of conclusions:

- **Research conclusions.** These summarise your understanding of the processes and dynamics of the subject you have researched. They provide the explanations that answer your research questions.
- **Strategic conclusions.** These summarise your judgements about what, if anything, should be done in response to your strategic questions. The strategic conclusions should be based on the new understanding that the research conclusions provide. The research conclusions may provide a context for answering the strategic question but it is your judgement, your ability to decide options and actions that are critical at this stage.

- **Recommendations.** These are the practical steps that need to be taken to implement the strategic conclusions. Recommendations are not always necessary or appropriate in a Master's dissertation. Whether they are needed or not will depend upon:
  - The aims and topic of the dissertation. Some dissertations directly address problems and issues, others do not. Only in the former case would recommendations be necessary.
  - The rules and regulations of the institution you are studying at. Some institutions may ask for recommendations in dissertations, others may not.
  - The informal expectations of some institutions may discourage students from making recommendations, preferring they concentrate on issues of academic understanding.

The conclusions are the link between understanding and action. This link does not arise automatically. It is forged by the writer of the dissertation. The writer chooses the link. Two practical consequences emerge from this perception of conclusions.

- **The test of conclusions is a pragmatic one.** This test holds that a belief is true if it proves useful in the long run. Usefulness is not sufficient, however. It is also important that there is a sensible explanation of why the belief will be useful (Mounce, 1997: 50–51). Let us imagine that we have been studying the impact of a particular management technique. Our research has suggested that companies that implement this technique do better than those that do not. It would be useful, therefore, to act on this belief and use the technique in our own organisation. But before we do so it would be sensible to check whether there is a sound explanation of why this technique is successful. Perhaps the success was not due to the technique. It could be, for example, that the companies we studied were just lucky and would have done well even if they had not introduced the technique. Or it might just be that it was the quality of the managers in these companies that brought success, not the application of the technique. However, if a sound explanation can be given that shows it most likely was the technique that caused the companies to perform well, then the belief that the technique works should be accepted as true. True conclusions are ones that are useful and whose utility can be explained. This is one reason why the answers to research questions help validate conclusions. They explain why conclusions are useful.

  There is a danger in taking the pragmatic view. It is that we may accept as true anything that is expedient or convenient for us. The use of a pragmatist test therefore requires a ruthless honesty with ourselves. It may be necessary to recognise the value of 'truths' that we personally find discomforting.

- **Drawing conclusions requires a creative leap.** Henry Mintzberg (1979), as have many others, recommended an inductive approach to managerial and organisational research. This involves working from the detailed research findings to new discoveries of general interest and application. A two-stage process is involved:

  1. The first stage involves detective work, tracking down patterns, consistencies and inconsistencies in the research material. This stage has been covered in Chapter 4 and the first part of this chapter.

  2. The second stage involves what Mintzberg refers to as 'generalising beyond one's data' or the creative leap. 'Every theory requires that creative leap, however small, that breaking away from the expected to describe something new. There is no one-to-one correspondence between data and theory. The data do not generate the theory – only researchers do that – any more than theory can be proved true in terms of the data. All theories are false, because all abstract from data and simplify the world they purport to describe. Our choice then is not between true and false theories so much as between more and less useful theories. And usefulness to repeat stems from detective work well done, followed by creative leaps in relevant directions' (Mintzberg 1979: 584).

Not all creative leaps are true.

Having encouraged you to make leaps of judgement, a note of caution is necessary. Not all bright ideas are true. The need for care in drawing conclusions is explored in Exercise 5.7.

Exercise 5.7

The cash register

Read the brief account given below and then answer the questions asked about it. Circle 'T' if you think the statement is true, circle 'F' if you think the statement is false and circle '?' if you think it is impossible to say whether the statement is true or false.

The story
A businessman had just turned off the lights in the store when a man appeared and demanded money. The owner opened a cash register. The contents of the cash register were scooped up and the man sped away. A member of the police force was notified promptly.

Statements about the story

1	A man appeared after the owner had turned off his store lights.	T	F	?
2	The robber was a *man*.	T	F	?
3	The man did not demand money.	T	F	?
4	The man who opened the cash register was the owner.	T	F	?

Exercise 5.7 *continued*

5 The store owner scooped up the contents of the cash register
   and ran away.   T F ?
6 Someone opened a cash register.   T F ?
7 After the man who demanded money scooped up the
   contents of the cash register, he ran away.   T F ?
8 While the cash register contained money, the story
   does *not* state *how much*.   T F ?
9 The robber demanded money of the owner.   T F ?
10 The story concerns a series of events in which only three persons
   are referred to: the owner of the store, a man who demanded money,
   and a member of the police force.   T F ?
11 The following events in the story are true: someone demanded
   money, a cash register was opened, its contents were scooped
   up, and a man dashed out of the store.   T F ?

Source: Pfeiffer and Jones (1975). This material is used with the permission of
John Wiley and Sons Inc.

Suggested answer

True – statement 6.
Not true – statement 3.
All the rest are 'don't knows' or 'can't says'.

1 The businessman is not necessarily the same person as the owner.
2 It is not known whether a robbery took place. All that is known is that the contents of the cash register were
   removed.
4 The owner who opened the cash register was not necessarily a man.
5 It is not known who scooped up the contents of the cash register.
7 It was not necessarily the same person who carried out all three actions.
8 It is not known whether the cash register contained money.
9 It is not known whether there was a robbery.
10 It is not known. The owner and the businessman may not have been the same person.
11 It is not absolutely certain that the store in which the lights were turned off was the same place as the one in
   which the other events took place.

The lesson from this exercise is that people love to make patterns from the material presented to them. In the
absence of pattern, the mind is predisposed to impose one. People often claim many of the above statements are
true because their mind unconsciously provides the missing information necessary to create a satisfying narrative
from the scant material provided. As a consequence it might be thought, in the words of Francis Bacon (in the
Novum Organum of 1620), that the intellect

   must not … be supplied with wings, but rather hung with weights, to keep it from leaping and flying.

However, once people realise this is what is happening, they then jump to the opposite position and refuse to
believe it is possible to draw a conclusion about any of the statements – even those such as questions 6 and 3 that
are indubitably true or false – or are they?
   When drawing conclusions you need to strike a balance between creative leaps and scepticism.

Problems of implementation

Research conclusions are useful because they give a better understanding on which to base judgements and actions. Sometimes it may be appropriate to frame the judgements as strategic conclusions and recommendations for action. If you do this you need to make sure that you have considered the practicability of your recommendations. You will need to think about such questions as:

- the degree of support or opposition to the recommendations;
- the availability of the money and resources needed to implement the recommendations;
- whether a business case can be made that would release the necessary resources;
- the practical and logistical difficulties that implementation of the recommendations might entail;
- the processes by which the recommendations should be sold to interested parties;
- the timetable for implementation.

Never underestimate the difficulties of implementing recommendations. Aaron Wildavsky (1973, quoted in Anthony and Herzlinger, 1975: 335) wrote a tongue-in-cheek piece about the problems of implementing IT systems. Although IT systems have changed hugely since 1973, it would appear that the problems of implementing them have hardly changed at all. Here are Wildavsky's rules for implementation. I suspect they have relevance beyond IT.

- **The rule of scepticism** No one, especially the consultants, quite knows how to do the task.
- **The rule of delay** If it works at all, it won't work soon.
- **The rule of complexity** Nothing complex ever works.
- **The rule of thumb** If the procedure book or manual is thicker than your thumb the system will never work.
- **The rule of childlike innocence** When discussing a scheme to be implemented always ask the childlike questions you feel too embarrassed to ask.
- **The rule of length and width** If there are more than two or three links in a vertical or horizontal chain of communication, the messages will get lost.
- **The rule of anticipated anguish** a.k.a. Murphy's law, which states, 'if it can go wrong it will'.
- **The rule of the known evil** The existing system may be rubbish but people know how to estimate the 'fudge factor' and use it to make the system work. The new system may be better, but will people know how to work it?

- **The rule of the mounting mirage** Can be seen at work in the following quotation. 'We are doing badly, we need better information to perform better. We set up a costly new system. The costs of the system appear immediately but the benefits only emerge in the medium term. Therefore, in the short term we are doing worse, so we need a better information system to help us improve.' Ad infinitum.
- **The tenth rule** The hypothetical benefits of a new system should out-weigh the costs by ten to one before we decide to implement.

Exercise 5.8

Potential problem analysis

This exercise is based on an old technique developed by Kepner and Tregoe (1965). It is a useful way of thinking about the practical problems of implementation that might arise from your recommendations. It could be a useful framework for discussing issues of implementation in your dissertation. The technique is applied by asking and answering the following questions in sequence.

1 What problems could occur that would hinder the successful implementation of your recommendations? Make a list of them.
2 Assess the likelihood that each of these problems will occur. Rate them on a prob-ability scale of 0 (totally impossible) to 1 (absolutely certain).
3 For each of the most likely problems identify a number of preventative actions you might take to reduce the chances of the problem occurring.
4 Reassess the probability that a problem will still occur even after preventative actions have been taken, again by using a probability scale.
5 If the residual probability that the problem will arise is still high enough to cause anxiety then prepare a contingency plan. A contingency plan defines the action you will take to minimise the consequences of a problem should it happen.

Accepting the limitations

Michael Bassey, once a professor of education at Nottingham Trent University, proposed the following law. There are, he argued, three charac-teristics of a research conclusion in the social sciences. It can be:

- true
- generalisable
- simple.

But Bassey's law states that a conclusion can only be two of the three at any one time. If it is simple and true, it cannot be generalisable. If it is simple and generalisable, it probably is not true. If it is generalisable and true, it is not simple. However, as Bassey's law is simple, and appears to be a general law, it cannot be true.

Summary

- Be aware that there is no automatic and correct way of interpreting research findings, although there may be many silly and wrong ways.
- Consider carefully, and clearly explain in your dissertation, the interpretive grid you are using.
- Avoid lazy sentences that imply more than you claim.
- Include in your dissertation a discussion of the issues of validity affecting your research findings.
- Try to apply some of Winter's six principles when making sense of your research material.
- Do not disguise the apparent contradictions in your research material; use them as doorways to a deeper understanding of complex processes.
- Remember that quantitative material needs interpretation just as much as qualitative material.
- Do not be afraid to make creative leaps when framing your conclusions.
- But do not construct overelaborate theories that are more complex than the material requires.
- Consider the practical problems of implementing your conclusions and recommendations.

Suggested reading

Richard Winter's book (1989) is very good on the topics covered in the section on interpretation in this chapter, but it is a demanding read. It is also set in the context of education and this makes it a little more inaccessible to management students; but try Chapter 4. Pat Cryer's book has a chapter on creative thinking that might be useful when making your creative leaps. Johnson and Duberley (2000) is the best book if you want to follow up on the epistemology of organisational and managerial research.

References

Alvesson, M. and Skoldberg, K. (2000) *Reflexive Methodology*, London: Sage.

Anthony, R.N. and Herzlinger, R. (1975) *Management Control in Nonprofit Organisations*, Homewood, Ill.: Richard D. Irwin.

Bayard, P. (2000) *Who Killed Roger Ackroyd? The Murderer who eluded Hercule Poirot and deceived Agatha Christie*, London: Fourth Estate.

Belbin, R.M (1981) *Management Teams: Why they Succeed or Fail*, London: Heinemann.

Billig, M. (1996) *Arguing and Thinking. A Rhetorical Approach to Social Psychology*, 2nd edn, Cambridge: Cambridge University Press.

Christie, A. (1993) *The Murder of Roger Ackroyd*, London: HarperCollins.

Collier, A. (1994) *Critical Realism: An Introduction to Roy Bhaskar's Philosophy*, London: Verso.

Cryer, Pat (1996) *The Research Student's Guide to Success*, Buckingham: Open University Press.

Eco, U. (1984) *The Name of the Rose*, London: Picador.

Eco, U. (1994) 'La bustina di Minerva', *Espresso*, 30 September. Available on the World Wide Web at: http://www.themodernword.com/eco/eco_mac_vs_pc.html (and many other sites). Site visited 24 May 2006.

Eco, Umberto, with Richard Rorty, Johnathan Culler and Christine Brooke-Rose, edited by Stafan Collini (1992) *Interpretation and Overinterpretation*, Cambridge: Cambridge University Press.

Fisher, C.M. (2001) 'Managers' perceptions of ethical codes: dialectics and dynamics', *Business Ethics: A European Review*, vol. 10, no. 2: 145–156.

Franklin, P. (2001) 'Is strategy still relevant?' *The Internet Journal of Strategy and Planning*, (online). Available at: www.strategyfirst.net (accessed 28 July 2002).

Johnson, P. and Duberley, J. (2000) *Understanding Management Research: An Introduction to Epistemology*, London: Sage.

Kepner, C.H. and Tregoe, B.B. (1965) *The Rational Manager: A Systematic Approach to Problem Solving and Decision Making*, London: McGraw-Hill.

Lee, N. and Hassard, J. 'Organisation Unbound: actor-network theory, research strategy and institutional flexibility', *Organisation*, vol. 6, no. 3: 391–404.

Leopold, J.W. and Hallier, J. (1999) 'Managing the employment relationship on greenfield sites in Australia and New Zealand', *The International Journal of Human Resource Management*, vol. 10, no. 4: 716–736.

Lincoln, Y.S. and Guba, E.G. (1985) *Naturalistic Inquiry*, London: Sage.

March, J.G., Cohen, M.D. and Olsen, J.P. (1972) 'A garbage can model of organisational decision making', *Administrative Science Quarterly*, vol. 17: 1–25.

Massey, D. (2004) *For Space*, London: Sage.

Mintzberg, H. (1979) 'An emerging strategy of "direct research"', *Administrative Science Quarterly*, vol. 24, December: 582–589.

Mounce, H.O. (1997) *The Two Pragmatisms: From Peirce to Rorty*, London: Routledge.

Pawson, R. and Tilley, N. (1997), *Realistic Evaluation*, London: Sage.

Pfeiffer, J.W. and Jones, J.E. (1975) *A Handbook of Structured Experiences for Human Relations Training*, vol. 5, San Diego: University Associates.

Phillips, C. (1999) 'A review of CCTV evaluations: crime reduction effects and attitudes towards its use', *Crime Prevention Studies*, vol. 10: 123–155.

Pollitt, C. and Bouckaert, G. (2000) *Public Management Reform: A Comparative Analysis*. Oxford: Oxford University Press.

Ramazanoglu, C. (1992) 'On feminist methodology: male reason versus female empowerment', *Sociology*, vol. 26, no. 2: 207–212.

Subramaniyam, V. (2001) 'Critical realism and development programmes in rural South India', *Journal of Critical Realism* (incorporating *Alethia*), vol. 4, no. 1 (May): 17–23. Available at: http://www.journalofcriticalrealism.org/index.php?sitesig=JCR&page=JCR_040_JCR_19982003&subpage=JCR_009_JCR_(Alethi).

Tietze, S. (2005) 'Discourse as strategic coping resource: managing the interface between home and work', *Journal of Organisational Change Management*, vol. 18, no. 1: 48.

Tilley, N. (2000) *Realistic Evaluation: An Overview*, paper presented at the Founding Conference of the Danish Evaluation Society, September 2000. Available on the World Wide Web at: http://www.danskevalueingsselskab.db/pdf/Nick%20Tilley.pdf (accessed 28 January 2006).

Van Maanen, J. (1988) *Tales of the Field: On Writing Ethnography*, London: University of Chicago Press.

Walsham, Geoff, Sahay, Sundeep (1999) 'GIS for district-level administration in India: problems and opportunities', *MIS Quarterly*, 1 March, 1999, vol. 23, no. 1.

Webley, S. and More, E. (2003) *Does Business Ethics Pay?* London: Institute of Business Ethics (IBE).

Weick, K.E. (1995) *Sensemaking in Organisations*, London: Sage.

Weick, K.E. (2001) *Making Sense of the Organisation*, Oxford: Blackwell.

Wildavsky, Aaron (1973) 'Review of Brewer's *Politicians, Bureaucrats and the Consultant*', *Science*, vol. 28, December: 1335–1338.

Winter, Richard (1989) *Learning from Experience: Principles and Practice in Action-Research*, Lewes: Falmer Press.

Chapter 6 ● ● ● ●

Framing arguments and writing up

Contents

● ● ● ● Introduction

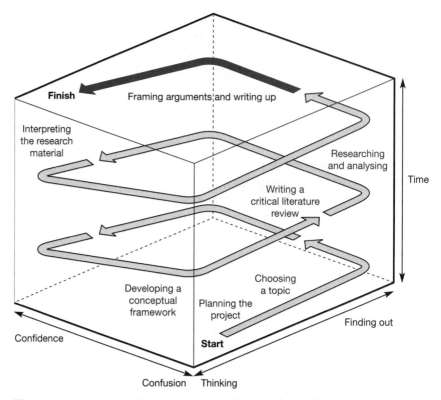

The processes of researching and writing a Master's dissertation

So, in this way of writing without thinking, thou hast a strange alacrity in sinking.

Thomas Sackville, Earl of Dorset (1536–1608)

This chapter is designed to help you write up your dissertation or paper, and to do some thinking in the process, and prepare it for submission for marking. There are three main sections:

1. Giving the dissertation structure, which gives advice about the chapter structure of your dissertation.
2. Writing a thesis, not just a dissertation, which is about making sure that the dissertation presents a clear and logical argument.
3. The style guide, which gives practical tips on writing up and presenting your dissertation.

There are more exercises in this chapter than in some of the earlier ones. This is because at this stage in the project you have gathered your material from the literature and research, and the exercises are designed to help you shape the material into good arguments that support a clear thesis.

Learning outcomes for the chapter

1 Readers will be able to give a logical and systematic structure to their dissertation or paper.
2 Readers will be able to create an overarching or narrative theme that will integrate the various parts of the dissertation or paper.
3 Readers will be able to support the main arguments presented in the dissertation or thesis.
4 Readers will be able to write the paper or dissertation in plain and clear English and in accordance with the requirements of the business school or other institution at which they are studying.

Structuring your dissertation

You need to plan the chapter structure of your dissertation. A default plan is given below, but it is not necessary or obligatory for you to follow this sequence slavishly. Feel free to develop a chapter plan that is relevant to the topic you are writing about. Papers do not have chapters and so this part does not apply to them.

If you are writing a traditional dissertation (i.e. not one based on action research), the following should provide a useful model to follow. Even if you follow this structure, you can give the chapters more imaginative titles:

(a) Introduction and objectives
  ● Explain the focus of the study and its object or purpose.
  ● Explain why the study is important and to whom.
    – Define the strategic question, if any, to be answered.
  ● Explain what you want to find out and why.
    – Define the research questions to be answered.
  ● Set the scene and describe the context, but not in too much detail.

(b) Critical literature review
  ● Identify the appropriate academic and/or professional fields of literature.
  ● Describe the main themes in the literature that are important and useful to your study.
  ● Identify the connections or discontinuities between the themes in the literature.
  ● Evaluate and critique the literature.
    – Check whether the ideas you wish to use are robust enough.
    – Challenge the assumptions.

- Question whether the literature might mean something other than it says it means.
- Create a coherent sequence of arguments from the themes drawn from the literature.

(c) The conceptual framework
- Using material from the previous chapter produce working definitions of the main concepts you will use in your study. If possible, form them into a conceptual framework, theory or hypothesis to be tested.
- Sometimes it is not necessary to have this section as a separate chapter. If this is the case, it can be included in the critical literature review chapter.

(d) Research methodology and methods
- Discuss the nature of the questions you are asking and choose an appropriate methodological stance for answering them.
- Describe, explain and justify the research methods you are using.
- Describe the practical and technical aspects of conducting the research.
- Discuss any ethical issues connected with the project.

(e) Presentation and analysis of findings
- Describe what you found out and what it means.
- Refer back to the literature review and your conceptual framework.
  - Use the literature to interrogate and evaluate your research material and vice versa.
- Presentation and analysis may require several chapters, e.g.:
  - one chapter for presentation and one for analysis; or
  - several chapters, each presenting a different case study;
  - and so on.

(f) Conclusions and recommendations
- Summarise the main argument, otherwise known as the thesis, of the dissertation.
- Either discuss the validity and reliability of the findings and arguments or reflectively critique the account provided in the dissertation.
- Frame the conclusions, and recommendations if appropriate.
- Discuss any issues concerning the implementation of the conclusions or any recommendations.

This structure is designed for an academic audience, the academic staff who will mark the dissertation. It would not necessarily be appropriate for a managerial audience, especially the managers in the organisation(s) that the dissertation reports on. In any case, a dissertation is normally too long for internal management purposes. Sometimes students prepare a short version of the dissertation for organisational use. The executive summary that students have to submit with the dissertation (see 'Dissertation, report and paper specifications' at the end of this chapter) may be sufficient for this purpose.

If you are writing up an action research project, something like the following structure might be more appropriate. A greater variety of structures can be seen in action research dissertations than in traditional ones. What they all have in common is a chronological or narrative form. In writing up action research, the story of the developing project is told from its inception, not forgetting to record the blind alleys that were entered and the false starts that were made. The structures normally follow through the cycles of action, monitoring, theorising and further action:

(a) Preparation
   - Introduction. Define the strategic and research questions the project will address. Explain the organisational and personal context.
   - Conceptual framework. Theories, concepts and literature.
   - Methodology and methods.
   - First-stage action: research material collection.
   - Reconnaissance. Collection and interpretation of evidence.
(b) Development of project
   - Review of strategic and research questions.
   - Review of conceptual framework and methods.
   - Second-stage action: material collection and analysis.
   - Interim conclusions.
   - Issues for the final stage.
(c) Further development and conclusions
   - Review of methods and conceptual framework.
   - Final-stage action: material collection and analysis.
   - Conclusions.
(d) Personal, reflexive critique.

This structure includes three cycles of action research, which is normally the most a Master's student would have time for. The first cycle would be based on a literature review and an initial reconnaissance. The second cycle (development of the project) would report on the main piece of action research. The third cycle gives an opportunity to refine the action and review the consequences.

Writing a thesis, not just a dissertation

A dissertation should also be a thesis. A thesis is a proposition that a person offers to maintain, or does maintain, by argument. In a well-ordered dissertation it should be possible to identify a chain of logic and argument that can be followed by the reader. It is often a good idea to signpost this development by frequent summaries of how the argument has developed and how it is going to be developed in the rest of the dissertation. The dissertation should have a beginning, a middle and an end. In journalistic terms the dissertation should be linked by a 'hook' or a theme. Exercises 6.1, 6.2 and 6.3 provide practice in framing a thesis.

Exercise 6.1

The press release – *Tony Watson and Colin Fisher*

- An article is being prepared on exciting research being undertaken by star Master's students.
- You are to submit a press release for this article.
- The purpose of the exercise is to focus your mind on what the project 'adds up to' – a notion of a clear underlying story with a clear structure leading to a clear 'thesis'.
- Write the press release in a style appropriate for the broadsheet press.

Prepare a summary of your ongoing project that a journalist could use to write a newspaper story. Give your story a strong narrative flow.

- What inspired you in the first place?
- What new things are you going to tell the world?
- How are you doing it?
- What is emerging?
- What awe-inspiring difficulties are you overcoming in your crawl along the frontiers of knowledge?
- What lessons can be learnt from your work?

Exercise 6.2

The pub bore test

Write an interesting account of your dissertation, in a few sentences, that you could use when someone in a pub asks, 'What's your research about?' It has to be something that would catch the listener's attention and, of course, it needs to be expressed in very simple English.

Exercise 6.3

A haiku

Write a haiku poem that captures the essence of the argument you will be presenting in your dissertation.

Haiku poems consist of, respectively five, seven and five syllables in three units. In Japanese, this convention is a must. In English this can sometimes be difficult to achieve and variations in the number of syllables are allowable. The cutting divides the haiku into two parts, with a certain imaginative distance between the two sections, but the two sections must remain, to a degree, dependent on each other. Both sections must enrich the understanding of the other. To make this cutting in English, either the first or the second line ends normally with a colon, long dash or ellipsis.

The MBA done:
With God as my witness, I'll
Not study again.

If you wish to change
And modernise companies –
Value the staff's views.

Constructing arguments

If you had difficulty in doing the exercises here is a technique for helping you sharpen up your skill in argument formation.

A four-stage sequence in developing an argument can be identified using a method loosely derived from the work of the US pragmatist philosopher C.S. Peirce (Mounce 1997: 17–18). It includes two terms that have already been discussed – induction and deduction (see p. 95). Sometimes dissertation students claim that they are following either an inductive or a deductive method. It is often dangerous to claim to be using one or the other exclusively. Most researchers use both. Peirce added abduction to the two and other writers added a further element taken from the idea of analytic induction (see Gill and Johnson, 2002: 152–159 for a detailed discussion of analytic induction).

The sequence is explained using the example of downsizing, as a management strategy, to improve financial performance, as the topic of an argument.

1. **Start by stating the problem you are researching**. Let us say we are interested in the issue of downsizing. We want to know why many of the companies that downsize do not appear to reap the benefits in terms of improved financial performance.

2. **Abduction**. Abduction means kidnapping. In this stage you raid your store of knowledge and reading to hunt for a possible cause of the problem. You just happen to have read a few journal articles that suggest that the people, the survivors, who remain in the organisation after their friends and colleagues have been made redundant, suffer from guilt and depression. They lose motivation and commitment. This might explain why companies perform less well after downsizing. You 'kidnap' the idea as a possible explanation.

3. **Deduction**. Deduction is defined, in this context, as the process of inferring particulars from a general statement. Well, if we think the survivor syndrome (as the sense of depression following downsizing is called) is an explanation, we should be able to deduce some observable consequences for the organisation. We might, for example, deduce that absenteeism and sickness rates would go up, productivity would go down, staff turnover would go up and people would report, in both exit interviews and staff satisfaction surveys, that their morale had diminished.

4. **Induction**. Having deduced some practical consequences, we can now go out and do the research to see whether they can be observed. If we find that our deductions are correct, then induction comes into play. Induction is the process of drawing general conclusions from specific and detailed findings. If we have discovered increased absenteeism and sickness rates and so on, then we can infer that our initial speculation was correct.

5. **Exceptional cases**. So far the process will have identified minimum, or necessary, conditions for a strategy of downsizing to result in a worsened financial performance. It will not necessarily have provided a sufficient explanation of the effect. In other words, there may be other factors, as yet unthought of and unconsidered, that need to be in place for the effect to occur. These conditions may have been present in the case study but had not been noticed or had not been looked for. One way to check for this possibility is to look for cases or instances where there has been downsizing, and all the symptoms of increased turnover and absenteeism and so on are present, but where the financial performance has improved. If no such cases are found, your explanation remains secure until such time as contrary cases are found. If such a case is found then the researcher needs to identify whatever other factors may influence the impact of downsizing.

If the findings do not support the general theory, then we have to return to the second stage and choose another speculative cause of the problem and begin again. I suggest that this sequence – problem definition, abduction, deduction and induction – could provide a framework within which you could construct the core arguments of your thesis.

Exercise 6.4

Constructing an argument

Choose a problem or issue that you are trying to explain in your research and use the framework outlined above to try to construct an argument.

Constructing dialectical arguments

In Chapter 5 the dialectic was suggested as a means of interpreting research material. Here I want to make a more general case by arguing that the dialectic can be used to shape your thesis. The dialectic provides an alternative form of argument that can be useful in an MBA or Master's dissertation. This is not as exotic as it sounds. Gareth Morgan (1997) recommends it as a useful metaphor for understanding organisations in his book *Images of Organisations,* and Pascale (1990: 142–143) used it to analyse Ford's (then) strategic success, in his best seller *Managing on the Edge.* Pascale used the form of the dialectic developed by Hegel, the German philosopher (1770–1831), rather than the Marxist version favoured by Morgan. In this section we will be using a much simplified version of the Hegelian dialectic. Its usefulness is suggested by an overheard remark by a student:

> Well I don't agonise over papers. What I say is always pretty much the same. First I wonder, 'What's the main thing in this book?' and then I wonder, 'What's its opposite?' When I write my paper, I claim that these two things, though they seem different, couldn't exist without each other; even that they are really two aspects of the same thing ... Near the end of your paper you have to say that your two things, whatever they are, are 'locked in an unstable but mutually constitutive relationship'. Profs just love that.
>
> (Eisaman Maus, 2001)

This remark neatly summarises the dialectical method of arguing, which consists of the following triad:

- **Thesis.** A formal idea, empty of content. An idea that is separate from the messy practicality of experience.
- **The antithesis.** The practical realities that undermine the formal idea in a practical application.
- **The synthesis.** This moves understanding of the idea up a notch so that the contradictions become unimportant at a higher and more sophisticated level of understanding.

The synthesis does not declare either the thesis or the antithesis the victor. Rather, it develops a new level of thinking in which the old opposition becomes irrelevant. The dialectical process goes through many such sequences. As soon as a synthesis is reached, new contradictions will arise and it becomes a thesis, a starting point for a new dialectic.

Hegel's most famous application of this triad is known as the dialectic of the master and the slave. In a very simplified form it goes as follows:

- **Formal idea.** The master is superior to the slave.
- **The antithesis.** The formal idea is contradicted by the following factors:
  - The master is dependent on the slave because he needs the services the slave provides.
  - If the slave were not there, the master could not express his superiority.
  - The master sees himself reflected in the slave. In other words, the master looks on to the inferior, and this diminishes him, but the slave looks at the master and is provided with ambition.
- **The synthesis.** The master and slave come to see themselves as mutually dependent equals and develop cooperation.

I am currently doing some work on attempts by western agencies to encourage organisations in the countries of the former Soviet Union to adapt to their new economic and political environment. In particular, I am studying the relationships between the western 'experts' brought in to lead the change, the change agents they select and train in the host country, and the local managers in the local organisations that they are encouraging to change. It deals with some of the issues discussed on pp. 145–48. I developed the dialectic structure shown in Figure 6.1 to present an argument about how the relationships between these three groups develop. The dialectic also acts as a conceptual framework for my research.

You can see that the middle dialectic in Figure 6.1 is based on the master and slave dialectic. One feature of this needs a little further explanation. The western experts and the local change agents had different ideas of friendship. The experts' view was that the obligations of friendship little exceeded the requirement for mutual amusement and support. The local change agents had a more eastern concept of friendship and hospitality, which placed greater demands upon friends. This required friends to spare no effort to support each other. Consequently the western experts expected little of their friends among the local change agents but the change agents expected their western friends to do all in their power to help them with foreign trips and obtaining jobs in the west. In consequence, the formally subordinate were in practice dominant because they were making the greatest demands. This social contradiction was reinforced by the western experts' dependence on the change agents' local knowledge that, again, made the formally superior practically dependent.

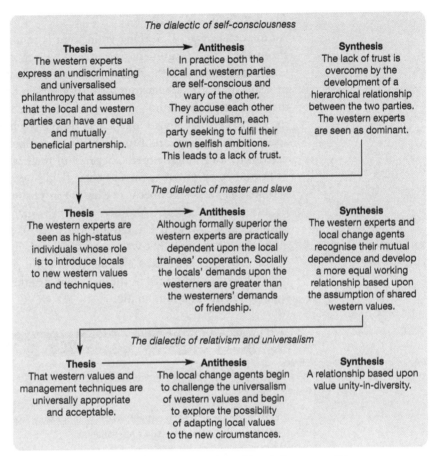

Figure 6.1 The dialectic of western experts and local change agents
Source: Fisher and Lovell, 2006, Table 11.7, p. 447.

If you have found any discrepancies between formal intention and actual practice in your research material, then the dialectic may provide a tool for analysing them.

Supporting your arguments

There are a number of ways in which you can support your argument when you write it up in the dissertation:

- authority – other writers have supported the position you take;
- evidence – selected examples drawn from your research material; and
- persuasive writing style.

Each of these is considered in turn.

Arguing from authority

An important way of arguing your point is to claim authority for it. You show that your argument is correct by reporting that one or more undoubted experts in the field has written that it is so. There are a number of issues that arise from this form of argument. First of all you need to make sure that the author you are citing is indeed an accepted authority in the field. This becomes a particular problem when, as is common in the social sciences, there are disputes between competing authorities. You also need to be aware that experts, because of their fame, are sometimes prone to pronouncing on areas outside their field of expertise. Other people are accepted as authorities because they are in positions of power rather than because they are expert. Another problem is that a student may well have misunderstood what the noted authority wrote and therefore is claiming authority for an idea that was never proposed. Exercise 6.5 looks at some of the problems caused by arguing from authorities. It reveals that some researchers use literature in the way that drunkards use a lamp-post: for support rather than illumination.

Exercise 6.5

Bad habits

What is wrong with each of the following examples of argument by authority and academic citation? The references are fictitious.

Chinese whispers

The principles of ethnographic technique espoused by Malinowski were ... (Anderson and Burns, 1989).

Showing off

The works of Habermas (1991, 1997) and Roy Bhaskar (1983, 1993) support my main contention ...

The founding fathers

... this returns to the ideas of Weber as a core thinker in sociology.

Padding

... was influenced by organisational structure (Simon *et al.*, 1954; Bear, 1972 and 1979; Becher and Kogan, 1992; Berquist, 1993; Galbraith *et al.*, 1993); and institutional culture with five elements ...

Neophilism

The key writers on motivation and commitment of people at work are Bloggs (2002), Smith (2003) and Jones (2004).

Canonicity

Let us begin with the idea of a decision (Caputo, 1993; Chia, 1994; Derrida, 1978).

Exercise 6.5 *continued*

Suggested answer

Chinese whispers

If Malinowski is the key authority it is better to cite him directly rather than through a third party. The problem is that the intermediary may have misrepresented the *echt* (authentic) author. However, this is not a truly wicked crime and in the case of obscure or difficult authors it can be acceptable to quote someone who provides an accessible account of the maestro's work.

Showing off

This is a development of Chinese whispers. The works of Habermas and Bhaskar are large and very difficult and it is likely that most MBA students will not have had the time or inclination to study them. The suspicion is that the writer is merely showing off by claiming to have read works they have not. If the writer has read them, they could indicate this by giving page references to the places where Habermas and Bhaskar make the points the writer claims they do.

The founding fathers

Some authors, such as Weber, are so universally admired that dissertation writers believe that it is necessary to cite them. It isn't.

Padding

The writer is so insecure in their argument they have to call on large battalions to support them. This becomes very tedious and it raises doubts about whether the writer has actually read all the works being cited. It would be better to provide arguments rather than lists in support of the proposition.

Neophilism

Citations can never be more than three years old, and any old work should never be cited. This of course is nonsense.

Canonicity

This assumes that something is a universally agreed position or starting point when it may not be.

Arguing from evidence – *Alistair Mutch*

Using references is one way of supplying evidence to support your arguments. You will also use evidence that you have gathered directly. Evidence used appropriately can be very powerful. However, there are some pitfalls to be aware of.

Theory is underdetermined by data. This point might best be illustrated by an example. Galileo's theory about the movement of the planets made predictions about planetary positions that could not be observed using the telescopes of the time. It was only when such telescopes were developed (prompted by the need to test the theory) that the essential correctness of Galileo's predictions was confirmed. In other words, the theory preceded the data. For your work, the message is that just presenting data by themselves is inadequate.

The 'facts' do not 'speak for themselves'. Not only does the approach we use determine which 'facts' we will use (and, indeed, which we may have created by our observations) but any 'fact' needs interpretation. Remember that during the process of research you will become very close to your material. What seems obvious to you may be very unclear to your reader. You cannot stop the readers from making their own interpretations, but you can at least be clear about your own. This means explaining why you are using particular bits of evidence, rather than assuming that the readers will work this out for themselves. What it also means is that you will have to think carefully about the following:

- classification strategies that make sense of your evidence – which should be derived from your conceptual framework;
- ways of presenting the data (tables, charts, diagrams) that fit the data being presented and make the point in a clear fashion.

Do not 'pile it high'. The end result will often not contain all the material that you have collected. This can be very frustrating, but you have to be selective. It is important that you do not make the reader do the work of selection. Putting large chunks of interview transcripts into your text, for example, may help the word count but not the reader's patience. *You* have to do the preliminary interpretation and selection, not the reader. Do not be tempted to take the course of putting all this material in an appendix, 'just in case'. Your main text should contain the key points, the appendix essential supporting material. Thus, say you had carried out a survey in which only three questions out of twenty had produced interesting results. You might discuss these three questions in depth and summarise the rest of the results in an appendix. You would not put all the returned questionnaires in the appendix. What is more common is to put interview transcripts in an appendix, but this is not necessary. If we want to see them, we will ask for them.

Weight of evidence. An occasionally successful rhetorical strategy is the piling on of example after example until the reader caves in under the weight. Some historians employ this strategy very successfully, but it has great dangers. It needs to be used sparingly and in the context of a clearly developed theoretical framework. Without this it is in danger of becoming a tedious list. Remember that what is fascinating to you may hold little charm for a wider audience. The meander down a byway that fascinates you but nobody else is one of the most frustrating perils that can snare the researcher.

Persuasive style

In universities in the Middle Ages, learning how to make persuasive arguments, taught under the heading of rhetoric, was a major part of students' curriculum. Rhetoric is re-emerging as a serious topic. Whether you are aware of it or not you will use some of the skills of rhetoric when you are writing your dissertation.

The classical teachers of rhetoric identified five stages in the preparation of an argument:

1. Invention – choosing the materials and arguments to be used.
2. Arrangement – putting the arguments and materials into a proper order.
3. Style – choosing an appropriate style for the audience.
4. Memory – learning the arguments and material is necessary for a spoken presentation but not for a piece of written work.
5. Delivery – making the presentation or writing the dissertation in a persuasive manner. There are many courses available to help you learn these skills.

Exercise 6.6

Establishing an audit trail

- What are the main findings or conclusions of your dissertation?
- What support do you have for each finding/conclusion?
  - authorities
  - evidence.
- How reliable and valid is the evidence?

The previous sections have dealt with the invention and arrangement stages. In this section, style and delivery will be considered. The ancient teachers of rhetoric identified many devices or figures for encouraging an audience to accept the arguments being presented. Technical names were given to many of the persuasive devices. Some are familiar today, such as metaphor and rhetorical question, but others such as epanorthosis have sunk, probably rightfully, into obscurity. It is not necessary for you to know the technical terms but you should be aware that there is an art to constructing convincing arguments. Some of a puritanical temper argue that rhetorical devices should be ignored because they are no more than tricks designed to lure the innocent into accepting ideas and arguments that cannot stand on their own. They tend to contrast rhetoric with reality. It is probably more realistic to accept that rhetorical skill is an inevitable part of all speech and communication, as may be illustrated in Exercise 6.7.

The text in Exercise 6.7 uses rhetorical devices and skill without the back-up of sound argument and evidence. You should aim to use both. The moral of Exercise 6.7 is not that rhetoric is to be despised but that it should be used in support of a good thesis.

Exercise 6.7

Rhetorical devices

1 What is the main thrust of the argument?
2 By what steps does the argument proceed and what rhetorical tricks are used in each?
3 Can you find examples of the following rhetorical figures?
   – Metaphor – comparison by referring to one thing as another: 'Life's a beach'.
   – Oxymoron – placing two ordinarily opposing terms next to each other: 'jumbo shrimp'.
   – Rhetorical question (erotema) – a question asked for any reason other than obtaining the answer. 'Why me, God?'
   – Antithesis – juxtaposing contrasting words or ideas: 'It can't be wrong if it feels so right.'
   – Epitrope – turning a thing over to the audience in such a way as to suggest a proof without actually giving one: 'Go ahead, make my day.'
   – Sarcasm – a taunting remark.

Burton's (2000) website provides an intriguing guide to the exotic world of rhetorical figures of speech.

The call for papers

In the world of today, change is said to be the only constant. Knowledge travels fast, through a variety of distribution channels, many of which were unknown only a few years ago. Therefore knowledge can be a highly perishable commodity. An important objective of the dissemination of knowledge will always be to ensure that it arrives fresh after the shortest possible route. Academic research within the areas of business administration and economics has often been criticised by the business community, which claims that much of it is mainly directed at the establishment of researchers themselves, who reply to and discuss it within the establishment instead of distributing it to the business community. Students may often wonder whether they are studying yesterday's knowledge, instead of being continuously updated on current and relevant research. The proliferation of learning opportunities (for example, information technology) today makes learning for tomorrow even more complicated. In our global society success or failure in business frequently depends on which party has the most current knowledge of the issues and facts involved.

As universities and corporations attempt to prepare management to be alert to future changes, improved (and even brand new) teaching methodologies are required. The main focus of the sixth ERGOT conference will be on the distribution and selection of new knowledge. How can business educators deliver new knowledge to students and the business community more rapidly than before? How should we define the core business curriculum when new knowledge becomes old knowledge?

Suggested answers – Alistair Mutch
1. The main argument
The argument is that changes in the world mean changes in both the nature of knowledge and the way in which this should be taught. All three components of this argument:

Exercise 6.7 *continued*

- the nature of changes in the world,
- that forms of knowledge are changing,
- that changes in teaching are required,

are extremely contentious and there is no necessary connection between them. However, the thrust of this argument is that the links are self-evident. This is achieved through a number of 'dodgy arguments'.

2. The steps

A note of caution: this was a call for papers and not a published paper or an assessed report. Some of the strictures below might seem a little harsh. However, the central issues about the status of the arguments, you might think, apply to any piece of argument.

1. *In the world of today, change is said to be the only constant.*
   We might point out three things about this sentence:
   (a) Is it true? Hasn't the world always been changing? (You might want to look at Henry Mintzberg's (1994) scathing comments about this in *The Rise and Fall of Strategic Planning*, where he notes that, for example, managers in the Great Depression had to cope with a far more turbulent world.)
   (b) Who says? The word 'said' is being used to give a spurious authority to this statement. In an essay you would expect an idea of who has done the saying, so that the reader could judge the respect to be accorded to this assertion. Here we cannot tell, but in passing over it quickly we may get some of the aura of a reference.
   (c) It is a cliché. We might want to follow George Orwell's (1962: 156) advice (although it is not easy!) to 'never use a metaphor, simile or other figure of speech which you are used to seeing in print'.
2. *Knowledge travels fast, through a variety of distribution channels, many of which were unknown only a few years ago.*
   The effect here is cumulative, with the change of the previous sentence emphasised by *fast* and *only a few years ago*. The impact of an argument may rest in this rather vague, cumulative impression.
3. *Therefore knowledge can be a highly perishable commodity.*
   There is no support for the *therefore*, other than as a rhetorical device to convince you that there must be a connection. Even if the two sentences were accepted, they say nothing about the perishable nature of knowledge. It could change and travel fast, but still not perish.
4. *An important objective of the dissemination of knowledge will always be to ensure that it arrives fresh after the shortest possible route.*
   Our acceptance of this assertion depends on the *therefore* of the previous sentence and our subsequent acceptance of the perishable nature of knowledge.
5. *Academic research within the areas of business administration and economics has often been criticised by the business community, which claims that much of it is mainly directed at the establishment of researchers themselves, who reply to and discuss it within the establishment instead of distributing it to the business community.*
   This may or may not be true, but here it is being used to add authority to the argument. We may not be convinced by the previous argument, runs the sub-text, but here is an influential group, so we had better be convinced.
6. *Students may often wonder whether they are studying yesterday's knowledge, instead of being continuously updated on current and relevant research.*
   The crucial contrast here is between *yesterday's* (bad) and *current and relevant* (good), which implies the couplet of 'old' and 'irrelevant'. The use of *relevant* is designed to touch an emotional nerve – we all want to be relevant, don't we?

Exercise 6.7 *continued*

7. *The proliferation of learning opportunities (for example, information technology) today makes learning for tomorrow even more complicated.*

   Bringing in the powerful symbolism of technology reinforces the relevance argument, as does the emphasis on *today* and *tomorrow*.

8. *In our global society success or failure in business frequently depends on which party has the most current knowledge of the issues and facts involved.*

   The final sentence of the paragraph uses a few more loaded words to emphasise the point – *global*, *business* and *current*.

9. *As universities and corporations attempt to prepare management to be alert to future changes improved (and even brand new) teaching methodologies are required.*

   We reach a new paragraph bludgeoned into submission! Who could object to this contemporary, up-to-date account? This might prevent us seeing that some very broad assumptions are being made about the equivalence of universities and corporations. We might think that *methodologies* rather than *methods* or even *ways of teaching* lend some scientific authority to this brave new world.

10. *The main focus of the sixth ERGOT conference will be on the distribution and selection of new knowledge. How can business educators deliver new knowledge to students and the business community more rapidly than before? How should we define the core business curriculum when new knowledge becomes old knowledge?*

    You might think that there are deeper questions here concerned with what the real purpose of business education is. However, we see the familiar buzzwords of *new* and *rapidly*, confirming the whole emphasis of the piece on the speed of change. The use of words is geared to giving an overall impression of speed and change – try counting the occurrence of words that support this.

Finally: I have been making an argument here. I have used some rhetorical devices of my own, especially bringing in authority figures, such as Orwell. I think this passage is badly thought-through and uses weak arguments (not necessarily consciously) to make its points. We are led through a chain of sentences that seem to have a logical coherence but that do not. I think the choice of words is made to reinforce a particular point. I think this is sloppily done – but feel free to construct a counter-argument!

3. Rhetorical figures – *Colin Fisher*

There seem to be many rhetorical figure employed in this piece, some of which I cannot put a name to. But here are some that I could identify:

Metaphors

Knowledge as a perishable commodity that has freshness. Knowledge seen as fruit and veg.

Teaching methodologies as a brand in 'brand new' and therefore a product.

Oxymoron

'change is the only constant'.

Antithesis

'when old knowledge becomes new knowledge'.

Rhetorical question

'How can business educators deliver new knowledge to students and the business community more rapidly than before?' Less an enquiry than a call to action.

Sarcasm

'yesterday's knowledge', especially with its echoes of the political campaign slogan 'yesterday's men', just about counts as a bitter taunt.

Epitrope

The last two sentences are implicitly handing the task over to the delegates at the conference.

It is most important when writing your dissertation to have a clear image of the readers and to write it in a style that they will find attractive and persuasive. The most important readers of your dissertation are the academics who will mark it. It should be written for them. You may, however, if you also want to use the dissertation to convince managers in your organisation to take action based on your findings, have to write another version that is designed for their consumption. This will need to be much shorter than the dissertation and be written in a report format. Exercise 6.8 looks at different styles of academic writing and should help you decide which style to adopt in your dissertation.

Exercise 6.8

Focusing on your readers

There follows three extracts from fictitious articles on a business and management topic. They are each in very different styles. The emphasis of this task is on the style of the writing and not on the content. In the following passages, therefore, the arguments are not intended seriously and may indeed be nonsense. The citations are invented. In terms of their content treat the extracts as caricatures. Your task is to:

- identify the similarities and differences in how they are written;
- decide what sort of reader each is best suited to;
- decide which is the closest to the style you think you should adopt when writing your dissertation.

Extract 1 From *The dialectics of neo-institutional processes and the forms of rationality*
The rationalised myth, according to neo-institutional theory (Weiskopf and Chin, 1976, Bullock and Lamb, 1985, Sweetens *et al.*, 1989 and Huckleberry and Finn, 2002), provides the leitmotivs against which organisations seek isomorphism, although recent writers (Hazelcroft and Tonningen, 1999) have argued about whether institutional or rational forces have primacy in the shaping of organisations and their cultures. When western change agents seek, through metropolitan led and funded change programmes, to change the rationalised myths that were dominant in Soviet organisations, competing dimensions of rationality are exposed within the rationalised myths. To understand these agons it is necessary to return to Webber's perspectives on different forms of rationality, as interpreted by Kautilya (1994), that provide a conceptual framework to analyse the responses of organisations in post-Soviet countries to the globalising pressures of the western rationlised myth of free markets and rational choice. Webber (1929 and 1932) distinguished deontological rationality, which is concerned with actions based on certain values, from utilitarian rationality, which is based on a means–ends calculation (Bloch and Simon, 1996). It will be argued that within post-Soviet organisations the conflict between the substantive value rationality of the Soviet order and the formal rationality of the globalising agenda creates, as Webber predicted, a gap into which instrumental rationality moves. Organisational actors adopt the globalising myth because it moves them towards the goal of economic success but their commitment is mechanical and superficial as their substantive rationality leads them to prioritise the cultural sphere over the economic ...

Extract 2 From *To Boldly Go: Counter-institutional strategies in transforming post-Soviet economies*
Case studies of turnarounds in successful western companies can provide lessons for those involved with major change programmes in post-Soviet countries that are designed to encourage a culture of entrpreneurialism and a commitment to market-led growth. Close study of how three internationally admired companies have moved from basket cases to world-class financial performers have identified five **counter-institutional** strategies that act as drivers of cultural change in post-Soviet organisations.

Exercise 6.8 *continued*

Anatomy of a counter-institutional strategy

1 Supply and mould revolutionaries
2 Develop new internal brands that challenge the old ones
3 Create new safe zones
4 Adapt existing vales to new ends
5 Create western minders for host country change leaders.

Savvy incumbents of change agent roles in post-Soviet organisations reduce the collateral cost of culture change by leveraging the existing contra-cultural undercurrents that exist within any culture. Worldron Inc. transformed itself to respond to global competitive pressures when its charismatic CEO finessed the inventiveness of its young Turks in the derivatives trading division and brought about a new commitment to improving financial returns.

Strong leadership from the top is an important driver in all the case studies.

Extract 3 From Cross-cultural dynamics in western change projects in countries of the former Soviet Union

Institutionalism and modernisation projects

Smith and Smith (2001: 29) used the concept of institutionalism to theorise about the change processes in modernisation projects in countries of the former Soviet Union. The values, practices and structures of a society form its institutions. Institutionalism is the theory that organisations conform to these institutions. This process is not automatic. It is caused by the choices and actions of people within the organisations. Choice makes it possible for organisations to conform to institutions other than those of the society organisations are located within. Modernisation projects are designed to substitute global (or western?) institutions for local Soviet institutions as the templates against which organisations should model themselves.

Others argue that managerial rationality is more important than institutional pressures in influencing the forms of organisations (Hazelcroft and Tonningen, 1999: 235–256). An organisation is designed rationally if its form is as efficient and effective as possible. Local institutions would not figure in managerial rationality. This debate will be considered later in the paper. At this stage the concern is how modernisation projects can be understood in terms of institutionalism.

In case studies Smiles (1996), Dubrovsky (2001) and Aliev (2002) identified five difficulties experienced during modernisation projects. These will be discussed in turn.

1 Western experts employed on modernisation projects are too ignorant of the local culture and language to engage the sympathies of the local managers they are working with. Modernisation projects cannot, argued Aliev (2002: 203–204), involve the re-institutionalisation of indigenous organisations alone. The western experts of the project teams also need to respond to the values and practices of local institutions. A synthesis that creates a mutual process of learning is needed. Local managers respond more positively to western values if the western experts are not dismissive of the local culture.

Suggested answer

Similarities and differences

Use of references

Extract 1 has a very heavy use of references including several multiple references. Extract 2 has none at all. Extract 3 has a smaller number of references with fewer multiple citations. The third extract often gives page numbers so that specific arguments in a book can be easily located.

Exercise 6.8 *continued*

Use of academic jargon

The first extract uses much academic jargon but gives few definitions or accounts of the concepts. The author assumes the reader to be familiar with the ideas and with the debate in the literature. The second extract is clear of academic jargon. The third extract does use technical terms but mostly gives a brief explanation of them at or near their first use.

Use of management jargon

The second abstract uses managerial jargon extensively. The jargon is taken to be straightforward; but words such as 'drivers', 'leveraging' and 'world-class' can become mere habit. When this happens they may imply assumptions that ought to be questioned. The extract also uses colloquial terms ('savvy') in an attempt to empathise with the presumed reader. Such approaches can badly misfire. The other two extracts are free of managerial jargon.

Theory, research and anecdote

The first extract is entirely theoretical, although typically in this type of paper there will be some empirical material in the middle before a return to theory at the end of the paper. Both of the other papers have theoretical concerns but in the second extract theory is seen as a guide to action and in the third extract there seems to be a more balanced integration of the case study material and the theoretical issues. Although the second extract refers to its empirical material as case studies it looks more like anecdotes. The case studies mentioned in the third extract look more like rigorous and systematic accounts.

Critical tone

The first extract is critical in the sense described in Chapter 2 as radical critique. It is challenging the purpose and moral status of the modernisation projects. The second extract is more enthusiastic than critical. There are no doubts or nuanced discussions about the ideas being put forward. People are being invited to 'buy into' them and put them into practice. The third extract does identify doubts and arguments about some of the key concepts that are used.

Sub-headings and visual tricks

The first extract favours large solid blocks of text. The second extracts assumes that readers will be terrified of this and breaks up the texts with figures, illustrations, bullet points and extracts of key points printed as aphorisms in boxes. The third extract also uses sub-headings and numbered lists but does not avoid solid paragraphs. The items in the lists consist, not of one or a few words, but of sentences.

Ease of reading

The Flesch reading ease scale rates a text on a 100-point scale. The higher the score, the easier the text is to read. The recommended target for standard texts (which may exclude academic texts) is between 60 and 70.

Extract 1
Flesch Reading Ease Scale	0
Average number of sentences per paragraph	7
Average number of words per sentence	35.1

Extract 2
Flesch Reading Ease Scale	22.3
Average number of sentences per paragraph	1.5
Average number of words per sentence	25.8

Extract 3
Flesch Reading Ease Scale	20.8
Average number of sentences per paragraph	4.7
Average number of words per sentence	15.3

Exercise 6.8 *continued*

As a general rule, keep your sentences short and your paragraphs long. The third extract is the easiest to read but even in this case the sentences are still rather long. The number of sentences per paragraph is acceptable although at the lower limits of desirability.

The readers
The first extract is written for a small number of highly specialised academics who understand their subject's jargon and are familiar, and indeed have probably been involved with, the debate. The second extract is for managers who would be scared or suspicious of anything they thought academic. The third extract is probably accessible to the academic and the practitioner, although it would be too academic for managers with academiphobia. It is aimed, to use a very old-fashioned phrase, at the interested and educated lay reader.

Which style would be best for your dissertation?

I would recommend the style of the third extract. Academics will mark your dissertation and although they will have a familiarity with your broad field of study they may not be specialists in your research topic. It is best to treat them as interested lay readers. Also, if you adopt the technique of explaining and discussing your terms, it helps the markers assess whether you understand them. Many markers would find the style of the second abstract to be unscholarly and full of assumptions that ought to be challenged. The style of the first abstract is almost as hard for a full-time academic to read as it is for you. I doubt you would be tempted to write like this, but in any case don't.

● ● ● ● Style guide

Dissertation, report and paper specifications

There are a number of practical issues concerned with writing up a paper or a dissertation. This section details the house style that Master's students are expected to follow in the business school I work in. You will need to conform to the requirements of the institution you are studying at.

Paper or report specification

A paper or report can be informally bound, that is to say, spiral bound or with a glued and taped spine and soft covers. Binding in a report cover bought from a stationer would be fine.

The front cover should include:

Title	OBTAINING VALUE FOR MONEY IN SKEGMOUTH DEVELOPMENT CORPORATION
Full name	POLLY TITIAN Conference paper submitted in part fulfilment of the requirements of The Nottingham Trent University for the degree of [appropriate degree title]
Institution	NOTTINGHAM TRENT UNIVERSITY
Date	SEPTEMBER 2007

There should not normally be a need for tables of contents and such like for a document of this length, but do include:

- an abstract or executive summary (about 150 words);
- references;
- appendices if appropriate and necessary.

Dissertation specification

The dissertation shall be bound in hard black covers with gold lettering. The front cover should include:

Title	ECONOMIC MISMANAGEMENT
Full name	POLLY TITIAN
Institution	NOTTINGHAM TRENT UNIVERSITY
Date	SEPTEMBER 2007

The spine of the document should include:

Initials and surname	P. TITIAN
Course	M.Sc.
Year	2007

Contents of the bound dissertation

The following should be bound in with the dissertation:

- title page;
- acknowledgements (only if you insist, but try to avoid mawkishness or bad jokes);
- an abstract (also known as an executive summary) of approximately 300 words;
- table of contents;
- list of tables and figures (these are discretionary);
- main text;
- references;
- appendices (these are discretionary).

Submission

Normally two bound copies of the dissertation are required for assessment purposes, one of which will be retained by the university. Check your institution's requirements.

Style hints

Typing

The dissertation should be printed on white A4 paper with 1.5 spacing using a font size no larger than 12. We have no preference for font, but choose something classy. There used to be, believe it or not, a British standard, BS 4821 (1990), for academic dissertations. However, this has now been withdrawn.

Layout

The dissertation should be printed with a left margin of not less than 40 mm, the other margins should not be less than 15 mm. Normally the default settings on your word processor will be fine. The pages should be numbered consecutively.

Title page

The title page of the documents shall give the following information:

- the title of the document;
- the author's name;
- dissertation submitted in part fulfilment of the requirements of Nottingham Trent University for the degree of [appropriate degree title];
- month and year of submission.

Headings

The use of headings and sub-headings, in addition to chapter headings, is encouraged. Decide your own sequence of typographical features for defining the various levels of headings. For example:

MAIN SECTION

Blah blah blah blah. Blah blah blah. Blah blah blah blah, blah blah blah; blah blah blah. Blah blahblah blah, blah blah blah, blah blah.

Sub section

Blah blah blah blah. Blah blah blah. Blah blah blah blah, blah blah blah; blah blah blah. Blah blahblah blah, blah blah blah, blah blah.

Sub-sub section

Blah blah blah blah. Blah blah blah. Blah blah blah blah, blah blah blah; blah blah blah. Blah blahblah blah, blah blah blah, blah blah.

Sub-sub-sub section

Blah blah blah blah. Blah blah blah. Blah blah blah blah, blah blah blah; blah blah blah. Blah blahblah blah, blah blah blah, blah blah.

Paragraphs

The dissertation or paper should be written in paragraphs. Each paragraph should normally be longer than one sentence and will often take up about a third of a page. If the average number of sentences per paragraph in your writing approaches one, you should do something to remedy the situation. If you are using Microsoft Word you can set the spelling and grammar check to show readability statistics, including the average number of sentences per paragraph. To set this option click on **Tools ... Options ... Spelling and Grammar** and finally tick the **Show readability statistics** option. The statistics will appear when you have finished the spell and grammar check.

Paragraphs often have a linking word such as 'next' or 'furthermore' near their start. These linkers, to use Perry's (2000) term, lead the reader from an established idea to a new theme or idea. Each paragraph should begin with a theme sentence that explains the new theme or idea. The rest of the paragraph is dedicated to developing and describing the theme or idea. Each paragraph should deal with only one main idea.

Numbering

Do number the sections if it makes you content. However, I have a personal antipathy to the decimal numbering systems that give each paragraph a number. A reference to 5.6.4.8.ii looks to me as if it belongs to a statute rather than to a dissertation. My suggestion, if you must use numbering, is to use no more than one or two decimal places. If you insist on using a decimal numbering system to the nth degree, the end result will be that every sentence has a number.

Bullet points

Bullet points are acceptable but are no substitute for chunky paragraphs full of argument. So use bullet points for summaries and genuine lists and not as a way of avoiding debate. The following would not be acceptable:

- People are an organisation's most important asset.
- Empowering people means energising an organisation.
- Empowered organisations are more effective.
- Empowered people have freely chosen to do what the organisation requires them to do.

Each of these statements is contentious and ought to be argued through.

Quotes

If they are brief include them in the main text. If they are more than one line long, indent them as follows:

> Blah blah blah blah. Blah blah blah. Blah blah blah blah, blah blah blah; blah blah blah. Blah blahblah blah, blah blah blah, blah blah.
>
> Blah blah blah blah. Blah blah blah. Blah blah blah blah, blah blah blah; blah blah blah. Blah blahblah blah, blah blah blah, blah blah.
>
> (author, date, page number)

Indented quotations should be in single spacing.

Footnotes

Do not use these for providing citations. Use them very sparingly for comments or information that, while not part of the main flow of argument,[1] have sufficient merit or amusement value to raise a wry smile on the reader's face.

Tenses

Perry (2000) recommends that the introductory chapters and the conceptual framework chapter should be written in the present tense. The literature review and the student's own research should be written in the past tense. Conclusions should be in the present tense.

The personal pronoun

I have no objection to people writing in the first person singular. The more your research is in the ethnographic or action research style, the more appropriate it would be. However, the author recognises that in more traditional research cultures its use would be regarded as unprofessional. C.M. Fisher argues that an excessive use of 'I' is a symptom of egomania.

Appendices

Appendices are very useful. They are not counted against the dissertation word limits. They are places to put subsidiary information (such as the summary of results from a questionnaire), which it is good scholarship to make available to the reader but which is not necessary to the flow of the argument. Appendices that are thicker than the text are a sign of heap making and are best avoided. As Nennius wrote in his ninth-century *History of the Britons*, 'Coacevarvi omni quod inveni'.

Foreign languages

The documents should be in English. If you use quotes in other languages, please provide a translation. Just in case your Latin is rusty the quotation in the previous paragraph says 'I made a heap of all that I found'. This may have worked in the Dark Ages but it is no longer a good academic strategy.

---

[1] It seems unlikely but someone has written a history of the footnote (Grafton, 1998). He argues that the unwashed read the text but the learned read the footnote.

Tables, diagrams and boxes

Tables and diagrams should be included in an appropriate place in the text. They should be numbered consecutively with separate sequences for tables, figures and boxes. They should only be placed in the appendices if they are so bulky that they would disrupt the reader's flow of understanding. The use of boxes to contain illustrative material within the text is fine.

Clichés

Clichés, as in Exhibit 6.1, which can be seen on many office pin boards, are best avoided. Especially when, as in the case of this ancient Roman he never actually said it; see: http://www.research.att.com/~reeds/petronius.html.

Exhibit 6.1

As Petronius Arbiter did not say:

We trained hard ... but it seemed that every time we were beginning to form up into teams we would be reorganised. I was to learn later in life that we tend to meet any new situation by reorganising; and a wonderful method it can be for creating the illusion of progress while producing confusion, inefficiency and demoralisation.

Vocabulary and jargon

There is a grave danger, when writing dissertations, that we lapse into bizno-bollocks speak, such as in the following example:

> It is our job to continually leverage others' performance-based methods of empowerment.

Or its scholarly equivalent, professorial pompous talk:

> The premise of capitalist narrative states that reality is used to reinforce the hegemony of capitalism. If neo-capitalist narrative holds we have to choose between the semiotic paradigm of discourse and the textual paradigm of consensus.

Both of these examples are extreme because they were written by computer programs[2] that use random methods to generate text. They look as if they mean something profound but, because they are randomly generated, they are clearly nonsense. It is easy to find examples of both conditions in management reports and in academic journals. Business and management students are more likely to suffer from bizno-bollocks speak

---

[2] See the Dilbert mission statement generator at http://www.unitedmedia.co./comics/dibert/career, and the postmodern essay generator at http://www.csse.monash.edu.au/other/postmodern.html.

than its academic equivalent when they write. It is easy to fall into the trap of using management jargon because it sounds impressive. However, as it involves little thought, it generally means little or nothing. The purpose of this section of the chapter is to help you to be more careful about what you say, especially when you are writing a report or dissertation.

The general rule to apply is 'only use words you understand'. This probably excludes the use of bizno-bollocks speak, unless used ironically or within quotation marks. Also be careful with academic jargon. Terms such as 'deconstruction' are frequently used in ways that reveal the writer's ignorance of their meaning. Neologisms, however, would be allowed according to this rule. If you have invented the word it can be assumed you know what it means; but let the reader in on the secret. One good piece of advice, which I frequently ignore, is to allow yourself only one fancy piece of vocabulary per document, and that only in the last paragraph.

Grammar

There are many 'how to write good English' manuals available in libraries and bookshops and on the World Wide Web. I recommend you use them. Unquestioning reliance on Word's grammatical checker is not a good idea. Here are some of the more common mistakes[3] to watch out for:

- Verbs has to agree with their subjects.
- Prepositions are not words to end sentences with.
- And don't start a sentence with a preposition (well, not a paragraph anyway).
- It is wrong to ever split an infinitive.
- Avoid clichés like the plague.
- Also, always avoid annoying alliteration.
- Be more or less specific.
- Parenthetical remarks (however relevant) are (usually) unnecessary.
- No sentence fragments.
- Contractions aren't necessary and shouldn't be used.
- Don't use no double negatives.
- Eschew ampersands, abbreviations, etc.
- Eliminate commas, that are not necessary.
- Never use a big word when a diminutive one would suffice.
- Kill all exclamation marks!
- Use words correctly irregardless of how others use them.
- Use the apostrophe in it's proper place and omit when its not needed.
- Puns are for children, not groan readers.
- Proofread carefully to see if you any words out.

---

[3] There are many versions of this list on the World Wide Web, which helps obscure its origins. William Safire (2002) wrote and/or collected some of them in *Fumblerules*, first published in 1990. An earlier claim to have invented the form and some of the rules is that of George Trigg (1979). A useful starting place for exploring these rules through the Web is: http://www.yaelf.com/aueFAG/miffmblrlsdntsndbl.shtml. Otherwise just type in a distinctive phrase from one of the rules into a search engine to begin to experience the number of versions of the rules available on the Web.

Martin Cutts (1999: Ch. 12) argues that several of these crimes should no longer be regarded as serious.

Citation and referencing

On a point of the purest pedantry I want to distinguish between a list of references and a bibliography. You must put in your documents, under the title of references, a list of all the works cited in the document. This is not the same thing as a bibliography, which is simply a list of books that you may or may not have cited. Bibliographies, therefore, are generally unnecessary.

There are three main systems of citation and referencing: the footnote system, the Harvard system and the Vancouver system.

The business school or other institution that you are studying at will have a policy on which system of citation and referencing to use. It is important not to mix up the systems. The use of ibid. (short for *ibidem*, the Latin for 'in the same source') and op. cit. (short for *opera citato*, the Latin for 'in the work already mentioned') belong to the footnote system and should not be used in conjunction with the Harvard system, which is the most common one in use in business and management studies and the one I will go on to describe. Business schools may require you to follow their own specifications. I have used Fisher and Hanstock (2002) as a guide. The Harvard system cites work in a text by mentioning the author(s) and the year of publication. Only these details are needed. An alphabetical list of the works referred to is then given at the close of the text, which includes full details of the work and its publication. The great advantage is that, unlike with the footnote system, the full bibliographic details do not have to be typed out every time a work is cited.

References in the text

Here are some tips about citing works in a text.

- If the author's name is included in the sentence, then all you have to do is provide the year of publication in parentheses (brackets), e.g. 'many have argued that Smith (2003) has misunderstood the issues'. Many students feel they must include the author's initials (Smith, C.M. 1975), but this is unnecessary and should not be done.
- If the author is not mentioned in the text, then include it with the year of publication in the parentheses, e.g. 'It has been argued that correct citation is a mark of scholarship (Smith 1999).'
- If there are two authors, give both names (Smith and Jones 2003); if there are more than two give the first name followed by *et al.* (Smith *et al.* 2001). You must give all the authors' names in the list of references.
- If you are referencing two or more works by the same author that were published in the same year, use letters of the alphabet to distinguish them, e.g. (Smith 2002a, Smith 2002b).

- If the author is an organisation or an institution, give as much information as necessary to identify it, e.g. (Chartered Institute of Management Accountancy 2002). If the organisation is better known by the abbreviation of its full name, then this can either be added in parentheses or used instead of the full title.
- The reference in the text should include page references if you are giving a source of a quotation, a particular piece of information or an argument. This is so that the reader can easily check back to the original material. There is some latitude about the format of this, e.g. (Smith: 29), (Smith 2003 p. 29). Where you refer to several pages the numbers should be given in full (Smith 2003: 245–289).

The list of references

The function of the list of references is to allow the reader to track down and read the material you use in the dissertation. The reference should therefore include all the information needed to achieve this purpose. Note that to make the list of references easy to read, the second and subsequent lines of the reference should be indented.

Normally this includes, for books:

Author(s) surname(s), initials or forenames, date of publication, title, edition, place of publication, publisher, pagination when only a part of a work is cited.

And in the case of journal articles:

Author(s) surname(s), initials or forenames, date of publication, article title, journal title, volume number, part or issue number (if available), start and finish page numbers of the article.

With this information, the reader should be able to go unswervingly to the source.

Here are some examples of layout and format for references. There are allowable variations. Titles of books and journals can be underlined or **emboldened** rather than *italicised*. There are other variations you will come across:

- Sometimes the date of publication is given in parentheses.
- Sometimes details of journals are spelt out, e.g. vol. 34, no. 6, pp. 235–245; sometimes they are abbreviated, e.g. 34(6), 235–245.
- Sometimes the authors' initials are given; sometimes their forenames are given. Avoid mixing the two.
- Sometimes the titles of works are typed in 'title case' in which the first letter of all the words (except minor ones) is capitalised. Alternatively sentence case is used, in which only the words at the beginning of sentences are capitalised. The important thing is, having chosen a style, to be consistent.
- And several other variations that you can discover for yourself.

Books

Badaracco, J.L. Jr (1997) *Defining Moments: When Managers Must Choose Between Right and Right*, Boston, MA: Harvard Business School Press.

Baldwin, S., Godfrey, C. and Propper, C. (eds) (1990) *Quality of Life: Perspectives and Policies*, London: Routledge.

British Airways (2000) *British Airways Social and Environmental Report 2000*, London: British Airways.

Eastwood, A. and Maynard, A. (1990) 'Treating Aids: is it ethical to be efficient?' in S. Baldwin, C. Godfrey and C. Propper (eds) *Quality of Life: Perspectives and Policies*, London: Routledge.

Journal articles

Carroll, A.B. (1990) 'Principles of business ethics: their role in decision making and an initial consensus', *Management Decision*, vol. 28, no. 8: 20–24.

Guerrera, F. (2001) 'Huntingdon seeks nominee structure to protect shareholders', *Financial Times*, 12 May: 25.

Official publications

The proper way of doing this is as follows:

Great Britain. Department for Education and Employment (1997) *Setting Targets to Raise Standards: A Survey of Good Practice*. London: Department of Education and Employment.

But it is not unusual, and appears to be acceptable, for the initial 'Great Britain' to be omitted. If you are citing works from the European Union or countries other than your home country, then you should use European Union or the name of the body or government as the author of the work.

Conference papers

Fisher, C.M. (2000) 'The ethics of inactivity: human resource managers and quietism', *Proceedings of the Third Conference on Ethics and Human Resource Management*, Imperial College School of Management, London, 10 April.

Kärreman, D. and Alvesson, M. (1999) 'Ethical closure in organisational settings: the case of media organisations', 15th EGOS Colloquium, *Organisations in a Challenging World: Theories, Practices and Societies*, The University of Warwick, 4–6 July.

World Wide Web and other electronic resources

There is less standardisation in citing electronic resources. The following examples show what information should be provided. It is often difficult to discover the author of a web page, in which case it should be referenced by title.

Transparency International (2001) *The 2001 Corruption Perceptions Index*, Berlin: Transparency International. Available online at: http://www. gwdg.de/~uwvw/2001Data.html (accessed 20 September 2001).

Journal articles downloaded from the Internet can be referenced as follows:

Fisher, C.M. (2001) 'Managers' perceptions of ethical codes: dialectics and dynamics', *Business Ethics: A European Review*, vol. 10, no. 2: 145–156. Available from Business Source Premier (online) (n.d.). Ipswich, MA: EBSCO.

Hammersley, M. and Gomm, R. (1997) 'Bias in social research', *Sociological Research Online* (online) vol. 2, no. 1. Available at: http://www.socresonline/2/1/2.html (accessed 13 June 1997).

A problem can arise if you view the article in html format rather than in pdf. The original pagination is lost and it can be difficult to cite page numbers for quotations. If you have a pdf file, then you have a facsimile of the original article, as if you had photocopied it from the journal. In this case I think it is acceptable to reference it as if from the original. This saves you the trouble of tracking down the bibliographic details of the database and including them in the citation, as in the Fisher reference above.

You can reference all kinds of other electronic resources such as TV or radio programmmes:

Father Ted (1995) Episode 1, Good Luck Father Ted. Channel 4 TV, 21 April.

Referencing software

There are software products available that make the chore of preparing the references a lot easier. It is probably only worthwhile using such software if you begin to use it from the start of your dissertation project. If you do this you can build up a database of the references you use, in the format your institution requires. This means that you only have to type the full reference into the computer once. The software can be set up, for example, so that when you write the author and publication date of a work in your dissertation the software automatically copies the full reference from your database into the list of references for the document you are working on. Many UK universities give their students free on-campus access to a software programme called EndNote. More details on the wider uses of referencing software can be found on p. 255.

Binding

At the end of the programme the dissertation will have to be properly bound according to the institution's guidelines:

- The binding shall be of fixed type so that leaves cannot be removed or added; the front and rear boards should have sufficient rigidity to support the weight of the work when standing upright.
- In at least 24-point type, the outside front board (in black) shall bear the title of the work, the name and initials of the candidate, the qualification, and the year of submission.
- The same information (excluding the title of the work) shall be shown on the title of the work, reading downwards. All lettering shall be in gold.

Summary

- Have a clear chapter structure for the dissertation.
- Make sure there is a clear line of logical argument, or a strong theme, that links all parts of the dissertation together.
- Have logical arguments as well as arguments from authority.
- Write the dissertation in clear, plain English.
- Avoid bizno-bollocks speak and its academic equivalent.
- Use rhetorical skill to enhance your style.
- Keep to the house rules on presentation and citation.

Suggested reading

Fairbairn and Winch (1996) are good on constructing arguments and writing a dissertation. Chapter 13 of Saunders *et al.* (2002) is good on writing up. For the tricks of creating a narrative flow in your dissertation see Raimond (1993). Martin Cutts (1999) is a good, quick guide to grammar and writing style. *Troublesome Words* (Bryson, 1997) helps with all the words that confuse people and is also good on punctuation and grammar. Perry's (2000) notes for presenting a thesis are useful even though they were written for PhD rather than for Master's students. If you are interested in the layout and design of a report, see Orna and Stevens (1999).

Bryson, B. (1997) *Troublesome Words*, London: Penguin.

Fairbairn, G.J. and Winch C. (1996) *Reading, Writing and Reasoning: A Guide for Students*, Buckingham: Open University Press.

Orna, E. with Stevens, G. (1999) *Managing Information for Research*, Buckingham: Open University Press.

Raimond, P. (1993) *Management Projects: Design, Research and Presentation*, London: Chapman & Hall.

Saunders, M., Lewis, P. and Thornhill, A. (2002) *Research Methods for Business Students*, 3rd edn, Harlow: FT Prentice Hall.

References

(NB If a work mentioned in the examples and illustrations in this chapter is not included in this list of references it is because it is fictitious.)

Burton, G.O. (2000) *Silva Rhetoricae*. Available online at: http://humanities.byu.edu/rhetoric/silva.htm (accessed 24 November 2000).

British Standard Institution (1990) *Recommendations for the Presentation of Theses and Dissertations (BS 4821)*, Bracknell: British Standards Publishing.

Cutts, M. (1999) *The Quick Reference Plain English Guide*, Oxford: Oxford University Press.

Eisaman Maus, K. (2001) 'Why it's fun to be smart', *Times Literary Supplement*, 25 May, no. 5121: 24.

Fisher, C.M. and Lovell, A. (2006) *Business Ethics and Values: Individual, Corporate and International Perspectives*, Harlow: FT Prentice Hall.

Fisher, D. and Hanstock, T. (2002) *Citing References: A Guide for Users*, Oxford: Blackwell.

Gill, J. and Johnson, P. (2002) *Research Methods for Managers*, 3rd edn, London: Paul Chapman.

Grafton, A. (1998) *The Footnote*, London: Faber & Faber.

Mintzberg, H. (1994) *The Rise and Fall of Strategic Planning*, Hemel Hempstead: Prentice Hall International.

Morgan, G. (1997) *Images of Organisations*, London: Sage.

Mounce, H.O. (1997) *The Two Pragmatisms: From Peirce to Rorty*, London: Routledge.

Orwell, G. (1962) *Inside the Whale and Other Essays*, Harmondsworth : Penguin.

Pascale, R. (1990) *Managing on the Edge: How Successful Companies Use Conflict to Stay Ahead*, London: Penguin.

Perry, C. (2000) *A Structured Approach to Presenting a Thesis: Notes for Students and Their Supervisors*. Available online at: http://www.literaticlub.co.uk/Writing/theses.html (accessed 12 July 2001).

Safire, W. (2002) *Fumblerules: A Lighthearted Guide to Grammar and Good Usage*, New York: Barnes & Noble.

Trigg, G.L. (1979) 'Grammar', *Physics Review Letters*, vol. 42, no. 12: 747–748.

Index